The Cambridge Introduction to
Russian Literature

Russian literature arrived late on the European scene. Within several
generations, its great novelists had shocked – and then conquered – the
world. In this introduction to the rich and vibrant Russian tradition,
Caryl Emerson weaves a narrative of recurring themes and fascinations
across several centuries. Beginning with traditional Russian narratives
(saints' lives, folk tales, epic and rogue narratives), the book moves
through literary history chronologically and thematically, juxtaposing
literary texts from each major period. Detailed attention is given to
canonical writers including Pushkin, Gogol, Dostoevsky, Tolstoy,
Chekhov, Bulgakov, and Solzhenitsyn, as well as to some current
bestsellers from the post-communist period. Fully accessible to students
and readers with no knowledge of Russian, the volume includes a
glossary and pronunciation guide of key Russian terms and a list of
useful secondary works. The book will be of great interest to students of
Russian as well as of comparative literature.

Caryl Emerson is A. Watson Armour III Professor of Slavic Languages
and Literatures at Princeton University.

Cambridge Introductions to Literature

This series is designed to introduce students to key topics and authors. Accessible and lively, these introductions will also appeal to readers who want to broaden their understanding of the books and authors they enjoy.

- Ideal for students, teachers, and lecturers
- Concise, yet packed with essential information
- Key suggestions for further reading

Titles in this series:

Map of Imperial Russia

The Cambridge Introduction to
Russian Literature

CARYL EMERSON

CAMBRIDGE
UNIVERSITY PRESS

CAMBRIDGE
UNIVERSITY PRESS

University Printing House, Cambridge CB2 8BS, United Kingdom

Cambridge University Press is part of the University of Cambridge.

It furthers the University's mission by disseminating knowledge in the pursuit of education, learning and research at the highest international levels of excellence.

www.cambridge.org
Information on this title: www.cambridge.org/9780521606523

© Caryl Emerson 2008

First published 2008, 2011
4th printing 2012
Second Edition 2012
Reprinted 2013

A catalogue record for this publication is available from the British Library

Library of Congress Cataloguing in Publication data

Emerson, Caryl.
The Cambridge introduction to Russian literature / Caryl Emerson.
    p.   cm. – (Cambridge introductions to literature)
Includes bibliographical references and index.
ISBN 978-0-521-84469-7 (hardback) – ISBN 978-0-521-60652-3 (pbk.)
1. Russian literature–History and criticism.   2. Russian literature–Themes, motives.
I. Title.   II. Series.

PG2951.E47 2008
891.709–dc22   2008006275

ISBN 978-0-521-84469-7 Hardback
ISBN 978-0-521-60652-3 Paperback

For Nicholas,
wonderworker

Contents

Illustrations

Acknowledgments

This is a book for the advanced beginner. It is not presumed that the reader has taken any courses in Russian literature or history, nor studied the Russian language (although I do introduce a number of Russian words for which there are no precise cultural equivalents; these words are gathered in a glossary at the end). All works discussed exist in English translation and most enjoy considerable name recognition outside Russia. But the beginner is nevertheless not entirely a blank slate. Most readers, hopefully, will have read a story or seen a play by Chekhov and know something by Tolstoy (perhaps *Anna Karenina*) or Dostoevsky (*Crime and Punishment, The Brothers Karamazov*). If the name Solzhenitsyn is familiar at all, it sounds less dissident today, in Putin's Russia, than it did in the post-Stalinist Soviet Union. The reader might have heard that Aleksandr Pushkin is their greatest, most perfect writer, but having come across a piece of his in translation, can't figure out what all the fuss is about. (If Pushkin is appreciated, probably this is due to the famous operas built off his works: Modest Musorgsky's setting of Pushkin's play *Boris Godunov*, and two Tchaikovsky operas inspired by Pushkin's texts: *Eugene Onegin* and *The Queen of Spades*.) Readers will most likely also know that Russians endured an absolutist autocracy until the early twentieth century; that the enserfed Russian peasantry was liberated around the same time that the North American states freed their black slaves; that a Bolshevik *coup d'état* took place in 1917; and that this communist regime fell apart in 1991. Further contexts are provided in brief timelines prefacing each chapter or along the way.

Because the book is for beginners, those professional colleagues who helped me by reading drafts, prodding out errors, and advising me on what to delete know a great deal more than the book's target audience. And yet they kept their erudition in check, remembering that the purpose here is to introduce and seduce, not to resolve some scholarly debate. Of those who donated their page-by-page insights and services to this project I thank, above all, my Princeton colleagues Michael Wachtel (whose *Cambridge Introduction to Russian Poetry*, 2004, preceded this volume by several years), Olga Peters Hasty, Simon Morrison, Ksana Blank, Ellen Chances, Serguei Oushakine, and Petre Petrov.

Many hundreds of Princeton undergraduates in my literature courses over the past twenty years have helped me to see what texts did (and did not) speak to the curious, but still "common" reader. For scrutiny and scholarly feedback from outside the Princeton community, I am indebted to three of my most astute longstanding readers, Kathleen Parthé, Donna Tussing Orwin, and (in a class of her own as stylistic editor and critic) Josephine Woll, whose untimely death from cancer in March 2008 makes the imprint of her intelligence on these pages all the more precious.

Then there are my own teachers, in print as well as in person, whose traces are everywhere and edgeless: George Gibian, Sidney Monas, Victor Erlich, Robert Belknap, Michael Holquist, Robert Louis Jackson, Richard Taruskin, Donald Fanger, Joseph Frank.

In this as in other Cambridge University Press projects, Linda Bree has been the exemplary editor, ably assisted this time round by Maartje Scheltens, Elizabeth Davey, and Jacqueline French. At the final inch, which became a very demanding mile, Ivan Eubanks provided indispensable editorial, formatting, and research services. Jason Strudler helped me cut 23,000 words from the final draft without batting an eye.

Debts to my family this time round are deeper than ever. To my ever support-ive and enabling husband Ivan Zaknic, my parents, and my siblings, the usual gratitude for accepting the fact that the wisdom and provocation of the Russian literary tradition has been my lodestar for as long as I can remember, obliging them to make allowance, decade after decade, for odd priorities and monu-mental blind spots. Special thanks are due to my father David Geppert, who is the sort of reader and interlocutor that most writers can only dream about, and to my sister Trisha Woollcott, certified nurse-midwife, who persisted in calling Nikolai Gogol "google" and whose no-nonsense diagnostic skills detected all manner of verbal obfuscation. To my grandnephew and godson Nicholas, born in 2004 and thus also a beginner, this volume is lovingly dedicated.

Introduction

Russian literature is compact, intensely self-reflexive, and always about to forget that it is merely made up out of words. Imagined characters walk out of fiction into real life, while real-life writers are raised to the status of myth. Myths consolidated first around saints, then around cities (St. Petersburg and Moscow), then around biographies of writers, finally around ethical and ideological systems. When measured against the subcontinents – Europe and Asia proper – that flank Russia to the west, south, and east, this tradition is remarkable in two respects: its extreme brevity, and its lateness. Chinese literature is calibrated in millennia. Masterpieces in Arabic date from the fifth century. Dante wrote his *Commedia* in the early fourteenth century and Shakespeare his unparalleled English works at the end of the sixteenth. But Russia as a literary nation entered into consciousness (her own, and the world's) only two hundred years ago.

From that point on, the rise was unprecedentedly swift. Within two decades, from 1815 to the end of the 1820s, two paradigm-shifting events came to pass that provided prime binding material for national myth: Russia's most perfect military victory (the expulsion of Napoleon, from 1812–15) and the maturity of her most perfect poet, Aleksandr Pushkin (1799–1837). These achievements were not the crowning peaks of a national history but its beginning, and they shaped the public face of modern Russia and of Russian literature. It was a two-faced Janus. Pushkin came to represent a style of creativity so cosmopolitan that a Russian man (or woman) of letters was presumed to be at home, linguistically and culturally, anywhere in Europe. During those same years, however, Napoleon's defeat and its aftermath led to a chauvinistic closing-down of Russia as a sociopolitical entity, and to a pattern of suspicious confrontation with the West that has continued, with small windows of relief, into the twenty-first century.

Such was the visible point of origin. A scant fifty years after Pushkin's birth, Russians were producing works of prose fiction that not only were translated into every major world language, but whose authors, most spectacularly Leo Tolstoy (1828–1910), became international celebrities and media stars, as much for their lives and philosophies as for their art. The self-consciousness of this

1

tradition was furthered by a steadily rising literacy rate, the emergence of a mass press, and also by recurring national trauma, censorship, and an edgy, often defensive "exceptionalism" – that is, by the insistence that Russia was so special that she could not be judged by normal (which is to say, Western European) standards of progress, health, or success. "Normalization" at some non-catastrophic level became a possibility only for post-communist Russia. But many Russians – and Russia-watchers as well – have feared that rudderless freedom and the abrupt dethroning of literature's role as arbiter of national identity might spell the end of the Russian literary tradition.

This book is predicated on the assumption that such fears are unfounded. A literary tradition can crack, interbreed with alien elements, be subject to massive purging and parodies of itself, incessantly predict its own demise, and still remain robust. Indeed, purgings and parodies need not discredit the corpus but can become identifying traits and even load-bearing structures within the tradition. The enduring core of this tradition is called the "literary canon." The phrase requires some explanation. The canon of a nation's literature – its best-known texts, plots, fictional characters, plus the mythically enhanced biographies of its writers – does not have the force of a religious doctrine or a legal code. It changes constantly, but slowly, more by accretion and decay than by fiat. A given canon looks different, of course, to native speakers raised inside the culture that gave birth to it, than it does to outsiders who speak another language and depend upon translations. The literary canon of any national culture works in approximations. Ask any dozen interested readers to identify "canonic works" from a given culture, and each will come up with a different list. But chances are excellent that all lists will contain some works in common. Our goal is to stick close to that common core.

As used here, the phrases "literary tradition" and "literary canon" refer to works of creative fiction that satisfy three criteria. First, these are the created worlds (or writers' biographies) that generations of Russians have been raised on and are expected to recognize, the way English speakers recognize the shape of one of Shakespeare's plots (*Hamlet, Macbeth, Romeo and Juliet*) and Spanish speakers the tribulations of Don Quixote. Merely mentioning the name is enough to bring up the story, for these are common denominators, a sort of cultural shorthand. Although these plots are themselves often of international (or pan-European) origin, the Russian canon is unusually rich in common denominators that peaked first in other national literatures and then were adapted, with fierce enthusiasm and particularity, as Russia's own (the "Russian Hamlet," the "Russian Don Quixote").

Second, texts become canonical when they are repeatedly referenced, recycled, and woven into successive artistic worlds so that they never entirely fade from view. Tolstoy's *War and Peace* (set between 1805 and 1819) had an impact in its own time (the 1860s), inspired an opera (by Sergei Prokofiev in the 1940s), a steamy parodic sequel titled *Pierre and Natasha* (in the 1990s), and along the way a mass of reverent and irreverent illustrations, films, spin-offs, caricatures, and comic strips. Natasha Rostova has now become a personality that can enter other stories (including real-life ones); she is not limited to the plots that Tolstoy created around her.

And finally: the literary canon is proof of the legitimating aesthetic judgment of readers over time. Of course politics, censorship, taste, prejudice, accidents of loss or discovery, and approved reading lists play a role in the canonizing process. But overall, canonic works survive because they are excellent. Excellence in an artwork is both formal (that is, due to its efficient aesthetic construction) and "psychological" – that is, we recognize a classic because it has rewarded multiple interpretations of itself from multiple points of view, over generations.

During the century that it has existed in adequate English translation, the Russian canon of novels and plays has acquired a reputation and a certain "tone." It is serious (that is, tragic or absurd, but rarely lighthearted and never trivial), somewhat preacherly, often politically oppositionist, and frequently cast in a mystifying genre with abrupt or bizarre beginnings and ends. The novels especially are too long, too full of metaphysical ideas, too manifestly eager that readers not just read the story for fun or pleasure but learn a moral lesson. These books are deep into good and evil even while they parody those pretensions. If there is comedy – and Russian fiction can be screamingly funny – there is a twist near the end that turns your blood to ice. Russian literary characters don't seek the usual money, career, success in society, sex for its own sake, trophy wife or husband, house in the suburbs, but instead crave some other unattainable thing.

How one should respect this reputation and received "tone" is a delicate issue. In the literary humanities, an Introduction is a subjective enterprise. It has a shape of its own, which means big gaps and broad leaps. It is not a history, handbook, encyclopedia, digest of fictional plots or real-life literary biographies, and even less is it a cutting-edge textbook summarizing, as science textbooks can, the "state of the art." No in-print genre today can compete with search engines or updatable online resources for objective information of that sort. An Introduction probably works best as a tour guide, pointing out landmarks, road signs, and connecting paths. Since its purpose is to lead somewhere more complex than the point at which it began, it should introduce names, texts, and themes that an interested reader can pursue elsewhere in more detail. A non-Russian author inviting a non-Russian audience to enter this territory is thus obliged, I believe, to select as exemplary those literary texts and tools that are accessible "from the outside." They must exist in decent translations, survive as genuine works of art in their target languages (here, English), and be capable of accumulating cultural weight beyond Russia's borders.

With minor exceptions, this defines the transposable Great Russian prose canon, plus perhaps a dozen plays. It neglects the empire's cultural minorities. This prose canon contains very few women (the Russian nineteenth century had no Jane Austen, George Eliot, or George Sand) – although groundbreaking research on Russian women's writing over the past three decades has brought to light many formerly invisible authors and works. For reasons of space, the Russian émigré community is excluded from this book (together with the aristocratic and very Russian genius of Vladimir Nabokov, who has stimulated a Russo-American industry of his own).

The most significant compression in the present volume, however, occurs in the realm of Russian poetry, which can only be a secondary presence in the story. The *Cambridge Introduction to Russian Poetry* has already been written, by Michael Wachtel; the present book can be seen as a companion to it. Our tasks are quite different. Wachtel notes provocatively in his opening sentence: "The achievements of Dostoevsky and Tolstoy notwithstanding, Russian literature is a tradition of poetry, not prose, and Russian readers have always recognized it as such."[1] Russian readers, yes – but not the rest of the world. Europe ignored the Slavic tongues. Highborn, educated Russians of the imperial period were raised bilingually, spoke French in polite society, and many knew English and German as well. Europeans by and large did not presume that any benefits could be gained by learning Russian. And why should they? The Russian officers who occupied Paris in 1814 spoke French as purely and elegantly as their defeated foe. Some Russian writers, like Pushkin's friend Pyotr Chaadaev as late as the 1830s, argued that the Russian tongue was unsuited to refined philosophical thought. This imbalance in language competencies contributed to a curious, and not unjustified, superiority complex in many great Russian writers. Most insistent in this regard was Fyodor Dostoevsky in his journalism of the 1870s. We can translate you, Dostoevsky proclaimed, but you cannot translate us. We can grasp, absorb and transfigure your legacy, but ours is mysterious, potent, for us alone. When the quatralingual Ivan Turgenev, living in Paris in the 1870s, presented some poems by Pushkin in his own French translation to Gustave Flaubert, the latter shrugged: "Il est plat, votre poète" [He's flat, your poet].[2]

To set poetry at one pole and "the rest of literature" at the other is a familiar reflex in literary studies, and it comes at a cost. It satisfies our intuitive sense that the most marvelous aspects of a poem collapse outside its original language, or must be wholly recreated by a translator-poet of equivalent gifts, whereas prose is somehow wide open, serving raw experience more than form. This binary view, unfair to the resources of both poetry and prose, leaves out rich stretches of artistic writing in between – ornamentalist prose, rhythmic speech, and "prose poems," for example. But it nevertheless touches on an important truth. Prose is deficient in criteria and tools for precise measurement, whereas poetry has an agreed-on descriptive and critical vocabulary, beginning with rules of versification. In his *Introduction to Russian Poetry* and elsewhere, Wachtel argues that poets cite, converse, and bond with one another (that is, come together in a tradition) most intensely at the level of what is lost in translation. The reality of the work, its substance, is this complex of rhythmic patternings and specific aural cues. Only later does that technically identifiable mass come to be associated with certain themes (feelings, images, narrative experiences).[3]

How do prose writers bond and cite? Shared themes and images are important for both poetry and prose, but unlike the lyric poem, fused to the language and rhythms of its birth, prose and dramatic genres are presumed to be more resilient – orphaned without trauma and adopted with gratitude into new families. Novels, stories, and plays are routinely "realized" outside their original languages, garnering international fame in all manner of translations, to audiences that have no idea of the context or sound of the source. (Occasionally one even hears the comment that a translation can, and should, *improve on the original*. A variant on this position was voiced by the Czech-French writer Milan Kundera in 2007, when he argued that the aesthetic value of a given novel could be appreciated fully only in the "large context of world literature," which for him meant by those "without a knowledge of the original language."[4]) Confounded by the success of their product and uncertain about the specificity of their tools, professional prose analysts frequently default to plot summaries, the work's "message," the perspectives of its narrators, its reflection of real-life events, and how its fictive personalities do or do not cohere as people who resemble us, their readers, and their friends. These are all valid categories and inquiries. But they apply as readily to philosophy, sociology, politics, cultural anthropology, psychology, and simply getting through the day as they do to verbal art.

This profligate applicability of stories to life was one reason why the Russian Formalists, attempting to professionalize literary study in the 1920s, took up the challenge of narrative prose with such missionary fervor. They devised technical categories for its analysis that were deliberately, polemically blind to personality and to ethics: objective terminology and procedures that would qualify artistic prose as a self-consciously "literary" (or "poetical") construct. It is of enormous significance that the most aggressive and fertile of these Russian prose theorists,

Viktor Shklovsky (1893–1984), wrote brash and influential essays on the artistry of Miguel Cervantes, Charles Dickens, Arthur Conan Doyle, Laurence Sterne, all the while working solely, and apparently with full confidence, in Russian translation. Shklovsky did not know Spanish, English, or any foreign language. Did he consider his monolingualism a handicap? His practice as an analyst of prose suggests that in his view, a higher-order authenticity residing in the very structure or movement of literary narrative permits it to transcend the specific material out of which it is made. No verse theorist could take seriously the "scientific" results of such a method applied to his chosen subject matter.

In balancing these two wings of the Russian tradition, the poetic and the prosaic, Flaubert's remark to Turgenev about that "flat poet, Pouchkine" has been a warning to the present volume. Flaubert was not wholly wrong. Pushkin taken out of Russian becomes two-dimensional with treacherous ease. Part of the reason, surely, is that his lyric gift was not especially pictorial. He tended to avoid metaphor, which is among the easiest elements of a poem to be transferred out of one language into another. Instead of image and metaphor, Pushkin manipulated for poetic purposes various grammatical categories, largely case endings and the verbal aspect peculiar to Slavic tongues – all the while delivering a lucid, pure, almost conversational speaking line.[5] Other great poets of thicker, more startling texture, such as Marina Tsvetaeva (1892–1941), built so inventively out of Russian phonemes that each verbal unit literally explodes on the ear with a mass of lexical and rhythmic associations. Such effects can hardly be registered outside their native element. But some genres of poetry (longer narrative poems, ballads, and many types of verse satire) communicate powerfully in translation, and these will be selectively stitched in to the chapters that follow. Perhaps most important, the *lives* (and deaths) of poets – heroic, sacrificial, prophetic – are themselves texts of the utmost centrality to the Russian literary canon.

There is a final intriguing paradox. Michael Wachtel is surely correct that Russian poets cultivate a highly formal communal identity out of aural and rhythmic reminiscence. But prose writers seem to have cultivated the opposite, a form-*breaking* impulse. Several high-profile Russian writers celebrated their resistance to, if not downright defiance of, all the received forms or genres out of which Western literary canons were built. To cite only the most famous, Leo Tolstoy, writing in 1868 upon the conclusion of *War and Peace*: "the history of Russian literature since the time of Pushkin not merely affords many examples of deviation from European forms, but does not offer a single example of the contrary . . . In the recent period of Russian literature not a single artistic prose work rising at all above mediocrity quite fits into the form of a novel, epic, or story."[6] Because Ivan Turgenev wrote trim little novellas that resembled

French and Italian prose classics, he was viewed with suspicion as a renegade, insufficiently disobedient and exotic to be truly Russian. The same charge was later leveled against his well-trained, formally disciplined, Western-friendly compatriot in music, Pyotr Ilyich Tchaikovsky.

Russian spokespersons for the canon have long been protective of its eccentric, high-risk, rebellious profile. The greatest writers seemed always to be in trouble with their regimes, and the worst regimes in turn felt threatened by writers. But a persecuted or martyred writer could be posthumously cleansed of ideological impurities and elevated to approved, even to cultic, status in a series of state-sponsored Jubilees. This happened massively with Pushkin (d. 1837) at the end of the nineteenth century, with Tolstoy (d. 1910) beginning with the centenary of his birth in 1928, and with the great Futurist poet Vladimir Mayakovsky (d. 1930), glorified by Stalin's decree five years after he had committed suicide. A writer privileged to be part of this pantheon could be alternately repressed and sponsored, shoved into the limelight and just as suddenly yanked back into the shadows. One can only wonder, looking back at the process from a freer time, how much of that heroic story of literature's centrality to Russian culture was itself manipulated. How might Russian identity have developed without these violent enthusiasms and constraints?

Such thought experiments are sobering. For of the three major forces that disseminated literature and compensated writers – the ruling court (tsarist or communist), the aristocratic salon, and the bookseller's market – "royal patronage," with its hectoring censorship and selective sponsorings, has probably done the most to foster the high-minded texts that we associate with the immortal Russian classics. But did the average Russian citizen in times of distress really recite poetry like a mantra? How many readers actually desired to change their lives, as those great novels (and novelists, and literary critics) constantly urged them to do? The story of the two-hundred-year rise of Russian literature became its own bestselling novel – although, some now suggest, largely among the elite groups invested in the story.

This hazard is inherent in discussions of any canon, but of the Russian more than most. Among the virtues of Jeffrey Brooks's path-breaking study *When Russia Learned to Read* (1985) is its conclusion that the majority of ordinary Russian consumers of literature in the latter half of the nineteenth century resembled our own sensation-seeking, escapist Western readerships far more closely than the morally saturated, often mournful high canon would lead us to believe.[7] When, for example, adventure, crime, and detective fiction began to attract a mass Russian market in the 1890s and again in the 1920s, the cultural intelligentsia took fright: escape and thrills were not compatible with the mission of the Great Tradition. For all that this turf war raged over keenly valued goods, Russian "high" and "low" cultures were not isolated from each other. Plots, fads, and literary devices moved in both directions. Among the services rendered by recent scholarship is to remind us that most people, including great writers who live in authoritarian or "closed" regimes, have everyday lives and non-heroic appetites. The pull of pleasurable distraction interrupts the grimmest political threats as well as the temptations of tragedy and high significance. Pushkin, lofty persecuted poet, loved comic opera and formulaic verse comedy throughout his life. Sergei Prokofiev, repatriated to the USSR on the brink of the Great Terror, had long courted commissions (from Hollywood and elsewhere) for the frothiest film music. It was this rigid aspect of Russian reverence for its canonical writers and writings that began to loosen up in the 1980s, most frequently through affectionate irony, occasionally through abuse, but always with the sense (thrilling to some, terrible to others) that the stability of a massive and precious edifice was at stake.

Such, then, have been the major anxieties informing this project: the status of the "high" canon; the indispensability of the Russian language to it; and the self-mythologization of Russia's literary tradition. For each anxiety, compromises were eventually found. Some parts of poetry survive admirably in translation, because form has many ways of making itself felt. It was my working assumption that the major literary works of a cultural tradition do submit to a technical treatment more rigorous and interesting than a paraphrase of plots, feelings, and ideas. Tools of analysis can be devised. Alongside the evolution of poetically analyzable structures – the ode, ballad, elegy, blank-verse lyric, revolutionary "stepladder verse" [lesenka] of Mayakovsky – one can also note a sturdy evolution of Russian prose from the middle of the eighteenth century to the present. These "prose units" are partly thematic and generic (prose comedy, travel notes, society tales, ghost stories, newspaper gossip columns, the naturalistic "sketch," the factory novel) and partly a matter of authorial voice and intonation (satire, travesty, confession). Genres borrowed from Europe encountered a body of Russian traditional (pre-Enlightenment) plots that had long circulated in urban and rural areas, some native to their regions and some trickled in from the south and west: incantations to the powers of the earth, miracle tales, stories of ritual sacrifice, Jesuit school drama, adventure plots, all of which survived well into the modern period. Evolution of these Russianized hybrids occurred within a larger familiar framework of pan-European literary "periods" of which Russian writers were keenly aware, the sequence from Neo-classicism → Sentimentalism → Romanticism → Realism → Naturalism → Symbolism → Modernism → Postmodernism. Irregular pockets of the pious, the baroque, the grotesque, and the absurd interrupt this spectrum. At least one movement (socialist realism) was deliberately designed to debunk, relativize, and humiliate European literary models.

Let me return in closing to the anxiety about "rudderless freedom" raised in the opening pages. Does Russia's partially "normalized" post-communist literary life, which has greatly diminished the role and status of the creative writer, threaten the integrity of the tradition? Perturbations have been severe, but apocalypse is nowhere in sight. In-print verbal art continues to have splendid survival advantages, regardless of sinister twists in Kremlin politics and even in competition with today's image-saturated, instantly accessible cybernetic world. To its immense good fortune, literature does not need the big budgets, collective efforts, or approved public spaces required to realize symphonic music, visual art exhibits, cinematic productions or large-scale architectural projects. Its more compact forms can be carried in the pocket, composed (and also carried) in the head. Heroic legends abound concerning this latter mode of survival under the most recent Old Regime. Nadezhda Mandelstam, widow of the great poet, committed her husband's entire poetic corpus to memory "for safekeeping" during the Stalinist years, until it was no longer dangerous to write it down. Since literary texts are so very dispersed and so inefficiently, individually, privately processed, inertia tends to be huge. One can blow up an offensive monument but cannot gather up and burn all copies of a published novel. A state bureaucracy can ban a film or mutilate an opera, but it cannot prevent us from memorizing and mentally re-experiencing a poem in all its fullness.

And finally: unlike the progressive, falsifiable sciences or (at the other extreme) the capriciously marketed world of fashion, great literature does not date. It accumulates contexts rather than outgrows them, for literature is designed to speak to the current needs of the person who activates it. Who are these "activators"? Although today's Russian school curriculum might no longer require *War and Peace* or Mikhail Sholokhov's *The Quiet Don* – too many other texts compete, and time is in shorter supply – the great Russian novels continue to be read around the world with undiminished fervor.

With that fact in mind it is worth asking, in Milan Kundera's spirit, whether a literature need belong to its own nation at all. Russian lovers of the word are of two minds on this issue, professing two ideals. In the first, that peculiar chauvinism exemplified by Dostoevsky, Russian literature is a common denominator for the world, yet only Russians are privileged to understand it. Fifteen years after the collapse of the Soviet Union, some leading Russian sociologists still see in the Russian national character a "negative identity" driven by self-deprecating exceptionalism, ennui, sentimentality, constant expectation of catastrophe, and an alarming xenophobia.[8] It is indeed true that these character traits read like a home page for the darker sides of Dostoevsky's novels. But it is also true – and this is the second ideal – that Russian literature long ago slipped out from under the tutelage of the nation that produced it. Russian artists – in literature, theatre, dance, music, film – have inspired more disciples and "schools" around the world than any other single national culture. Since the early 1990s, a bit of that openness has been coming home.

Chapter 1

Critical models, committed readers, and three Russian Ideas

"Apart from reading," Dostoevsky's Underground Man complains, "there was no place to go."[1] The metaphor is striking. So central was proper reading to the cultured Russian's self-image and sense of reality that poetry, fictional literature, memoirs, diaries, even personal letters from and among great writers almost constituted a *place*. The authority of these fictive or quasi-fictive residences was compelling and truth-bearing. What is the best point of entry into these alternative worlds?

Several models were considered for this book. The first was the most conventional: selected writers and their works juxtaposed to one another in chronological sequence. A second model suggested itself around distinctive Russian genres: saint's life, fairy tale, war epic, "notes" or casual jottings [*zapiski*], prison memoir, dysfunctional utopia, industrial production novel. Yet another structure emerged when the focus shifted to recurrent Russian heroes (or anti-heroes): righteous persons, fools, rogues, wanderers, frontiersmen, Europeanized fops, nihilists, superfluous men, salvational women, the merciful or tyrannical tsar. Special note was made of those types that did *not* take root in Russian soil or appeared only late on her literary horizon: the beautiful sinner, the chivalric knight, the virtuous merchant, the benign or productive bureaucrat. Each of these three formats raised interesting questions. How are we to explain the enduring popularity of the unconsummated love story or the epic that ends in defeat or dissolution of the goal? What about "heroless epic narrative" – the attempt to paint humanity on a vast historical scale and dispense with personal agency? However intriguing those questions were, ultimately the last two models, focusing on genres and heroes, were stripped down to a "glossary" of representative types in Chapter 2. Chapter 3 was then given over to the traditional narrative forms – often undated or anonymous – that dominated cultural life up to the modernizing reign of Peter the Great (d. 1725). The remaining chapters then unfold chronologically.

Several factors led to this compromise decision. First, Russian literary "types" do not cluster especially well in the abstract. They are historically conditioned and best grasped within those conditions. What is more, the practice of clustering heroes is usually unfair to the fictive personalities involved. As proof it is sufficient to consider the innocent, by now pedestrian label "superfluous man," routinely applied to a certain style of Russian nineteenth-century male protagonist. The epithet would have been incomprehensible to the most famous heroes who bore it (Pushkin's Eugene Onegin, Lermontov's Grigory Pechorin) – unhappy men, perhaps, but surely not willing to be classified as unnecessary or redundant to the only life they knew. The phrase was devised decades later and applied to them only retroactively, by writers and critics who decided that a more socially responsible, productive (that is, "positive") hero was morally preferable for Russia's social development. Thinking by type is always crude, but historical context can help us avoid the worst abuses. One good illustration of the necessity to read Russian types historically might be the myth of a "salvation-bearing peasantry."

Early Russian images of the rural underclass were raw and satirical. In the 1790s, in imitation of the European vogue for pastoral idylls, Russia's first pre-Romantic writers began to sentimentalize the peasant. This myth took on weight in the 1830s–40s after the appearance in Moscow of a Slavophile movement glorifying the archaic Russian past, and thereafter was kept alive by a conscience-stricken, serfowning "repentant gentry" up to and beyond 1861, the year Tsar Alexander II emancipated the peasantry from personal bondage. One writer's long life could encompass several stages of this evolving image. Leo Tolstoy, for example, portrays a shrewd, ethnographically diverse, ethically neutral peasantry in *War and Peace* (1860s), an idealized peasant in his didactic fiction of the 1880s (such as "The Death of Ivan Ilyich" and "Master and Man"), and brutally naturalistic village life in his peasant plays, especially in *The Power of Darkness* (1887), written in folk dialect. Dostoevsky, whose imagination was overall an urban one, idealized the common people for reasons related largely to his own prison term in Siberia (1850–54), spent among murderers and thieves of peasant origin. The high-born and wealthy Turgenev was haunted throughout his life by his tyrannical mother's violent, capricious treatment of the family's serfs, and his sympathetic portraits of peasants in *A Sportsman's Sketches* (1852) reflect this agony and painful memory. It fell to Anton Chekhov, grandson of a serf, to demythologize Russia's commoners thoroughly, both urban and rural – before the working class was re-mythologized in the Marxist-Leninist state.

For most writers of the Soviet period, the factory worker and front-line soldier were the commoners of choice. Only in the 1960s and 1970s, when official ideology began to fray, did "Village Prose" writers offer an alternative to those two ideologically sanctioned groups in a stoic, heroic peasant who had survived modernization, collectivization, and total war to become the moral standard of the nation. The 1976 novel *Farewell to Matyora* by Valentin Rasputin (b. 1937), tells the story of a 300-year-old peasant village on a remote island on the Angara River in southern Siberia, doomed to disappear when a hydroelectric project floods the area. The final seasons of the Island are related from the dual perspective of an old woman grieving over the fate of the ancestral dead in the village cemetery, and of the Master, the Island's guardian folk spirit. The peasant had been reinvented as an archaic hero, although no longer prettified or pastoral.

Another sensitive cultural marker is the battlefield. Types of heroes and heroism have been closely tied to Russia's major (and minor) wars – aggressive and defensive, nation-threatening as well as the routine border conflict. Distinct literatures developed around the years 1812 (Napoleon's invasion, called the "First Fatherland War"), 1854–55 (Crimean War), 1878 (Russo-Turkish War), 1904–05 (Russo-Japanese War), 1914–18 (The Great War), 1918–21 (Civil War), 1941–45 (World War II or "Second Fatherland War"), and, from the nineteenth to the twenty-first century, the interminable bloodletting in Chechnya. The close integration of the military class (officers and soldiers) with civilian society throughout the imperial period (1725–1917) not only permeated literature with the martial values of sacrifice, courage, obedience, duty, and patriotic death, but also fostered a tradition of literary plots built around crises in the public domain. In the Russian context, a great writer like Marcel Proust would find no readymade place.

The Russian literary canon developed as a dialogue in time. Here I use that overworked word "dialogue" literally, not in its more metaphorical meaning that would apply, say, to the dispersed English or Italian literary traditions, each with a leisurely thousand years of distantly spaced texts. Russian literature since 1820 was a real person-to-person dialogue taking place almost entirely in two cities, St. Petersburg and Moscow, the cultural capitals of a vast but highly centralized empire. All the main publishing houses were there, the reading public was there, and the rest of the country was still imperfectly mapped and largely mute. Writers knew, responded to, revered and parodied each other within their own lifetimes and the living memory of their readers. Succession rites were often overt. As an old man in 1815, the eighteenth-century court poet Gavril Derzhavin formally consecrated the teenager Pushkin to poetry. Mikhail Lermontov stepped out to fame in 1837, in the aftermath of an outraged poem he composed on the occasion of Pushkin's death in a duel that same year. Dostoevsky in the 1840s fashioned his first literary heroes out of prototypes created by Nikolai Gogol a decade earlier – and to underscore the debt, he obliged his own heroes to read, react to, and measure themselves against fictive characters created by Gogol and Pushkin. Maksim Gorky (real name Aleksei Maksimovich Peshkov, 1868–1936), who knew both Tolstoy and Chekhov personally and revered them both, lived to become Lenin's comrade, Stalin's uneasy cultural commissar, and the Party's official sponsor of socialist realism in 1934. We can speak here of a tradition so concise, responsive, and linear that chronology is its natural framework.

Literary critics and their public goods

Russia's stunningly rapid literary rise and its importance to her sense of identity made literary activity highly self-conscious. Almost before there was a literature, Vissarion Belinsky (1811–48), Russia's founding literary critic, was promoting indigenous talent and debating, at times ferociously, the nature of a writer's duties. The Romantic-era notion authorizing literary critics to supervise artistic creativity and instruct the nation's readership enjoyed a long life on Russian soil. "All our artists would wander off along various paths, because it is only the critic-journalists who show them the way," wrote the radical critic Nikolai Shelgunov in 1870. "Novelists merely collect the firewood and stoke the engine of life, but the critic-journalist is the driver."[2] Poetry was celebrated and novels serialized in literary periodicals, the so-called "thick journals." For most of the nineteenth century, the circulation of each of these omnibus literary almanachs rarely exceeded 700 subscribers – and this tiny readership "conversed" with itself around emerging fictional masterpieces. Successive chapters of *War and Peace* and *Crime and Punishment* appeared in the same thick journal, *The Russian Herald*, during the mid-1860s; traces of Tolstoy's 1805 war turn up in the mouth of the police investigator Porfiry Petrovich while he is interrogating Raskolnikov.[3] These were the dialogues that endured.

When dialogue was desired with the transitory (non-fictive) world, readers became skilled in a pre-emptive interpretive strategy known as "Aesopian language." It assumes that Russian authors, unfree to state in print what they really mean, don the sly mask of the fabulist Aesop and encode each utterance with latent content, intended for those with ears to hear it. A curious relationship then developed between literary authors and Russia's fledgling civic and professional discourses – the quasi-public speech of salons, theatre foyers, student circles, meetings of medical societies, scholarly gatherings, jubilee anniversaries for famous artists or scientists, lawyers at public jury trials.[4] This growing professional class adored literature and relied on its heroes and themes to authenticate their public statements. The respect was often not returned: literary authors, in their fiction, continued to portray "group" and public speech either satirically – or criminally. It would appear that many creative writers considered civic speech, mediated by institutions and a rising corporate consciousness, an unwelcome rival.

Although intellectual freedom in the public sphere constricted at times to the choking point, Russian thought about literature broadened and became more systematic in the twentieth century. Russian theories burst upon the world, with ambitions of being applied to the world. Russian Formalists in the 1920s made claims about the nature of *all* narrative; the structuralist Roman Jakobson about *all* language; cultural semioticians in the 1960s–70s (Yury Lotman and his Tartu School in Soviet Estonia) about *all* sign systems; and the ideas on dialogue, carnival, and literary time-space of an obscure provincial professor, Mikhail Bakhtin, came to be embraced by a vast global community a decade after his death. In deference to this rich critical tradition, whenever the need arose for some organizational framework I have sought to use categories or paradigms developed by Russian thinkers. In the post-communist period, this includes the work of some bicultural émigrés – Mikhail Epstein, Boris Gasparov, Mark Lipovetsky, Vitaly Chernetsky – who continue to work as "culturologists" on material from their native land. Such an application of Russian categories to Russian creativity is intended to anchor these chapters without falling into that least wholesome of all theoretical habits: imposing, on defenseless primary texts, alien instruments devised in some context distant or indifferent to them.

Three major approaches to literary expression achieved currency beyond Russia's borders in the twentieth century: the Formalist, the Dialogic, and the Structuralist-semiotic. From each of these schools I have chosen one concept to help focus our literary juxtapositions and link them up into a more coherent national narrative.

From the Formalists, in particular Viktor Shklovsky (1893–1984) and Yury Tynyanov (1894–1943), comes the idea of "respectful" parody. The idea grows out of the Aesopian defense discussed above. Many authors and critics in the latter half of the nineteenth century believed that a protest literature, one that exposed social ills and assigned blame, was the only morally justified position for a writer. But by the century's turn a reaction had set in against this civic-minded – and usually stridently materialist – mandate, first among Symbolist poets and critics seeking a more mystical reality, then among a group of Petrograd literary scholars, known as the Formalists, who sought to defend the autonomy of art against all such ragged, ill-formed obligations to "real life." Formalists did not preach "art for art's sake." They acknowledged that art and life were interdependent. Shklovsky stressed this symbiosis in his twin ideas of "estrangement" and "automatization," by which he meant the duty of art to "make everyday objects strange" so that our habitual perceptions would be jolted out of their drowsy rut and we would wake up to life anew. As he put it in 1916: after viewing nature – or people, or ideas – through the lens of art, "the sun seems sunnier and the stone stonier"; without art, our automatized life would "eat away at things, at clothes, at furniture, at our wives, at our fear of war."[5] This is definitely art in the service of life. Overall, however, it was not the "wake-up" function that the Formalists advocated for verbal art as much as a higher degree of autonomy.

Literature, they insisted, was a profession and a craft. It could even become a "science" (in Russian, the word for science, *nauka*, refers not only to empirical hard science but to all scholarship, and to systematic or methodologically consistent thinking in general). Literary creativity – or as the Formalists preferred to call it, "literariness" – had an arsenal of techniques and devices for achieving its effects. Writers cared about life's problems, of course, but mostly they cared about learning how to write. For this to happen, they needed to master the tools of their trade. Some Formalist critics, like Boris Eikhenbaum (1886–1959) in his study *The Young Tolstoi* (1922), went so far as to claim that Tolstoy's obsessive "self-improvement lists" and periodic condemnations of his own behavior in his diaries, as well as his elaborately public, exaggerated confessions later in life, were tasks more intrinsic to "literariness" than to conscience. Diaries of the sort Tolstoy produced were designed to experiment with various literary forms of punitive self-exposure, not really to combat, or repent of, the actual sins being recorded – which often continued unabated. This skeptical verdict on Tolstoy's spiritual quest was an extreme Formalist position, and Eikhenbaum himself later backed off from it. Mostly the group sought to understand the role of formal strategies or "devices" in a literary tradition. Apprentice writers studied devices for portraying character, plot, imagery, and emotional tone that had been developed by their predecessors. In their own creative writing they worked subtle changes on these earlier formulas, expecting their readers to recognize when an old, worn-out, automatized device was being brought to the surface and replaced by something else. To "lay bare" an old device was one of the tasks of parody.

In a 1921 essay on Dostoevsky and Gogol, "Toward a Theory of Parody," Tynyanov insisted that parody is not the same as satire, travesty, farce or burlesque. All those forms involve a struggle against outdated behaviors and forms, to be sure. At some level all strive to make us laugh. But parody need not imply any mean-spirited disrespect. Within the tightly laced spiral of the Russian tradition, the old was understood as essential to appreciating the new. The early Dostoevsky "parodied" Gogol but worshipped him and could not have existed without him. The novelist and playwright Mikhail Bulgakov (1891–1940), writing a century later, perceived himself as a direct heir (indeed, almost a contemporary) of both Gogol and Dostoevsky. The best Decadent and Symbolist-era novels, such as Fyodor Sologub's *Petty Demon* (1904) or Andrei Bely's *Petersburg* (1916/1922), are saturated with the nineteenth-century classics, in dense networks of allusion recombined and often distorted so that tragic motifs become comic and comic motifs tragic. *Pushkin House* (1971) by Andrei Bitov (b. 1937) portrays the Russian intelligentsia, betrayers of culture who are themselves betrayed by communism, through the affectionately garbled lens of masterworks by Pushkin, Gogol, Lermontov, Turgenev, Dostoevsky: the real and enduring Russia of the literary imagination. One trademark device of the postmodernist poet and performance artist Dmitry Prigov (1940–2007), author of over 35,000 poems, is to swallow up and re-accent other poets' words: his spectacular recitation of Pushkin's novel in verse *Eugene Onegin* as a Buddhist mantra always brought down the house. For such indefatigable inventiveness with cultural artifacts of the past, Prigov won a Pushkin prize in 1993. Such parody does not discredit or overthrow its predecessors, but addresses and confirms them. The point of this address is not to displace the writers who came before, a futile and impoverishing exercise, but to become worthy of *joining* them.

The Dialogic school is represented by Mikhail Bakhtin (1895–1975). Bakhtin was a profound student of parody, in which he heard a rich "double-voicedness" and thus the potential for achieving that most difficult human virtue: responsible, or answerable, freedom. His readings of Dostoevsky from this perspective are highly provocative. Respectful parody also permeates the Bakhtinian idea of carnival as open-ended, two-way or reciprocal laughter. More central than freedom or carnival to our discussions, however, will be Bakhtin's less flashy, more workmanlike notion of the chronotope. Bakhtin adapted this neologism ("time-space") from Einstein's insights in physics and then applied it to the life sciences – where, in Bakhtin's capacious view, literature should probably be classified. Verbal narrative resembles a living organism of a highly advanced type. It regulates itself internally on the basis of responsive feedback (from its author, its readers, and the fictive characters within itself). It respects laws of causality and plausibility. It can manipulate categories of time and is capable of producing surprise, that is, the unpredictably new. The major difference between a work of creative literature and organic life is that literature, although meticulously individualized as an organism, does not die. Its life is sustained by its chronotope.

Bakhtin was a Kantian. He assumed that before any world could be represented or structured, the structuring mind makes assumptions about the workings of time and space. That matrix then determines, or conditions, the kinds of events or evaluations that can happen within its borders, as well as the personalities that "come alive" in response to these events. Authors must decide how much liberty they will allow their narrators to exercise in the process of "coming to know" (penetrating, consoling, violating) the fictive consciousness that quickens inside this time-space. For unlike the Kantian practice, Bakhtin's time-space is never transcendental or abstract. Seeing and speaking – Bakhtin's minimum for experience – require a concrete body. A valid chronotope thus always delimits, individualizes, and evaluates the point of view from which any story is experienced and then told. It puts edges and eyes into the literary word. Bakhtin argued that the difference between literary genres is not to be found in formal features such as length, theme, rhyme scheme, acoustical patterns or the prose/poetry boundary. The sense of a genre is determined by its chronotope, whose primary task is to provide a breeding ground and viable environment for the growth of consciousness.

The Structuralist-semiotic perspective in this book is represented by Yury Lotman (1922–93) and his Tartu School of Cultural Semiotics. They contribute one big concept to the present study: the binary opposition. Binary structures – often resolved into a triad awaiting new bifurcation – were comfortable for Russian intellectuals, who had been enthusiastic about the Hegelian dialectic ever since the 1830s and who were battered by the obligatory "Marxist-Leninist dialectic" for most of the twentieth century. Opposing polarities is a controversial method, however. It feeds in to the proverbial (and oversimplified) image of Russian culture as a place solely of black-and-white extremes and maximalist ideals. Possibly for Aesopian reasons, in their writings from the 1970s Lotman and his colleagues limited their binary interpretations to the more formulaic texts and behaviors of the Russian medieval world (twelfth to seventeenth century), which could indeed be explicated effectively in terms of sacred versus demonic, high versus low, East versus West, old versus new. Applied to later eras or more complex texts, the binary can be distorting. Lotman himself, in the final years of his life (which were also the final years of the Soviet regime), began to question the wisdom of a binary worldview for Russia, comparing it to a stool on two legs – exciting because always on the brink but unstable and chronically vulnerable, liable to collapse after a single shockwave. Perestroika, he implied, was that "explosion or rupture necessary for the transition in Russian culture from a binary to a ternary cultural formation."[6]

    That being said, natives as well as outsiders have long organized Russian literary space according to polar oppositions. Among the most durable of these poles have been: court poets versus prose satirists in the eighteenth century; Slavophiles versus Westernizers in the 1840–50s; utilitarians versus aesthetes in the 1860s (and again in the 1890s); proletarians versus the relics of "bourgeois" art in the 1920s; and official party-minded art versus underground dissidents in the Soviet period. Bakhtin's "carnivalesque," the biggest bestseller ever to come out of Russian cultural theory and justly celebrated for its tolerance, openness, and malleability, paradoxically rests on one huge unbridgeable binary: the "official serious classical body" versus the "unofficial laughing grotesque." In such polarized models, each extreme sustains and defines the other – while reducing the other, unavoidably, to caricature. Only in the last three decades has this for-or-against infrastructure definitively broken down, replaced by a rich assortment of asymmetrical, legally coexisting postmodernist alternatives. Relief as well as confusion has been immense.

My use of the binary model in the present book is intended to be more suggestive than analytically rigorous. Each chapter identifies two major authors, text types, or worldviews that represent fundamentally different forms of literary expression during that period. These anchor the two poles and delimit the field. Sometimes the two poles are mediated and pushed out into a triad. Key episodes in a work (or a small cluster of works) are then discussed chronotopically – that is, with an eye to how time, space, interpersonal relations (author-narrator-hero-reader), and consequently human values are structured within it. Where the story line of a literary text promises to be obscure to non-Russian readers, plot summary is provided (for an Orthodox saint's life, warrior epic, medieval Faust tale, prose comedy from the eighteenth century, Stalin-era production novel or fairy-tale play). For the "first-bench canon" (name recognition at the level of Pushkin, Gogol, Tolstoy, and Dostoevsky), episodes must suffice.

These literary works or episodes are then linked to one another through parody, taken in the appreciative sense discussed above: a respectful homage and a reworking. Each of the six chronological chapters has its theme. For the eighteenth century (Chapter 4), it is satire and hybridization: how French-style neoclassical prose comedy and the picaresque novel were transposed to "barbaric" Russia, and how one synthesis of Russia and the West took powerful root at the end of the century. The Romantic period (Chapter 5) is organized around two distinctly different poles. The "Pushkin side" is the world of public codes, game-playing, and the duel of honor; the "Gogol side" is governed by the opposite dynamic, a private world of evasion and concealment, abundant in texts of embarrassment and exposure. During the Realist era (Chapter 6), these themes of honor and embarrassment inflate, change shape, and take on a more strident intonation. In Tolstoy, the duel broadens out into the battlefield, where honor is eclipsed by courage and the playful narrator is replaced by stern no-nonsense moral authority. In Dostoevsky, concern for privacy can reach insane, pathological, conspiratorial proportions, cunningly masked by self-defensive narrative shields and comic narrators. For the Symbolist and Modernist period (Chapter 7), our theme is the city and its devils – which yields up the greatest Petersburg novel, the greatest Moscow novel, and a dystopian city-state that distils the myths of both these great Russian capital cities. For the Stalinist era (Chapter 8), we consider the doctrine of socialist realism and how it impressed itself upon three genres: the construction novel, the dramatized fairy tale, and the "suspended" lyric materialism of Andrei Platonov. Beginning with the first post-Stalinist Thaw (Chapter 9), the ideology of the canon relaxes somewhat. Literature is officially allowed to acknowledge prisons and labor camps. Authors rechannel familiar high-canon scenarios through gratingly domestic contexts – our examples include the Dostoevskian underground from a harassed female perspective. New heroes appear: Asian businessmen who are also mystics, lyrical alcoholics, starched-collar detectives, serial killers, the tsarist secret police as role model, storage sheds that commit suicide. Certain constants survive from chapter to chapter: honor and humiliation as paths to a viable identity, the death of children.

For some periods, the benchmark writers anchoring the edges of literary space are so different from each other that each begins his own literary tradition. This is the case with the Romantic era, where the "Pushkin" and "Gogol" lines are antipathetic. But in other periods, a great writer will combine elements of both poles in a conscious quest for new and healthier hybrids. Under such conditions, one can speak almost of a "dialectical" development of characters and themes. The task of the mediating author is to challenge the oversimplification that is endemic to binary thinking and thus to re-complicate the field. To take only one example, the most timeworn binary in all of Russian literature: Tolstoy versus Dostoevsky. Like Pushkin and Gogol from an earlier period, these two were seen as incompatible geniuses. But writers appeared – one thinks of Anton Chekhov – whose gift it was to bridge, test, break down, and transform the most canonical hero types and legacies. Just as Pushkin reworked the clichés of European Romanticism in his short stories of the 1830s, so did Chekhov provide explicitly modest, non-melodramatic reworkings of bigger-than-life, tragic Tolstoyan plots in the 1880s and 1890s. Chekhov's characters (like every other literate person alive in Russia) have read *Anna Karenina* and envy its profound insights. But they aren't living in that novel. As creatures of Chekhov's pen, to react in a Tolstoyan way to their plight can be part of their problem, even if it was part of Tolstoy's solution. On occasion, a more recent author at the end of the chain can turn prior inherited worlds inside out or upside down. One example is Andrei Platonov (1899–1951), who, in 1930, suspended socialist realist time-space and – dreamily, as if in a trance – inverted a Stalinist-style production novel into a construction pit that eventually became a grave. In no way are these inversions or syntheses assumed to be superior to the benchmark authors who flank them. They are simply complex in a different way, for the intelligence of a literary tradition is not linear or progressive. It constantly grows in all directions without invalidating its earlier truths. For that reason there is no single optimal place from which to view it. But some students of the Russian tradition have seen in it a darker and more severe pattern than the binaries and triads offered here.

One such skeptic is the cultural historian Steven Marks, in his 2002 book titled *How Russia Shaped the Modern World: From Art to Anti-Semitism, Ballet to Bolshevism*. By what criteria, he asks, does the cosmopolitan common reader sense a work as "Russian"? Not by its length, setting, characters, spirituality, moral demands – in other words, not by a stable list of traits or revealed truths. "Russianness," Marks argues, is a special attitude toward the outside world, one that is dismissive or condemnatory. When nineteenth- and twentieth-century Russian ideas caught on around the world – and catch on they did – it was not because they "worked" or were "true" in any practical (or even moral) sense, but because they were designed to startle, destabilize, and negate. This nay-saying was practiced at a very sophisticated level. From Napoleon's defeat to the defeat of Gorbachev, in Marks's reading, the refrain was the same: resent the bourgeois, consumer-oriented, progress-bewitched West. Out of such restlessness and resentment came Russian maximalism, irrationalism, messianism, mysticism, utopianism. On censored Russian soil, these unruly ideas were either promptly banned, or else co-opted by the state and turned to sinister purpose. But they were a source of inspiration to revolutionaries and dispossessed people everywhere else around the globe. This ecstatically nihilistic edge to so many Russian achievements in art is key to their enduring success.

Marks has been praised as well as censured for this thesis. His book has been taken as a tribute to the dynamic creativity of Russian culture, to its infectious pan-humanism, and also as a slanderous insult to it. One negotiation of his hostile binary might be offered. Contempt for what the "civilized West" considers normal, healthy, or prosperous need not be the sole (nor even the primary) motivating force of Russian artists and thinkers. Russian nay-saying might more fairly be seen as a protest against any fixed idea of normalcy, against the belief that "normalcy" is or must be the norm or the ideal, and that sufferings and exceptional passions are painful diversions from the balanced, healthy condition that everyone would choose if given the option. In Russia's more nonconformist tradition, from the earliest Orthodox saints to the most celebrated Dostoevskian novels, pain and passion have been considered necessary to both wisdom and consciousness. But Marks has nevertheless grasped a basic truth. What returns us to Russian literature again and again is the chance to savor risk-taking at the extreme edges of an idea. And even those writers who parody these extremes (like Chekhov) or who despair at surviving them (like Boris Pilnyak [1894–1937]) are unsympathetic to the goals, behaviors, and humdrum activity that result from a disciplined or calculated pursuit of material prosperity.

What Marks explores in his book is one flamboyant expression of the "Russian Idea." It too is part of the story of Russian literature. This Idea, born in Moscow in the 1830s among Russian Romantic disciples of Schelling, has had a long gestation. The émigré philosopher Nicolas Berdyaev (1874–1948), in a mood shaped equally by nostalgia and despair, codified the Russian Idea for Western consumption in a book of that name published in 1947, on the ruins of World War II.[7] In it he emphasized Russia's divinely inspired mission on behalf of all other peoples through her passivity, apocalypticism, collectivism, distinctly feminine softness (receptivity and forgiveness), indifference to political grandeur and private property alike, and her anarchic preference for the depths of personality over the superficialities of institutional identity. The work of great novelists and poets was recruited selectively as evidence.

Three Russian Ideas

As Russian imperial pretensions were enfeebled and discredited in the final decades of the twentieth century, these cosmic ambitions contracted. In 2004, an anthology of present-day Russian opinion on this time-honored, oft-maligned topic appeared as *The Russian Idea: In Search of a New Identity*, edited by a Canadian scholar of religion after seven years spent teaching at Moscow State University.[8] By that time, of course, political caution was gone, Aesopian language was gone, the centralized management of culture lay in shambles, and Russians were routinely invoking Western cultural theorists to discuss their native experience. Even in this anthology, however, traditional value-categories prove resilient. No literary work can wholly escape their shadow. To complete this chapter on critical models and their readers, then, I sketch out three "Russian Ideas" (cultural invariants) that have recurrently served to distinguish this literature from any other. These are the Russian Word, Russian space, and their meeting ground on the human face.

The socially marked, quasi-sacred Word

In the Beginning was the Russian Word. This word has always been perceived as more than a means to communicate the merely transitory needs or truths of the current day. Russia understood herself as having come to consciousness (as a mute infant comes to consciousness) through language. This Romantic-era conviction has had enormous staying power, and to some extent explains the charismatic grip of the Poet on Russian culture. Writers frequently attributed to the Russian Word "such values as self-consciousness, self-reflection, perception, intentionality" – as if the word itself and by itself were a person.[9] In one's native language, the wandering self could find its abiding home. Kathleen Parthé opens her book *Russia's Dangerous Texts* (2004) with "ten common beliefs" about the relationship between literature and politics in pre-1991 Russia.[10] These include the truisms that Russians read more than any other people; that in Russia all serious "politics, prophecy and identity" took place through literature; that a single literary text (licit or illicit) would galvanize the attention of all reading Russians at a given time, providing an electrical current of common language; and that the great writer, by definition, must avoid cooperating with "power" [*vlast'*]. The flip side of a country that exiles and shoots its poets is a culture that nurtures an image of the writer as prophet, philosopher, a person with the status of (in Solzhenitsyn's words from his novel *The First Circle*) a "second government." Even when the word fails in its mission – as many post-communist writers now feel it did, and perhaps should have – that failure is predicated on immensely high expectations. In his retrospective book on writers and readers post-1995, *Remaining Relevant after Communism* (2006), Andrew Wachtel opens his chapter on "The Writer as National Hero" with the reminder that "a good definition of Eastern Europe would be the part of the world where serious literature and those who produce it have traditionally been overvalued."[11] Two broad explanations have been suggested for this word-centeredness in Russian culture: one spiritual, the other secular.

At first glance the spiritual primacy of the word might seem paradoxical, for in Russian high medieval culture up through the late seventeenth century, literacy was low. The visual image and the miracle-bearing relic had far more potency than the written word. Eastern Christendom – first Byzantine, then Russian – revered icons even more intensely than did Roman Catholicism, especially after the Eastern Church decisively refuted the iconoclast movement (triggered by the charge that icon worship was akin to idolatry) in the eighth century CE. What is more, signed, authored literature was undervalued and at times even demonized. "Authorship was not one of the recognized activities of Old Russia," D. S. Mirsky writes in his *History of Russian Literature*. "There were no 'writers,' but only bookmen [*knizhniki*]."[12] Books were valued, but as artifacts to be inherited, copied, memorized, not created anew. Although Western medieval culture shared many of these values, Russia – which experienced no Renaissance or Reformation – upheld for much longer the idea of the divinely received Word as the measure of all things, as a sort of Absolute.

Newness was suspect. For this reason, the qualities of visuality, palpability, and fixedness were compatible with a Russian cult of the word. In fact, they served it. As Kathleen Parthé reminds us, the sacred, immutably "thing-like" qualities of the Old Russian word – the importance placed on the design of its alphabet and proper spelling; its incantational potential – imbued it with magic or miracle-working powers.[13] On Old Russian soil, then, word and image tended not to compete but to collaborate in a tight moral alliance. The great nineteenth-century Realist writers inherited this tradition. Once uttered, words were not mere means to an end but already, in some sense, ends – deeds in themselves. These traditions fed richly into the revival of Russian poetry in the early twentieth century, and, ominously, into an equally rich cult of forced or fanciful political denunciations in the Stalinist 1930s.

Secular reasons for Russia's word-centeredness echo these sacral concerns. A magically potent Word was a word worthy of being closely watched. From the mid-eighteenth to the end of the twentieth century, state censorship could reach a degree of suspiciousness and capriciousness hard for us to fathom in terms of the labor-hours required to impose it. Of course, there was always freedom by default: bureaucratic carelessness, networks of protection and politeness, regal arbitrariness, mercy, and the sheer vastness of the administrative task – but all the same, not even a rudimentary system of safeguards for individual expression in the public realm ever existed. In principle, every scrap of newsprint, every line of verse could be scrutinized, by secular and church authorities, with separate, successively more severe filters for in-print genres and theatrical performance. This quest to root out unapproved ideological content was made even more virulent by a worship of the shape and sound of the specifically Russian word. When Pushkin was exiled to the south of Russia in 1820 for penning some revolutionary verse, Russia's sophisticated bilingual elite must have noticed that the sentiments in his offending poems did little more than repeat the abstract clichés of French liberationist rhetoric on which the reigning Tsar Alexander I had himself been raised two decades earlier. But when Pushkin addressed local realities and applied his glorious Russian to those banally familiar turns of phrase, they became startlingly new, authoritative, and impermissible.

Russian space: never-ending, absorptive, unfree

It is a truism that vis-à-vis the Western nations, Russia has always lost in time and triumphed in space. Space saved Russia from Napoleon and Hitler. The broad expanse of Siberia saved Dostoevsky's Raskolnikov (and Dostoevsky himself) from crimes against body and spirit committed in crowded, stifling cities. The "bird-troika" invoked by Gogol to save his trickster Chichikov at the end of *Dead Souls* thrills us precisely because it rises up out of the dust so unexpectedly, terrifying all who witness it, and then soars away into the distance while, in the final phrase of the novel, "all other peoples and nations stand aside and grant it right of way." Russian land never runs out. The need to control this potent surplus of space and tie its wandering population down to the tax rolls justified the centralized autocracy. In the opinion of Marshall Poe, writing a decade after the 1991 collapse, if the Russian state looks like a failure it is probably because we stubbornly insist on classifying her as a borderline European power, in which context she is indeed always "behind." But in fact the Russia of the tsars and Soviets was a remarkable geopolitical enterprise, the modern world's most successful West Eurasian empire.[14]

Space is forever forward, but time is an embarrassment. "Backward" for Russia has conventionally meant "not yet caught up with the progress made by France, Britain, America." In part because of such invidious comparisons, novelists as diverse as Tolstoy, Dostoevsky, Olesha, and Solzhenitsyn have been united in their contempt for European "progress" – acquisitive, morally stupefying – and eager to discredit it. But the humiliation and vulnerability remained, and communism attempted to alter both. Time, too, would be forced to move to Russia's advantage. When Valentin Kataev wrote his Modernist industrial novel *Time, Forward!* (1932), which chronicles the construction of a huge metallurgical plant in the Urals city of Magnitogorsk, his choice of title resonated. We learn in Chapter 2 of that novel that Kataev's engineer hero, David Lvovich Margulies, always awakes before his alarm clock rings. There is no Chapter 1. It was, we read, "omitted for the time being." Life is moving too fast; no time for it!

All the same, that abundant and reliable parameter, Russian space, could be deceptive. Just as a reverence for the Russian word can lead paradoxically to its obsessive monitoring and even enslavement, so triumphant Russian space has been accompanied by a sense of being trapped, tied down, crowded together in tiny communal apartments in cities with permanent housing shortages or herded into prison cells scattered over an open plain. Since so many literary narratives, from fairy tales to epic poems to postmodernist science fiction, are built on this paradox of vast but constricting Russian space, let us consider some of its dimensions.

First, size does not mean power or safety. Geophysically speaking, Russia is a wide, flat, overexposed, underdeveloped plain, with her major rivers running north–south, into foreign ports or frozen marsh. Her huge spread has been a constant source of national pride, but the lack of fixed boundaries or natural obstacles on her land borders has encouraged aggression by other peoples and a wanton imperialism pressing outward from her own core. Since industrialization has a great deal to do with access – with extracting resources or manufacturing goods and then moving them to ports and markets – Russia's immense physical resources, for most of her history, were not translated into efficient productivity or national security.

It was easier to exile dissidents to Siberia than to integrate them, to trash and move on rather than to recycle, negotiate, and conserve. "Because Russia had become accustomed to solving its historical problems geographically," Mikhail Epstein writes, "it came to occupy an area so large that finding its place in time became somewhat difficult."[15] In a country this large with an overall climate so severe, transit time is enormous. Setting out, there is no assurance one will ever arrive. In a 1996 essay on Russian destiny and the Russian Idea, Mikhail Ilyin speaks of two governing images for this continental empire, the first "the rush from one valley to another through dangerous and threatening stretches of forest or steppe" and the second, a specter that has proved equally anxiety-laden, that of "roadless space," or "the myth of the road going nowhere."[16] These two images so debase the movement and goal of any human activity that the end recedes, the reward disappears, and there remains only the texture of an exhausting, short-term present. One recalls the slogans that filled Russian street posters soon after the implosion of communism in 1991: "Seventy-two years on the way to nowhere."

"Making the rush" from one secure valley to another encouraged a distinctive spatial binary in traditional folk consciousness. Cities, those dots on a plain, were protected by their churches and Christian saints; everything outside the city fell under the sway of pagan gods. Space was divided into what was known and protected – what had its patron saint or spirit – and what was unprotected and unknown, the uncharted roaming grounds of various demons, imps, and mischievous spirits. Russian expanse was deified as Moist Mother Earth, but not after the manner of most gods. It is a remarkable fact, one of perennial concern to Russia's great poets, that this most successful continental empire, which at its zenith covered one-sixth the land mass of the globe, never glorified a god of war and never produced a genuinely affirmative, appropriately chauvinistic war epic.

The enormity, flatness, insecurity, and low population density of the Eurasian continent had socioeconomic consequences that conditioned all domestic Russian narratives. Those who worked the soil did not initially stay put. To guarantee the tillable land its laborers, the army its soldiers, and the state its tax revenues, peasants were tied down to their villages in the late sixteenth century and then gradually enserfed as the personal property of the gentry and noble class. Of course the Russian serf was neither racially marked nor "imported" from another continent, as was the case in the northern hemisphere of the New

World. But with Peter the Great, Russia in effect became two countries in an equivalently explosive way. Peasant villages adopted a siege mentality against the cities and towns. When urban outsiders appeared at the edge of a village, it was not to trade, educate, heal, but always to bring the bad news of recruitment or taxes: always to take something away.

Eighteenth-century prose dramas mercilessly satirized country bumpkins. Of equal or greater weight to these comic scenes were the tragic or angry variants. The peasant imprisoned on the plain at the mercy of "city meddlers" became the protagonist of a wide number of narratives, from Mikhail Chulkov's savage 1792 sketch on the bureaucratic cover-up of a mass peasant murder ("A Bitter Fate") through the conscience-stricken outrage of Aleksandr Radishchev (1749–1802), the sentimentalism of Nikolai Karamzin (1766–1826), Turgenev's evocative *Sportsman's Sketches*, Tolstoy's "Alyosha the Pot," and Chekhov's rural tales ("In the Ravine," "Peasants"). In his 1885 story "The Culprit," Chekhov relates the criminal trial of one Denis Grigoriev, peasant, accused of sabotage against the railways and sentenced to prison because he had unscrewed a nut that held the rails to the ties – for how, mutters Denis, can any decent fish be caught without a sinker? Of course he would not have unscrewed *all* of them. In his 1905 memoir of Chekhov, Maksim Gorky relates how the author of "The Culprit" was cornered one day by a young, freshly uniformed prosecutor who insisted that progressive society had no choice but to imprison the Denis Grigorievs if Russian trains were to run safely – and how mournful Chekhov became, hearing him out. This image of an uncomprehending and trapped peasant (sometimes innocent, sometimes defensively sly), victimized by a callous city dweller with a sheaf of laws in his briefcase and an arrest warrant in his hand, became a painful nineteenth-century genre scene. This geophysical binary – urban seats of power against the countryside – reached its apogee in the collectivization campaigns of the first Stalinist Five-Year Plan (1928–32). By that time, of course, writers were no longer free to describe it. It has been said that only during the war of 1941–45 did enough Russians succeed in suffering together to heal this split between the tiny, rich, exploiting cities and the broad laboring plain. Surely this was one reason why World War II narratives remained a vigorous literary genre in Russia long after the other combatants in that conflict had moved on to other themes.

This abrupt distinction between city life and life everywhere else has proved tenacious. The refrain of Chekhov's *Three Sisters*, to get somehow "To Moscow!" so that real life can begin, is gently mocked in that play. But significantly we do not know where the Prozorov family estate is: is it four miles from that dreamed-of Moscow, or forty, or four hundred? Despite the telegraph and occasional stretch of train track, the space between habitations remained mythical, without gradation. Roads were (and are) a disaster. There is little tradition of the civilized suburb. To this day, surprisingly close to the city limits of Petersburg and Moscow, "the provinces" begin – unmowed, unpaved, out of touch. To leave Moscow or Petersburg has always meant not only to go out in space but also to go back in time. This too reinforces the sense of space being primary and pockets of time negotiable, set down like the cities, as islands in a sea.

Even this excessive, untamable Russian space had its edges. In 1829, Pushkin slipped out from under police surveillance to visit the Russian army skirmishing on the Caucasus–Turkish border. As he later described this episode in his droll travel notes, *A Journey to Arzrum* (1836), en route to join the Russian troops he happened upon a small river which, a Cossack informed him, was the boundary. "I had never before seen foreign soil," Pushkin wrote of this encounter. "The border held something mysterious for me . . . Never before had I broken out from the borders of immense Russia. I rode happily into the sacred river, and my good horse carried me out on the Turkish bank. But this bank had already been conquered: I was still in Russia."[17]

Pushkin was never allowed out. This scenario of sealed borders around an immense, unmappable world became another theme, both hair-raising and comic, that lasted right up until the end of the Soviet Union. Russia, so this thesis went, is so big, her borders so impenetrable, her censorship so pervasive, her people so gullible, and her ability to construct whole countries inside herself (with space to spare) so difficult to detect, that the authorities could simply *fake* the existence of everywhere else. In his 1992 novella *Omon Ra*, Viktor Pelevin (b. 1962) tells the story of a young Muscovite training for a suicidal space program, only to discover that there is no program, no broadcast from outer space, only a shabby stage set strewn with empty vodka bottles down in the metro and a black drape with holes poked out for stars. In a chapter titled "Imaginary West," the cultural anthropologist Alexei Yurchak discusses this fantasy-zone in terms of a "politically faked travelogue," a literary genre productive as late as 2002. A simple factory worker from the Urals circa 1970 is finally allowed to go to Paris. But "after a few euphoric days in the French capital" he bumps into a painted canvas stretched on a huge frame. It had all been a theatrical backdrop, "Paris simply did not exist in the world. It never had."[18]

If a real and inaccessible outside perhaps did not exist, then an "accessible inside" to Russia has proven itself real on several levels. I have in mind Russian spatial utopias. Most cultures, Russia's included, have utopias in time – a Golden Age in the past, a Promised Kingdom in the future. But Russia also has a vital minor tradition of timeless, salvation-bearing utopias in space. These utopias refuse to accept the reality of Russia's physical defenselessness, the porousness of her borders, her inability to protect her population from chronic and devastating invasion. And thus they manipulate space – that inexhaustible Russian resource – to overcome the vulnerability of space.

Yury Lotman, who devoted a good portion of his scholarly life to spatial topographies, discusses this mythical geo-ethics as codified in Russian medieval texts.[19] The model has had impressive lasting power. Dostoevsky drew on it in his great novels (reverently for his righteous persons like the Elder Zosima, symbolically for his seekers like Raskolnikov, in travestied form for his petty devils), and traces of this value system survive in Stalin-era socialist realist texts. Geo-ethics combines the high status of physical matter in the Eastern Orthodox Church with the moral implication of the compass. Lands to the east are pagan, to the west are heretic: only at the Russian center can one find holiness. Righteous persons [*pravedniki*] wander through this space, colonizing it with their humility and charity, aware that all corruptible matter encountered down below can be resurrected in a heavenly space that is continuous with it. Eternity is not the absence of matter or the transcending of matter, but its absolute triumph. Up there, matter lasts forever. Lotman sees this "eternally thing-like" nature of salvation as an intensely Russian invention. Among the most celebrated sites of geo-ethics in Russian culture is the Invisible City of Kitezh on the bank, or the bottom, of Lake Svetloyar.

Great Kitezh was built in the Yaroslavl-Volga region northeast of Moscow in the twelfth century. In 1239 it was destroyed by the Mongol Khan Batu, grandson of the great Ghengis. No contemporaneous account of the battle mentions any survivors; the city simply vanished. To counter that unacceptable fact, popular legend decrees that the city exists but at the final moment was "transposed," not lifted to Heaven but sunk into the lake to be saved, where its bells and golden domes are still audible and visible to the righteous person. In successive Russian times of trouble, the Kitezh legend revives and Lake Svetloyar becomes again a place of pilgrimage.

The populist Vladimir Korolenko (1853–1921) wrote an ethnographic sketch on the region in 1890. The Symbolist Dmitry Merezhkovsky (1865–1941), in his 1905 novel *Anti-Christ. Peter and Alexis*, linked the invisible city to all in Russian culture that Peter the Great had attempted to destroy. In his pantheistic opera *The Invisible City of Kitezh and the Maiden Fevronia* (1904), Nikolai Rimsky-Korsakov created Russia's most perfect artistic tribute to *dvoeverie*, dual pagan-Christian faith, with a final scene set in the radiant deathlessness of the resurrected city. The Symbolists warmed to the apocalyptic resonance of this miraculous place, and twentieth-century history bore them out. A "Kitezh poem" was written by Maksimilian Voloshin in August 1919, when General

Denikin's White forces were moving on Moscow during the darkest days of the Civil War; another was composed by Anna Akhmatova in 1940, as Nazi troops were annihilating Poland. In the opening lines of her poem, Akhmatova calls herself a *kitezhanka*, a resident of that doomed, saved, sunken city. Essential to the myth is that the city indubitably exists – only we who now gaze upon it are insufficiently pure to hear it or see it. In her work on the Kitezh legend, Ksana Blank suggests that the myth of this Invisible City is structured as anti-Petersburg and set in the hidden, apocalyptic, backward-looking space of the seventeenth-century schismatics or Old Believers, where it refutes the very idea of linear, temporal progress in the visible public realm.[20]

A family of human faces

Kitezh makes itself visible to the face that gazes on it, but only if that face is seeking communion and purification. With this image, we arrive at our final Russian idea, or cultural invariant, that might be said to link the Russian Word and Russian space: the concept of *lik*. *Lik* (pronounced *leek*) is one of several Russian nouns for the human face, and etymologically the most basic. The word signifies visage, countenance, a responsive face that contains eyes that gaze out on other faces, ears that receive others' words. Eyes on such a face transmit divine light.[21] Saints portrayed on icons possess a *lik*. The noun *lik* is more spiritually elevated than *litso*, the generic Russian word for face, and directly gives rise to the word *lichnost'*, the abstract noun palely rendered in English as "personality" but which, in Russian spiritual philosophy, always implies moral and interpersonal responsibility. At any point *litso* can degenerate into *lichina*, a mask that refuses to communicate, that looks (and is) lifeless, whose beauty becomes rigid and demonic. Dostoevsky's Nikolai Stavrogin, the estranged, doomed hero of his novel *Demons*, possesses precisely such a beautiful and terrible *lichina*.

Leo Tolstoy felt these distinctions keenly, if intuitively, when creating the characters of *War and Peace*. Female beauty fascinated him. Eventually he came to fear it, but not before he had analyzed its workings thoroughly in Natasha Rostova, Hélène Kuragina-Bezukhova, and Marya Bolkonskaya. Natasha enchants, but she is not beautiful. At moments of crisis her face is described as positively ugly, misshapen, "absurd," with its large mouth gaping atop her scrawny neck and shoulders. To the highest degree, however, this face is responsive, porous, a *lik*. Natasha's mobility, receptivity, and joy in the present become the magnet that draws others in. Everything she does and says has the stamp of her own eccentric face on it (the Russian word for "personal" is *lichnoe*, "belonging to that face"). In contrast, an unresponsive, lacquered beauty is always *im*personal, a *lichina*. Such is Hélène's static "marble beauty" and complacent self-absorption; like the terrible beauty of Dostoevsky's Stavrogin, it will degenerate into active debauchery and evil. Tolstoy awards to his beloved Princess Marya a third type of female face: an ugliness so severe that men turn away in embarrassment and she herself despairs before the mirror. But again and again Marya's radiant eyes, the eyes of the Mother of God on a holy icon, have the capacity to transform her plainness – never to make it formally beautiful, which in Tolstoy is never a virtue, but to express love toward others, forgiveness, compassion, and access to a higher spiritual sphere. When, during Prince Andrei's final days and death, Natasha and Marya at last overcome their mutual antipathy, their two positive variants of a receptive human face (immediate joy and contemplative depth) supplement one another in a passionate friendship. Only a mix of the two families can produce the fertility of the novel's Epilogue.

Nikolai Gogol, our final exemplar in this Russian family of human faces, adds a third variant: neither the radiant iconic *lik* nor the hollowly deceptive *lichina*, but something more monstrous and comic at the dynamic peripheries of this sacred/demonic binary. Gogol specializes in the face that is still being assembled (its parts not yet fixed in place: a floating nose, an unfinished chin, even a face like an egg with a certain phosphorescence but no distinct features) or the face that is already spoiled and rotting (Plyushkin's from *Dead Souls*). At times Gogol even gives us "a hole in place of a face."[22] The astonishing elasticity of Gogolian faces is his contribution to overcoming the separation of body and spirit, always so uncongenial to Russian Orthodox thinking.

The speaking, receiving face is the only force competent to bridge great Russian distances. It does so directly, eye to eye – not through intermediaries, representatives, or impersonal "blind" laws, for the idea that "justice is blind" is incomprehensible and counterintuitive to the logic of *lik*. The desired direct intuition occurs either in close spatial proximity to others or else in a sort of sensually felt collectivity, what Russians have traditionally called *sobornost'* (conciliarity, togetherness) or *tselostnost'* (wholeness). Central to this complex of ideas is that wholeness does *not* mean homogeneity or sameness. Every face is different, every personality is distinct, but each needs the other (or many others) in order to realize the contours of its own self. It is significant that the Russian language has no native word for privacy, and also that Russian culture did not develop the metaphysical image so productive in Western Christendom, that of the soul imprisoned within the body. The body (and especially the face) was not a prison but a vehicle, a responsive mirror, the "soul made flesh." Light moved through that body and sanctified it. Twentieth-century Bolshevik literature seized upon this sacral collectivist tradition and politicized it, first into a cult of the people's communal heroism and then into a cult of party-mindedness, shearing off the heterogeneity at the core of the Orthodox idea. The success of such a campaign, for all its brutality, betrays its deep organic roots.

As Tolstoy correctly divined, the two master plots in Russian socio-literary history are *War* and *Peace*. How they are won is peculiar to this nation. War is won by space, although usually at ghastly human expense. Peace is registered as a victory of face-to-face intimacy, clustering around the kitchen table, samovar, nursery, whispered or outlawed poem. For most of Russian literature, the battle-field and the hearth have been enduring polar values. Cultural anthropologists at work today on Russian communication patterns note the genres of litany and lament that develop freely only in the space of small (often communal) apartments, bathhouses, and run-down country dachas barricaded against the hostile outside world.[23]

The same binary might be said to govern more strictly aesthetic realms. In his 2005 book on the codes of Russian musical culture, Boris Gasparov argues that Russian nineteenth-century creativity in several fields – philosophy, literature, and music – was characterized by a single unified striving: the desire to escape the trappings and obligations of Russia's external empire, with its spectacles, masquerades, pomp, whims of patronage, and to reconsecrate intimate, non-theatrical, sentimental space.[24] Thus the whole world feels at home in the Great Russian Novel, which so often ends as a comedy – that is, as a ritual of fertility and family reconciliation. Successors to that great novel in the twentieth century were pressured to redefine this ritual out of the nuclear family into some larger, equally compelling unit that could serve communist ideology and motherland. When that model failed or proved insufficient, the family became Russian Literature itself, "Pushkin House."

There are spaces, however, that the Empire and the Hearth do not cover, which Russian literary culture has traditionally not endowed with a sympathetic face. These are the middle spaces: commercial classes such as merchants, bankers, and Jews; professional classes such as lawyers and professors; and bureaucratic classes of every sort. The compromised heroes here range from the local thieving mayor and his cronies in Gogol's play *The Government Inspector* to Anna's unhappy spouse Aleksei Karenin, government minister made ridiculous by his desire, cruelly satirized by Tolstoy, to improve the plight of human beings through an official commission. If the bureaucrat is modest and oppressed, like the clerk Akaky Akakievich in Gogol's "The Overcoat," then we might see (after a fashion) a human face. If a learned person is of low enough rank, like a provincial tutor or schoolteacher, then some virtues might be mixed in with the weakness and vice. But let any of these middlemen flourish, and they lose all possible positive qualities. One challenge for twentieth-century Russian literature was to devise an acceptable sort of success for the pragmatic and disciplined wage-earner, state servitor, or career bureaucrat in modern civic culture, without losing the enormous energy contained in the sacrificial, spiritually rich hero.

If this was a difficult task for the Soviet century, it will be even more daunting for the more fragmentary and less cohesive twenty-first. But full stops, failed apocalypse, and looking out the window at empty space going nowhere are completely familiar to this cultural tradition and easily accommodated by it. This Introduction opened on the assertion that the Russian literary canon is "always about to forget that it is merely made up out of words." Assuming that is true, surely Russia's literature will talk itself out of this trap too.

Chapter 2

Heroes and their plots

In the preceding chapter we introduced Bakhtin's chronotope. It might be helpful in this chapter, before discussing some favored Russian character types, to review the services it can provide.

Bakhtin devised the chronotope as an aid for "walking into" and co-experiencing the time-space of a fictional world. Prose fiction is a field. Usually it is populated by more than one consciousness and designed to be experienced over time. In all but the most disorienting fictional environments – the absolute absurd, for example, or literature of terror and trauma devised to frustrate all attempts at communication – readers will seek to talk, interact, or empathize with characters inhabiting this field. The character can be a talking frog if we're inside a beast fable, personified Vice or Virtue if inside a medieval mystery play, an alien from outer space if inside a science fiction, or a recognizably human being: the physical wrappings of consciousness are incidental. Both the type of creature and the rules for relating to it depend upon the conventions of the literary genre. What feels strange in one environment can be wholly unmarked in another. In all cases, however, time and space in the chronotope are fused. Some sorts of time – say, in old-fashioned comic strips and soap-opera serials – never add up. Hours, days, years pass, but people do not age; characters might not even remember from one episode to the next. Accordingly, the space that accompanies such time is abstract and non-historical.

Some sorts of time permit the hero to change, but only at miraculous, isolated moments (say, tales of metamorphosis or religious conversion). The qualities of the surrounding space may or may not change to accord with the abruptly altered hero. In other chronotopes, the outside world changes in a variety of ways, but the people residing in that time-space are "ready-made" from the start. Their potential is predetermined. They may be tested by events, but they do not learn or mature as a result of such testing; they merely unfold as a pre-formed bud unfolds into a given leaf. Fully novelistic heroes (Bakhtin's favorites, such as he sees in Goethe, Dickens, and Dostoevsky) both change themselves and presume that they live in a changing environment, which will present them with unexpected challenges to which they must respond.

In Bakhtin's view, the vigorously functioning, free personality (fictive or real) needs open-ended time more than open-ended space. It is no surprise, however, that the most durable parameter in many Russian chronotopic situations is space, with the temporal dimension a secondary, often dysfunctional afterthought. "Growing up" properly can appear difficult or dead-ended. Developmental time simply stops: through early sacrificial death, in capped or arrested adolescence, or on the far side of threshold moments that commit the hero to an unchanging revealed truth. Conversely, space-based trajectories or metaphors remain fertile and attractive options in a variety of secular as well as sacred genres: "setting out in search of something," being exiled or displaced, waking up after thirty years of immobility and "going on the road" to slay Russia's enemies (the plot of Ilya Muromets, Russia's favorite epic hero). Start with the spatial imperative, and time will tag along. Even when the journey is parodied beyond repair, as in the tragicomic alcoholic fantasy *Moscow to the End of the Line* (1970) by Venedikt Erofeyev (1938–90), the illusion of movement is the indispensable starting point. Leo Tolstoy, Russia's great demystifier and debunker of all the bad habits we live by, spent decades writing narratives that showed how people are doomed if they try to escape their truth or their fate by running away – from *The Cossacks* (1863) through *Anna Karenina* (1873–78) to his late stories "Master and Man" (1895) and "Father Sergius" (1898). And then a week before his death, he himself boarded a train to get out.

In addition to a general preference for changing one's fate by moving through space, the very concept of evil was scattered and diversified. In traditional Russian folk culture, the devil [*chort*] was small: omnipresent, petty, devious, often a changeling, miserably ugly and unheroic. Traditional Russian culture had a bigger devil [*dyavol*] – an abstractly ominous black body – but no humanized, grand Miltonic Satan; native Russian demons were "not tragic or avuncular or nobly doomed free spirits."[1] Such anthropomorphized images of evil, largely Romantic in origin, arrived from the West only in the early nineteenth century. Instead, a myriad of tiny folk devils hovered around your body, eager to crawl down your throat when you yawned, up your birth canal while you were delivering your infant, into your ears during an unguarded moment. Against this onslaught of small exhaustions and seductions one could apply numerous folk charms and incantations. But the best defense against demonic temptation was "righteousness."

Righteous persons [*pravednik* (m.) / *pravednitsa* (f.)]

To be a "righteous person" is more an attitude than a deed. Christian faith often informs this righteousness, but the type was frequently secularized and re-sacralized. A righteous person usually requires an enemy to fight against – the Mongols, Napoleon, Hitler, capitalists as a class, the Antichrist – but a big, showy Foe is by no means necessary. The enemy as well as the task can be very small. Dostoevsky's radiant *pravedniki* (pl.) in *The Brothers Karamazov* (the Elder Zosima and the youngest brother Alyosha) are of this sturdy everyday sort, fending off doubts with a spiritually healthy mind. Success in the deed is not essential, but steadfastness is.

In her discussion of righteousness in *Russia's Dangerous Texts*, Kathleen Parthé remarks of this sort of hero that the righteousness is "inflexible but unselfish."[2] A righteous person can stay home and instruct by example, but often, "unable to bear the injustice of the world," he or she becomes a wanderer [*strannik/strannitsa*]. Central to the type is always a willingness to suffer – but regardless of torment self-inflicted or imposed, a *pravednik* does not change his mind or his soul. He cannot, for he is inseparable from his truth. He can become a righteous person after a sinful youth (as does the elder Zosima), but like Saint Augustine, once he has seen or arrived at the truth, he does not develop further. For this reason, Parthé remarks, Russians of more liberal or ironic temperament have been wary of this peculiar sort of heroism (pp. 148–49).

The prototypical *pravednik* is a martyred saint. He may choose to cooperate with the state, rescuing it heroically in its hour of need, but he cannot be owned by any earthly power and often boycotts existing governments altogether. This "hagiographic [saint's life] type" experienced a minor boom during the reform decade of the 1860s, when dozens of devotional publishing houses were founded.[3] In any era, the *pravednik* tends to adhere to archaic, backward-looking truths, valuing the impulses of the heart over the pride of the intellect or the cleverness of the machine. The righteous almost always prefer the village to the city. Aleksandr Solzhenitsyn (b. 1918) fashioned himself into the twentieth century's greatest exemplar of this type, both in his life and his art.

Unsurprisingly, after the 1917 Revolution the Bolshevik government made strenuous attempts to recruit righteous sufferers for the cause of forward-looking communism. Precedent was not difficult to find. Chernyshevsky's utopian novel *What Is To Be Done?* (1863), which Lenin called "the greatest and most talented representation of socialism before Marx," includes in a cameo role one political activist-ascetic, Rakhmetov, who sleeps on nails to harden his resolve. Revolutionaries shared many traits with medieval saints. Among them are the ideal of bodily discipline (fasting and chastity), a transcendence of brute matter (miraculous visions, impossible work quotas), and a biographical progression that begins with a separation from society, is followed by initiation into the divine mystery, and ends with a potential for "return" and reintegration.[4] One common sign of a specifically ascetic Russian hero-saint, modern as well as medieval, is that he does not return. He perfects himself and withdraws further, into increasingly remote geographical spaces. Others may follow him into that wilderness, but the hero does not need others to realize his truth. He is complete in himself.

We might say, then, that relations between righteous persons and their Truth remain stable and unambiguous, but relations between a *pravednik* and other human beings can differ widely – both inside fiction, and between fictional characters and the reader. Consider some examples from famous Russian novels. Sonya Marmeladova in *Crime and Punishment* is a *pravednitsa*; she never doubts the rightness of her views over the vacillating anguish of Raskolnikov. But she rarely preaches, either to him or to the reader. Only when directly interrogated does she share the grounds of her faith, and then reluctantly. She is aware of her truth unconsciously, in action, because she is fused with it. Her concern and love are directed at all times toward saving the tormented hero. Such self-effacement is a trademark of Dostoevsky's righteous people, whose gestures are turned wholly outward, and who (unless ill with epilepsy and raving) tend to be short on words. The chattering, opinionated confessant in Dostoevsky is rarely worthy of trust.

Tolstoy's variants on the truth-bearing type are different. His heroes tend to be oriented inward, constantly talking to themselves or "thinking out loud," and they address their truth to the reader (whom they wish to persuade) more directly than to their fictive co-characters. Autobiographical heroes such as Konstantin Levin from *Anna Karenina* or Dmitry Nekhlyudov from the novel *Resurrection* (1898) are genuine seekers who come to know Truth. But the urgency of this search to their own desperate selves is such that they have no energy to attend to others *as* others; other people's needs and experiences serve largely as a backboard against which to enlighten their own consciousness. (Tolstoy was of course alert to this selfish, self-inflating dynamic, and strove helplessly throughout his life to attain an *un*conscious humility.) It is characteristic of the gentler, more tolerant Chekhov that he created stories designed to truth-monger in reverse, showing a greater wisdom in *losing* one's righteousness than in proving it. *The Duel* (1891) is an exemplary tale in this regard: each antagonist begins confident that he knows and can expose the fraudulence of the values that the other lives by – and manages to do so very skillfully. But at the end, both admit that "No one knows the whole truth."

Very occasionally a failed *pravednik*, for all the indisputability of his failure, utterly wins the sympathy of the reader, the author, and the fictional world in which he lives. He can even be rewarded, although not with salvation. Such is the eponymous novelist-hero of *The Master and Margarita* (1940) by Mikhail Bulgakov (1891–1940). This extraordinary novel takes place simultaneously in three different spaces (Stalinist Moscow; Jerusalem during the crucifixion of Jesus; and some stratospheric metaphysical space undated and unmarked). The Master is tested and found wanting in fortitude – he cannot protect his novel against the hostile outside world – but ultimately he is empowered, as a writer, to create the new word that alters Divine history. His mistress Margarita, who has bargained with Satan to get him back, emerges as a *pravednitsa*, a truth-bearer for whom loyalty and love do not merely work miracles, but are themselves the miracle.

Bulgakov's Margarita, the unfaithful wife whose virtue is fidelity, and the saintly prostitute Sonya Marmeladova, whose "soul made flesh" hardly registers the degrading effects of her profession, are two models of the *pravednitsa*, or female carrier of truth. But there are others. Like Sonya, most have their source in Mary, Mother of God (in Eastern Christianity, Mary's protective mercy is emphasized rather than her virginity). As did Rome, Russia domesticated this revered Marian image, but along somewhat different lines from the Western or Catholic Madonna, who was eroticized as early as Dante and became a cult in Europe during the Age of Chivalry. The Beautiful Lady arrived late in Russia, on the brink of the twentieth century. Even in her secularized guise, the Marian *pravednitsa* transcended sexuality as often as she incorporated it. Two of her most popular manifestations were as maiden or bride, and as mother.

As "bride" – even if this status exists only in the fantasies of the girl – the Russian heroine blended with the enlightened female protagonist created by the French feminist novelist George Sand (1804–76). This hybrid inspired a decade of stern, earnest female heroes, perfected by Ivan Turgenev in a triad of early novels: *Rudin* (1856), *A Nest of Gentlefolk* (1859), and *On the Eve* (1860). Each features a naïvely idealistic woman who loves and resolves to serve (that is, to save) a flawed, weak, "superfluous," and ultimately doomed man, who inevitably fails her. The Russian source for such heroines is Pushkin's Tatyana Larina from *Eugene Onegin*. While pointedly not sacrificial, Tatyana's path is, for a love story, dazzlingly renunciatory; traces of a saint's life glint affectionately through her childhood. Unconsummated love stories – being simpler, more controllable, and in their own lofty way, more selfish – are characteristic of truth-carriers.

The *pravednitsa* did not have to be a maiden or a nun. Wives and mothers in Old Russia were revered and formally canonized. Maksim Gorky's novel *Mother* (1907, first published in the USA in English) became the most influential incarnation of the Russian maternal saint in its forward-looking, atheist variant. In this founding text in the "Bolshevik tradition of secular hagiography," the sacrificial and salvational subtext is wholly restored.[5] Through love for her revolutionist son, the mother Pelegeya Nilovna outgrows both the resignation bred into peasant life and her own possessive nuclear-family love, becoming a comrade, a *pravednitsa*, and a radical activist for the working class. The Mother's spiritual transformation also altered the image of the Pietà – for if Pelegeya Nilovna enacts the Madonna at the Cross, then Christ has become a social revolutionary. Gorky's novel ends as the son is exiled and the mother is beaten to death while proclaiming the truth of socialism in a May Day demonstration.

Fools

Russian culture produced three types of fool. None coincides precisely with fools further west. In common with Western Europe, Russia has the fool of the folk tale, the *durak* (in Russian *Ivanushka-durak*, Ivan the Fool, the youngest, laziest, bumbling yet lucky third son). Old Russia also knew medieval jesters, the trickster or *shut* (pronounced *shoot*), and a wandering minstrel-acrobat-actor, the *skomorokh*. All were associated with pagan magic and the demonic. Finally there is that peculiar Russian variant on a Byzantine saint, which has amazed European visitors ever since the sixteenth century: the *yurodivy* (fool in Christ, holy fool) or *blazhenny* (blessed one).

If in Europe the fool tended to be a dunce or a rogue, laughed at and held in low esteem, then Russians displayed both a reverence for folly and a tolerance for the physically grotesque and mentally deranged.[6] Under Peter I (r. 1682–1725), moronic or grotesque dwarfs did enjoy a brief vogue, but far more commonly, powers of clairvoyance and prophecy were bestowed upon the eccentric or dim-witted. The tradition of the cleverly spoken fool, the fool as sidekick, confidant, or court buffoon to the king, was weakly developed in Russia, enjoying a brief stage life only in the imitative eighteenth century. For many reasons Leo Tolstoy despised Shakespeare and in particular the tragedy *King Lear*, but he took special offense at the Bard's punning, pontificating Fool.

Andrei Sinyavsky (1925–97), Modernist prose writer, dissident, and émigré professor at the Sorbonne, drew an engaging portrait of fools and jesters in his lectures from the late 1970s, published as *Ivan Durak* [Ivan the Fool].[7] Well into adolescence, the Fool lies "on the stove" (the warm sleeping-shelves to either side of the large bricked peasant chimney), doing nothing but blowing his nose or catching flies. If unable to avoid a task set by his older and smarter brothers, he does it stupidly, without forethought, to further his own comfort (not, note, out of kindness or passivity: Ivan the Fool can punch, kill, lie, sew up innocent people in sacks and dump them into the icy river without a second thought). Central to his nature is an openness to many paths, living for his pleasure in the present, and seizing opportunity on the fly. Setting out, he doesn't know his destination – but various miracles always come to his aid. To be called a *durak* is usually an insult, but the fool, typically, is open to that possibility too: if he notices the offense, he doesn't care.

Sinyavsky's own irreverent writings, for which he suffered a prison term before emigrating to France in 1973, often feature a *durak*. Equally prominent in them, however, is the folk-tale thief and *shut-skomorokh*. Like the folk fool, the jesting, pilfering thief travels light and lives in a perpetual present. He robs, but since he never accumulates wealth for himself – he either loses it, or gambles or drinks it away – openness and a sort of honesty adhere in him too. *Skomorokhi*, the Russian wandering minstrel-mummers, constituted a more established profession, almost a guild. Hired as professional merry-makers to perform at feasts, weddings, and funeral ceremonies, they plied their trade even at the tsarist court. Such regal employment was controversial, however, because the hugely popular *skomorokhi*, a blend of Eastern mimes and *Spielmänner* (itinerant medieval singers of Central Europe), were associated with pagan – and thus demonic – activities: instrumental music, theatre, dance and acrobatics, juggling, sorcery, the training of bears, obscene or blasphemous storytelling. As part of a more general ban on public levity, the Orthodox Church outlawed them in 1648. Many practitioners masked their activities and went underground. In a strange conflation, *skomorokhi* became associated in some areas with the act of writing and the art of bookmaking. Psalters have been found dating from fourteenth-century Novgorod, for example, where the initial letters are illuminated by *skomorokh* figures dancing, playing stringed instruments, or wrapped around the letters of the alphabet in lithe acrobatic pose.[8] This infiltration of pagan energy into holy writ must have lent an exciting, sinister cast to the very act of writing, which also tapped supernatural powers. *Skomorokh* speech, too, was creative and potentially poetic – full of elastic triple rhymes and deceptively sly double meanings. In his drama *Boris Godunov* (1825), Pushkin creates a dissolute wandering monk, Varlaam, who, when a little drunk, starts speaking in triple rhymes. In a later scene the playwright has his own ancestor, Gavrila Pushkin, remark that in Russia a poet is treated no better than a *skomorokh*. By the time the play passed the censor (1830), that naughty line had been edited out.

The jester/clown or *shut* often overlapped with the rogue. But a *shut* was more self-consciously costumed and theatrical. His links to Italian *commedia dell'arte* and to the Petrushka of itinerant puppet shows made him a key figure for Symbolist theatre and Russian Modernism.[9] Prior to that renaissance, Russia's richest repertory of jesters had been created by Dostoevsky – whose greatest creation in this genre is the dissolute, sly, self-deprecating, repulsive, and irritably vain Fyodor Pavlovich Karamazov. Significantly, the noun *shut* also means "joker," one who tells a joke [*shutka*], and is a common euphemism for the devil. Devils played jokes as well as told them; "mocking laughter could often be heard as man was led astray."[10] Russian cautionary proverbs frequently rhyme *smekh* [laughter] with *grekh* [sin]. But pagan devil-jesters and ecclesiastical (church-recognized) devils tended to laugh for different reasons. Sinyavsky notes that in Russia, even holiness often had a "*shut*-like" quality about it (p. 59). This enigmatic comment brings us to the most curious of the Russian fools, the *yurodivy* or "holy fool."

Holy foolishness originated in Byzantium but was greeted with increasing reverence as it moved north. The *yurodivy* was a wanderer, an ascetic, a renouncer of goods, home, family, social standing, even the resources of reason. If a holy fool did seek temporary residence, his peasant host was honored as a *pravednik*. The *yurodivy* went around barefoot, winter and summer, dressed in rags and often bruised across the back, shoulders, and loins by heavy chains. He was foolish (or feigned madness) not for his own benefit, and not always even for the sake of some concrete good, but in order to stimulate others toward a moral reassessment of their actions or attitudes. Not all holy-foolishness was perceived as *yurodstvo Khrista radi*, "folly for the sake of Christ." But in all cases it attested to one's liberation from the immediate environment and its confining perspectives. The holy fool lived in another time-space and had access to its truths.

For this reason the fool's utterances, even the most incoherent, were presumed to carry prophetic meaning. A *yurodivy* could speak the truth to tsars without fear of reprisal. In addition to its sly *skomorokh*-monks, Pushkin's *Boris Godunov* also contains a holy fool who confronts Tsar Boris with his crime (the murder of Tsarevich Dmitry) publicly on Red Square and emerges unscathed, even after refusing to pray for the "Herod-tsar." The *yurodivy*'s role is paradoxical. He must live in permanent insecurity and homelessness, despising all hierarchy, fixing his focus not on this world but on the other world, yet he is not a hermit or recluse. He is a social and public figure. It is difficult to represent this type in a psychological novel, because the author (and the reader) cannot get inside its consciousness. There is no coherent, mappable inside. Holy foolishness is entirely performative, symbolic, and specular.

The type fascinated Dostoevsky. At one point in his confession to Sonya, Raskolnikov – wondering what sustains her in the squalid, beggarly underworld of Petersburg – calls her a *yurodivaya*. He fears that further contact with her will cost him his reason and perhaps even turn him into a holy fool himself. In the novel *Demons*, the grotesque fool, wanderer, and "prophet" Semyon Yakovlevich becomes a popular tourist attraction for bored young people of the town: is this a realistic portrait or a parody? Dostoevsky – the most frightening, most hilariously comic master of all types of fool in Russian literature – built his greatest plots on the edge of blasphemy. He did not hesitate to breed a *shut*, Fyodor Pavlovich Karamazov, with an abused, weak-minded orphan girl ("Stinking Lizaveta"), whom her seducer cynically calls a holy fool. The result of this union is the depraved offspring Smerdyakov, family cook and epileptic, who commits parricide.

Must Russian fools be subversive, and are they always comic? Not necessarily; the tone of a foolish narrative can be lyrical, delicate, laden with pathos. But fools must always be strange, governed by rules that others cannot grasp, or else by no rules at all. For this reason fools proliferate when cultural norms break down. In the decade following the death of Stalin (1953), there was such an explosion of eccentrics, dreamers, and wanderers – charismatically portrayed in the work of the short-story writer and film actor-director Vasily Shukshin (1929–74) – that some critics declared the *chudak*, the oddball or misfit, to be Russia's new contemporary hero.[11] Female fools and madwomen realize a different symbolic trajectory. In her 1998 novel *Little Fool* [*Durochka*], Svetlana Vasilenko (b. 1956) continued the tradition of "violated, pregnant holy fools" initiated by Dostoevsky.[12] The heroine Ganna-Nad'ka, a young mute girl with Down's syndrome who performs miracles and is persecuted by everyone she meets in her provincial town, sings to the surrounding evil or flees it with animal-like cries. At the end, heavily pregnant, she ascends to heaven to give birth to a new sun on the brink of the Cuban missile crisis, 1962. "Nad'ka had saved us," the narrator suddenly realizes, "there would be no nuclear strike, no missiles . . . There would be no death!"[13]

Do holy fools always intercede for sinners, and do secular fools always stumble their way to success? That indeed has been the convention. But in the 1980s, the declining moments of the Soviet regime, a strange and colorful group of "foolish" performance artists emerged in Leningrad who targeted precisely that rosy plot – and all the plots by which our various types of Russian fool have lived. They called themselves, after their founder the Petersburg artist Dmitry Shagin, the *mit'ki*. They shunned work, earned next to nothing, accepted everything with a smile of good-natured irony and gentleness, and ignored all the usual standards of victory or success so as to have time for art, conversation, drink, and recitation of oral epics based on their life. In keeping with their passivity and professed "aesthetics of failure," they dressed in grubby striped sailor shirts resembling prison garb and adopted as Russia's defining historical event the Battle of Tsushima in the Russo-Japanese War (1904–05), when the Russian navy was defeated – that is, sunk – in several hours, a military event of unprecedented national humiliation. On principle, *mit'ki* neither produced

nor condemned. They refused to consider the loss of worldly goods or reputation a bad thing. Somewhat like Charlie Chaplin (a figure much beloved by
Russian audiences) but politically far more confused, the *mit'ki* turned personal
bumbling into an art form. Unlike the lucky loafer of the fairy tale, however, in
a proper *mit'ki* epic no one ever wins anything. Theirs was a post-heroic, post-
communist ideal, equally alien to sacrificial activity, acquisition for one's own
sake or for others, masculine posturing, and meaningful protest. The *mit'ki*
have been called "a late-Soviet inversion of Ivan the Fool."[14] Even at its most
eccentric, however, their behavior displayed some didactic and salvational overtones. In 2001 the group gave up drinking altogether and sponsored the first
free-of-charge rehabilitation center for alcoholics in post-communist Russia.
A series of images of Mitya Shagin has been painted in canonical iconographic
style.

The *pravednik* is innerly whole and single-voiced. He can be apocalyptic or
merciful, an irritant to society or the savior of it. Fools, however, are double-
voiced and sly. They *must* be ridiculed, abused, misunderstood by others. At
times they present their protest as an alternative to the righteous. But holy fools
are also numbered among the righteous, for they elevate moral consciousness
in those who witness them. Only those pure instruments of amusement, the
shut and *skomorokh* (jester and minstrel), are pagan enough to serve solely
themselves, and for that reason so often blend with the rogue.

Frontiersmen

Between the fifteenth century and 1991, despite devastating invasions, the
Russian state expanded steadily. There was always more frontier. As distances
increased, however, political power was not dispersed. The highly centralized
Russian Empire continued to be run from its two capitals, each of which,
by the early nineteenth century, had developed a cultural mythology of its
own. Pushkin's 1833 narrative poem *The Bronze Horseman* and Gogol's surreal
Petersburg tales of the 1830s–40s represent the apex of the imperial Petersburg
Myth, which was launched soon after the city's founding in 1703. The myth
of Moscow, although attaching to a far older city, took longer to consolidate,
focusing in 1812 around the city's occupation and burning by the French.
Countering the myths of these two metropolises, the myth of the ever-widening
edge became home to all those heroes who, abandoning the center or exiled
from it, explored the periphery.

Three peculiarities of this expansion are worth noting.[15] First, a continental
empire of Russia's vast and thinly populated sort, bordered by hostile Catholic

or Protestant peoples to the west and hostile Islamic or pagan cultures to the south and east, gave rise to what might be called the "contiguous exotic." But unlike the classical overseas empires of Spain, Portugal, or England, it was accessible by land, even by foot, and thus could be made familiar in routine and unspectacular ways. Colonizers could creep into it, could reside comfortably on its edges and spread out in them. Expansion involved violence, of course. But many narratives interwove peace and war. One example with an 800-year pedigree is the twelfth-century *Lay* [epic song] *of Igor's Campaign*.

Written soon after the event, the *Lay* describes the ill-fated incursion by a minor prince named Igor Svyatoslavovich into hostile territory controlled by pagan Polovtsian tribes to the southeast of Kiev. In imagery of great lyrical power, the anonymous author of the *Lay* rebukes Prince Igor for his rash adventurism and laments his capture by the enemy. But historically, matters were not that tragic. By autumn 1187 Igor had escaped, and two years later his son Vladimir, who had also been taken hostage, married the daughter of Igor's captor, Khan Konchak. The alliance made good military sense: quasi-Russified Polovtsians could then be deployed as warriors and spies against hostile tribes further east. The eastern frontier did not become culturally significant for its pragmatic military alliances, however. In the mid-1870s, the composer Aleksandr Borodin (1833–77) turned this ancient epic song into a Romantic orientalist opera, *Prince Igor*. In this new musical context, the "enemy to the east" became thoroughly eroticized, redefined as sensuousness and associated with savage, arousing dance. A century later, Aleksandr Solzhenitsyn exploited another, more sinister aspect of this myth of the permeable Russian frontier. In Chapter 50 ("The Traitor Prince") of his 1968 novel *The First Circle*, Russian scientists imprisoned in a research institute re-enact, as barracks entertainment, the sequence of conquest–captivity–treason–intermarriage–alliance from the *Lay of Igor's Campaign*. The performance unfolds in a fictional format well known to the Stalinist era, and to these incarcerated men personally: a mock show trial. Armed with the proper sections of the Criminal Code, the inmates condemn to prison or death "Olgovich, Igor Svyatoslavich," double-agent and spy, together with his collaborationist family, the composer Borodin, and the anonymous author of the *Lay*. These two famous artistic transpositions of the Igor Tale illustrate a second peculiarity of Russia's frontier narratives: their indebtedness to Western European narrative.

Our third peculiarity concerns the compass. In the modern period, we tend to think of Russia's frontier tensions in terms of East–West. But in fact, the North–South axis has always been equally pronounced and productive of plots. Until the twentieth century focused our attention, unhappily, on survivor narratives from Siberian prison camps, Russia's most vibrant boundary in terms of aesthetic texts had been the southern tier. The Caucasus mountain range, Russia's domestic Alps, was the birthplace of her native tradition of the Sublime. The discovery of awe-inspiring natural beauty on home territory raised Russian literature in its own eyes vis-à-vis the West, which helped to compensate for other perceived backwardness.

"Frontier heroes" lend themselves to exemplary binaries, of which probably the most robust are the categories of *free* versus *unfree*. On the free side we find the monastic frontier communities, homesteaders, pilgrims, adventurers, commercial travelers, heroes of Romantic *Wanderlust*, and – after the founding of the Russian Academy of Sciences in 1725 – scientific expeditions. The classic Russian homesteading text, Sergei Aksakov's *Family Chronicle* (1846), describes the travails of a patriarchal household that emigrated eastward into the Ufa region in the Urals, bordering the Bashkir steppe. To this same "free" line belong all Soviet-era narratives of virgin-soil settlers, Trans-Siberian railway workers, and founders of new industrial centers in the Ural mountains. On the unfree side belong the exiles and prisoners.

Two astonishing early autobiographies by *pravedniki* (one religious, the other political) anchor the punitive Russian frontier narrative. The first, "The Life of Archpriest Avvakum, Written by Himself" (1670s), was composed in a vigorous vernacular Russian appropriate to its message of hunger, pain, mud, resignation, compassion, and spiritual courage. Avvakum's "Life" is the self-accounting of a charismatic religious conservative or "Old Believer" who was persecuted, together with his family, by the official church. His travail through Siberia and then the Far North ended in martyrdom in 1682, when he was burned at the stake. The second autobiography is the 1767 memoir of Princess Natalya Dolgorukaya, who was exiled by order of Empress Anna in 1730 four days after marrying into a disgraced family. It details their 2000-mile deportation to a central Siberian settlement north of Tobolsk on the Ob River. In 1739, after her husband was broken on the wheel and beheaded for treason, Dolgorukaya's discipline and courage held together the wrecked lives of their large clan. In such punitive narratives as Avvakum's and Dolgorukaya's, the scaffolding of evil events is imposed exclusively from without. Under such conditions, to sustain oneself and survive without doing harm to others is the maximum that can be asked of the victim by way of a moral goal. A hero or heroine need take no other initiative. Solzhenitsyn's prison-camp laborer Shukhov, hero of *One Day in the Life of Ivan Denisovich* (1962), speaks for the optimal plot expectations of this type of hero on the book's final pages: because so many potentially awful things did *not* happen to him in his Siberian work gang during that stretch of hours, it was an "unclouded day, almost a happy one."

This paradox of happiness achieved through unfreedom in wide open space, of salvation through imprisonment on Russia's vast frontier, has proved spiritually very fertile for Russian literature. Raskolnikov confesses his murder in Petersburg – but only repents of it in Siberia, in prison, gazing out over the empty steppe. A story with similar geographical shape was so dear to Tolstoy that he wrote it twice, once as the peasant Platon Karatayev relates it to Pierre Bezukhov, prisoner of the French, in *War and Peace* (1863–68), and then later, in 1872, in the free-standing parable "God Sees the Truth, But Waits." A man unjustly accused of murder serves twenty-six years as a convict in Siberia, meets the real murderer there, refuses to betray him when the latter tries to escape, and both men die spiritually content. In such narratives, the unfree Siberian exile is Everyman, by birthright a sinner, for whom release into true freedom is release from life itself.

Other organizing binaries for the frontier might include civilian versus military, or the scientific explorer (cartographer, naturalist, cosmonaut at the edge of the known mapped world) versus the supernaturally assisted traveler "beyond seven seas" in the magical folk tale. Let us consider only one final contrast: *settlers* versus *wanderers*. Here the relevant distinction is between those who set out with the goal of arriving somewhere, of putting down roots in a new home, and those for whom space itself is their destined and undifferentiated home, their ultimate residence.

Wanderers can be secular or religious. The secular wanderers in Russian literature were largely borrowed from European Romanticism: restless, alienated Byronic heroes, who kept "travel notes" and died beyond the boundaries of the story line. The religious variant of wanderer, the *strannik*, was a figure of some spiritual stature. In Dostoevsky's *Demons* (1872), the foolish buffoon-father Stepan Trofimovich Verkhovensky, having sired a demonically destructive son, decides, after decades of posing and sponging, to take to the open road with backpack and staff. He ends his life as a *strannik* in the company of a Bible-vendor, which casts a faint but authentic aura of wisdom over his otherwise parodied and indulgent person. And at the spiritual center of Tolstoy's *War and Peace*, Princess Marya reveres the wandering God's folk who visit the Bolkonsky estate at Bald Hills. Her brother Andrei and her stern industrious father must ridicule these visitors, but Tolstoy's central hero and seeker, Pierre Bezukhov, is sympathetic and curious about Marya's guests. Seekers are drawn to wanderers.

Wanderers are not obliged to arrive anywhere, but their natural end is a monastery. In a strange mock epic written in 1873 titled *The Enchanted Wanderer*, Nikolai Leskov tells the story of a vigorous young man, born a serf, who carelessly commits several murders, suffers remorse, and in a vision is commanded to wander through Russia, the Tatar lands, and the Caucasus, constantly exposing his life to danger before being deemed worthy to become a monk. Maksim Gorky (1868–1936) tapped into the same tradition, when he launched his career as a writer in the 1890s with bestselling stories of itinerant dockworkers and charismatic tramps.

The wanderer or displaced person during war constitutes a terrible and vital subset of Russian heroes, one that remained vigorous in literature and film up through the end of the Soviet era. Its human parameters stretched from helpless children to cold-blooded killing machines (Bolshevik as well as enemy). A rich Soviet literature of the (literally) embattled frontier emerged out of the savagery of the Civil War (1918–21), which was fought simultaneously on dozens of fronts: on the Western frontier among Poles, Cossacks, and Jews, portrayed in the violent miniatures of Isaak Babel (1894–1941) in *Red Cavalry* (1924–26); throughout Siberia, Mongolia, and along the Chinese border in the brutal war stories (most notably *Armored Train 14–69*) of Vsevolod Ivanov (1895–1963), himself of mixed Polish, Mongolian, and Russian ancestry. Total war allowed these writers to bring into focus Russia's huge ethnographic expanse through fierce personal close-ups that were at once lyrical, shockingly naturalistic, and unsentimental. When, in the 1930s, experimental war prose gave way to more conservative and expansive models – exemplary are the *Quiet Don* epics by Mikhail Sholokhov (1905–84) – the prototype again reverted to Tolstoy's classic, Russocentric *War and Peace*. But all Russian war literature has tended to be read as a parable on Russia herself, a land in which experience could never be made short, painless, or small.

Rogues and villains

Our previous three hero types – righteous people, fools, frontiersmen of the ever-expanding and never-pacified edge – have noticeably Russian chronotopes. To an important degree, each is space-and-time-specific to the Russian culture and continent. With the rogues and villains we move into more pan-European territory. The Russian rogue [*plut*, pronounced *ploot*] shares much with the Spanish *picaro* [rascal], his genetic cousin. But the Russian rogue exhibits some unmistakably national traits, which come into focus at those points where a rogue becomes a villain. In the Russian context, certain acts came to be considered villainous that would not be so quickly condemned elsewhere.

Rogues are not virtuous, of course, but neither are they evil. What gets in the way of evil is their buoyancy, self-confidence, sense of humor, high level of responsiveness, and the fact that they live off the land. If they prosper, it is because their human surroundings are corrupt, greedy, foolish, selfish – or simply amoral. Rogues are survivors; they live by symbiosis and take on the color of the terrain. There is something of Ivan the Fool in them, rooted in the immediate present, although rogues are far more energetic and entrepreneurial. Often we cannot help feeling gratified at a rogue's success. A villain, in contrast, creates victims.

Consider the most famous Muscovite exemplar, "Frol Skobeyev the Rogue," set in the 1680s. Frol is a poor solicitor. He wants to marry Annushka the *stolnik*'s daughter (a *stolnik* is a high-ranking court official who served the tsar at table). So he bribes Annushka's nurse to let him attend her sleepover party dressed as a girl. He ends up in bed with Annushka, who, at first shocked, rapidly develops a liking for her seducer and their mutual sport. By means of various minor blackmails the couple manages to elope. The parents are scandalized; the tsar is alerted; Frol confesses his heinous deed to his in-laws with a shrug. The incensed parents ban their daughter and son-in-law from their house. The daughter fakes illness to win over her parents, at which point the parents send an icon to heal her because "apparently God himself has willed that such a rogue be our daughter's husband"; and Frol, without effort or apology, ends up the heir to all the *stolnik*'s estates.[16] Are we to condemn Frol Skobeyev, or secretly admire him? Both at once, perhaps. Much in our answer depends on context, tone, and the rogue's own capacity for moral growth. These can vary widely. One study of early Russian rogue tales identifies four career trajectories: the rogue repentant, rewarded, punished, and "unresolved."[17] With their ability both to titillate and to admonish, rogue tales proved immensely popular. In the nineteenth century, Nikolai Gogol became godfather to the greatest rogues' gallery on Russian soil.

Gogol's swaggering tricksters had sprawling progeny in the twentieth century, all with fanatic cult followings. This colorful family includes the Jewish gangster-hero Benya Krik in the Odessa tales of Isaak Babel; the free, illegal, comic spirit of Ilf and Petrov's Ostap Bender, conman and impostor of the early Soviet years; the justice-bearing troublemakers Koroviev and Behemoth from the Devil's entourage in Bulgakov's *Master and Margarita*. Two things must be noted about this class of rogue. First, in keeping with the traditional Russian virtues of hospitality, generosity, communality, circulation of wealth – and also their inverse, Russian intolerance for profit-making schemes and hoarding of any sort – the Gogolian rogue is overwhelmingly a mercenary one. The tests that he puts to others, and the tests that the narrative puts to him, concern proper and improper uses of money. Pavel Chichikov, the conman in *Dead Souls* who buys up and then tries to mortgage deceased serfs, is shallow and unappealing. But his flaws pale in comparison with Plyushkin, the miser in that novel, whose hoarded wealth turns to rot and whose person becomes paranoid and beggarly. Plyushkin is beyond rogue or villain, a black hole that sucks in every material thing and immobilizes it. He is absolutely unredeemable. Greed of this paralyzing scope is so disrespected that rogues who redistribute wealth by any means, on any pretext, can easily become noble outlaws, or cease to be outlaws at all.

This Russian discomfort with material accumulation provokes our second comment. According to Vladimir Nabokov, Russian roguery – at least in Gogol's fictional gallery – boasts a special sub-type, the *poshlyak* (from the adjective *poshlyi*: vulgar, trivial, banal), designating a self-satisfied materialist, a mediocrity, the ultimate consumer mentality. This mediocrity knows neither heights nor depths; he is cautious, acquisitive, narrow-minded. To bolster his weight in the world, he would always prefer to buy than to spend. In *Crime and Punishment*, Pyotr Luzhin (his name derives from *luzha*, "mud puddle," and also suggests the German *lügen*/Russian *l'gat'*, to tell a lie) is one such figure, whose economic pragmatism degenerates rapidly into moral villainy. In *War and Peace*, Tolstoy forgives the extravagant, impulsively generous and financially bankrupt Rostov family, even when their fiscal irresponsibility causes a great deal of grief. He marries the profligate survivors, Natasha and her brother Nikolai, to wealthy heirs and heiresses. But Tolstoy does not forgive the elder Rostov daughter Vera and her shallow, calculating husband Berg for decorating their apartment out of the spoils of war. He does not even forgive Sonya – the loyal, thrifty, morally astute ward of the Rostovs – for caring about the family's expensive carpets when their carts are being unloaded to make room for wounded officers during the evacuation of Moscow. No capital value can accrue to a thing, only to a life.

Following Dostoevsky's lead, twentieth-century Russian satire of Western societies tended to target one aspect especially: bourgeois prosperity. Such satirists routinely ignored (or discredited as sham) whatever civil liberties or political freedoms they saw, emphasizing only the triviality, conformity, and tedium of a comfortably provisioned life. One good example is *The Islanders*, a novel of British life written in 1918 by Evgeny Zamyatin (1884–1937), by profession an engineer who supervised the construction of Russian icebreakers in England during World War I and later authored the anti-utopia *We*. In a celebrated moment near the end of Solzhenitsyn's great novel *The Cancer Ward* (1968), the camp (and cancer) survivor Gleb Kostoglotov, just released from the hospital ward, overhears in a department store a man ask for a shirt with a size fifteen collar. He is staggered. "Why return to this life?" he asks himself. "If you have to remember your collar size, you'd have to forget something else, something more important!" The widespread Western idea that life can be difficult, useful, and morally demanding while also being well ordered and prosperous is not easy to defend against this very Russian fear of becoming a *poshlyak*. Indeed, the abstract noun from *poshlyi* – *poshlost'* – is one of two Russian words that Nabokov insisted had no "Western" equivalent.[18] (The other word, *toska*, refers to a peculiarly targetless Russian melancholy.) Part of the translation difficulty begins with the Eastern Orthodox Christian model of society, which makes no provision for a Protestant elite that justifies its accumulation of wealth (with or without the work ethic) as proof of God's favor. Quite the opposite: an excess of possessions can lead only to smugness and spiritual inertness. Material security – a morally neutral background texture for many literary plots in post-industrial countries – has aroused far greater irritation and suspicion in Russian culture.

One category of roguishness was not well developed in the Russian context: the professional roué or sexual rogue (Don Juan or Casanova for men, femme fatale for women). This important type entered Russian high literary culture only during the Romantic period, and even then long retained the flavor of a European import. When Pushkin tried his hand at the Don Juan legend (*The Stone Guest*, 1830, one of his four "Little Tragedies" in verse), it was with the intent of demonstrating that Russian authors, and the Russian language, could deal confidently with the most cosmopolitan European plots. But characteristically, Pushkin awards his Don Juan lofty poetic dimensions that undercut the covetous physical aspect of his pursuit and add aesthetic luster to it. If Pushkin cleanses and poeticizes the purely sensuous, then Tolstoy darkens and coarsens it. When he touched upon the femme fatale type with his own Helen of Troy, Hélène Kuragina-Bezukhova in *War and Peace*, she became perversion incarnate, a one-dimensional woman unworthy of psychological investigation. It can even be argued that Tolstoy's Anna Karenina – whom he most certainly did deem worthy of subtle psychological treatment – is brought to suicide not by the fact of her infidelity and not by the loss of her son, both long familiar facts of her life with Vronsky, but by jealousy nourished, to her horror, by an uncontrollably growing sexual appetite.

Intriguingly, it might have been Dostoevsky, that chronicler of the "accidental family," who came closest to achieving what we might call carnal dignity. He created several unforgettable portraits of the beautiful, hungry, wounded, and predatory female (Nastasya Filippovna in *The Idiot*, Lizaveta Nikolaevna Tushina in *Demons*, Grushenka in *The Brothers Karamazov*). The final woman in this sequence, the temptress Grushenka, under pressure of Mitya's arrest and imminent Siberian exile, evolves before our eyes into a loyal helpmeet, almost a *pravednitsa*, but – and this is key – without losing any of her earlier, sexually alluring skills. This should not surprise us. Key to Dostoevsky's extraordinary popularity in his own time was his genius at devising solutions to social ailments that were hopelessly clichéd in Europe (concubinage, libertinage, unjust inheritance, urban crime) through the righteous and foolish heroes of the Russian tradition.

The villains of Russian literature – those heroes or anti-heroes who attack a readership's most precious values – are to some extent continuous with the rogues, especially, as we saw, in the economic sphere. From the Baron in Pushkin's "Little Tragedy" *The Miserly Knight* (1830) through Gogol's miser Plyushkin to Dostoevsky's despicable Luzhin, healthy lives are polluted and destroyed by hoarders. If these hoarders hurt strangers or obstruct tax-collectors sent by an impersonal state bureaucracy, their sin is not so heinous. They can become attractive rogues and sometimes even positive heroes. But if their hoarding destroys their family, it is unforgivable. Albert, the miserly Baron's neglected son, complains bitterly that money, for his father, is neither servant nor friend but a master whom the Baron serves "like an Egyptian slave," like "a dog on a chain": the gold quietly glistens in its chests while his father sustains himself on "water and dry crusts, never sleeps, runs about and barks." Albert's first impulse is to spend, which is a form of giving. Money, like love, only has value if it circulates. Pin it to yourself and you will lose everything.

The nadir of such greed and money-driven villainy is reached with the darkest nineteenth-century novel, *The Golovlyovs* (1870s), by the civil servant and satirist Mikhail Saltykov-Shchedrin (1826–89). The tone is set by its grasping matriarch Arina, successful businesswoman. She doles out pittances to her eldest and youngest sons (depraved, resentful, drunken) while the hypocritical middle son, Porfiry *Yudushka* [Little Judas], sweet-talks his way into the entire inheritance after his brothers' deaths. The second generation slips into prostitution, Siberian exile, suicide. On the final pages Porfiry is found frozen to death en route to his mother's grave, in an attempt to ask forgiveness. But of whom? As with Gogol's Plyushkin, the money vice leaves no values behind. Thus the practitioners deserve no mercy and can be rubbed out. Villains at Golovlyov levels of greed were revived officially in the early Stalinist period as kulaks ("fists": well-off peasants) and as cartoon-strip Western capitalists. Popular support for their extermination was easy to incite. From the perspective of the terrorized economics that governed Russia's modernizing – but at the same time re-medievalized – Soviet 1930s, it is sobering to recall a seventeenth-century didactic verse written by the court poet Simeon Polotsky (1629–80), on the theme of the cheating, profiteering, speculating "Merchant Class":

> The merchant class can hardly keep from sinning.
> The Evil Spirit to his ways is winning
> ... Shady business practices lead to Darkness Eternal,
> deprived of the Lord's Light in punishment infernal.[19]

Evil takes more than economic form, however, and we might note two other categories. One is the "Gothic villain," originating in the horror novels of Horace Walpole, Ann Radcliffe, and Matthew "Monk" Lewis,[20] whose sensational cruelties were imitated in early Russian Romantic fiction and later popularized in the serialized press through gruesome crime and bandit tales.[21] When Realist-era literature absorbed this type – again most stunningly by Dostoevsky – it was with a crucial difference. Consider the most famous portrait, Nikolai Stavrogin from *Demons*. This appropriately tall, handsome, dark-haired and mysterious hero, no stranger to the sexual abuse of children and profligate with other men's wives, is (also appropriately for the genre) a man with a mask [*lichina*] rather than a communicating face [*lik*]. But Stavrogin becomes progressively weaker as a result of his amoral profligacy, not stronger. The authentic Gothic villain does not weaken. Vigorous to the end of his evil life, he can – like the sadistic Ambrosio in Lewis's *The Monk* – rape his own sister in the charnel house of a convent and then go on to other things. Dostoevsky's parody on this type of villain might be *rumored* to have attempted such feats (and he might even boast to himself of them). But in a Russian cosmos, evil rewards him with impotence.

Our final category is the political villain, the villain backed by governmental power. In a country as poorly managed as Russia, this type of villainy abounds – together with high-minded exposés of it. Thunderous denunciations of tyrants have had a place in Russian letters ever since Ivan the Terrible's illustrious general, Prince Andrei Kurbsky, defected to Lithuania in 1564 and sent blistering letters back across the border to his former master, condemning his villainies. This Terrible tsar [lit. *Groznyi*, "terrifying to his foes"] was long a Russian touchstone for the political villain, albeit often sentimentalized with Gothic or melodramatic traits in historical drama and opera. His rehabilitation as an exotic, patriotic, divinely decreed precedent for Stalin, in a campaign that began in 1937 and recruited the best talent in literature, film, and music, formed the aesthetic backdrop for those fabricated charges of treason that claimed the lives of so many artists during the Great Terror. The greatest poets fought back literally with their lives. In the autumn of 1933, after witnessing the effects of collectivization in the south of Russia, Osip Mandelstam (1891–1938) composed his "sixteen line death sentence," the so-called "Stalin Epigram," in which he compared the fat fingers of the "Kremlin mountaineer" to "slimy slugs," the tyrant's face to "cockroach whiskers laughing," and his pleasure at ordering executions to a red berry squashed against his savage chest. Six months later the poet was arrested, exiled, given a reprieve, and required to produce an "Ode to Stalin." Then in 1937 Mandelstam was re-arrested, to meet his end near Vladivostok in winter 1938. The tyrant in Russia has always been threatened by acts of straightforward outrage and feats of more private loyalty. But tyranny has also been successfully undone by more double-voiced means – through parable, satire, the fantastic, the absurd, and perhaps with greater effectiveness.

Chekhov delivers one such parable of despotism in his "Ward Number Six" (1892), a provincial hospital ward-turned-madhouse-turned-prison. Its fulcrum is the doorman Nikita, an impenetrable bully with the power to lock in or lock out as commanded by his superiors. It is Nikita who redefines a slothful, recalcitrant doctor first into a patient and then into an inmate. This story was one of a handful of tales that turned Lenin into an implacable enemy of the tsarist state. Laughter can be equally terrible, especially with its demonic undercurrent. When the evil is off to the edge of the action, behind a closed door, seen imperfectly by some naïve folksy narrator, the story becomes all the more truthful and terrifying for being only partly understood by its teller. In Leskov's 1881 yarn *Levsha* [The Left-handed Craftsman], a provincial's hilariously misspoken account of competition between the Russian and British empires unfolds blandly against the brutal, violent, wasteful Russia of Nicholas I. In the comic masterpiece *Sandro from Chegem* (1979) by the Abkhazian-Russian writer Fazil Iskander (b. 1929), we glimpse Stalin and his NKVD henchman Beria at a drunken feast through the eyes of a member of a Georgian dance troupe brought north to entertain their former fellow mountaineers in the Kremlin. And finally: avant-garde drama is well acquainted with political villainy. In the Kafkaesque playscript *Elizabeth Bam* (1927) by the absurdist writer Daniil Kharms (1905–42), two men behind a closed door accuse a woman of murder "in the name of the law" – and until the last moment it seems as if she will be saved from these thugs outside by the impossibly fantastical room in which she is trapped. But that room turns out to be reality.

Society's misfits in the European style

Our final category of heroes is more familiar to a Western readership. These are the "European-style misfits" of the Sentimentalist and Romantic eras: the "man of nature" escaping the city, the "hero of sensibility" oppressed by society, the noble outlaw, the figures of Faust, Hamlet or Don Quixote. Many of these alienated heroes were simply transplanted. During the Realist period, they evolved into distinctly Russian nihilists, utopians, and other idea-driven reformers or eccentrics. From the outset a cutting-edge of parodic reassessment characterized Russian borrowings from Europe. By mid-century, these types had coalesced under the umbrella term "superfluous man," *lishnii chelovek*, a phrase coined in print by Ivan Turgenev with the publication of his *Diary of a Superfluous Man* (1850, in Paris). The idea caught on among Russian critics and was retrofitted to heroes of the Romantic era. To be superfluous meant to be defeated along three parameters: to fail to win the woman one loves, to fail in health (Turgenev's protagonist is dying of tuberculosis), and to fail to find a productive niche in society. But the Russian idea of "superfluity" is itself curious when measured against many Western norms. Its perspective is largely that of society, not of the individual. It moves, as it were, from the "outside in," considering the needs of the social body primary and the rights of the misfit almost not at all. If the European Romantic-era misfit was an egoist, outcast, rebel, and proud of his rebellion – proud even to fail in that rebellion, if need be, for the attempt and the quest were all – then Russian variations on the Byronic hero were more contemplative, passive, and resigned. They were less deluded (which is why Onegin and Pechorin thrill us even today with their intelligence), but they were frail. By default, this frailty brought them back into the fold.[22] An interesting tension emerges between native heroes (righteous people, fools, wanderers) and these European imports. Traditional Russian culture valued communality and wholeness. As we have seen, however, this culture was also highly tolerant, even protective, of eccentricity: it admired holy fools who spoke their truth to tyrants (or even who spoke gibberish), wanderers who abandoned their homes and goods, Ivan the Fool who was lazy, dunce-like, cruel without cause, and ended up on top of the heap. The Westernized eccentric or outsider on Russian soil was not so fortunate. He was featured but neither pitied nor respected, and usually he did not survive. The "society misfit," an ambitious, even glamorous category of protagonist in most West European literary traditions, becomes superfluous more quickly in Russia and rarely delivers a wise or unambiguously redeeming word. We limit our discussion here to three Russian variants: Napoleonic, nihilist, and utopian.

The Russian Napoleon myth evolved in several stages, each with its own literary signature.[23] For several years after the devastation of 1812, the fallen Emperor continued to be demonized in the popular consciousness as a destroyer, villain, and Antichrist. By the 1820s, national trauma had faded and the cult of Napoleon had begun: in the stifling civil and military bureaucracy of St. Petersburg, a self-made man and merit-based career was an exhilarating, illicit dream.

Pushkin had been only thirteen when Moscow was occupied and burned, too young (by two years) for military service or exploits against the foe; in his various poems on Napoleon, the poet already saw the Frenchman more as a liberator and democrat than as a scourge. As the myth matured in the 1830s, however, it again darkened. Insignificant clerks in Gogol's and later Dostoevsky's Petersburg tales went mad with Napoleonic delusions. In *Dead Souls*, Gogol evoked the Napoleon image as farce: when the townspeople groped for some alibi for this cipher-imposter Chichikov, one option was "Napoleon returned, in disguise." Significantly, the "little Napoleons" who retained their sanity were motivated not by the honorable Romantic goals of pride, honor, egoism, empire, but rather by greed and paltry identity crises of their own making.

This "bourgeoisification" of the Napoleon myth began with Pushkin's 1833 story "The Queen of Spades." Germann, gambling hero of that tale whose dark ambitions are compared to Napoleon's, does not want military glory, a woman's love, freedom from lowly birth; he wants a fortune. This mercantile reduction of the myth reached its culmination in Raskolnikov's self-loathing reflections on the great Frenchman: Napoleon loses an army in Egypt and doesn't look back, and here I crawl under a wretched pawnbroker's bed, looking for trinkets! During the mid-1860s, while *Crime and Punishment* was being serialized, Tolstoy was recreating in his *War and Peace* the saga of the 1812 invasion (replete with its cardboard Napoleon) – and already Tolstoy was nervous that the wheel might be turning again, that the French Emperor was regaining his aura and would have to be debunked. In several decades, this proved true. The Symbolist generation admired Napoleon anew.

The Napoleonic hero had a cyclical trajectory in Russia, one tied to the mystique of the West and to the nightmare (and the nostalgia) of foreign invasion and heroic self-defense. In contrast, and somewhat paradoxically, the nihilist hero – who doubts and negates everything – was nourished by rumors of positive internal reform. The foundational text here, Turgenev's *Fathers and Children* [*Ottsy i deti*: not, as the familiar translation has it, *Fathers and Sons*], appeared in 1862, one year after the enserfed Russian peasantry had been liberated by imperial decree. Turgenev's hero is Evgeny Bazarov, the "New Man." He is a skeptic, a materialist, a medical man and researcher who, in order to respect himself, "believes in nothing," "respects nothing," and "regards everything from a critical point of view." In place of received belief, Bazarov puts utility: if a tool or an idea works, it is worthy of being affirmed. Only by applying a utilitarian standard could a rational human being escape the disillusionment of the Byronic hero and the delusions of Napoleonism. Although the world might still consider such a nihilistic hero "superfluous" – Bazarov does indeed fail in all the ways that Turgenev had laid out a decade earlier, losing the woman he loves, dying before his time, finding no useful role in society – still, Bazarov is convinced that only with his priorities and values can humanity progress. "Nature is not a temple, but a workshop," he insists, thus placing himself outside the realm of the traditional Russian hero who prefers to rely on righteousness and miracle. Bazarov's death at the end is a remarkable variation on the plot of Turgenev's earlier novels, in which a weak man is tested by a strong woman and fails the test. Bazarov falls in love against his will (he doesn't believe in love), and the woman lacks both energy and inclination to test his devotion. Turgenev was pilloried by the radicals for presenting so negative a view of Russia's new "sons," a charge that appalled and embittered the novelist. It is the fathers who are the brunt of my satire, Turgenev insisted in letters to his friends; and as regards Bazarov, "I don't know whether I love him or hate him."[24]

The rather lyrical literary image of the nihilist in Turgenev soon degenerated – or matured – into something far more dangerous and violent. The first attack on the life of the Liberator Tsar Alexander II, by a domestic terrorist organization, occurred in 1866, and it promoted the nihilist from metaphysical portrait to political threat. Political assassinations rose steadily in Russia until the outbreak of the Great War. But in literature, the apogee of the nihilist was reached in 1872 with Dostoevsky's *Demons* (although a Nietzschean afterglow of the type suffuses several Symbolist and Decadent novels). In 1913, on the occasion of a dramatization of *Demons* by the Moscow Art Theatre, Maksim Gorky declared Dostoevsky himself "superfluous" to the needs of the new Russia. In Gorky's Marxist-Leninist view, Russia had outgrown those Dostoevskian *pravedniki*, Prince Myshkin and the Elder Zosima. There was also no use for cynical, nay-saying nihilists in the spirit of the Underground Man. "Russians have no need now to be shown Stavrogins," Gorky wrote in his 1913 essay "More about Karamazovism." "The teaching of courage is needed, spiritual health is needed – action, and not self-contemplation, a return to the source of energy . . . to the people, to civic activity, and to science."[25]

Gorky on Russia's new optimism is a good bridge to our final exemplary "Western" import, the utopian hero (and its anti-utopian shadow). Literary utopia has a lengthy European pedigree, beginning with Sir Thomas More in the early sixteenth century. But utopian thinking remained robust longer in Russia than in the West. Again paradoxically, the eagerness and acuity with which Russian heroes debunked their surrounding reality, and the impatience with which the nihilist discredited *all* options (practical, impractical, pragmatic, corrupt) fed their tolerance of "re-utopianization." For if every alternative was always fatally deficient, perhaps it made better sense to stick with the ideal. Idealist logic was the reverse of Bazarov's scientific nihilism, which required above all that the material world be made to "work." But it is characteristic of these utopias that the reader can never be convinced that the scenario is not simply a sly undercutting of the entire idea. Even the most famous of revolutionary utopias, Chernyshevsky's 1862 *What Is To Be Done?*, has a gabby, unreliable, digressive narrator who prompts the attentive reader to constant disbelief. And properly so: this romance about a high-minded Petersburg girl who sets up a seamstress cooperative with the help of several devoted, non-possessive men-friends, punctuated with marvelous dreams of an idyllic future life given over to love and leisure in crystal palaces, is governed by no accountable economy at all. The novel is a dream, free of the anxieties of a workable political blueprint, and no wonder Lenin was so fond of it.

Anti-utopias, it turns out, are as double-voiced as utopias. It is both impossible to remain as we are, and impossible to survive in a society where our current vices have been eliminated. Vladimir Mayakovsky (1894–1930) was a Bolshevik poet, committed in word and deed to the futuristic slogans of the new regime. But in the final scene of his dystopian comic drama *The Bedbug* (1929), when the pre-Revolutionary hero is unfrozen and displayed in the zoo as a relic of ancient times, he cries out to the audience with genuine pathos: "Friends! Brothers! Why am I alone in this cage?" In his 1927 novel *Envy*, Yury Olesha (1899–1960) ridicules the self-satisfied New Soviet Production Manager Andrei Babichev – a virtuous, well-fed, public-spirited *poshlyak* – but discredits even more the envious, superfluous sponger and social relic who is telling the tale. And finally there is the most famous Russia anti-utopia, a Modernist forerunner to Orwell's *1984*: Zamyatin's *We* (1921). The protagonist and diary writer of *We* is liberated by his rediscovery of the first-person singular – and simultaneously appalled by it. The prototype for all these threshold dystopias is Dostoevsky's 1864 *Notes from Underground*, where the indeterminate narrator is suspended verbally as well as spatially between principled denial and a denial of that denial. It is no surprise that this underground hero has no discernible face.

The heroes we might yet see, and what lies ahead

This gallery of favored Russian heroes has not been strong in certain categories widespread in Western fiction. Virtuous merchants and productive bureaucrats are few, beautiful sinners are rare. Has the twenty-first century already irreversibly changed this repertory? After the collapse of cultural controls, the classics ceased to be lavishly subsidized and the boundary between "high" and "low" literature began to erode. Russian literary space openly welcomed persons and themes that had always been on the brink of taboo: detective fiction featuring state security personnel or the ruling dynasty or party; crime where the state is to blame; wars that Russia has lost or is losing (like Afghanistan and Chechnya); attractively snappy capitalists. And also, to be sure, explicit pornography, violence, and misogyny. Whereas the tsarist-era and Soviet canon held women's rights sacred (and preferred salvational women to superfluous men), that prejudice is now gone. Instead we begin to see a partial return to the bawdy mixed prose of the eighteenth century, to wide-open (not Aesopian) satire, and to the amoral ethics of the folk tale. These and other narratives of the pre-Pushkin era are the subject of our next two chapters.

Chapter 3

Traditional narratives

862:	Viking chieftain Ryurik invited to rule Novgorod (Ryurikovich dynasty lasts until 1598)
988:	Kiev: Prince Vladimir converts Rus' to Eastern [Greek] Orthodox Christianity
1015:	Martyrdom of Boris and Gleb
1223:	Mongols reach Kiev and destroy it ["Mongol Yoke" lasts until 1480]
1242:	Alexander Nevsky defeats Teutonic knights on frozen Lake Chud
1563:	First printing press in Moscow authorized by Ivan the Terrible
1580s:	Boris Godunov sends eighteen young men abroad to study; none return, nor do their assigned spies
1598:	Election of Boris Godunov as tsar
1606:	Assassination of Tsar Dmitry (called "The Pretender"); "Time of Troubles" begins
1613:	"Troubles" end, Mikhail Romanov elected tsar (Romanov dynasty lasts until 1918)
1636:	Moscow: Patriarch orders musical instruments burned
1652:	Moscow: all foreigners required to live in a single district (the "German Quarter")
1650s–60s:	State-sponsored church reforms leading to Schism [Raskol] and breaking-away of Old Believers
1672:	First stage play performed at Moscow court
1682–1725:	Reign of Peter the First, the Great

Russian medieval culture was rich, but not in the printed word. Folk and religious art was visual and aural: folk tales, epic and everyday songs, round dances, charms for healing the sick, rituals for marrying and burying, laments for men lost to the army during recruiting season, saints' lives and the liturgy. In 1563, Tsar Ivan the Terrible allowed a printing press to be set up in Moscow. The first book published in Russian on Russian soil, an elaborate edition of readings from the Apostles for use in the liturgy, appeared in 1564. In 1565, the press was destroyed by a mob incited by clerical authorities. Accused of heresy, the master printer Ivan Fyodorov "fled for unknown lands" – but printing continued under the protection of Tsar Ivan himself.[1] This cautionary tale, in which an absolute ruler pushes through a modernizing reform against the popular will, resonates throughout Russian history. Although printing made steady gains, until the late seventeenth century, the small number of literate Russians preferred scrolls to printed books.

Traditional texts were performed in connection with specific communal rituals. This sense of the "oneness" of a literary work with its experienced environment remained an ideal for many Russian writers, long after the triumph of the privately authored, privately consumed book. In his final years, Leo Tolstoy (1828–1910) provocatively declared a wedding song and a well-timed anecdote or joke preferable to a symphony or a novel. At the time of his death, the visionary Symbolist composer Aleksandr Scriabin (1872–1915) was planning a vast choral work of divine revelation, *Mysterium*, which would synthesize all the arts in a single performance, usher in the apocalypse, and herald the birth of a new world. Tolstoy as a peasant primitivist and Scriabin as a religious ecstatic might be seen as two possible twentieth-century end points for traditional (pre-modern, pre-print) Russian narrative. One is the down-to-earth, profane wisdom of folklore and the folk tale [*skazka*], rooted in a partially Christianized paganism. Its master plot is survival. The other is the revelatory, didactic, transfigurative saint's life. Its master plot is intercession and salvation. In between are various hybrids: oral legends, cautionary tales, and the folk epic [*bylina*] where the epic hero, or *bogatyr*, is part warrior, part saint, part superman, and at rare moments even partly a folk-tale fool.

All of these narratives – ecclesiastic and folk – could accommodate miracles and the supernatural. Russian medieval genres did not know the distinction between fiction and non-fiction, only between entertainment (profane stories) and edification (sacred stories). As in most pre-modern oral cultures, if a given legend did not seem true for its contemporary audience, this was no proof that it was "made up"; it had been true for grandparents or ancestors, who had witnessed it first hand or heard it from a trusted second party. All events, consciousnesses, and narratives were linked in a single, integrated continuity, told or experienced. Just as no person could stand alone, fully outside a clan or community (for every person at least has parents), so no literary work stood alone.

But integration did not mean homogenization or a dissolving of the one into the many. Just as every individual is born of two discrete parents but does not duplicate either of them, so was every medieval text perceived as indispensable to the integrity of the whole. No body was excluded from a community merely because it happened to be orphaned or deceased. Churches were understood also to be bodies – or more precisely, human faces with eyes, ears, and heads (onion domes rose up roundly on necks; *oko* [eye] gives rise to *okno* [window]).[2] The Russian word for spiritual togetherness or communality, *sobornost'*, is built off the word *sobor*, which means both a collective and a cathedral.

From this animated and integrated cosmos, we will discuss only a small number of text types: the saint's life, the folk- or fairy tale, and two famous hybrids: the folk epic of *Ilya Muromets*, and the Russian Faust narrative *The Tale of Savva Grudtsyn*.[3] At chapter's end, we review two important modes of causation operative in these traditional texts: miracle and magic.

Russian saintly prototypes originated in Byzantine Christianity but mutated while moving north. Reasons for this mutation have been found in Russia's peculiar time-space. Her official conversion to Christianity was abrupt. It affected cities and towns but hardly registered in the countryside. As Christian stories and motifs spread slowly over the Russian plain, they blended with, rather than replaced, pagan worldviews. This fused belief system came to be known as *dvoeverie* or "dual faith."[4] Its hybrid hierarchy of demons, godlets, earth spirits, patron saints, the Holy Trinity and Mary Mother of God never experienced the astringent cleansings of a Renaissance or Reformation – two European cataclysms that did not reach Russia and whose echoes registered only much later, in altered form. The dark agents of dual faith went under the collective name of *nechistaya sila*, the "unclean force," that which causes mischief or induces us to sin. The distinction between mischief and sin is important. In the Russian hagiographic tradition (the Christian side of dual faith), saints are radiant and singular; devils are small, devious, and many. Devils are always drawn to the challenge of bringing down a saint.[5] Arguably more fundamental to the unclean force, however, were the archaic folk devils on the pagan side: nasty but not necessarily evil, possible to placate with the proper magic or bribe, often thought to possess creative power – and thus linked more with fear (or thrill) in the face of the unknown than with sinful behavior.[6]

East Slavic paganism was the product of a landlocked agricultural empire. Gods of sun, moon, stars, and wind did exist, but prayers were directed down to the life-giving black soil rather than up to celestial deities. Bodies did not "rise" after death but were reabsorbed into the womb of *Mat'-syra-zemlya*, Moist Mother Earth. The body was understood to be a seed; thus failure to bury a dead body was a grievous sin. The pagan Greek pantheon was not well known in Kievan or Muscovite Russia, and many of the central Greek gods had no equivalent in the Russian religious imagination. There was no aggressive god of war, for example, and no goddess of female beauty (only of grass, flowers, birch trees, ponds, lakes, rivers, and swamps). Mother Earth Herself had no discernible face.[7] Russian "dual believers" would not have considered the anthropomorphized antics of Mount Olympus, fueled by rage, jealousy, revenge, rape, and meanness of spirit, either natural or normal – and certainly no model for human behavior. Kindness, fidelity, and the capacity to nurture were valued over freedom or valor.

The center of human life, the peasant house, was embedded in four elements, the same four known to the medieval West. Two were mythical-metaphysical, masculine in gender, intangible, and behaved "vertically" (that is, they "rose"): air [*vozdukh*] and fire [*ogon'*]. Two were more material-physical, female in gender, solid, and behaved "horizontally" (they fell, filled up or flowed): land [*zemlya*] and water [*voda*]. Both pairs were obligatory, but their energies did not mix. Nor did they fundamentally change. The idea of progress was not part of the peasant worldview; the very word for "time," *vremya*, is derived from the verb *vertet'sya*, "to revolve," spin or spiral around. Since time was not progressive but cyclical, whatever change we see can only be superficial – the work of wizards, masks, or shape-shifters.

Since native Russian paganism had no established priesthood and Russian villages no temples, it was easily "conquered" by Christianity. But the pagan cosmos was pragmatic and overall tolerant. It made room for the officially new and then re-coalesced around the well, the barn, the hearth. Up through the eighteenth century, Church and state authorities in the cities attempted to stamp out pagan "survivals" in Russian rural culture – much as the Bolsheviks attempted to stamp out Christian "survivals" in the first half of the twentieth. But in the nineteenth century, the authorities gave up trying. Precisely that century witnessed the phenomenal flowering of a Russian literature that freely integrated motifs of paganism, Christian monotheism, and modernization. All of Dostoevsky's great novels must be read in these three dimensions at once.

Saints' lives: sacrificial, holy-foolish, administrative, warrior

The first type of Russian Orthodox *vita* or saint's life [in Russian, *zhitie*] is that of the "passion-sufferer" [*strastoterpets*], an innocent martyr, often a child. In imitation of Christ, this innocent sacrifices its life – but for the sake of national unity or domestic peace, not for the salvation of all humanity. The concept of original sin is not central to Russian Orthodoxy; its punitive aspects are not obsessively dwelt upon. The Fall is less a story of sexual guilt than of prideful autonomy. The founding text for this meek type of Christian biography – doubled in two siblings, focused on family loyalty – was recorded in the eleventh-century Kievan Primary Chronicle as "The Martyrdom of Boris and Gleb" (in Z, pp. 101–05). Boris and Gleb, two teenaged sons of the Kievan Prince Vladimir, Baptizer of Russia, were slain in 1015 by their elder brother Svyatopolk (later known as "the Accursed") in a preemptive succession struggle. Both brothers had armed retainers and thus the power to defend themselves; they chose not to do so, which is essential to the potency and pathos of their story. When Svyatopolk's men arrived to commit the deed, Boris chanted the Psalter and prayed that this sin not be held against his eldest brother. Gleb, when informed of the murder of Boris, burst into tears and resolved also not to resist the assassin's knife. These two youthful martyrs – who had accomplished nothing for the faith except to assent unresistingly to death – were soon venerated as "interceders for the new Christian nation." Their submissive act freed the fledgling and vulnerable Kievan state from threat of civil war.

This non-violent, self-negating response to evil has nothing of the masochistic or epic-heroic about it. The boys did not wish to die. To *seek* suffering or to glorify it would have been a prideful sin. But undeserved death by another's hand, which generates compassion rather than glory, caught the imagination of the Russian Christians. Russia's steady secularization begun by Peter the Great did not obstruct the growth of a cult of martyred tsars (Paul I, murdered in 1801; Alexander II, assassinated in 1881; Nicholas II, shot in 1918). No matter how immature their royal persons or how flawed their reigns, a violent, passively received death ennobled them. The Boris-and-Gleb model of sacrifice resonates behind the most atheistic of patriotic Soviet fictions. In her classic study of the Stalinist novel, Katerina Clark notes that martyrs remained the privileged means by which History moved toward its preordained end.[8]

The second saintly prototype is the canonized holy fool or Fool in Christ, the *yurodivy*. In Chapter 2 we introduced this type as the most spiritualized in Russia's rich trove of national fools; here we emphasize the religious dimension of their illogical or extra-logical speech, physical handicaps, indifference to comfort, and unpredictable politics. One of the earliest and most beloved of these figures was a monk from Klopsko near the northern city of Novgorod in the first half of the fifteenth century, canonized in "The Life of St. Michael, A Fool in Christ" (in Z, pp. 300–10). Michael occupied a cell in the monastery for forty years, living on bread and water, sleeping on the bare earth, and facilitating a series of miracles during local famines and droughts. Two details are worth noting about his holy-foolish career.

At this time Moscow was "gathering together" (that is, subduing in genocidal campaigns) the scattered Russian lands, including Novgorod. Michael advised his city to sue for peace. Holy fools intervened "illogically" in politics – but not always in defiance of the crueler, more powerful side. Sometimes, as did Michael, they saw reality more sensibly than the politicians. And second: Michael's unexpected appearance at the Klopsko monastery was marked by what would become a characteristic exchange. Upon seeing this strange monk, the abbot inquired: "Who are you, my son, a man or a devil? Why did you come to us? Where are you from?" And the as-yet-unnamed Michael responded: "Are you a man or a devil? Who are you? Why did you come to us? Where are you from?" (Z, p. 302). This mirror or echo-dialogue is an instructive example of holy-foolish discourse, which, dressed up in more literary garb, will become the verbal dynamic of carnival, of certain types of dissident speech, of avant-garde poetry and the Russian Absurd. The interrogator asks a question confidently because he (unlike, he presumes, his interlocutor) is in his right place, a stable and recognized identity. The interrogated party responds by casting back the question unchanged, thus turning a hierarchical inquiry into a horizontal pan-human one, the *litso* [face] of the interrogator into a potential *lichina* [mask]. Ushering from another world, "foolish" words radically equalize all parties.

Not all observers of "foolish" behavior responded positively to it. We provide here only one post-medieval example. In Chapter 5 of his quasi-autobiographical *Childhood* (1852) Leo Tolstoy describes, from the perspective of a ten-year-old boy, the visit of the *yurodivy* Grishka to a Westernized aristocratic estate. Entering the house, Grishka strikes the floor with his staff, breaks into a grotesque laugh, and begins to mutter incoherently. The father of the family expresses (in French) his keen distaste "for fellows like this" who, he insists, deceive honest educated people, refuse to work, and should be put under arrest. The mother (whom Tolstoy eventually immortalizes as the meek, pious Princess Marya Bolkonskaya in *War and Peace*) answers him in Russian. She expected this skepticism and parries it. "I find it difficult to believe" – she sighs – "that a man, despite being sixty years old, who goes barefoot winter and summer and under his clothes wears chains weighing over seventy pounds, which he never takes off, and who more than once has refused offers of a quiet life with everything taken care of – it is difficult to believe that such a man does all this out of laziness."

No nation can live by sacrificial martyrs and holy fools alone. Our remaining two saintly types are more survival-oriented and pragmatic. Saint Theodosius, who founded the Caves (or Crypt) Monastery in Kiev in 1074 and then became its abbot, represents the monk-administrator. He was an essential figure in Moscow's steady expansion east and northward across a vast continent. The monastic complex, Russia's omni-purpose civilizing and colonizing structure, served at various times as military fortress, place of worship, and prison. The task of its administrators was not to jolt or confound society – the duty of the confrontational fool – but the opposite: to organize, discipline, and inspire it to prayerful and productive labor. With his own monks, Theodosius proved himself a gentle and patient advisor. His Life, written by the chronicler Nestor (Z, pp. 116–34), portrays him as an astute psychologist who counseled monastic residents on the virtues of self-control and self-reliance. To his enemies, however, Theodosius could be uncompromisingly severe. In his youth, those enemies included his own possessive mother, who fought tenaciously to keep him within the biological family fold, beating him without mercy when she discovered he had girded his loins with iron chains. He escapes her, of course, for his vocation is preordained. When his mother tracks him down, she discovers that she will have access to him only if she enters a convent. Her love drives her to it – and eventually she provides the chronicler Nestor with her son's story. This model of a working male community under threat at the edge of the civilized world, led by a spiritual ideologue who must overcome (among much else) the protective and procreative instincts of the family, will combine with the traditional Russian epic hero (*bogatyr*) to inspire the Soviet construction novel. In Chapter 8 we discuss its prototype, Fyodor Gladkov's 1922–24 novel *Cement*, the saga of a ruined factory restored after the Civil War under the charismatic leadership of a returned soldier-engineer named Gleb.

Our final exemplary saint's life, that of the first Russian warrior saint, also had a revival during the Stalinist period. Alexander (1220–63), later called Nevsky because of his 1240 victory over the Swedes on the Neva River, became Prince of Novgorod in 1236. Two years later, Mongols were at his doorstep, but a miracle of spring flooding made the swamps impassable and kept the fierce horsemen at bay. Alexander reigned for sixteen years, fending off the attacks of Swedes, Lithuanians, and Teutonic knights from the west while buying off the Mongol overlords with tribute to the south and east. His Life, composed around 1280, is the first hagiography of a secular prince and military leader. It is titled "Tale of the Life and Courage of the Pious and Great Prince Alexander" (Z, pp. 224–36). Wherein lies the courage?

In the Russian context of exposed borders and the nightmare of an all-front war, courage for a virtuous state-builder meant knowing when to subdue one's pride in the interests of national survival. Against the well-armed, highly aggressive Catholic nations to the west, Alexander fought lightning-swift, strategically brilliant battles. In such maneuvers, pursuit of glory was possible and appropriate. (Before one such battle, recalling the partisan gods in ancient Greek warfare, Saints Boris and Gleb appeared in a vision to one of Alexander's allies – less as martyrs of non-resistance than as heroes of national unity.) But a very different strategy was required to fight Khan Batu, Genghis Khan's grandson, whose "Golden Horde" came to occupy most of Eurasia after the fall of Kiev in the 1220s. The steppe frontier was endless and could not be defended. Thus the Church blessed Prince Alexander in his journeys of taxpaying tribute to the Mongol capital on the Volga River. Two centuries later, when internal rivalries fractured the Horde, Muscovite tsars pitted one khanate against another and reunited the Russian lands.

In the Stalinist period, Saint Alexander Nevsky was rehabilitated. Sergei Eisenstein's epic film *Alexander Nevsky*, released in 1938 with Prokofiev's stirring score, became propaganda art in the Party's campaign to replace proletarian internationalism with Russo-centric heroes in the shadow of Hitler's growing might. As Eisenstein had intended, enthusiastic moviegoers saw in the "Germanic" Teutonic knights close relatives of the contemporary fascists. When Stalin and Hitler concluded their non-aggression pact in August 1939, *Alexander Nevsky* was immediately withdrawn from the movie houses, to be just as rapidly reinstated in June 1941 after the Nazi surprise attack.

In times of national trauma, it is common for governments to turn to military heroes as patriotic rallying points. For this purpose Russia's warrior saints have proved surprisingly durable, even during officially atheistic periods. Throughout the post-communist 1990s, a reinvigorated Russian Orthodox Church won enthusiastic new converts among Russia's armed forces, humiliated and impoverished by the loss of the Soviet empire.[9] In 2004, the Air Force and the Patriarch (with the full approval of President Putin) jointly celebrated the ninetieth anniversary of the world's first heavy bomber unit (the fighter plane *Ilya Muromets* of 1914), a ceremony that included a blessing of the troops and, in 2005, the consecration of 160 new bombers in Russia's Long Range Aviation Forces. The emergence of a faith-based army in this once officially atheistic country will most certainly affect the plots of Russian war literature and its prototypical heroes.

Folk tales (Baba Yaga, Koshchey the Deathless)

The Russian folk tale [*skazka*] obeys a different logic than does the saint's life. In his study of the European folk tale, Max Lüthi notes a cardinal difference between it and more didactic narrative such as legendry. "The saint's legend wants to explain, it wants to comfort," Lüthi notes. "It demands faith in the truth of the story and in the correctness of its interpretation. The folktale, however, demands nothing. It does not interpret or explain; it merely observes and portrays . . . It is precisely this relinquishment of explanations that engages our trust."[10] This insight helps us to see why the greatest of Russian psychological novelists, Leo Tolstoy, exhausted by writing *War and Peace* and temporarily sick of his own hyper-hortative literary voice, turned to folk-tale speech in several

stories in 1872, especially his brief prose tale, "A Prisoner of the Caucasus."
"If you try to say anything superfluous, bombastic, or morbid, the [common
people's] language won't permit it," he wrote his friend Nikolai Strakhov in
March of that year.[11] Tolstoy was certainly not surrendering his right to instruct
his readership. But he suspected what Lüthi noticed above, that neutrality
inspires trust whereas narrative exhortation does not – and Tolstoy wished to
be trusted.

Among the distinctive features Lüthi finds in European folk-tale language are
one-dimensionality, lack of depth, and an abstract, detached style. Recasting
Tolstoy's auto-critique in Lüthi's terms, what is "not permitted" in folk narration is thick description and a conflicted inner life marked by doubt or self-pity.
What is it like to live in a depthless world? The hero has one clear, linear task. At
the end of it lies his reward, usually a princess. While accomplishing the task,
he encounters various helpers, whose gifts or services are all palpably material.
Helpers and obstacles appear from nowhere and disappear without a trace; a
dark void opens up on either side of the narrow path of the plot. Whatever is
on that path, however, is lit up in brilliant primary colors: metallic reds, golds,
blues. Throughout his travails the hero expresses no astonishment, curiosity,
longing, or fear, and apparently does not experience pain. He never reassesses
his goal or his reward.

Many of these pan-European traits are common to the Russian *skazka* as well.
Conventionally it is divided into three types. "Tales about animals" address
human behavior but with animal or vegetable actors – all greedy, sneaky, self-
serving, duplicitous, for whom the prime value is survival at any cost. More
edifying are the "wondertales" that test and transform a hero, usually by dis-
patching him on a quest and always by relying on supernatural help. Finally
there are "tales of everyday life," focused around the home or hut (center of
the peasant cosmos) and featuring a sexual or financial plot – in which a devil
might be outwitted, but without any transfiguration of the heroes. As a rule,
sexual themes are not treated erotically or chivalrously. Russian folk tales are not
incipient love stories, as they frequently were in Western cultures. The Russian
fairy-tale princess is often mute, unwilling or passive in the beginning. Once
moved to act, however, she is matter-of-fact, inventive, alert to what it takes to
survive trial and temptation, and far less sentimental than her Tsarevich Ivan.
The *skazka* is a dual-faith narrative, mixing pagan and Christian motifs. The
villain controls major celestial and geophysical forces (frost, wind, thunder,
water), but the hero or heroine can always win the services of small animals by
acts of kindness. Many Russian folk tales are linked to incantations, spells, and
nature worship.

The most famous Russian folklore villains are Koshchey the Deathless and
Baba Yaga. Koshchey, the simpler of the two, is an archaic figure, a sorcerer, often

portrayed as a skeleton (his name is related either to the word for bone, *kost'*, or to *koshch'noe*, the Slavic kingdom of the dead). Koshchey's task is to thwart the hero in his pursuit of the reward (the princess). The only way to foil this immortal creature is to reunite him with his own death. The hero must find this death (usually hiding in a duck's egg in an oak stump floating in the sea) and smash it against Koshchey's forehead. Although stubborn, vain, and dangerous – his foul breath can turn a person to stone – Koshchey is not very intelligent and easily outwitted. His tactics suffer from his innate inability to sympathize with others. Consider Nikolai Rimsky-Korsakov's folk opera *Koshchey the Deathless* (1902). Unusually for folk tales but conventionally for opera (which requires, in addition to the romantic soprano, a mezzo or contralto as secondary love interest), the villain has a beautiful daughter, Koshcheyevna, who by various charms almost seduces Ivan-Tsarevich, thereby interrupting his quest to regain the captive princess. The princess, being human, can empathize with her rival. Out of compassion she kisses Koshcheyevna on the forehead. For the first time in her life, Koshchey's daughter begins to weep – turning her into a willow tree. The Koshchey element can revert to plants or trees but cannot be fully humanized.

Baba Yaga, "Old Woman Yaga," is a far more ambiguous and powerful figure.[12] Witch, cannibal, earth goddess, Mistress of the Forest, she lives in a hut on chicken legs that rotates in expectation of the unwary visitor. This quasi-animate dwelling is surrounded by a fence made of stakes readied for human heads. Inside her hut, Yaga's sprawling grotesque body cannot move; one leg is always of bone (or iron), the other often of excrement, her nose is hooked to the ceiling, her breasts hang over a rod, her genitals foam. Outside her hut, she travels in a mortar and pestle. (The famous ninth episode – or "picture" – in Musorgsky's 1874 *Pictures from an Exhibition*, "The Hut on Hen's Legs [Baba Yaga]," depicts her ferocious ride in this strange kitchen vessel.) Baba Yaga can be Koshchey's consort or his sister, but she can also do battle with him. And significantly, she can be the "donor" or enabler of the hero, the one who insures his success against Koshchey in quest of his lost princess. But Baba Yaga extends her help to a hero only after he has been tested for manliness. First she announces that she will eat her visitor (his bones will be ground up in that mortar) – and waits to see how the guest responds. If he ignores her hideousness and demands proper hospitality, she will feed him and provide him with talismans and secrets for his journey. If he trembles and goes limp with fear, she will destroy him.

We will now consider two variants of the same exemplary tale. The first, "Faithful John," was collected by the Brothers Grimm; the second, "Koshchey the Deathless," by their Russian counterpart Aleksandr Afanasiev. Placed side by side, they suggest how a specific folk-tale plot might change in emphasis and value system as it migrates east. The most prominent difference between the two variant tales is the presence of Koshchey and Baba Yaga.

From a Russian folk perspective, "Faithful John" is a very Western plot. The many European versions of this tale – including the French "Old Fench" from Lower Brittany and the Swedish "Prince Faithful" – all open as an incipient love story. All are fueled by mercantile interests and test the hero in the manner of a knight from the Age of Chivalry. The old king dies, leaving his adolescent son in the care of Faithful John. The new young king is allowed access to everything in the palace but the room with the portrait of the Princess of the Golden Dwelling. Of course the king glimpses the portrait and falls instantly in love. To court her, he orders that five tons of family gold be crafted into various artifacts. He packs these into a ship, and he and Faithful John sail across the sea to the princess. She adores gold and is persuaded to come on board to view the wares of this "merchant." Only after the ship has sailed away does she discover that the merchant is a king; swayed by the gold, the royal lineage, or perhaps even the prince himself, she consents to be his wife.

While still at sea, Faithful John overhears three ravens predict that the young king will not consummate his marriage. He will mount a horse that will fly off, his bridal costume will burn him to death, and his bride will faint away during the nuptial ball. Interventions and antidotes are possible against these disasters, but anyone who warns the king in advance of them will be turned to stone. John intervenes in the first two temptations and the mystified king tolerates it. But when Faithful John revives the insensate queen by sucking three drops of blood from her right breast, the king loses his temper and condemns his servant to the gallows. Then John tells all and turns to stone. He is only brought back to life several years later when (such are John's terms) the king agrees to behead his own twin sons with his own sword. The sons are beheaded, the stone statue revives, John replaces the children's heads, and all five dwell together in happiness.

As this well-known folk tale migrated throughout Eastern Europe, it absorbed local motifs and amplified different virtues. One commonly anthologized Russian variant appears in conjunction with a "Koshchey the Deathless" tale. A number of crucial details are altered. Romantic love is far less in evidence. There is no positive mercantile theme (no courtship that exploits the princess's appetite for gold), no ships at sea (Tsarevich Ivan sets out in search of his bride on foot). A great deal more casual violence is encountered on the way – and the tests administered to hero and heroine alike come from the world of untamed nature, not from the realm of domesticated animals or manufactured goods. The tsarevich comes upon his "Faithful John" – here, Bulat the

Brave – while the latter is being flogged in a public square for non-payment of a debt to a rapacious merchant. The tsarevich is informed that the man who redeems Bulat will lose his wife to Koshchey. All the same, Ivan pays the debt, and from then on Bulat manages everything. He courts the destined bride Vasilisa the Beautiful with the wing of a chicken, a duck, and a goose (she is frightened, silent, and Bulat must negotiate for her by supplying both their voices). He abducts her from her tower. Twice Bulat slays the pursuers sent by Vasilisa's father. But even Bulat cannot straightaway slay Koshchey, who steals Vasilisa while Ivan (like most tsareviches, kindhearted but singularly inept) is asleep. The two men eventually locate Vasilisa in Koshchey's hut – and remarkably, separated from her father and childhood home, the silent bride has become the wise and crafty female force, the "donor," or helping aspect of Baba Yaga. Through three deceits, Vasilisa seduces her bony, braggart captor into revealing the location of his death. Ivan and Bulat set out in search of it. Along the way, various animals are almost killed for food (a dog, an eagle, a lobster) but then at the last minute spared; they become the indispensable helpers. The death is found in the egg, Koshchey is reunited with it, and at this point the contour of the Grimm tale resumes.

Twelve doves, relatives of Koshchey, inform Bulat that his master will be killed by his favorite dog, or horse, or cow. He who enables the tsarevich to avoid these threats will be turned to stone. The threesome returns home, the marriage is consummated, and the tests begin: Bulat slices the threatening dog in half, then decapitates the horse and cow. Incensed, Prince Ivan orders Bulat to be hanged, and the faithful helper, confessing, slowly turns to stone. In this version too, only the blood of the two slaughtered royal children (a son and a daughter), smeared on the stone, will bring Bulat back to life. But one detail of this final episode is worth noting. In the German version, the king carries out the sacrifice of his two sons on his own and then tests his wife after the fact, to see if she would have consented to it. No such test of the female is necessary in the Russian tale. There, the prince consults with his wife *before* committing the double sacrifice. Once she becomes a wife, the Russian heroine (nourished on the roasted wings of birds and tested against Koshchey the Deathless) is wiser, stronger, and more autonomous than the gold-coveting trophy wife and consort queen we see in Grimm.

There are other East–West divides. European Cinderellas run themselves ragged for their evil stepmothers (one senses a work ethic here), even though they never lose their beauty while doing so. Russian Cinderellas tend to be more realistic as regards the effect of unremitting physical labor on human bodies. Idleness and laziness is never a virtue, of course, but many Russian heroines happen to have magic dolls from their mothers who miraculously do everything, permitting their own hands to remain attractively soft and white. On the male side of the genre, Western Prince Charmings tend to be enterprising young men, whereas the Russian Ivan-Tsarevich is a bumbler not unlike Ivan the Fool, relying on helpers or miracles. The cosmopolitan Pushkin, barely out of his teens, burst into fame in 1820 with his first long narrative poem *Ruslan and Lyudmila*, a mock fairy-tale epic of unprecedented bawdiness. He provided four princely suitors for the abducted princess in hopes of getting one who could complete the job, even though (a wise sorcerer informs us early on) Lyudmila is in no serious danger: the evil dwarf Chernomor is impotent. In Chapter 8, we will see how the resilient, predetermined plot of the folk tale – both simple-minded and sly – was adjusted to the Stalinist stage.

Hybrids: folk epic and Faust tale

To complete this rudimentary literacy in Russian traditional narratives, it remains to consider two hybrids. The first is the *bylina* or "Russian folk epic."[13] A *bylina* was chanted rhythmically to a simple melody (often with spoken inserts) and featured the exploits of a *bogatyr* [warrior-hero]. Highly formulaic, these songs were governed not by plot suspense but by descriptive detail and texture. Like the folklore hero, epic heroes were external agents only, devoid of psychological motivation; for this reason, a *bylina* cycle was often organized around a historic city rather than a personality. Kiev played this anchoring role during the first wave of Mongol attacks in the thirteenth century. Later, the northern medieval city of Novgorod became home to an epic cycle built around the wealthy merchant Sadko and his dealings with the Sea Tsar.

Some of the earliest mythological *byliny* reflect a struggle between the *bogatyr*, the male hero-warrior mounted on a swift steed, and the immobile, invincible depths of Mother Earth. In one widespread variant, Earth gives birth to a hero, "Svyatogor" [Sacred Mountain], so huge that she cannot bear the weight of her son. Svyatogor is a swaggerer, a braggart, who tosses his mace to the sky and never fails to catch it on the way down. Among his claims is the curiously Archimedean boast, provocative considering the person of his Mother, that he could lift the entire earth if only he could find a point of support. One day, riding through the steppe, he finds a small *skomorokh*'s [minstrel's] bag in the open field. It is too heavy to pick up from the saddle. Svyatogor dismounts, but still he cannot lift the bag; instead, he sinks up to his knees in the earth. In some variants his horse hauls him out, but at other times the giant *bogatyr* interprets this failure to attach a pouch (a womb) to his own belt as the beginning of his death.

With the collapse of the Kievan state by the middle of the thirteenth century, these early heroic songs migrated to central and northern Russia. To their familiar repertory of enemies (nomads or heathens from the eastern steppe) the Kievan epic heroes then added villains of the darkened forest and swamp. One such foe was the highway bandit Solovey ["the Nightingale"], who lived in a huge tree and whose very whistle could deafen or kill a passerby. North or south, the defense of Russia remained the *bogatyr*'s primary task. The most famous saga of all is the dual-faith tale of Ilya Muromets, Ilya of Murom on the Oka River, halfway between Moscow and the Urals city of Kazan.

Ilya was a poor peasant's son, born a cripple. Or in other versions, Ilya, like the folk hero *Ivan-durak*, faked his disability, preferring to warm himself on the stove rather than work. For thirty (in some versions, thirty-three) years Ilya lies on the stove. One day, while the rest of his family is in the fields, several wandering beggars (in the Christianized variant, three wise men) drop in on him and command him to rise from his bunk. He protests; they insist: "Get thee up and give us to drink!" Ilya rises and finds that his strength is boundless. His visitors tell him what to avoid, whom to appease, what to attack, and how to equip himself with a horse. Taking leave of his astonished parents and tying a clod of soil around his neck (a talisman of the moist Earth that bore him), he sets off to Kiev to serve Prince Vladimir. Along the way he liberates the city of Chernigov from the Mongols and captures the bandit Solovey. In one variant, Ilya encounters the huge Svyatogor, challenges him to a duel, but the giant only plucks Ilya up and puts him in his pocket. The two become friends. However, when they stumble across an enormous coffin on the road "destined for the person who fits it," Ilya is unable to protect his fellow *bogatyr* from the death pre-measured for him.

Motifs from the life of Ilya of Murom pervade Russian culture – inverted, parodied, or stylized, depending on which phase of his career is highlighted. For his *Brothers Karamazov*, a strikingly "male" novel of fathers, sons, rivals, merchants, monks, lawyers, and adolescent boys, Dostoevsky chooses the name Ilya for Captain Snegiryov's young son, the brooding boy who dies mysteriously of a crippling ailment; the novel ends on Alyosha's injunction to Ilya's grieving schoolboy friends to remember "his face, his clothes, his poor boots, and how he bravely rose up for his sinful, unfortunate father." In a comic vein, the eponymous hero of Ivan Goncharov's novel *Oblomov* (1859), famous for a sloth so profound that he cannot get out of bed (and then unwillingly) until the middle of Chapter 8, is named Ilya Ilyich [Ilya son of Ilya]. Immobility can be comic, but elevated to the status of nation, it displays its epic and implacable side. The world's first mass-produced bomber aircraft, the "Ilya Muromets," was a huge four-engine biplane designed in Riga in 1913 and adopted by the

Imperial Russian Army in August 1914. The heroic Muromets squadron flew 400 sorties between 1914 and 1918, until its designer Igor Sikorsky abandoned it for a more manageable aircraft to be called the "Alexander Nevsky."

Each expanding border, greeted by a patriotic cheer, also brought an increased vulnerability. The traditional types of "survival heroism" sampled so far – that of Ilya Muromets, Alexander Nevsky with the Mongols, Boris and Gleb, even the gentle colonizing abbot Theodosius – developed primarily in response to the demands and threats of the northern, eastern, and south-eastern frontier. In that arc of confrontation facing the Eurasian land mass, both Kievan and Muscovite Russians viewed themselves as civilized enlighteners against pagans and nomads. Our final exemplary hybrid text comes from another sector, the Catholic and Protestant West.

These heretics to the west – well-armed, educated, cultured, carriers of the European Renaissance – presented a very different threat to Russian integrity than did the Tatar khans, who taxed heavily but in principle tolerated the Orthodox Church. The theological academies of Kiev were already important centers of Latin literacy at a time when books were being banned and musical instruments burned by more conservative Orthodox authorities in Muscovy further north. The Northwest–Southwest cultural border remained highly porous to all modes of entertainment and aesthetic expression. A century before Peter the Great, literate Russians had access to love poetry, Jesuit school drama, satires, popular histories, picaresque narratives, Faust tales, and chivalric romances in crude Russian versions. Bowdlerized adventure tales of European, Greek, or mid-Eastern origin were hawked in the towns in the form of woodcut prints [in Russian, *lubok*], primitive pocket-sized graphic novels with a minimal story-line text. The influence of all these genres is reflected in the final pre-Petrine narrative we will consider, a prose tale recorded in Muscovy in the seventeenth century, *The Tale of Savva Grudtsyn* (Z, pp. 452–74).

The Grudtsyn-Usovs were a well-known north Russian merchant family and the tale is precisely situated, historically and geographically. In 1606, during Russia's inter-dynastic "Time of Troubles," the senior Grudtsyn moved east with his wife and son to Kazan to escape the invading Poles. When Mikhail Romanov became tsar in 1613, Savva was twelve years old. His story is a quasi-secular – and sexually explicit – multiple hybrid, with components of documented history, witchcraft, Faust tale, adventure story, travelogue, jousting bout, and an Intervention of the Holy Virgin, all framed by the redemptive formulas of a Russian Orthodox saint's life. Integrated into one biography, it is the life of a sinner whose courage during the drawn-out torments of his repentance permits the storyteller to reframe demonic experiences as a sacramental trial. Its plot divides into three phases.

The first is the period of Savva's seduction, fall, and pagan bewitchment. Apprenticed in the city of Oryol, Savva is befriended by a wealthy elderly citizen, Bazhen Vtory, who has a young beautiful wife. The wife seduces Savva so successfully, and he cooperates so enthusiastically, that the young man, startled at his own appetite, resolves to refrain from carnal activity (at least for the duration of one holy day) for the sake of his soul. The wife, enraged, devises exquisite punishment: having slipped him a magic love potion to increase his desire, she connives with her unknowing husband to expel him from their home. Savva grieves and begins to waste away.

The second phase begins when Savva summons up the devil: "If someone would do something so that I might again take sexual pleasure with this woman . . ." Suddenly a young man appears, offers to intervene, asks Savva to provide a brief written note renouncing Christ, and again Savva is welcome in Vtory's house. The wife is not exactly in league with the devil. She is "incited" by him – and one of the fascinating aspects of the tale is its ambivalent, borderline treatment of human responsibility. The externalized medieval model of "an angel on one's right shoulder, a devil on one's left," battling over possession of the helpless human soul, coexists with a more modern internal explanation: "Human nature knows how to lead the mind of a young man into iniquity" (p. 455). Is human nature the victim, the carrier, or the willful initiator of the vice? Is the body choosing to pursue its pleasure, or has the body itself been taken captive and thus deserves our sympathy? This archaic image of an outside "devil doing it to us" remained vital, deep into Russian literature's maturity: in the art of Gogol and Dostoevsky, in the mystical poems and stories of the Symbolist poet Zinaida Gippius (1869–1945), and in plays and novels by the Soviet-era Mikhail Bulgakov, all of which combine folk devils and grand Lucifers with astute human psychology and rigorous moral accounting.

The two "brothers," Savva and his false friend, become inseparable. They travel to the friend's home – which is Hell, of course, but on the horizon of earth, a city of gold – to present Satan with the God-rejecting letter. At this point the tale veers off to the west, much as the leaner Grimm tale, "Faithful John," had opened up to absorb a Koshchey-the-Deathless subplot when that famous German folk tale moved east. *Savva Grudtsyn* incorporates Muscovite military history as well as a Polish chivalric subplot. The two brothers join the tsar's mercenaries fighting to recapture Smolensk from the Poles (an historically documented battle from the early 1630s). Savva jousts with three giant Polish knights, defeating them (although not without some wounds) with the devil's help. Then Savva falls ill. The final phase begins.

Several aspects of this remarkable final segment prefigure the later, great moral Realists, most notably Leo Tolstoy, whose 1890 story "The Devil" begins with a similar psychological dynamic. Savva both knows, and does not wish to know, the true identity of his patron. His dilemma is at the core of traditional Russian religious thought, which values self-discipline and believes in the transfiguration, rather than the condemnation, of the human body. The devil depends for his effectiveness on a mix of outer stimulation and inner inclination. We know that evil has triumphed within us when we lose control, when our desire cannot be satisfied, when it becomes insatiable and thus unstable. This is the truth that the gentle Russian ascetics such as Abbot Theodosius (and Dostoevsky's Elder Zosima) speak to the fanatics among their flock. The devil exploits the bad habits of the undisciplined body, but it is still our body and we still must answer for it. This lesson, which became central to the Russian psychological novel, registers in lapidary fashion on the body of Savva Grudtsyn.

Savva has fallen ill, and he is persuaded by a "wise, God-fearing woman" to take confession. The devil-brother immediately appears to him, waving the contract. For days, weeks, Savva undergoes the most awful physical tortures: he is thrown against the wall, onto the floor, throttled "until he begins to gasp and foam comes from his mouth" (p. 470). The bystanders can do nothing. Nor – significantly – do they attempt to do anything. The tale is marvelously dry-eyed. The Tsar is informed, so that there will be no ugly litigation should the courageous youth "die in such miserable plight" and those who are attending him be held accountable. All parties understand that Savva's repentance must be paid for in the currency of the initial sin. For every hour of pleasurable uncontrolled lust, he will undergo an equivalent hour of torment.

In the final step of his return to life, Savva has a vision that the Mother of God will save him on Her holy day – but only if he agrees to take monastic vows. He is carried, crippled with torment, to the door of the church. A voice commands him to get up and enter the sanctuary; like Ilya Muromets, he rises to his feet as if he had never been ill. Suddenly, a "most marvelous miracle" occurs: the God-rejecting letter flutters down from the cupola, and "all writing was erased" (p. 473).

Miracle, magic, law

This survey of saints' lives, folk tales, one epic *bylina*, and one hybrid cautionary tale barely taps the richness of Russian medieval literary forms. It omits many vital genres: chronicle histories, homilies, sermons, apocrypha, early travel literature, Kievan epic and Old Believer autobiography. The militant reformers of Peter the Great's revolutionary era will redefine Russia as separate from this ancient heritage, in an attempt to start the culture anew. Before we survey this eighteenth-century divide in Chapter 4, can any generalizations be made about Russia's traditional dual-faith culture?

Medieval versus post-Petrine Russia is often discussed as part of a larger question, "Russia versus the West." Yury Lotman, together with his colleague in cultural semiotics Boris Uspensky, offered a highly provocative and controversial schematization of this binary in two now-classic essays from the late 1970s.[14] The first essay, "Binary Models in the Dynamics of Russian Culture" (1977), argues that traditional Russian culture had no concept of "progress" in the tentative, gradualist, Western sense of the term. It could not, they reasoned, because the archaic Russian mentality does not acknowledge "neutral zones" where value has not yet been assigned. Either a space is "protected" and monitored by the appropriate saint, or "unprotected" and open to all manner of devils and mischievous spirits. How a given culture organizes its profane time-space is reflected in the structure of the otherworld or afterlife that it projects. And it is significant, so Lotman and Uspensky argue, that the Russian Orthodox wing of Christianity never accepted the Roman Catholic concept of purgatory, nor developed its own analogue for it.

Purgatory shares with other transitional chronotopes the idea of a "surplus," a "free tomorrow" during which the nature of our destiny can be altered by our own efforts (or by the efforts of those praying for us). Precisely that idea was lacking. Rather than such linear progress, historical motion in the Russian context more resembled an oscillation between fixed positive and negative poles. If, in tenth-century Kiev, a pagan temple was torn down, the Christian equivalent had to be built *on the same site*, in order that the pagan or heathen god be literally and spatially replaced, squeezed out of its space. The Russian impulse is not to "try it out and see" in pragmatic fashion, but rather to define, cleanse, and re-occupy.

"Doubled" or superimposed sites are rich concentrators of meaning, but they are fragile. In the blink of an eye and with no explanations or intermediate steps, they can flip from godly to demonic, from clean to unclean – and back again. One good example, consonant with the temples mentioned by Lotman and Uspensky, comes from the early, ebullient post-communist 1990s: the rebuilding of Moscow's gargantuan Cathedral of Christ the Savior, demolished by Stalin's order on December 5, 1931.[15]

In 1994, on the initiative of the Russian Orthodox Patriarch Aleksy II together with Moscow's ambitious Mayor Luzhkov, it was resolved that an exact replica would be reconstructed on the precise site of the original cathedral. The church had been dynamited to make way for a massive Palace of Soviets, eight meters taller than the Empire State Building, topped by a 6,000-ton statue of Lenin. But for two decades, nothing went up. Construction accidents were common. In the popular imagination, the denuded site was seen (with a mix of irony, superstition, and reverence) as "sacred" and thus its new profane mission cursed; it was rumored that a local holy fool visited the construction pit and predicted that nothing would rise out of it. In 1958, Khrushchev ordered the huge hole in the ground refitted as a heated swimming pool. Considerable public debate over the future of the site went on during the glasnost years, beginning in the mid-1980s: suggestions ranged from an empty site with a play of light to a small chapel or museum commemorating the victims of Stalinism. The Millennial Anniversary of the Baptism of Rus'(988–1988) gave fresh impetus to a "sacred" solution. The final decision to rebuild the cathedral, taken by secret decree, played in to a massive revival of Moscow's elaborate mythology of sacred towers, Kremlin walls, and twelve gates – proof of her status as the Third Jerusalem, heir to Constantinople, in fulfillment of the Heavenly City prophesied in the Book of Revelation.[16] The completed structure is topped by a huge golden cross on its cupola, symbolizing the repentance of the Russian people; its underground levels feature a business center, oversized parking lot for foreign cars, luxury sauna, and restaurant. The reconsecration of the cathedral in 1997 was a major victory for the energetic and enterprising patriarch, the culmination of his campaign to return nationalized property to the Church and reassert control over confiscated saints' relics. This reclamation of "lost" relics was relatively easy for Aleksy to arrange, since he had been elected Patriarch in 1990 after thirty-two years in the church hierarchy with simultaneous service in the ecclesiastical subsection of the secret police, the KGB. Without such collaboration, he could not have risen through the ranks of the Church to wage battle with the remnants of the atheistic state.

Lotman's second essay devoted to the East–West divide deals more with psychology than with the demonics of time-space. It has an intriguing title: "'Contracting' [*dogovor*] and 'The handing over of oneself' [*vruchenie sebya*] as Archetypal Models of Culture" (1980). To grasp the dynamics of this peculiar binary, we should review the distinction between two pre-modern explanatory strategies: magic and miracle.

Magic (incantations, charms, spells, curses, talismans) is a formula, a "contract" drawn up with a concrete goal. It should be distinguished from divination – the reading of stars, moon, thunder, numbers, marks on the body – which is the "attempt to predict something or to reach a correct decision about it rather than to cause it."[17] Magic always works against a fixed or closed future: it desires to make something happen. It presumes that the proper recipe or artifact, invoked by a qualified practitioner, will produce that desired result. If a given charm fails to work, this does not mean that charms don't work, only that the recipe was wrong for this particular application and the practitioner must learn the correct one. Magic is predictable. Belief in it gives rise to signs and to publicly accessible codes. In his classification of medieval Russia as a magic-driven culture, Lotman supplies four defining factors: reciprocity (the magician and the natural force respect each other); compulsion (the proper formula will compel the force to obey); equivalence (in the transaction between magician and nature, each side has a measure of responsibility and power); and a contractual relation (which can, of course, be "broken" through misinformation or deception). Contracts bind.

Magic is necessary because the workings of the world are fixed but hidden. Miracle, as Orthodox Christian believers understood it, was freer, less symmetrical, and thus less reliable than magic. It depended on intangibles and immeasurables: divine grace, strength of belief, the unknowable. The founding miracle for Russian believers was the Resurrection of Christ. During the dread and risk of that original Passion, for Jesus as well as for His disciples, there was no proof that anyone would rise again. (It might be said that into this slender stretch of time, the "second day" between the Crucifixion and the Resurrection, Dostoevsky fit all of his great novels.) A sense for the miraculous could restore hope to the desperate in spirit. But one has no right to *demand* a miracle. Believing Russians (and this is the other side of Lotman's binary, "handing over of oneself") assumed that a religious act was an unconditional gift, a voluntary, one-sided sacrificial offering of one's whole person, quite the opposite of a contract. Since miracles are precisely *un*predictable, they cannot entail compulsion and do not wait on reciprocity. If magic gives rise to mutually agreed-upon signs and codes, then miracle gives rise to symbols. There is no single way to make them mean for all members of a community, nor to communicate that singular, symbolic meaning. A miracle binds each witness on its own terms.

In closing this chapter, we might expand on some implications of Lotman's models. Vis-à-vis Russia, defenders of Western liberal democracy habitually feel rational, secular, "advanced," progressive, law-abiding, tolerant of others' rights – in a word, politically mature. But in the eyes of a Russian believer with the worldview Lotman has described, that bundle of liberal-political virtues is simply archaic or pagan magic, at a lower level of civilization and spiritual sophistication. Pagan Rome, together with the principles of pagan Roman law, was "magical": compulsive, contractual, enforceable, imperial, and inevitably violent. The logic of magic tends to standardize all parties and variables, to remove the irreducibly individual human face. It is no accident that the Devil, a master at demanding the written contract, believes in conventional signs.

But miracle itself has no logic. Nor is it dialogic. It is an unconditional gift, an orientation of myself to the world regardless of how the world treats me back.

Lotman's two essays suggest a final lesson to be learned from model biography, useful for the watershed of the eighteenth century: that moral guidance can be provided by a culture in two valid but fundamentally opposed ways. Each aspires to a different ideal. The first way is guidance through a relatively fixed and impersonal system of law. This law is codified, "blind," and legitimized to the extent that it applies to all, precedes the individual case, and follows its own rules. The second way is guidance through an integrated human personality. This personality – or face, *lik* – is assumed to be swayable by the needs, vagaries, and intonations of the petitioner. Compassion and mercy are essential to it and cost it nothing, since it does not worry about setting precedents. Mentors in this mode function face-to-face and one-on-one. Without question the second model is mainstream for the nineteenth-century literary canon, and for much of the great dissident literature of the twentieth. But the first, more severely juridical option is also present in Russian literary culture – although not always in forms immediately familiar to a Western reader. It expresses itself through comedy and satire, but of a stern sort, contained inside a neoclassical frame. The eighteenth century is its birthplace.

Chapter 4

Western eyes on Russian realities: the eighteenth century

1682–1725:	Reign of Peter I, the Great
1701:	First theatre troupe (German) invited to Muscovite Russian court by Peter I
1703:	Peter I founds city of St. Petersburg
1708:	Reform of Slavonic lettering system into a civic alphabet
1714:	Education made compulsory for all sons of nobility and gentry
1722:	Peter establishes a Table of Ranks
1725:	Founding of Russian Academy of Sciences
1755:	Founding of University of Moscow
1757:	First Russian theatre company established at imperial court
1762–96:	Reign of Catherine II, the Great
1769:	Catherine II permits publication of satirical journals
1773–75:	Peasant/Cossack uprising under Emelyan Pugachov
1789:	Outbreak of revolution in France and political crackdown in Russia

The Russian eighteenth century left little trace on any literary canon beyond Russia's borders. It is remembered as a century that borrowed its forms, themes, and expertise from the West, first from Protestant Europe and then from France. To borrow, translate, codify or imitate an alien cultural canon was not considered inappropriate, however; quite the contrary. "Originality" was neither a value nor a virtue. Reason and human nature were presumed to be universals. The poetics of neoclassicism, which ruled the European continent, relied on an idealized imitation of ancient models. What *was* self-consciously emerging as a value in Russian upper-class culture by mid-century were quests for national identity. Russia, an outlying border state, lagged some 200 years behind Western Europe, at least when measured by such "progressive" historical markers as a Renaissance, a Reformation, and a Counter-Reformation, epochal events for Europe in which Russia did not participate. If universality was a prerequisite for entering civilized history, Russia would have to show that she reflected it in her own way.

Russia's special path began in religious history. The Catholic and Protestant countries of Europe shared a lingua franca in Latin. "Underneath" that largely static foreign tongue, vigorous local vernaculars developed that were sophisticated enough by the sixteenth century to produce literary masterpieces. In contrast, Russian Orthodox Christianity had always conducted its liturgy – and communicated its texts – in an archaic Old Church Slavonic. Its writing system (called "Cyrillic" after the ninth-century Thessalonican missionary Cyril and his brother Methodius) had been adapted from the Byzantine Greek alphabet, supplemented with new letters devised for uniquely Slavic sounds.[1] This abstract, ecclesiastical language, vaguely comprehensible to its dispersed congregations but native to none, suited the needs of a borderless continent with migrating populations and contiguous, shifting dialects. But it increased Russia's isolation from the West. With Church Slavonic as their linguistic "binder," there was little impetus among the Orthodox Slavs to master Latin or Greek, the portals to pan-European culture. When language reform began in earnest under Peter the Great, as part of his ambitious attempt to order and rationalize all aspects of Russian life, the initial tactic of the reformers was to work with this chaotic but familiar "Old Slavonic mass": cleansing it, simplifying it, and defining high, middle, and low styles according to the proportion of archaic words that each layer contained.

In 1700, the Russian language, both spoken and written, was porous, receptive, shapeless, and lacked fixed norms for orthography or pronunciation. Polonisms, Latinisms, and Germanisms abounded. Tsar Peter – a regimenting mentality in all things – staffed his Foreign Office with corps of regulators and translators. Dictionaries, glossaries, and lexical commentaries became the rage at court. But no number of tsarist decrees could create a linguistic equivalent when the concept was lacking in the Russian language or in native Russian culture, which was the case for most technical terms and many abstract words. Even the forward-driving impetus of linear narrative, with its values of novelty and suspense, lacked a dignified literary container. More common for written texts in the Russian pre-modern era was "word-weaving" [*pletenie sloves*], a dense fabric of ornamental epithets, alliterations, and assonances that aspired to reflect the unknowability and inexpressibility of God's grace (or of a given saint's blessedness) through purely poetic resources. Word order could be very free, sentences monstrously long, "plot" of negligible relevance. On occasion, however, this porous ecclesiastical texture provided an author with a rough-and-tumble freedom. Protected from Western intrusions and mandated stylistic levels, Church Slavonic could absorb racy colloquialisms and even bawdiness, fuse these images with bookish formulas or realize biblical allegory in a strikingly crude, realistic manner. A minor thread in the work of major poets (from Gavril Derzhavin in the eighteenth century to the cubo-futurist Velimir Khlebnikov [1885–1922] and the great Marina Tsvetaeva

[1892–1941] in the twentieth) kept alive this vigorous archaic stratum of militant, "unintegrated" language, full of wild metaphoric associations and primitivist sound patternings, deployed to almost surreal effect.

By the eighteenth century, state-approved innovations in technology and bureaucracy had boosted the production of secular texts. The printing press was an accepted reality. Ecclesiastical censorship lost its monopoly in 1700. But the core problem of inter-cultural translation remained. How can a word, which makes sense in the context of its own source culture, be recreated in empty semantic space? The translator could provide a paraphrase in the form of a definition – a bulky solution. More common was the practice of "doublets," embedding the foreign word (usually transliterated into Cyrillic) in the Russian text, followed by a parenthetical explanation (if one could be found – although often the Russian equivalent had an entirely different aura). Translators were most successful with concrete physical things. When a paraphrase or approximation could not be found, often the foreign word just sat there, in its own alphabet and alien script, grammatically uninflected and unresponsive to the rules of Russian declension or conjugation.

The difficulty of orienting oneself in this unmonitored polyglot sea was one reason why the Russian upper classes, by the second half of the eighteenth century, arranged matters so that their children learned to speak French from infancy, relying upon that language for all "civilized" society interactions. The wealthy families had multilingual teams of nannies and tutors on their estates (consider Tolstoy in the nineteenth century, Nabokov in the twentieth); the poorer nobles and gentry could generally afford only one miserable, underpaid, often ignorant immigrant from France, Polonized Ukraine or the German states. It is no surprise that some of the best neoclassical comedy in the eighteenth century was *language* comedy. Foreign language fakery, mutually incomprehensible dialogue, and linguistic snobbishness (primarily "Gallomania," a frenzy or mania for all things French) will be a focus for the first half of this chapter.

Our exemplary genres are limited to two irreverent literary experiments, one dramatic and one prosaic, followed by one end-of-the-century response to them that transformed this irreverence into respect. The first genre, Russian prose comedy, was especially adept at ridiculing Gallomania; the second, Russia's primitive picaresque novel, broadened the ridicule to include, among many other targets, literary pretense and high court poets. Triumphant over both these satiric projects was Sentimentalism, which took French influence seriously, even piously, and integrated it into a new prose style that swept up the Russian readership. All three genres – prose comedy, the picaresque, and Sentimentalist prose – enjoy a vigorous afterlife in the nineteenth century.

All three parody that problematic eighteenth-century mandate, "pursuit of national identity by means of imitation." To remind us of that mandate and as backdrop to this circuitous assimilation of European forms, one mid-century Russian tragedy will suffice.

When Aleksandr Sumarokov (1717–77), codifier of Russian neoclassicism and a prolific tragedian, published his Russian-language *Hamlet* in 1748, he was proud of the fact that its plot did not resemble Shakespeare's nihilistic and decadent one. In Sumarokov's version of the play, Polonius is not a bumbling counselor but the masterminding villain, Ophelia is being forced to marry the usurper Claudius, and Hamlet arrives as leader of a popular mutiny just in time to rescue his beloved from that invidious marriage. The end of the play is edifying as well as happy: Polonius commits suicide, thus releasing his daughter from the need to choose between wicked father and virtuous lover. But some trace of that tension was necessary, as a tribute to the mandatory neoclassical conflict between love and honor, the passions conquered by reason. Russian tragedians were expected to portray a victory of virtue over vice. Not only pity and fear but also "admiration" was a crucial source of tragic emotion.[2] In tragedy, with its abstract characters, heightened rhetoric, and familiar plots distanced in time and space, "Russianness" (and in this case, Shakespeare-ness too) mattered little.

The chronotope of comedy was different. Self-improvement was the goal here as well, but upright behavior or abstract edification was insufficient for it. In 1747, in his so-called "Second Epistle," Sumarokov addressed this question. Comedy, he wrote, should "correct manners by mockery; to amuse and bring [moral] benefit is its basic law." Satire should cut along the same lines, only deeper: its task was to "censure vices" and ridicule "passions, follies, wit-lessness." Sumarokov's own twelve verse comedies were poor instantiations of this ideal, however, remaining trivial, weakly plotted caricatures (often of Sumarokov's personal enemies) that only rarely rise above farce. His failure here is significant. Tragedy addresses the lofty and eternal, whereas "manners" remain a local affair. And how could *Russian* manners – and Russian follies – be attacked effectively in a comedy adapted from an alien culture? A favorite source for themes and character types was Voltaire. But what in the specifi-cally Russian landscape could speak to the creations of this skeptic and secular humanist? As another prolific author of Russian comedies, Vladimir Lukin (1737–94), put the problem in his preface to two adaptations from the French prepared for the 1764–65 Petersburg season: our spectators receive little benefit from "comedies based on foreign manners," especially if the European settings and names remain unchanged, because Russian audiences "assume it is the foreigners being laughed at, not them."[3]

Foreign models were nevertheless assumed to be indispensable. Not only did the codes of neoclassicism advocate it, but Russia had no well-developed native tradition of genteel scripted comedy. "Going to the theatre" was not part of early modern Russia's upper-class culture. When Muscovite envoys were posted to fifteenth-century Florence or Elizabethan London, they either did not see plays or poorly understood what they saw.[4] In the early eighteenth century Peter the Great tried to create, under imported German management, a state-sponsored public theatre in Red Square. Ill-wishers sabotaged the construction, audiences had to be bribed to attend, and the plays were uniformly rendered in an archaic biblical style completely at odds with their content and with spectators' interest (p. 48). Like the printing press under Ivan the Terrible, it would appear that theatre, too, was destined to be a "reform from above," a Western craftiness foisted on the unwilling populace by a visionary autocrat – or tyrant.

The three empresses who succeeded Peter passionately loved masquerade and theatre. The most gifted of them, Catherine the Great (r. 1762–96), wrote plays herself on a variety of themes: satires on religious hypocrisy, adaptations of Shakespeare to Russian conditions, even folkloric opera libretti (including one on Baba Yaga and a *bogatyr* from the Novgorod *bylina* cycle). Catherine dismissed her dramas as "trifles." But the Empress's literary pastimes lent prestige to playwriting – as long as this activity entailed no political threat to her or her absolute power. The individual abuse could be targeted, but not the institution enabling that abuse. As astonished Russian poets noted in the nineteenth century, "abuses" were displayed on the public stage in the 1760s and 1770s with far more candor and outrage than in later eras, when the institutions in question (absolutist autocracy, serfdom) were no longer perceived as part of an ordained, immutable social order (pp. 123–24).[5]

Neoclassical comedy, Gallomania, cruelty: art instructs life

In 1769 Catherine II, in imitation of the Enlightenment, encouraged self-correcting domestic satire by personally sponsoring a satiric journal. The timing was delicate. Two years earlier the Empress had decreed that no enserfed peasant could lodge a complaint against his master (owner) – a momentous step in the transformation of serfdom into fully legalized slavery. This juxtaposition of a retrograde social policy with tolerance in the literary sphere was not lost on Catherine's liberal-minded aristocratic critics. The most famous of the publisher-journalists, Nikolai Novikov (1744–1818), sparred with the Empress for two decades in his irreverent journal *The Drone* – until the French

Revolution provided startling proof that ideas could result in the decapitation of monarchs. Catherine had Novikov arrested and incarcerated in Peter and Paul Fortress in 1792. He was freed only in 1796, after her death.

In an absolutist state, the balance between acceptable, self-improving mockery and the unacceptable censure of political realities is a fragile one. For the next two centuries, Russian culture and Russian prisons would be populated by writers, artists, stage directors, and composers who gambled and lost while negotiating this tightrope. The practice of comedy under Catherine the Great is a good test case, because the rules for its composition and the range of its character types were so uncomplicated – and also because the very idea of a secular literary establishment was still so fresh. The tense relationship that later became "Poet versus Tsar" was still Poet *and* Tsar for most high-culture literary forms. In certain ways, neoclassical comedy was just as conventionally structured and ideologically collaborationist as the solemn ode.

Russian playwrights imitated two popular French models: the *comédie de caractère* (a "comedy of character" focusing on a single eponymous universal vice, as in Molière's satires on the Miser or Misanthrope) and *comédie de moeurs* (a "comedy of manners" satirically portraying contemporary society). The gallery of fixed types for such comedies includes an obedient heroine and a virtuous (often clueless) hero, an obstacle to their union (venal or dimwitted false suitors, parents or guardians), corrupt officials, foolish pedants, witty and resourceful servants, confidantes, and a *raisonneur* [a "person of good sense" who expresses the moral views of the author]. Virtue must triumph, usually in some sort of public showdown. En route, these types do not so much interact – few events actually occur on the neoclassical comedic stage – as "inter-talk," that is, expose themselves, scene after scene, through words, either in monologues (often becoming tirades) or dialogues (often dysfunctional). These verbal masks rarely become more complex as a result of any unexpected plot events; if they do, the audience perceives such change as superficial or untrustworthy.

Some Russian "manners" were relatively safe to address simply by mocking an isolated targeted vice. Such was Catherine II's strategy in her comedy *O! The Times!* (1769), which ridicules religious hypocrisy, gossip, greed, and faking a knowledge of foreign languages. The Empress followed the convention of giving characters "speaking names" to announce their essence: "Khanzhakina" [Hypocrite], "Vestnikova" [Tattler], "Nepustov" [Not-Empty, Not-Shallow]. Satire could be quite vicious as long as the vice or injustice in question was resolved harmlessly. Because satire and "reform from above" were so intimately interwoven in neoclassical comedy, the limits of the permissible can be tested through three dramatic works that go somewhat against the grain of royal patronage. Two are comedies. One (both blacker and more tuneful) is the libretto for a comic opera.

Denis Fonvizin (1745–92) was a translator, statesman, and liberal political philosopher as well as the author of Russia's two best eighteenth-century comedies, *The Brigadier* (1769) and *The Minor* (1781).[6] (The Russian title of the latter is *Nedorosl'*, the technical term for an adolescent who had not yet passed the basic literacy examinations qualifying him for obligatory state service – an intensely unpopular Petrine reform, because a young man could not marry until the state exam was passed.) While writing *The Brigadier*, Fonvizin was working as secretary to Ivan Elagin, director of the Russian Imperial Theatres. By the time of his second play, however, Fonvizin was thoroughly disillusioned with Catherine's rule. He had entered the employ of Count Nikita Panin, leader of the aristocratic opposition. Unusual for his era and station, Fonvizin advocated broadening the notion of state service to include not only the military but also commercial and mercantile activity undertaken by the noble class. He was certainly no radical, however, and *The Minor* is a rather obedient comedy. It broke new ground not in its politics but in its realistic portrayals: of an obsequious, ignorant German tutor and his two serf assistants (one an honest ex-soldier, the other a dishonest rogue), a provincial matriarch as violent as she is obtuse, and a setting immediately recognizable as Russia – however universal the vices exposed.

The plot delivers no surprises. Indeed, the "speaking names" attached to the characters at once reveal their virtues and vices. The virtuous ward Sofya [Wisdom] is separated from her beloved Milon [Dear One] by the machinations of her repulsive host family with its two false suitors: the loutish sixteen-year-old "minor" Mitrofan [Greek, "mama's boy"] and his uncle Skotinin [Mr. Pig or Brute]. The true lovers are duly united in the end, thanks to the device of the heroine's uncle, Starodum [Old-Thought], who returns from Siberia in the nick of time to provide a dowry for his niece, join up with the righteous government inspector Pravdin [Mr. Truthful], and expose the evil-doing of the play's villain, the abusive serfowner and doting mother Prostakova [Mrs. Simpleton]. In the final act, Prostakova fails in her naïve attempt to kidnap Sofya for her worthless son. Her wealth is confiscated by official decree, at which point even Mitrofan casts her out. All these threats and moral cleansings happen in the most improbably well-timed way. Defeated villains immediately collapse into craven beggars. Neither the fate of the lovers nor the exposure of the tyrant – both foregone conclusions – provides the moral infrastructure. That function is filled by the sermons of the old-fashioned moralist Starodum, one of the play's two *raisonneurs*, who directs his maxims not to the fools on stage but to the audience.

For Fonvizin's audience in the 1770s, the "old-thought" of Starodum was still rather recent. Starodum identifies himself as a product of Peter the Great's vigorous, masculine policies on universal service, economic progress, Western-style education, and enlightened patriotism so different – we are meant to infer – from the frivolous politics of bedroom and ballroom under the subsequent empresses. Starodum delivers his sermons on this energetic upright life as if from a pulpit. He does have interlocutors, but he rarely listens to or learns from them. His style and language belong to an enlightenment treatise, proclaiming on matters precious to Fonvizin: the proper education of youth (the lout Mitrofan being the negative example), the temptations of inherited wealth, one's duty to the fatherland, the value of personal honor above rank and of service above favoritism, and the virtue of independent economic initiative. Starodum's sojourn in Siberia prompts from him a paean to that region of Russia where "money is drawn from the earth itself," a place – unlike the imperial court – that "rewards labor faithfully and generously" and does not require a man to "exchange his conscience for it" (Act III, ii).

Performances of *The Minor* in later centuries often abridged or omitted altogether these cumbersome monologues as smug and devoid of dramatic interest. Fonvizin's negative portraits proved far more popular, enjoying a phenomenal afterlife in imitations, sequels, and adaptations. (Fonvizin was greatly beloved by Pushkin, who places a Skotinin, a Mr. Pig, among the guests at Tatyana's nameday party in *Eugene Onegin*, Five, xxvi: 5–7.) But the sanctimonious moralizing of Starodum and Pravdin appealed powerfully to audiences of their own eighteenth century. This fact should not be forgotten. At the end of that century, through the efforts of Nikolai Karamzin (1766–1826), literate Russia met and fell in love with the Sentimentalist narrator, a direct descendent of this anti-ironic, Starodum-style hortatory voice but now motivated more by feelings than by reasonableness. Sentimentalism as a literary movement also preached the innate goodness of human nature, our natural desire to empathize, repent, and self-improve. As part of his mission, Karamzin took Gallomania – heretofore ridiculed in comedies and placed in the mouths of fools – and dignified it. Methodically and with great skill, he created a narrative style that was permeated by French influence, even by French turns of phrase, but integrated smoothly into the texture of Russian discourse. In his wake, Russian prose became fluent, eloquent, lofty, sincere – a vehicle for the fictions of gentlefolk and even (after 1803, when Karamzin set to work on Russia's first history intended for a mass readership) a carrier of Russian national consciousness.

This shift from "Gallomania" to "Gallophilia" – from ridiculing French influence to loving it and relying on it – is one of the major watersheds preparing us for Pushkin. We return to Karamzin's achievement at the end of this chapter, for his Sentimentalism proved exceptionally durable on the Russian literary landscape, holding its own against irony and existential despair well into the twentieth century. But first we must sample the ridicule itself. Two targets were beloved by eighteenth-century satirists. One was the favorite of court playwrights: the French language as worshipped, parroted, and fractured by Russians. The other, embedded in crude prose, was more subversive, for it included among the targets of its parody the aristocratic court with its neoclassical genres and "acceptable" comedy.

Gallomania is nowhere more perfectly exposed than in Fonvizin's 1769 comedy of manners, *The Brigadier*. In a series of static tableaus, the two virtuous colorless lovers, Sofya [again, Wisdom] and Dobroliubov [Mr. Lover-of-Good], stand obediently off to the side, waiting for the fools to self-destruct. Chief among these fools is Ivanushka the Brigadier's son, called several times a *durak* [fool] to his face. He has been to Paris, despises all Russians, and sprinkles his pompous speech with French words or with Russian verbs built on French constructions, to the mystification of his parents and the amusement of the audience. This Ivan-*durak* is betrothed to Sofya but, offended at the thought of living with someone who does not know French, courts Sofya's silly young Frenchified stepmother instead (meanwhile, the Brigadier also courts the stepmother, and the Brigadier's dimwitted wife is courted by Sofya's father, a pious councillor). What fuels this comedy of multiple false suitors and utterly inept seductions is the fact that no one understands anyone else. Or rather, when they do manage to communicate, it is only to slander or snipe at one another. Malicious spousal relations are one startling aspect of this sort of comedy, contrasting oddly with the inevitable "happy marriage between lovers" hovering just beyond the final act and definitive for the comedic genre.

Well into the nineteenth century, Gallomania retained its moral resonance. The great successor to these satiric playwrights is the Gallophobic (and quatralingual) Leo Tolstoy in *War and Peace*, for whom speaking French in contexts where "Russian words would do" is an index not only of frivolity but of moral depravity. Characters of irrepressible spontaneity and intuitive ethical judgment, like Natasha Rostova, have stiff or artificial French. Hélène Kuragina-Bezukhova, foul seductress, feels at home only in the French-speaking salon. When, in the early 1940s, Sergei Prokofiev turned Tolstoy's novel into a sprawling opera, his librettist intensified this inherent Tolstoyan equation of moral corruption with "speaking (or living) a foreign language" through the simplified diction appropriate to a libretto, especially one composed in the suspicious and xenophobic Stalinist era. Natasha's illicit romance is musically propelled by the genre of the waltz, with its Viennese and French associations, to which

Prokofiev allots an intoxicating, dreamlike time-space separated from the surrounding action. These slightly off-balance waltzes can be seen (or heard) as visitations from the Sentimentalist tradition, and they condition the emotionally vulnerable Natasha to its dangerous fantasies.[7]

Soon after Fonvizin's *Brigadier*, the playwright Yakov Knyazhnin (1742–91) composed a two-act libretto, in prose with inserted arias, on the theme of Gallomania. It bore the odd title *Misfortune from a Coach*. Although comic libretti were often sung to any popular tunes of the day, in this case the court composer Vasily Pashkevich (1742–97) composed the music. The opera premiered before the Empress herself, in 1779. It was an immediate hit. Its plot type is the "peasant opera" made famous throughout Europe by Rousseau (upgraded to the manor house in such masterpieces as Mozart's *Marriage of Figaro*): two rustic or lowborn lovers are prevented from marrying by some villain of higher rank – a jealous bailiff, uncooperative parents, philandering masters. The cleverness of servants (or slaves) outwits the obtuse power of their superiors. It would seem that this plot, once Russified, could only strike at the heart of serfdom. But the opera did not deliver that message, even though the abuse was no laughing matter.

What was the "misfortune" caused by a coach? Two Gallomaniac landowners, the Filyulins (Mr. and Mrs. Ninny) desire to buy the latest fashionable coach from Paris. To get the necessary funds, they decide to sell some serfs to the army (a life or death sentence: the standard term of service was twenty-five years). Since the bailiff wants the peasant heroine Anyuta for himself, he selects her lover Lukyan as one of the serf recruits. Lukyan is promptly shackled and led away. The situation is saved only when, for a sizable bribe, the Filyulins' household jester Afanasy (labeled in the libretto simply "*Shut*," Jester) suggests to the two threatened serfs, who know a few foreign words, that they babble a bit in French in front of their masters. The Filyulins are delighted. Peasants who can utter French words must be creatures who know how to love. Keep these two serfs at home, the Filyulins conclude, let them marry, and Lukyan will be our coachman! The strangeness and Russianness of this little comic opera lies not in the reunification of the lovers – that end-point is mandatory for the genre – and not even in the capriciousness of the masters, but in the *Shut*.

This inserted Jester is a morally blank, unsentimental, folk-comic type. He sings two arias that owe little to the ethos of enlightened self-improvement – or even to the ethos of enlightened despotism – and much to the cynical, pragmatic, resigned ethics of a Russian secular fool. In his first-act aria, the Jester chides the two desperate lovers for not knowing how to joke. "Why be sad and why go moan?" he sings. "It's best to spit, spit on everything in the world, / It's all in knowing how to dance to someone else's tune / The trick's to be a jester and a rogue."[8] In the second act, the Jester urges the fettered Lukyan simply to die at the first opportunity, because: "It's really the best way; you can't imagine how bad this world is." And finally – after the Gallomaniac ruse works – he delivers another aria on Lukyan in his new role: "What joy it is, / What sweetness to the heart" to have a coachman who "Instead of shouting 'Here we come!' / will shout in French! / . . . and no one on the street will understand!" In the closing scene, the Jester gathers the grateful peasants around himself: "What were you crying about? Where the *shut* Afanasy is, there you have to laugh; you see, there's nothing in the world worth worrying about." And then the Jester introduces the refrain that all sing in ensemble: "A trifle destroyed you, / But a trifle saved you too."

Like Melancholy Jacques in Shakespeare's comedy *As You Like It*, Knyazhnin's Jester is a mournful realist, surprised at nothing. For him too, "All the world's a stage" – a world worthy of wry commentary, perhaps, but run by caprice and resistant to moral correction. This pragmatic amoral type was certainly familiar to the Russian eighteenth century. But it was not borrowed from Elizabethan drama. At this time, Shakespeare was still being read in edited French prose versions, tamed and cleansed. A truer, more durable inspiration for Knyazhnin's Jester might be the Muscovite rogue Frol Skobeyev. By the middle of the eighteenth century, Frol's ribald type of story had blended with Russian adaptations of foreign adventure tales, simplified in the illustrated woodcut book [*lubok*] or written up for commercial presses serving the newly literate population of Russian towns. One example must suffice of this new bestselling "vulgar prose": *The Comely Cook [Prigozhaia povarikha], or the Adventures of a Debauched Woman* (1770), by Mikhail Chulkov (1734–92). Chulkov was the most gifted of Russia's enterprising, pen-pushing pioneer novelists and the antipode of the values and patronage system of the aristocratic court. Unlike Russian neoclassical comedy, *The Comely Cook* left little, if any, legacy in subsequent centuries; it was reprinted in 1890 and then only sporadically during the Soviet period. Thus it did not become part of Russian literary tradition, only part of her literary *reality*. This fate is appropriate to the artifact, however. Literary fame, canonical status, and the neoclassical pretension that art can reform the manners and morals of life were themselves one satirical target of Chulkov's picaresque novel.

Chulkov's Martona: life instructs art

Mikhail Chulkov was of non-noble birth, an actor, journalist, and low-level bureaucrat who announced openly that his "pen was for sale." His activity as author and literary adaptor coincided with a controversy over the writing of novels that erupted in the 1760s. Was prose fiction serious literary art? Could novels and tales edify – or only entertain, distract, titillate, thus mocking the edifiers and self-improvers? In 1759, Sumarokov, then the director of the Russian Imperial Theatres, weighed in with the opinion that novels, unless elevated by dignity and usefulness, could cause readers a great deal of harm. Chulkov's eventual response to this lofty neoclassicist position was an omnibus narrative titled *The Mocker, or Slavonic Folktales* [*Peresmeshnik, ili slavenskie skazki*], a motley collection of chivalric romances, fantastic wondertales, pagan myths, and the occasional realistic account of abuses of serfdom transposed to the ninth century. Chulkov published his first novel proper, *The Comely Cook*, anonymously in 1770. In it he continued his earlier "undignified" and "useless" agenda, now integrated by a first-person voice and the thread of a single biography.

The heroine, with the unRussian name Martona, was probably modeled on Fougeret de Monbron's "*roman libertin*" *Margot la ravaudeuse* [Margot the Old-Clothes-Mender], a French rags-to-riches courtesan novel published twenty years earlier, in 1750. Martona begins her story as a beautiful, plucky nineteen-year-old, widowed after the Battle of Poltava (1709) and left without means. The battle reference is misleading, however, for the novel is not historical. Cast in the abstract chronotope of adventure tales and the picaresque, it is unified only by the appetites and adventures of its heroine. "I think that many of our sisters will accuse me of immodesty," Martona begins, "but since this vice is by and large natural to women . . . I shall indulge in it willingly."[9] For the first half of the novel, Martona moves from lover to lover, improving her position, re-pricing her services, surviving the occasional setback with aplomb (being beaten up by a wife, betrayed by a cad, thrown in prison by a jealous heir) and justifying her unscrupulousness – mostly robbing her clients – with pithy folk sayings. (If Fonvizin's Starodum spoke in Enlightenment maxims, then Chulkov's Martona, to justify *her* behavior, rattles off folk proverbs. The sinister culmination of such self-validation through proverbial wisdom comes with Leo Tolstoy's 1886 peasant drama, *The Power of Darkness*.) At one point Martona is forced to work as a cook. Most of the time, however, her lovers provide for her handsomely. Her most profitable position is with a lieutenant-colonel in his seventies, into whose wealthy house she smuggles a young admirer dressed as her older sister (a Frol Skobeyev motif). Before she can abscond with this new lover, however, he disappears with their mutually purloined wealth and she must return, humbled and penitent, to her "toothless Adonis," who is so delighted at her reappearance that on his deathbed he forgives her all.

Is the self-serving voice behind such a story in any position to mock the immoral behavior of others? Probably not, but such was hardly Chulkov's intent. Evidence from his other work suggests that *The Comely Cook* mocks not human folly – that comfortable target of neoclassical satire – but the humans gullible enough to think that folly can be eradicated by writing didactically about it. Chulkov's novel is prefaced by a mock dedication to a mock patron and an elaborate apology declaring everything (including his own book and its feeble author) perishable and mutable. The message of the preface is indeed debunking, but it is cast in the high style of the tragedian Sumarokov. Satire on all didactic literature, with its moral prescripts and self-righteous poet-practitioners, is woven into the events of the second half of the novel, where Martona is less a manipulator of others and more a witness.[10]

The novel hints early at its irreverent anti-literary end. One of Martona's lovers, an illiterate copy clerk, tells her of a neoclassical ode that turned up in their office; the chief secretary assured them it was "some sort of delirium, not worth copying" (p. 38). In a later episode, Martona befriends a merchant's wife who "writes novels with introductions in verse" (somewhat like Chulkov's own novel) and fancies herself a critic. "So busy was she at versifying," Martona notes, "she very seldom slept with her husband" (p. 58). This female friend presided over a literary salon, where nothing was natural or healthy: a decrepit old man seduces a thirteen-year-old girl, a young swain courts a toothless wealthy old crone, and in the midst of this "licentious brothel" a "short little poet," sweating profusely, "kept shouting verses from a tragedy he had composed" (p. 59). This fraudulent salon, which eerily prefigures the grotesque "Literary Fête" in Dostoevsky's 1870 novel *Demons*, is the portal to a series of other literary and real-life fakes, played out by Martona's lovers and servants as literal performances.

These performances are themselves parodies of the literary genres they pretend to be. The merchant's wife decides to get rid of her husband. On commission, Martona's servant concocts a poison that induces temporary insanity in the victim (the servant calls his harmless handiwork a "comedy"); he then proceeds to expose the wife's perfidious intent to the whole salon in a *skazka* [fairy tale]. Finally there is a fake tragedy, the staged suicide-by-poisoning of one lover following the presumed death of his rival in a faked duel. During this parade of malfunctioning genres, Martona herself does little except watch – and make sure that no one actually causes the death of anyone else. She stands for the amoral rights of life to its own preservation. As she confesses to this discredited crew, "even corrupt women are left with some sense of reason" (p. 50, trans. adjusted). The novel breaks off abruptly in the middle of one dramatic (and possibly faked) deathbed scene. Opinions vary on whether Chulkov intended this episode to be the novel's formal end. Either way, the truncated series of episodes in our possession suggests that a central message of the author – either

Martona herself, or whatever higher storytelling voice stands behind her – was premised on the fact that authors have nothing to "teach." Life's experience teaches. Chulkov's heroine, like every picaresque protagonist, is not a reader but a survivor.

Chulkov's Martona might have an even more potent (and more politically charged) rags-to-riches prototype than was earlier suspected. Recent research has suggested that Martona is modeled not only on a French clothes-mender who became a successful courtesan but also on Peter the Great's widow, Empress Catherine I, who, with the help of former lovers and allies, ruled Russia precariously from 1725 to her death in 1727.[11] The woman who married Peter I was a commoner, perhaps even a servant, in a Lutheran household. She is believed to have lost her first husband at the Battle of Poltava at the age of eighteen. Her first name was Marta; she was an excellent housekeeper and cook. Tsar Peter was only the most powerful in a series of increasingly distinguished lovers, and he was also the most constant. If this hypothesis about Martona/Marta-Catherine I is correct, then *The Comely Cook* is not only Russia's first picaresque novel, but possibly also the first Russian *roman-à-clef* (a novel in which actual persons appear under fictitious names). As befits Chulkov, it is a carnivalized *roman-à-clef* that travesties its lofty imperial subject.

Neoclassical comedy and the picaresque novel, enriched in the early nineteenth century by an explosion of interest in vaudeville, provide an essential backdrop to Pushkin's short stories, the dramas and narrative epics of Gogol, and Dostoevsky's great novels. These masterworks are most comic precisely at those points where stock characters or scenarios from eighteenth-century satire are recycled in the context of contemporary (and often more frightening) Russian reality. As we shall see in Chapter 5, Pushkin's *Tales of the Late Ivan Petrovich Belkin* (1830) are still cast in the neoclassical comedic mold of harmony, balance, wit, and good will. In Gogol's 1836 *Government Inspector*, the darker side of comedy comes to the surface. An unknown fop arrives at a provincial town and, faking every step of the way, terrifies the local bureaucracy into revealing and even intensifying its own corruption. (If the exposure of venality was Pravdin's straightforward mission in *The Minor*, Gogol's nineteenth-century "inspector" Khlestakov is now himself a fake.) In Gogol's *Dead Souls* (1842), a traveling salesman-rogue on the road must keep moving if he is to avoid exposure and disgrace – for clients and lovers with something to conceal must not meet one another, as Martona ruefully knows. In Dostoevsky's *Demons*, a young and pernicious dandy with a smattering of foreign education courts a silly self-important governor's wife in full view of her browbeaten spouse (a situation straight out of Fonvizin). Had she been alive to watch these stock-in-trade episodes on stage, the Empress Catherine II would have laughed heartily. Increasingly in the nineteenth century, however, fops and fakes are not only foolish. They are also lethal. Virtue no longer triumphs at the end. Manners are not corrected by mockery. Bouts of madness are not due to some magic potion slipped into an unsuspecting body from the outside. The madman has become shrewd, sly, multidimensional, manipulative, and this complicates our sympathy. Comic scenes in Gogol and Dostoevsky easily became demonic without the reassuring envelope of the Enlightenment.

Karamzin's "Poor Liza"

Nikolai Karamzin (1766–1826), prosewriter, literary reformer, essayist, and Russia's first major historian, almost single-handedly moved Russian literature across the century's divide. His prose fiction has not stood the test of time. But Pushkin and his generation could not have begun to write without him, and the plots, characters, and scenarios made famous by Karamzin surface uninterruptedly in all forms (poetry, short story, drama, opera) throughout the nineteenth century. Several factors contribute to his pivotal role.

Karamzin experimented with a wide number of genres. Uncommonly for the time, he favored English and German literature over the ubiquitous French, thus broadening the traditions on which Russian writers could draw (and also lessening the merciless heat focused on Gallomania). Among these pioneering works were his *Letters of a Russian Traveler*, based on his tour of Europe in 1789–90, his historical romances, sentimentalist love stories, Gothic horror tales, and hortative (but not treatise-like) critical essays. Each was a popular success, and for each he created a smooth, literary-colloquial intonation that came to be known as the "*novyi slog*," the "new style" – "new" in its elegance, emotionality, and politeness. Drawing creatively on French constructions, studiously avoiding both the piously inflected high style as well as the jarringly colloquial low style, Karamzin's prose strove to reflect "how people actually talked." Or more correctly, he created a model for the way Russian speech in the 1790s should sound among high-born, cultivated men and women in the upper-class salon – if they could be dissuaded from conversing in French.

Why was this task so timely? Fonvizin, we recall, wrote neoclassical comedies in the 1760s and 1770s remarkable for their racy dialogue and rudeness. These dramas were an enormous step forward from the stilted tragedies penned by his colleagues at Catherine's court. But Fonvizin's language-masks, for all their responsiveness, were brittle. The spectator's pleasure increased to the extent that the characters on stage did not understand one another, or made fools of themselves, or were indecorously exposed in public. Such negative types, which constitute the major delight of this sort of comedy, move without mediation from comic buffoon to violent bully to abject vanquished villain. Decency did not have its own voice. Karamzin sought to fill in the missing "decent" layers with a style that was appropriate for empathetic communication. Only then, he believed, could Russian prose become polite, witty, nuanced, playful, and thus a part of belles-lettres.

Some men-of-letters resisted these reforms. The so-called "archaists," or Russian-language patriots, preferred to develop the potentials of this eighteenth-century rawness rather than bleach it out. They feared, not without cause, that such prettified Gallicized Russian would become a linguistic "blandscape," even though the "old style" was an unspeakable amalgam of bookishness (at the upper end) and crudeness (at the lower). But even to these conservatives, Karamzin was indispensable. To him Russia owes the very concept of a "reading public."[12] Karamzin advocated universal literacy, for women and children as well as for "minors." He encouraged reading – *any* reading on any topic – as a dignified and honorable pastime. Unlike preceding playwrights or writers of odes, whose diction was public (either performative or rhetorical), Karamzin cultivated an intimate voice, one that sought out its readers privately and face to face. In their time, these priorities were considered quite provocative, even revolutionary. We consider only one example of the "Karamzinian revolution": his famous 1792 Sentimentalist short story "Poor Liza."

A peasant girl, Liza, living with her widowed mother on the outskirts of Moscow, is seduced by Erast, a young nobleman from the city. The seduction is roundabout. What first attracts the hero is Liza's virginal innocence, so unlike his carnal relations with women in town. But after some time spent on chaste kisses under the ancient oak, the two consummate their love (during the obligatory thunderstorm). Erast begins to lose interest once his ideal shepherdess becomes merely his mistress. Eventually he leaves her on pretext of going to war, gambles away his wealth, and arranges to marry a rich noblewoman. When Liza comes across his carriage on a Moscow street, Erast cannot avoid explaining matters – and then shows her the door with a hundred rubles and a farewell kiss. In despair, Liza drowns herself in the pond near the ancient oak. Her mother dies immediately of grief. Erast, the inconstant lover, cannot be consoled. The narrator hears this story from the miserable man a year before his death.

Such seduce-and-abandon plots are found in every culture. In the West today they survive robustly in serial soap operas, teenage romances, comic strips. When they were new, however, as they were for the Russian 1790s, they shocked and mesmerized the upper classes. Russian heroines might have behaved like this, but they had not been revered for it. A cult developed around the pond where Liza met her end. Still, "Sentimentalism" is inadequate to Karamzin's achievement. A better word would be "Sensibility," as in Jane

Austen's novel *Sense and Sensibility* (1811) – because the lachrymose suicide at the end is quite incidental. The story exists not in its events but in the tone given to those events by the narrator, a man of "sentiment." Like Rousseau, this narrator insists on the basic goodness of human nature (Erast, we read, has "a decent mind and good heart, only he is weak and frivolous"); in this sort of world, there are no truly evil villains. The "writer of sentiment" believes in the virtuousness of spontaneous feelings, which connect us to one another more readily and influence us more profoundly than can words, ideas, or our sense of duty. The successful Sentimentalist text, whatever its central event, must unite the author, narrator, hero, and reader in a mesh of co-sympathy, co-experiencing, and co-remembering of that event.

In Western Europe, Sentimentalism, or Sensibility, had a somewhat different profile.[13] Western novels – from Richardson's *Pamela* (1740) and *Sir Charles Grandison* (1754) to Rousseau's *Julie, ou la nouvelle Héloïse* (1761) and Goethe's *Sorrows of Young Werther* (1774) – were by and large moralizing sagas set among the bourgeois class, or on the border between bourgeois and upper-class values, replete with concrete realistic detail. In Russia, there was not much middle class. The "realistic," bourgeois, Sentimentalist novel of England and the continent was thus an unusable model for the pioneering Russian Sensibility. But the Russian peasant – largely unknown and thus available for idealization – represented a possible candidate for carrier of pure feelings. In this idyll, all individualizing traits disappear from bodies and words. Everyone speaks in the same emotionally heightened voice, peasant and nobleman alike. The time-space of idylls is severely constrained. Events unfold in a permanent present of emotional arousal or deflation. Liza, who makes a living by selling lilies-of-the-valley on Moscow street corners, is no recognizably Russian peasant and certainly no serf. Her family follows the biological conventions of folkloric and Romantic time, which deletes a generation: Liza is seventeen, but her mother is "in her sixties" – as if Russian women bore their first surviving children only in their late forties.

In the 1830s, Pushkin several times rewrote the Poor Liza plot, with varying degrees of affectionate irony. Dostoevsky, who knew his Karamzin thoroughly and loved all of it, gives us an urban "Poor Liza" as naïve prostitute in his *Notes from Underground*, a saintly Lizaveta as the pawnbroker's timid, hardworking half-sister (and co-murder victim) in *Crime and Punishment*, and an upper-class, sexually willing and sacrificial Liza in *Demons*. The plot was parodied and then reconstituted in sequential transpositions throughout the century. In Pushkin's 1833 "Queen of Spades," for example, the old Countess's ward [poor] Liza tries, but fails, to seduce Germann, the engineer-officer who is stalking her – for he is really only after the secret of the three cards. Thus Pushkin's

Liza survives, gets over her infatuation, and marries someone else. When Pyotr Tchaikovsky, a composer of profound Sentimentalist vision, turned Pushkin's tale into his opera *The Queen of Spades* (1890), he restored the heroine to her canonical Karamzinian fate: she drowns herself from love in a Petersburg canal. As we shall see in Chapter 9, the bestselling post-Soviet detective writer Boris Akunin explicitly structured the love subplot of his first novel, *Azazel'* [1998; in English, *The Winter Queen*] on Karamzin's "Poor Liza" – and hideously, she does not escape her canonized fate.

But the most complex commentary on all Russian seduce-and-abandon plots is surely Leo Tolstoy's final full-length novel, *Resurrection* (1898). What he dares to attack in this late novel is not only the vices of seduction and abandonment – familiar to the point of cliché – but the device of mutual forgiveness that sits at the core of Sentimentalism. For Tolstoy, it was no longer sufficient for the dishonored heroine to die so that the hero, en route to self-awareness, can repent, be redeemed, and weep together with narrator and reader. *Anna Karenina*, with its sympathetic portrait of the suffering Aleksei Vronsky in the Epilogue, still displays traces of that earlier dynamic. But by the end of century, letting Eros and Death do all the hard work of moral growth is no longer acceptable to Tolstoy. In his *Resurrection*, men and women must achieve the brotherhood, or sisterhood, that unites us into one human family by wholly other means.

In closing, let us note one paradox shared by neoclassical comedy, Chulkov's picaresque novel, and Karamzin's Sentimentalism. The high-minded, virtuous heroes in all three categories become, to later audiences, dismally boring. Starodum and Pravdin, Milon and Sofya, Erast and Liza, even Martona's lovers when they begin to behave, are one-liners with a one-dimensional afterlife. In contrast, the Brigadier, Prostakova, Skotinin, Mitrofan, Martona, Knyazhnin's Jester are unforgettably vital – and ubiquitous. This dilemma took its toll on many writers, most tragically Nikolai Gogol. Gogol's inability to portray a positive character was one factor contributing to his creative, and then physical, death. But Pushkin, Russia's other Romantic-era genius, will find several ways out. His true heroes are known not by their virtue, but by the more complex concept of honor. A personal friend of Karamzin and much indebted to him, Pushkin nevertheless undertook to roughen up Karamzin's prose, re-masculinize it, reclaim it from the salon and take it into the real outdoors. In the process, Pushkin the poet, prose writer, and dramatist became for Russia what Shakespeare is for the English-speaking world, an unsurpassed standard. To his astonishing century we now turn.

Sculpture of Aleksandr Pushkin by M. K. Anikushin, installed on
Arts Square in Leningrad in 1957.
Photograph by Michael Julius.

Chapter 5

The astonishing nineteenth century: Romanticisms

1801–25:	*Reign of Emperor Alexander I*
1812:	*Napoleon invades Russia and occupies Moscow*
1814:	*Tsar Alexander I enters Paris in triumph*
1820:	*Aleksandr Pushkin, age twenty-one, exiled to the south of Russia for subversive poems*
1825:	*Decembrist Revolt in Petersburg*
1825–55:	*Reign of Emperor Nicholas I*
1828:	*Nikolai Gogol moves from Ukraine to Petersburg at age nineteen*
1836:	*Gogol leaves Russia for Italy; lives mostly in Rome until 1848*
1837:	*Death of Pushkin in a duel at age thirty-seven*
1841:	*Death of Lermontov in a duel at age twenty-seven*
1852:	*Death of Gogol at age forty-three from self-induced starvation*

In the early nineteenth century, 5 percent of Russia's people could read. The fate of literature was in the hands of several dozen gifted, well-born, multilingual innovators, concentrated in the two capital cities and writing for one another. No literary "profession" existed, nor a "public opinion"; criticism of new poems or dramas took place in salons, theatre foyers, private correspondence. But this tiny community of cultured readers and writers, although cut off from the mass of their countrymen, never doubted that it was part of mainstream European culture. It passionately followed shifts in literary taste on the continent and, as neoclassicism gave way to cults of sentiment, furiously debated each step.

Like Romantics throughout Europe, Russian writers reacted against overly rationalistic views of human nature and the universalizing claims of the Enlightenment. The gothic and grotesque came into fashion. E. T. A. Hoffmann popularized cults of the poet, of creative madness and the fantastic; the early Dickens opened up the urban slum as an exotic locale with an ethnography of its own. Folklore, the unique spirit of one's native language, and national history began to compete with the neoclassical convention of borrowed plots and stock characters. Russia rapidly absorbed the major Romantic prose genres from Europe: society tale, novel-in-letters, "travel notes," "southern" (or orientalist) tale, diary and memoir, historical romance. But for all this cosmopolitanism, the two Russian Romantic-era writers who are the focus of this chapter – Aleksandr Pushkin (1799–1837) and Nikolai Gogol (1809–52) – are difficult to place on the European map. Although each endorsed the Romantic view of "poet as national prophet," neither embraced Romantic rebellion, or even Romantic individualism, as usually defined. With his impeccable taste, implied audience of insiders, and unquestioning faith in the power (and responsibility) of the poet to elucidate rather than mystify with words, Pushkin remained in many respects a neoclassicist, an eighteenth-century writer.[1] And as regards Gogol, no ready-made genre conventions apply. His Ukrainian folk and terror-tales, his humanoid caricatures and unclassifiable, out-of-control plots can pass from irrepressible laughter to unspeakable dread in the space of a phrase. Among the canonical Russian writers, the brief life of Mikhail Lermontov (1814–41) probably comes closest to reflecting the pan-European Romantic spirit.

During the reign of Alexander I, literary patronage came to an end.[2] Writers were obliged to seek other means of material support. Under Catherine the Great (r. 1762–96), the publicist Nikolai Novikov had stoutly refused to serve solely the interests of the empress – and to finance his publishing activities, he sold off inherited estates. Nineteenth-century writers were rarely so fortunate. They owned and managed (that is, mortgaged) serfs, served as military officers, worked as government bureaucrats. A commercially viable press began to function in the 1830s, but the best writing was not always the most marketable. Pushkin insisted on a decent price for his work, but he did not successfully make the transition from aristocratic to middlebrow readerships and was saddled with debts his entire life. Gogol scraped by on loans, subsidies from his mother's estate, and publishers' contracts. Occasionally a writer succeeded at a spectacular, high-profile imperial career. Karamzin, for example, was appointed to the salaried post of Historian Laureate in 1803, and until his death in 1826 he labored full time over his highly acclaimed *History of the Russian State*. The gifted poet Vasily Zhukovsky (1783–1852), illegitimate son of a wealthy landowner and a captive Turkish woman, rose in court to become tutor to the heir apparent. Aleksandr Griboyedov (1795–1829), author of Russia's finest neoclassical verse comedy *Woe from Wit* (1825) and a well-educated man of modest means, became a prominent diplomat; he was slaughtered together with the Russian delegation during a riot in Tehran following a peace treaty humiliating to the Persians.

Although the era of patronage was over, what remained, as a fact of life and a theme of literature, was Peter the Great's Table of Ranks. In 1722, Peter replaced promotion based on birth by a merit system with fourteen ranks, which provided the infrastructure to his decree on obligatory state service.[3] Mandatory service had never been popular and in 1762 it was rescinded by Catherine the Great's spouse, the ill-fated Peter III (r. 1762). But the basic structure of promotion, reward, and formal titles – which determined how a gentleman was addressed in public and what salaried positions he was allowed to pursue – remained in place, with small modifications, until the Bolsheviks abolished the Table of Ranks in 1917. Without a sense of this stratification it is difficult to grasp the dynamics of prestige, ambition, and humiliation in tsarist Russia. Its mechanisms of flattery and shame – the distinctive psychological fuel of much Russian Romantic prose – could function with grotesque precision, especially in the imperial capital. One's sense of honor and sensitivity to insult was conditioned by one's birth in conjunction with one's rank.

The fourteen ranks had three parallel branches: military, civil, and court (that is, "attached to the imperial court," "courtier"). Rank Fourteen was where one began. Any rank above Eight (after 1856, any rank above Four) bestowed hereditary nobility. Many benefited from this system; sons of the gentry and even of low-born scribes and secretaries could now work their way into the nobility. Some professions, however, had no rank assigned to them at all – such as musicians before the founding of a degree-granting conservatory in St. Petersburg in 1862 – and thus officially did not exist. One's rank guaranteed rights (such as existed in the Russian Empire): the right to own human property, the right to be exempt from public flogging. In official documents, a person's rank came first. When addressing a person formally it was procedurally obligatory to use titles, which were multi-syllabic, bulky, and intrusive (ranks One and Two were addressed as "Your High Excellency" [*vashe vysokoprevoskhoditel'stvo*], Three and Four as "Your Excellency" [*vashe prevoskhoditel'stvo*], Five as "Your Highly Born" [*vashe vysokorodie*], Six through Eight as "Your High Honor" [*vashe vysokoblagorodie*], etc.). Gogol gives us stretches of conversation consisting largely of a vacuous and sycophantic exchange of these formal titles. But more was involved than verbal courtesy or the currying of favor. Every branch of every rank had its required uniform, mandated down to the shape of the collar and color of the button, as well as hats, gloves, boots, weapons, the prescribed cut for facial hair, the dances one could perform at balls and the style of carriage one could drive. Petersburg was a heavily military city, with a large percentage of its adult males in uniform; many of its parks were de facto parade grounds. Visually, aurally, and behaviorally, one's rank bestowed one's identity.

Pushkin and honor (its reciprocity, roundedness, and balance)

Pushkin was acutely aware of the rewards and constraints of official rank. They often conflicted with two other values precious to him: professionalism as a writer, and noble birth. The poet possessed a distinguished genealogy of which he was very proud. On his father's side the Pushkins were an ancient, although impoverished and marginalized, boyar family. His exotic mother, known as "the beautiful Creole," was a granddaughter of Abram Gannibal, a black African who had been captured as a boy and educated as a favorite of Peter the Great (rising to rank Four, major general). Scarcely out of his teens, Pushkin was already celebrated as Russia's supreme poet. But he never "served the state" with distinction on *its* terms – indeed, he was arrested and exiled in 1820 for several free-thinking poems and remained under police surveillance for the rest of his life.

Pushkin was to rise only one notch above the miserably low rank assigned him upon graduation from his boarding school, St. Petersburg's imperial Lycée: the Tenth (civilian collegiate secretary). Many of his best friends were dashing officers. Pushkin felt his unglamorous official status keenly; but when the politically suspect and financially strapped poet volunteered for the army in 1829, he was turned down. In 1831 he was promoted to titular councilor (rank Nine), with access to imperial archives. He did receive one further dubious honor, however. On New Year's Eve, 1834, Tsar Nicholas, desiring to gaze on Pushkin's breathtakingly beautiful wife at imperial balls, named the poet a "kammerjunker" or Gentleman of the Bedchamber (court rank Eleven; the courtier ranks had no equivalent to civilian Ten). Pushkin considered this rank humiliating for someone of his years and stature, and furthermore it obliged him to escort his wife to palace events. Outraged, he avoided wearing the hated green uniform and (so it was said) even sabotaged it, ripping off a button and refusing to repair it.[4] After Pushkin was mortally wounded in a duel defending his wife's honor in January 1837, his widow bravely respected his wish to be buried in his frock coat, not in uniform – a gesture that greatly irritated the tsar. When his opponent, the young and well-connected French officer Georges d'Anthès, was eventually deported from Russia, the reason given was "for killing the kammerjunker Pushkin."

Birth, service rank, and social status came together for Pushkin in the concept of *honnête homme*, a man of honor. This image (or ego ideal) hovers constantly over Pushkin's heroes. It sits at the center of his historical novel on Pugachov's rebellion, *The Captain's Daughter* (1836), which is organized entirely around the nurturing, testing, and defining of honorable behavior. In the final scenes of *Boris Godunov* (1825), Pyotr Basmanov, the tsar's brilliant military commander and a man of non-princely birth, defects to the Pretender. He is urged to do so by Gavrila Pushkin, ancestor of the poet and military aide to the invading False Dmitry. Basmanov openly confesses that he feels trapped in the traditional Muscovite system, where a princely pedigree guaranteed incompetents a promotion while heroes like himself were passed over. Precisely such corrupt-ing "advancement by genealogy alone" was eliminated, one century later, by Peter the Great's Table of Ranks.

One's official title was tied to self-respect on more mundane planes. How promptly need one pay gambling debts – or any debts at all – to a person of lower rank? Is it a fresh insult to a dueling opponent to bring, as one's official second, a man of low birth or of lesser (or no) rank? Quite possibly the tragic subplot of Pushkin's novel in verse *Eugene Onegin* (1823–31) turns precisely on such details.[5] Onegin finds himself challenged to a duel by his best friend Lensky over a trivial indiscretion committed at a provincial name-day party. Onegin feels badly about the flare-up and seeks an honorable way out, in a stratagem designed to save Lensky's honor as well as his life. Lensky had chosen as his second one Zaretsky, a local landowner known to be a "pedant in duels" (Six, XXVI: 8). In a deliberately provocative move, Onegin brings along as *his* second not a gentleman (as the dueling code required) but his own valet, one Monsieur Guillot. Zaretsky should have canceled the event on a technicality. But for some reason Zaretsky does not enforce strict rules on this particular day. He is insulted but he only bites his lip. So the duel moves mechanically forward, honor is preserved, Onegin fires, a man is dead.

The duel of honor, initially devised to confirm aristocratic courtiers as a military-social class, was codified in the Italian Renaissance as a secular (and usually illegal) ritual response to perceived insults in which "extreme violence was meted out with extreme politeness."[6] As an institution it came late to Russian culture, which did not experience an Age of Chivalry and continued to prefer fistfights to formal duels up until the end of the eighteenth century.[7] Once arrived, however, the duel came to occupy an ambiguous place in nineteenth-century literature, not unlike gambling. In a society so stratified and closely watched, where every button was mandated, the right of a gentleman to duel became his right to define the limits of his own dignity and patience, to decide for himself how he would be punished and punish others. As soon as a challenge was issued, strict codes governed the response, whether or not the aggrieved party felt personal outrage. Failing to issue a challenge when provoked was also dishonorable. If a gentleman was insulted by a person who then refused to accept a challenge to a duel, or if a challenge that should have been issued for some reason was not, one means for the insulted party to restore his honor was to commit suicide, or at least to attempt it. In Tolstoy's *Anna Karenina* (Part IV, ch. 18), the humiliated Count Vronsky shoots himself soon after his mistress Anna, near death with puerperal fever and just delivered of Vronsky's child, is reconciled to her husband. As a *point d'honneur*, the deceived husband should have called out the lover. But Karenin, an enlightened government bureaucrat, refuses to be maneuvered by a military code he despises. Perhaps Vronsky, pressing his revolver to his chest and pulling the trigger, was in despair at losing Anna; but for certain he was desperate to restore his honor.

To duel and gamble meant to assert one's individual initiative and thus to act, and feel, more free – even though, paradoxically, the outcome was utterly out of one's control. Staking everything on a single bullet (or card) opened a person to arbitrariness and fate. Pushkin participated passionately in both duels of honor and games of chance. He favored high-stakes games and tended to lose heavily (his known losses at cards amount to 80,000 rubles, his wins to a mere 7,000); he had a reputation for playing honestly and for paying his large debts "conscientiously, even when his opponents cheated."[8] In Pushkin's most famous short story, "The Queen of Spades" (1833), the cautious hero Germann ends up in a madhouse after he fails to win on three cards (three, seven, ace) that he had been promised, in a dream, would yield him a fortune. He played them as per the instructions – but at the last moment, inexplicably, the ace turns into a Queen of Spades. Germann's error had not been gambling. It was his *refusal* to gamble, that is, his trying to fix in advance the results of a game of chance. Such calculation always struck Pushkin as servile and dishonorable.

"Chance, in Pushkin's view, was the servant of the greater thing that he called fate."[9] This seeming paradox lies at the heart of Pushkin's creative art and personal worldview (the poet was morbidly superstitious); it unites spontaneity and constraint in a fashion peculiar to this poet. Symmetry, often of dazzling complexity, governs his worlds. Events are balanced and circular; for all the easy banter, nothing is forgotten and no escape is possible from the choices and accidents that each hero must answer for. Exemplary here is Pushkin's novel in verse, *Eugene Onegin*, a perfectly proportioned genre hybrid. It partakes equally of novel and poem. The "novelistic" factors include a chatty and digressive narrator, abundant everyday detail, protagonists who mature over several years, and unimpeded conversation that fits effortlessly into lines of verse. The novel cuts off at mid-scene in a most capricious manner. Onegin is on his knees in Tatyana's boudoir. She has just rejected his advances and left the room. Her husband has just clinked his spurs in the doorway. At that moment "most dire for the hero," the narrator chooses to withdraw from the story. If the well-made novel ends with a wedding or a death, Pushkin gives us neither. The novelistic dimension encourages openness, surprise, uncertainty.

Representing the poetic aspect is, first of all, the Onegin stanza itself, the novel's structural "paragraph." As tightly coiled as the novel is garrulous and expansive, this stanza is remarkably flexible: a fourteen-line verse unit in iambic tetrameter, with a regular scheme of feminine and masculine rhymes, arranged in three differently rhymed quatrains (first alternating, then pair, finally "ring" construction) followed by a rhyming couplet (AbAb CCdd EffE gg).[10] Pushkin invented the stanza in May 1823, intrigued by Byron's verse narratives and most likely also inspired by the freely rhymed salacious verse of the seventeenth-century French fabulist La Fontaine. With several notable interruptions, eight chapters (over 5,000 lines) of these sturdy, intricately rhymed stanzas propel the plot of *Eugene Onegin* forward with an intoxicating and self-confident momentum. Each stanza-paragraph has a characteristic pace or spin: the opening quatrain and ending couplet are sedate and urbane; the middle stretch is blurred, excited, suggestive; the ending couplet snaps the paragraph shut.

The poeticality of *Eugene Onegin* pertains not only to its formal structure. Events also unfold in a mirrored way, although displaced in time. And meanwhile the unfolding story is punctuated by the narrator's repeated assertions – tinged but not tainted by irony – that no act is evil or good in itself but that timing is all: he or she is "blessed" who manages to live through life's challenges in the right order, at the right age, for the right length of time. This neoclassical sense of the proper place for things, the proper "pitch," pace, and rhythm that help us to see how one episode in a life might fit into a balanced and justified whole, is as crucial to Pushkin's writings in prose fiction and history as it is in a line of his verse. But what is this right order, and from what perspective can we know it?

Tatyana sends Onegin a lovesick letter in Chapter 3. He sends her lovesick letters in Chapter 8. He lectures her on the modesty befitting an honorable maiden in Chapter 3 (she listens but is silent). She lectures him on his duties as an honorable man in Chapter 8 (he listens but is silent). No one gets together, each slides by the other, each is in love with the other but not at the same time, and for this reason energy in the novel is stored, not squandered. Such precious, unspent pressure figured high among Pushkin's ideals for a well-balanced work of art, and he provides several metaphors for containing it. One occurs near the end of *Eugene Onegin*, in Eight, 1: the "magic crystal" [*magicheskii kristall*] or glass ball for guessing fortunes. The author admits to gazing into this crystal, many years earlier, seeking (in Nabokov's words) "the far stretch of a free novel." How can a free thing be sought in a closed, symmetrical structure?

Imagine a kaleidoscope: a tube with a set of mirrors at one end and a slot for the eye at the other. Life's myriad events, confusions, coincidences, accidents – what Pushkin called, collectively, *sluchai* ["chance"] – are a heap of brightly colored shards of glass on the novelist's horizon, the faceted mirrored surface at the end of the tube. The poet-novelist's task is to rotate the kaleidoscope so that these arbitrary shards, falling out in random heaps, are refracted within the funnel of the novel to form patterns. Pushkin did not write "psychological prose" that claimed access to every irregular, messy nook and cranny of another's consciousness (the pioneer in that realm is Mikhail Lermontov, still a decade away). His complexity lies in his juxtaposition of multiple reflecting surfaces. Pushkin produces consciousness and intelligence in his characters (and pleasure in his readers) by the intersection of many planes. Thus he attends fastidiously to how, when, and by whom story lines are cut off and then resumed, and when the reader is allowed to hook up the various parts. In *Eugene Onegin* these "stress-lines" of the plot criss-cross with a perfectly controlled poetic stanza. The effect is a sort of glittering visual mesh, suggesting depth but delivering a profusion of edges. Pushkin's ideals are the classical ones of public honor, duty, fearlessness in facing death, taking risks while young and letting go of one's fantasies when old.

Pushkin was a born poet who labored hard to learn the art of prose. Although he eventually managed to write lines that didn't scan, he never abandoned the symmetrical ideal. In his finished prose works of the 1830s (only four were completed out of thirty begun), roundedness – returning to the beginning, but at another level – became his compromise with the linear impulses of accumulation, conversion, and collapse. Delaying the reward, or stripping back a disguise to reveal that we remain what we have always been, could turn an incipient tragedy into a comedy and a mass of quotidian details into a potential poem. Of course Pushkin as prose writer employed so-called "situation rhymes" (the prefiguring and echoing of narrative events), but his poetic nature demanded more: not just the repetition of similar parts but a structural symmetry within the work as a whole, subordinating even free personality to its sway. *Boris Godunov* (1825) reveals just such a balanced construction, for example, when Grigory Otrepiev wakes up from a dream in scene 5 and then, as Dmitry the Pretender, falls asleep (and falls out of the play) five scenes before the end.[11] A "symmetrical situation rhyme" also frames *The Captain's Daughter* (1836). In its opening chapters Pyotr Grinyov meets a disguised Pugachov, the false monarch, and later benefits from his mercy; this "chance" happening is fastidiously reproduced in the closing chapters when Masha Mironova, also by chance, meets the disguised Catherine II, the true monarch, enabling the mercy-pardon of Grinyov and the survival of his line.

The primary task of prose writing (as Pushkin practiced it) was to design the maximally efficient action for the characters that would reveal the integrity and symmetry of their motives. In 1822, still exclusively a poet, Pushkin jotted down a few thoughts about prose. "Precision and brevity," he wrote, "these are the first virtues of prose. Prose demands ideas and more ideas . . . As regards the question, whose prose is best in our literature, the answer is: *Karamzin's*. And this, as yet, is no great praise."[12] Eight years later, at his Boldino estate, Pushkin first tried his hand at prose fiction for the literary market, in a set of five very short stories, *Tales of the Late Ivan Petrovich Belkin* (1830), linked by a common fictive editor. The style is laconic and spare; verbs outnumber adjectives. Its fourth tale, "The Stationmaster," will suggest how Pushkin moves a Sentimentalist plot – the subtext is "Poor Liza" – into precise, fast-paced prose.

Like Karamzin's story, "The Stationmaster" is a flashback told by an outsider. But unlike Karamzin's emotionally implicated narrator, Pushkin's author is drily reportorial. At no point do we know which way the story will go: "folds," slices, gaps, and overlappings in the narrative hide the end from view. The high-spirited, low-born heroine, Dunya, is seduced to the city by the dashing, smooth-talking officer Minsky. Her father the stationmaster (civil servant fourteenth class) is convinced that she is ruined – for how could she not be ruined? – and he trudges off to Petersburg to fetch her home. His worldview is reproduced in the woodcuts of the Parable of the Prodigal Son that hang on the walls of his station; quite naturally he sees himself as the magnanimous, all-forgiving father of that edifying tale. But Pushkin never allows a story to be seen from one perspective alone. Minsky won't give her up, and Dunya prefers not to come home. As it turns out, Minsky marries his Dunya, and her life with him is incomparably better than continuing to serve her father in that shabby station. The risk she took on impulse was the type of risk worth taking by the young; the timing was right, and not every prodigal act need have prodigal-son consequences. The embittered father dies of drink and the story ends on Dunya's visit to his grave, some years later, accompanied by servants, an elegant carriage, and three little children in tow. She is deeply sorry (we are given to believe), but not at all repentant. Dunya's escape with Minsky was a gamble against the odds of the seduce-and-abandon plot.

Pushkin loves to reward impulsively naïve actions with good luck. At times he does it "just so," with comedic simplicity, allowing his characters to be smarter (and luckier) than the plots they inherited from some earlier literary tradition – and that we think will trap or punish them. Usually, before the happy ending can be rounded off, unconventional heroines like Dunya must admit that their selfish behavior caused others pain, even if they do not regret their act.

The remaining four Belkin Tales work playful variations on clichéd plots of European Romanticism, with a subtle admixture of the poet's own anxiety about his social status and rank.[13] The delight and fantasy of each tale is how honorable or "healthy" behavior – usually young people of marriageable age trying to get together – so easily triumphs over obstacles of class or parental resistance. Thus we have a Romeo and Juliet story that ends happily, a dueling tale in which no one is killed, a stalled courtship where it turns out the boy and girl have been married to each other all along. There is a powerful core of pure, Shakespearean festive comedy in Pushkin. This comedy shares little with the didactic social comedy of Fonvizin or Knyazhnin from the 1770s–80s, although girl and boy get together in those scenarios too. Eighteenth-century comedy leaves its trace throughout the Belkin Tales (and throughout Pushkin's prose) in different, more decorative ways – in the secondary characters, for example, who are often quite "unRussian": the sassy maid as go-between for her mistress (a French *soubrette*), the ignorant or immoral provincial tutor. But there are no Sofyas or Milons in the leading roles. In Pushkin, positive characters exercise real initiative. They make choices and take risks. They must, of course, have an inborn sense of honor and loyalty, but they act in their own interests and according to their own naïve appetites. Only then will fate be on their side. Plots are rounded and people come home.

As we shall see, Gogolian time-space has a different shape altogether. Although also comic, it cannot support anything like a wholesome appetite or a circular, homecoming plot. Honor is not relevant to it, although rules most definitely are. Gogol is Russia's first Kafka, her supreme chronicler of bureaucracies and the insecurities of social life as it registers on the shy and the neurotic. He is the patron saint of heroes who linearly bolt out of a narrative and disappear. Before we move to Gogol's realm of Russian Romanticism, however, a few words are in order on the legacy of the first Belkin Tale, "The Shot." It links Pushkin's troubled consideration of the duel of honor in *Eugene Onegin* – the hero's failure to prevent his best friend's death – with a long Russian literary tradition of botched, parodied, or "estranged" duels. In each, the duel ends up testing some other sort of honorableness, some value deeper than a passing insult or a set of societal codes.

Duels

As love is displaced and misses its mark in *Eugene Onegin*, so are bullets displaced and (mercifully) go astray in "The Shot." The narrative structure of this tiny story is so ingeniously layered and jointed that we forgive its banal, fantastical plot. The gothic hero Silvio, insulted at a ball, calls out his rival, a handsome and wealthy count. Obsessively jealous and infuriated by his opponent's casualness at the duel, Silvio postpones his shot; the count graciously allows him to redeem it at any time. For several years Silvio plots his vengeance, awaiting a chance to test the courage of his opponent when the latter has something he fears to lose. A re-run of the duel finally occurs, in front of the count's new wife. We slowly realize that Silvio can never satisfy his honor because the issue is not an isolated insult but the count's whole personality, a blend of courage, self-respect, noble rank, and moral superiority. Such people are beyond testing. We discern a link between this Belkin Tale – a "little comedy," since no one is killed in either duel – and *Mozart and Salieri*, one of the four "Little Tragedies" that Pushkin wrote during the same Boldino autumn, 1830. Salieri too cannot abide the natural superiority (in this case the musical genius) of his junior colleague and rival. His envy of Mozart is not triggered by any single "insult," nor can it be answered by any single ritualized gesture. Both the confrontation and the insult are cosmic, so the desire to duel (combat between two men, equally armed) is replaced by the need to murder. When the duel becomes a test that goes beyond answering for an isolated deed, no manuals on dueling etiquette will help. The very existence of the superior rival constitutes the insult. This rival is unreachable, living on another plane. The envier can only look ridiculous (and knows he looks ridiculous) when he tries to "settle scores" with this more highly endowed being – regardless of the outcome of their duel.

The most subtle variant on the Silvio model in Russian literature after Pushkin is the duel between Pechorin and Grushnitsky in the "Princess Mary" segment of Lermontov's novel *Hero of Our Time* (1840). Grigory Pechorin is a Byronic hero, one degree more burnt out and malicious than his close literary relative, Eugene Onegin. Pechorin's friend Grushnitsky – a crooked shadow of himself, the double in the mirror he tries to avoid – is a fop, a conceited fool, a bad loser, far more juvenile and melodramatic than Onegin's naïve friend Lensky (perhaps because Grushnitsky is available to us only through Pechorin's diary). On a Caucasus mountain cliff, the two men duel over an innocent maiden's honor. But neither really cares about the maiden. At stake is their own honor, fatally mixed with injured pride. The duel has been rigged by Grushnitsky's cronies, and Pechorin, knowing this, nevertheless faces his opponent's bullet, survives the shot and secures his own honor. Pechorin then exposes the deception and brings the humiliated Grushnitsky to admit his guilt. But Grushnitsky refuses to apologize. "I despise myself and hate you!" he shouts; "Shoot!" Pechorin does so. He later averts his eyes from the blood-stained body on the rocks. Did Grushnitsky fail or pass the test that Pechorin had posed for him?

For Romantic ironists of Lermontov's sort, a duel brought relief. Such unanchored skepticism is not a dominant note in Pushkin, whom Lermontov worshipped. In no way could Pushkin be called naïve – but his irony was gentler, more forgiving of others, and for all his inflammatory response to attacks on his honor, he retained until the end his faith in the visionary Poet's ability to transcend the trivial spite of the mob with an inspired poetic word. Lermontov's prose and worldview are more brittle and bitter. Two lyric poems, each called "The Prophet" ["Prorok"], illustrate this difference between the two Romantic-era poets.

In 1826, Pushkin wrote his "Prophet," a biblical vision of terrible force. A six-winged seraph appears to a man "tormented by spiritual thirst" in the wilderness, rips out his tongue, installs the forked tongue of a wise serpent in its place, tears out his heart and replaces it with a smoldering coal. Then the voice of God instructs the benumbed man to "Rise, and see, and hear, / Be filled with My will, / and traversing land and sea, / Set fire to the hearts of men with your Word." In 1841, the year of his death, Lermontov wrote his own "Prophet," also in iambic tetrameter, picking up where Pushkin's vision had left off and most likely a disillusioned response to it. Lermontov's prophet peers into the eyes of people and sees nothing there but "malice and vice." His neighbors and closest relatives cast stones at him; he wanders the desert like a beggar, proclaiming his truths to the silent planets and stars. Back in town, he becomes a pathetic spectacle: elders point him out to their children with a smug smile. "Look at him: . . . The stupid fellow, wanted to persuade us / That God was speaking through his lips!"

Both prophets suffer, physically and spiritually. Both are outcasts. But for Pushkin, the public is a more transitory thing. His focus remains on the sacred mission of the Word, prophetic or poetic, indifferent to the vanities of the present audience – just as, in *Mozart and Salieri*, Mozart's focus remains on the mission of the "chosen few" in Music. No slander or poisoning can obstruct that reality. The prophet in Lermontov's poem allows his jeering detractors to define the duel between them on their terms. Such abdication of authorial pride Pushkin would never allow.

In an age that admired public display, the duel was a form of self-expression and even self-realization. But the scandals that electrified the Western European public – Victor Hugo's claim that Romanticism was "liberalism in literature," for example, or Lord Byron's outrageous personal behavior over several continents – were not practical options in Russia, where poets were more heavily censored and words (poetic or otherwise) were more quickly criminalized.[14] Throughout his brief life, Lermontov acted (and wrote) in a manner so insolent and provocative that by 1840 he had been reduced to a line battalion, twice exiled to the Caucasus, and assigned to a punishment battalion by personal order of Tsar Nicholas I. But Lermontov did not die in battle. In the spirit of his own fictional Pechorin, he provoked a challenge from a former schoolmate and was killed on the spot at the age of twenty-seven.

Pushkin provided another variant on the duel of honor, in Chapter 4 of *The Captain's Daughter*. While serving in a small frontier fort in Western Siberia, Pyotr Grinyov, hero of the tale, quarrels with Shvabrin, the villain, over an insult to the reputation of the captain's daughter. The two men decide to duel (this is the 1770s: the weapon is the saber). On the first try they are prevented from drawing swords by the crew of comic, commonsensical characters who run the fortress, the captain's wife ("What? Planning manslaughter in our fort?") and a one-eyed garrison lieutenant. The captain's wife locks up their swords in the kitchen pantry. Finally these two young hotheads manage to arrange a confrontation. But old Savelich, Grinyov's stubborn serf-servant, interrupts their sword fight, appalled that his young master is "poking at others with iron skewers" (a bad habit that Savelich blames on a dissolute French tutor). Why not punch each other out with fists in the Russian way, and forget it? Grinyov is badly wounded by Shvabrin's saber, but the tone of the entire event is comedic. Honor and the honorable testing of one's courage quickly cease to be the issue. Rather, the duel and subsequent injury clear the air so that authentically human relations can resume (in this case, the stalled love subplot). It teaches the participants some other more important lesson about life, unrelated to the original insult and the straitjacketed ritual that must answer for it.

This type of comic, or comically framed, duel produced a rich harvest in the second half of the century. In Chapter 24 of Turgenev's *Fathers and Children* (1862), the aristocratic Pavel Petrovich Kirsanov, a relic from the Romantic period, announces to Bazarov, the self-proclaimed nihilist, that "I have decided to fight a duel with you" because "you are superfluous here, I can't stand you, I despise you" (thus exposing, in one impatient gesture, the authentic motivation behind a Silvio-type duel of honor). Both men agree to dispense with the formality of a specific quarrel or insult. Bazarov wounds his opponent slightly in the leg, at which point the nihilist immediately ceases to be a duelist and becomes again a man of science and medical doctor. But this foolish, potentially dangerous pistol play between two men who simply dislike each other, which resolves nothing on the plane of honor, has highly productive consequences for the novel. The injured Pavel Petrovich, in his weakened and ecstatic condition, urges his brother Nikolai to marry the young commoner who has borne him a son. The novel's action ends on two fertile marriages, a bucolic celebration of the habits and economy of the Russian rural manor. This frolicking of parents and children sets the tone for the "happy" patriarchal ending that so infuriated the radical critics of the 1860s, who read this novel during the emancipation of the serfs and Russia's fraught Great Reforms.

Tolstoy devised a more complex variation on the duel of honor in his *War and Peace*. Unlike Turgenev's topical *Fathers and Children*, published in 1862 and set three years earlier (1859), Tolstoy in the 1860s was writing a historical novel that took place half-a-century before, during the Napoleonic Wars, when Pushkin was still a schoolboy. Tolstoy as author could look back on the institution of the duel and parody it. His fictive heroes, however, lived at a time when its hold over gentlemen of honor was absolute. In Book Two, Part I, ch. 4 of *War and Peace*, the insolent Dolokhov boasts that he is having an affair with Pierre's wife. Pierre, enraged, challenges him to a duel.

The actual event is a comedy of errors. Pierre has never handled a pistol in his life. The pine forest where they meet is so full of wet, deep snow and rising mist that bodies – even Pierre's immensely fat, bulky body – can scarcely be seen. Pierre's second dutifully attempts to reconcile the opponents, but even though Pierre agrees it was all "desperately stupid" he can't be roused to stop it, asks his second "what to shoot at," and then waves him away. Staggering toward the barrier, the nearsighted Pierre pulls the trigger, seriously wounds Dolokhov, and then, sobbing in remorse, exposes his broad chest to his opponent's bullet. Dolokhov fires and misses. As in Turgenev, the comic replay of a death-dealing ritual enables a breakthrough to otherwise unavailable wisdoms.

Up to this point, Dolokhov has been a scoundrel, cardsharp, and partner in mischief to the despicable Anatol Kuragin. Returning from the duel and perhaps dying, he confides to his friend Nikolai Rostov that everything is folly and lies except his "adored, angelic mother," who will not survive the news of his wound. Rostov – and the reader – realize that what was most important to this man had been invisible on the surface of his life, unsuspected throughout all these pages of the novel, until a bullet broke down his defenses. "To his utter astonishment, he [Rostov] found out that the rough, tough Dolokhov, Dolokhov the swaggering bully, lived in Moscow with his old mother and a hunchback sister. He was a loving son and brother."[15] Such moments of biographical revelation, triggered by the unpredictable outcome of a life-and-death event like the duel of honor, induce humility in Tolstoy's readers. Central to Tolstoy's Realistic message (inspired partially by the prose of Pushkin, the lesson of the Prodigal Son woodcuts on the stationmaster's wall) is that life never submits wholly to any single writing-up of it, and pockets of private experience, revealed by chance, can remake the perceived world. Episodes like this glimpse of Dolokhov's family, randomly made available to the heroes but carefully planned by the author, soften the effect of Tolstoy's overwhelming, panoptic narrative authority.[16]

Our final variant on Pushkin-era duels is Chekhov's 1891 novella, *The Duel*. Traces of the entire nineteenth century can be found in it. Turgenev's relatively civil dueling scene in *Fathers and Children*, between a late-Romantic-era aristocrat and a scientist-nihilist, has now mutated into something far less decorous. Layevsky, the vacillating, indolent "superfluous man," having fled with another man's wife to a coastal town on the Black Sea, is challenged to a duel by von Koren, marine zoologist and social Darwinist. They understand and despise each other. Layevsky has been borrowing money to escape from his mistress, who now bores and embarrasses him, and return to Petersburg; von Koren, after careful analysis of this useless parasitic type, is not averse to wiping him out. On an absurd pretext that flares up over dinner, they agree to fight. "Gentlemen, who remembers how it goes in Lermontov?" von Koren asks, since no one present has ever attended a duel before. "And in Turgenev, doesn't Bazarov have a duel with someone or other?"[17] Layevsky shoots into the air, but von Koren aims directly at his opponent's forehead. Suddenly a comic episode erupts, recalling the duel-side antics of the serf Savelich in Pushkin's *Captain's Daughter*. The local deacon, a man of irrepressible good humor for whom everything is hilarious, has been spying in the bushes. Unexpectedly, desperately, he shouts out. At that very moment, von Koren fires and misses. "But he was going to kill him!" says the deacon, radiant and shamefaced after the smoke has cleared. By the end of the tale, Layevsky has married his mistress and settled down to shabby real life, working as a clerk to pay off his debts. Von Koren is the one who leaves town, and the deacon congratulates him for "overcoming mankind's most powerful enemy – pride." The age of the charismatic duel is over.

Meaningful dueling scenarios that "remember one another" can be traced in a straight line from *Eugene Onegin* and "The Shot" through Lermontov to Turgenev, Tolstoy, and Chekhov. The roll call is significant. These great writers belong to the "Pushkin line" of Russian literature, where such issues as honor (variously defined), clarity, openness, civic decency, and public quests for a positive identity are central. The other great tradition to grow out of Russian Romanticism, begun by Nikolai Gogol and perfected by Dostoevsky, did not find the duel especially useful as a defense of personal dignity or private space. In Gogol, protagonists are too insignificant, non-noble, erratic, or caricatured to resort to dueling. Dostoevsky is more complex.[18] His heroes talk constantly of honor and insult. They worry obsessively about how to avenge bumps on the street or slaps in the face. References to duels are everywhere – but most of them fail or remain unrealized fantasies. Either the would-be challenger doesn't know the proper formula for calling a party out, or the other party refuses to accept the challenge. The Underground Man is too "hyper-conscious" to identify precisely the insult received (only "men of action" are obtuse enough to strike back vigorously when struck). Or worst of all, the aggrieved party might dimly realize that what insults him most profoundly and unanswerably is part of his own self, which must then be "called out" by other means (this is the task explored by Dostoevsky in his 1846 novella *The Double*). In *The Brothers Karamazov*, the threshold duel that turned Zosima from frivolous military officer toward a life of the spirit is buried deep inside the novel, in a luminous reminiscence recorded by Alyosha to glorify his mentor's teaching. This route to self-awareness and conversion is not available as an option to most Dostoevskian heroes.

The vagary of rank was not in itself an obstacle to dueling. Pushkin, at civilian rank Nine (titular councilor), was of the same low status as the poor clerks in

Petersburg tales by Gogol and Dostoevsky, perhaps even a little below. But a different dynamic operates in the "Gogol line." A larger role is played by laughter – an immense resource that the "Pushkinian" writers exploit only slightly, for brief stretches, and in a decorous, responsible manner quite foreign to the Gogol school. But also, for Gogol, a fundamentally different shape governs the fictional plot.

Public honor pursued through the dueling code requires that parties take themselves with high seriousness, stay put, and fire according to the rules. Having done so, a person "saves face." Further explanations or public confessions are inappropriate. Gogol prefers to work in more evasive, private realms. His heroes do not stay put. They move *through* spaces, quickly and linearly. They don't come home – or they don't have identifiable homes, a possibility that is concretely realized by Dostoevsky when he houses his heroes in crowded apartments that are in effect corridors, breeding places for "accidental families." (Tolstoy once remarked that Dostoevsky's characters all behave as if they lived at a train station.) When Gogol's heroes slow down, then the trouble starts, and to save themselves they must burst out. A happy ending, for Gogol, is an escape. If Pushkin is Russia's poet of honor, then Gogol is the unmatched master of evasion and embarrassment.

Gogol and embarrassment (its linearity, lopsidedness, evasiveness)

By temperament and upbringing, Pushkin was an aristocrat, thoroughly at home in European culture. Rank, honor, and pedigree were for him second nature. Nikolai Gogol, in contrast, was a provincial, the son of a minor landowner raised in Ukraine. His graduation certificate from public school conferred upon him the lowest rank, 'collegiate registrar' (civilian rank Fourteen). When Gogol moved to Petersburg at age nineteen, nothing in the imperial capital's estranged, glittering, regimented social system could have struck him as natural or organic. For Gogol – a brilliant stylizer of Ukrainian folk tales, which he filled with demons, witches, and gothic villains – Petersburg proved to be marvelous creative material. His stories quickly became foundational for the Petersburg Myth.

Before entering that urban landscape, however, with its caricatures in uniform and detachable human parts, we will consider one "provincial" anecdote (Gogol's shortest story, as it happens), which he intended for an almanac edited by Pushkin in 1835. It introduces in miniature the dynamics of a Gogolian narrative, psychological as well as spatial. This little stretch of text contains no fantastic or grotesque episodes of the sort we see in the Ukrainian folk tales or Petersburg stories. It passed unnoticed in the press. But Tolstoy later remarked that he was tempted to call it Gogol's best work, and Chekhov felt that these few pages were worth 200,000 rubles, so perfectly did they concentrate Gogol's genius. The anecdote is "The Carriage."

A cavalry regiment enters a provincial town, largely mud and pigs. The storyteller describes the town with hyperbolic relish. Gogolian digressions, it must be said, are not elegant or elegiac, as in Pushkin's *Eugene Onegin*; they are stuffed full of food (gorged or swilled), crude squawking sounds, the misbehavior of physical matter. A favored device of the storyteller is to fasten his eccentric roving eye on one inanimate thing (in this story, carriages) or one body part (bellies, moustaches) and stealthily, this one item becomes all on the horizon the reader sees. The general gives a banquet. Over cigars a local landowner, Chertokutsky, offers to sell his Excellency a carriage. The landowner invites the general and his officers to lunch the next day for a viewing. But then Chertokutsky stays on at the banquet, begins to play whist, "a mysterious glass full of rum punch appears before him," he plays and drinks, drinks and plays, "recalls winning a great deal, yet there appeared to be no winnings for him to pick up . . .".[19] At 3 a.m. he stumbles home. His pretty wife doesn't wake him in the morning, and only at noon does she hear the rumbling coaches of the general and his suite. Chertokutsky, in a panic, gives orders to say that he's gone for the day and hides out in his carriage. The general and his men arrive. Irritated at this defaulted invitation, the general decides to take a look at the item on his way out. Nothing special about it, he says. But maybe on the inside? His officer unfastens the coverlet:

> and there was Chertokutsky, hunched in a preposterous position and wrapped in his dressing-gown. "Ah, here you are!" said the general in surprise. And with that he slammed the door shut, pulled the apron back over Chertokutsky and drove off, with the gentlemen officers.
>
> (p. 157)

Thus does the anecdote end, in a perfect cul-de-sac of Gogolian psychology. The coverlet of the carriage is peeled back to reveal the error, the sin, the little white lie or the absentmindedness that we had hoped to conceal. We are exposed, and the audience departs. The effect here might be compared with the equally abrupt mid-scene blank-out that ends *Eugene Onegin*, prompted by the sudden appearance of Tatyana's husband in the doorway. Chertokutsky's crouching in the carriage resembles that moment in humiliation but exceeds it greatly in embarrassment. For the problem with embarrassment is that it cannot be answered. It cannot be made public or washed clean. One can remotely imagine Tatyana's husband challenging Onegin to a duel after finding his friend in his wife's boudoir. But what can Chertokutsky do, except wince? Or in Dostoevsky's more spiteful and malevolent variant on the scenario, gnash his teeth? Talk his way out of it? It will only get worse. The witnesses have already driven away. Since embarrassment cannot be remedied, its carriers must wear masks, or go mad, or (literally) come apart.

Consider Gogol's Petersburg fantasy "The Nose" (1836). A nose disappears from the face of a collegiate assessor (civilian rank Six), turns up in a barber's freshly baked roll, is seen strolling about the city, and then one morning for no reason reappears on its distraught owner's face. This much-loved story (Dmitry Shostakovich set it as a Modernist opera in 1930) has accumulated interpretations over the years ranging from Russia's first Absurdist work to clinical testimony on castration anxiety. But more scandalous for Major Kovalyov than the "absolutely preposterous smooth flat space" between his two cheeks is the fact that his nose, which he tracks down at prayer in the Kazan Cathedral, refuses to repatriate for reasons of rank. "You are mistaken, my good sir," says the Nose. "I'm on my own [*ya sam po sebe*]. Furthermore, there cannot be any close relations between us, for to judge by the buttons on your uniform, you must serve in the senate, or perhaps in the Department of Justice. Whereas I am in the Academy."[20] The narrator respects the desire of Collegiate Assessor Kovalyov to be called by the military equivalent of his civilian rank because "Major" has more status with the ladies. But how can Major Kovalyov show himself in public now? If a toe had disappeared, it could be covered up with a boot. When the surface defines the person, the definition of horror is an absence that cannot be hidden away.

In Gogol, the absurd aspects of rank blend with the sentimental and the frenetic. Each of these intonations is thickened by an "artless" storyteller who on occasion (as at the end of "The Nose") demands to know why writers choose such implausible incidents in the first place. But illogicality governs not only events; it permeates every level of the narrative, down to the sounds and punning components of words. A metaphor is developed so richly that it replaces the reality it was supposed to clarify. A non-logical combination of words is masked by sensible syntax. The hero of "The Overcoat" (1842) is a copying clerk and titular councilor (civilian rank Nine), Akaky Akakievich Bashmachkin. His last name comes from the Russian word for "shoe," *bashmak*. But, the narrator notes, it is not known how he got this name, although "his father, his grandfather, and even his brother-in-law wore boots . . ." The abrupt substitution of "boots" for shoes combined with that little word "even" impart a flash of madness to the whole.[21] Such garrulous wackiness on the part of the storyteller is matched, or undone, by the flatness and verbal uncreativeness of the hero.

Akaky himself is so timid he can hardly carry on a conversation, mumbling meaningless particles in place of nouns and verbs. He enjoys copying and is indifferent to rank. But the Petersburg frost makes a new overcoat imperative. He saves up for it, falls in love with it while the tailor is sewing it (or "her": the Russian word for overcoat, *shinel'*, is feminine in gender) – and she is stolen off his back by hoodlums the first night he wears her. Reprimanded by a general after futilely seeking help from the police, the depleted Akaky dies of humiliation and a chill, only to reappear as a vengeful ghost who pulls overcoats off shoulders of all ranks.

The clerk Akaky is meek. Other pathetic clerks in Gogol's Petersburg are ambitious. One such is the hero of *Diary of a Madman*, Poprishchin, pen-pusher and quill-sharpener. We watch him go out of his mind, entry by entry. Smitten with his boss's daughter, he gets access to her by purloining letters written by her dog. "Perhaps" – he writes in his diary a few days before declaring himself to be the King of Spain – "I'm really a count or a general, and am merely imagining I'm a titular councilor? Perhaps I really don't know who I am at all?" As we shall see in Chapter 6, Dostoevsky begins his career by literally rewriting these poor Gogolian clerks, who become the eyes and ears of his early worldview, growing gradually more self-conscious, shrewd, and cruel.

Like his madman Poprishchin and his con man Chichikov from *Dead Souls*, Nikolai Gogol also did not wish people to know precisely who, or where, he was. He had a dazzling gift for distortion and concealment. A brilliant mimic from early childhood, Gogol could create any role out of the most casual verbal prompt. He falsified personal events in his letters home. He left no diaries, memoirs, wife or close family. Even after he had become Russia's most famous prose writer, he was infuriated when a friend published a realistic portrait of him. Gogol perceived himself and his work in a messianic light. Until fully shaped, his person and message should shine through to others only darkly, if at all. Gogol abandoned Russia in 1837 and spent most of the rest of his life in Italy, writing and despairing of ever completing his epic *Dead Souls*.

Perhaps a private, evasive, deceptive psyche like Gogol's can be most accurately grasped by a creative writer of equivalent genius. Pushkin, with his brilliantly visible public life, is well served by several full-length biographies in English, most recently the fascinating and irreverent account by T. J. Binyon (*Pushkin: A Biography*, 2002). But arguably the best English-language biography of Gogol is still Vladimir Nabokov's *Nikolai Gogol* (1944), a slim volume extremely thin on events. Nabokov begins the story with Gogol's death in 1852 from malnutrition and gastroenteritis, huge leeches hanging from his nose, after he had burnt, in a frenzy of repentance and on the advice of his Roman Catholic confessor, Parts 2 and 3 of *Dead Souls*. "Gogol was a strange creature," Nabokov writes. His basic units were not ideas at all but "focal shifts," abrupt and irrational. "Steady Pushkin, matter-of-fact Tolstoy, restrained Chekhov have all had their moments of irrational insight . . . but with Gogol this shifting is the very basis of his art, so that whenever he tried to write in the round hand of literary tradition and to treat rational ideas in a logical way, he lost all trace of talent."[22] Respect for rank, good taste, clarity of confrontation, the straight line of honor that permits one to come back home with head held high: this is Pushkin's familiar landscape. And on the other side, we have Gogol: the sudden crooked "focal shift" of evasion and embarrassment, what Nabokov called "a jerk and a glide," with the hero darting away out from under our nose.

Pretendership (two authors, two plays, two novels)

As our final juxtaposition of Pushkin and Gogol we will consider, very selectively, four famous works – one novel and one play for each. Our focus for all four is "pretendership" – in Russian, *samozvanstvo* (literally, "self-naming"): the act of presenting yourself publicly as someone other than who you are. This gesture is relatively straightforward when the pretender in question is clinically mad, as is Poprishchin (protagonist of Gogol's *Diary of a Madman*) when he declares himself the King of Spain. Our upcoming examples are more complex. Both of Pushkin's pretenders are real historical figures in fictionalized garb. What they pretend to is the Russian throne. The two home texts for these adventurers are the drama *Boris Godunov* (1825), in which a young runaway monk, Grigory Otrepiev, invades Russia claiming to be the Tsarevich Dmitry, youngest son of Ivan the Terrible; and the novel *The Captain's Daughter* (1836), in which the Cossack chieftain Emelyan Pugachov claims to be Peter III, deposed and deceased spouse of Empress Catherine II. Pushkin's Pugachov, in conversation with the novel's hero Grinyov, remembers (from oral legend? from Pushkin's play?) Otrepiev's success at toppling the Godunovs and is inspired to imitate it.

In contrast to Pushkin, both of Gogol's pretenders – or better, imposters – are fictional creations with wholly civilian concerns. Khlestakov from *The Government Inspector* (1836) is a Petersburg fop who, passing through a provincial town, is mistaken for a police investigator by the gullible, corrupt local bureaucracy. Chichikov from *Dead Souls* (1842) is a trickster in the mode of traveling salesman – or better, buyer-up of deceased serfs. These two imposters are fictional in a deeper sense than the fact that Gogol made them up. They also make themselves up as they go along, as do all rogues, feeding off the foolishness or venality of the terrain. In Gogol's messianic vision, such inconstancy of personality was not creative or playful but unclean, demonic. Pushkin's historical pretenders, Grishka Otrepiev from 1604 and Pugachov from the 1770s, were in their time also perceived as "demonic," branded villains and Antichrists. Let us first consider the two plays.

Gogol's provincial town is taken up by identity crises of a comic and disreputable sort. The Mayor's primary anxiety is to determine whether this "inspector" is as corrupt as himself and therefore can be bribed into silence about the town's petty vice. In Gogol, extended contact between characters makes them (and us) increasingly nervous; people corrode one another as communication proceeds. Pushkin, in contrast, presents his pretenders as positive, even honorable personalities, men in whom value is allowed to accrete. They might be pretending, but the more time we spend with them, the truer and fuller they become. Let us begin at the point in these two plays when the freshly arrived "pretender" is receiving petitions. In Pushkin's *Boris Godunov*, this is the first Polish scene. The Pretender meets a Catholic priest (to whom he promises the conversion of the Russian people to the Roman faith), then a Polish noble, a Russian defector, a rebel Cossack leader, and finally a poet whom he rewards for Latin verses. Dmitry has the same golden effect on all. He listens to each petitioner and to each promises exactly what is required to gain their respect and support. He literally creates himself in their image of him, before our eyes. This buoyantly "attractive adventurer," as Pushkin called his Pretender, has been variously explained as the responsive spirit of poetic improvisation (a skill Pushkin greatly admired) or as a documented historical figure, Russia's first genuinely clement prince and the original embodiment of the utopian myth of a resurrected returning tsarevich.[23] Either way, Pushkin's False Dmitry does not strike us as a fraud. Historically, of course, Russian regal pretenders were all "exposed" (the False Dmitry reigned for a year and was assassinated; Pugachov was caught and beheaded). But within art, Pushkin deals very generously with their risk-taking and openness to fate, granting it full legitimacy. Pretenders took on other people's hopes and allowed them, for a time, to flourish. For Pushkin, *samozvantstvo*, "claiming for yourself a name not your own," was "not theft, embezzlement, expropriation, but exchange."[24] Since pretenders don't come with ready-made property, everything depends on inspiring trust and circulating it.

The opposite dynamic operates in Gogol. In *The Government Inspector*, openness to an identity that is not one's own has a bawdy, greedy, demonic quality to it. When a body is open, Russian folk wisdom teaches, mischief will crawl into it and everything begins to slip. Khlestakov – before he realizes that his mistaken identity can be turned to his advantage – is as frightened of going to jail as are the town officials, although for different reasons. The proper response of an audience to this devolving fiasco would be horror, released through a guffaw. Gogol was appalled at the stiffness of the 1836 premiere and insisted that the one positive character in the play had been overlooked: Laughter.

Pushkin's and Gogol's dramatic pretenders resemble each other in their restlessness, improvisatory skills, lightness, and ability to take on any number of verbal masks with no friction at the transitions. Khlestakov improvises, like Pushkin's Dmitry, but with opposite valence: he is successful to the extent that he can take value away. The relevant "petitioning" scenes in *The Government Inspector* occur in Act IV.[25] The officeholders of the town, in full dress uniform, have turned up to greet – and hopefully to bribe – Khlestakov, who is sleeping off a sumptuous dinner at the Mayor's house. At the end of Act III, in an intoxicated bravado, he had regaled the ladies of the house with a ballooning set of fibs about his life in Petersburg: his dinners and balls, the departments that scramble to serve him, his casual visits to the imperial court, his intimacy with Pushkin, how he is begged by publishers to contribute stories and plays (various works attributed to others are all in fact his). Now, sensing no barriers and pursuing no aim, he pushes his identity in every possible direction. Khlestakov gets whatever he can get away with.

In Act IV, the Judge, Postmaster, School Inspector, Warden of Charities, and finally the landowners Bobchinsky and Dobchinsky (Tweedledum and Tweedledee) drop by to "pay their respects." The judge bungles his bribe and Khlestakov, surprised, picks up the money from the floor and asks to "borrow" it. This success emboldens him. He hits up the postmaster for a loan outright, and with each visitor the requested sum rises. Finally Khlestakov barks in the first breath at Bobchinsky / Dobchinsky: "Got any money on you? A thousand rubles?" Getting away with pretense simply speeds up the scam; it never creates weight, shame, or a public face. Since all parties are equally nervous and guilty, all play the same game of hide-and-seek.

Against the advice of his manservant Osip ("get out while the going is good!"), Khlestakov lingers, as Chichikov will linger in *Dead Souls*. The playful masks begin to unravel – and what began as visitors with bribes becomes visitors with denunciations. Our false inspector slips out of town barely in time, just before the postmaster unseals Khlestakov's letter to a Petersburg friend describing the fools he has fleeced. At this point, a stretch of dialogue occurs that superficially resembles the final moments of the eighteenth-century "self-corrective" comedies by Fonvizin and Knyazhnin, where evil caves in and is exposed to public ridicule. The mayor admits to his gullibility, calling himself an imbecile and blockhead. But Gogol supplies no Pravdin or Starodum to receive sinners' confessions. Everyone is implicated. "What are you laughing at?" the enraged mayor shouts at the audience. "You're laughing at yourselves!" This Gogol line of pretenders will inspire buffoons, rogues, madmen, and nihilists of a severity and hilarity undreamt of by Turgenev's pure-minded Bazarov.

Pushkin fully appreciated Gogol's gift and nourished it. When in 1834 Gogol wrote to the poet asking for a real Russian anecdote to work up into a comedy, Pushkin obliged with one about mistaken identity based on his own experience: the poet loved being on the road and was once taken for a government official himself. But Pushkin's worldview was tethered to the aristocratic honor codes of his time. Remarkably, his criteria for honor remain stable regardless of the time and place: a military adventurer in 1604 or an illiterate Cossack rebel in 1774. In his historical drama, Pushkin presents Dmitry as false, but as useful and enabling to others. Only once, when he tries to be "true" in his confession of love to the Polish princess Maryna Mniszech, does his confidence falter. Pugachov too acts confidently, at times even magnanimously. Pushkin's pretenders have nothing to gain by running away and there is, in any event, nowhere for them to go; their stories are over.

For the two novels, *The Captain's Daughter* and *Dead Souls*, our point of departure is precisely this question of running away. Taking on an identity, for Pushkin, entailed responsibility, because his plots tend to circle around and come home. Pushkin's heroes might perform poetic improvisations, but they do not burst out to safety beyond the frame of the story, which is Gogol's favored route. In Pushkin, getting away with pretense *does* create weight, and this qualifies the pretender, during his brief sojourn on stage or in history, to be taken seriously, treated eye to eye as an equal, as someone who understands honor and deserves it. In one of his face-to-face encounters with Grinyov, Pugachov explains the morality he lives by in terms of an ancient Kalmyk tale. It is better, the pretender says, to live thirty-three years on fresh blood like the eagle than three hundred years on carrion like the raven. To which Grinyov responds: "Clever. But in my opinion, to live by murder and plunder is the same as pecking carrion." Both men fall silent. Not only does each live by his own truth, which is beyond the other's judgment, but only by speaking one's truth can a life be saved – one's own, or another's.

In Chapter 8, Pugachov demands that Grinyov recognize him as Tsar Peter III. "Judge for yourself," Grinyov responds. "You're a sharp-witted person: you'd be the first to realize that I was faking . . . I swore allegiance to her Majesty the Empress; I cannot serve you."[26] Pugachov is impressed by this sincerity (by this willingness to ignore hierarchy and address him eye to eye) and sets Grinyov free. A similar exchange occurs in Chapter 12. Pugachov has just liberated Masha Mironova from the clutches of the villain and traitor Shvabrin.

The humiliated Shvabrin reveals that Masha is not the priest's niece, as had been claimed, but the Captain's daughter. Pugachov turns angrily to Grinyov, who again decides to tell the truth. "Judge for yourself. Could I have declared in front of your men that Mironov's daughter was alive? They would have torn her to pieces" (p. 340). Pugachov bursts into laughter, agrees, and sets both Grinyov and his sweetheart free. These conversations resemble displays of honor between equals, between two enlightened noblemen – not an exchange between a young high-born officer and an illiterate Cossack rebel. To be sure equality does not mean endorsement. At no point, note, does Grinyov approve of Pugachov, his rebellion, or his wanton violence. But close up they speak the same language. They have nothing to conceal and can easily default to a language of trust. Such clarity and truth-telling will be interpreted, on the institutional level, as treason.

What, finally, about the pretender Chichikov in *Dead Souls*? Why must he run away? Chichikov's project is a bureaucratic ruse spread out along a road. Everything works as long as the hero keeps moving. In the first half of the novel – a series of one-on-one interviews with serfowners, distributed along this road – our rogue buys up legally alive but actually dead serfs so he can mortgage them for cash. Not only do the caricatured interviewees flesh out a number of venal sins (the sins that land us in purgatory: sloth, foolishness, wrath, gluttony, miserliness), but each has a natural home in past Russian literary genres or heroes, here exaggerated and parodied. We meet a Karamzin-style Sentimentalist (Manilov), a comic Baba Yaga of the folk tale who, disappointed in her guest, will be the immediate cause of his downfall (Korobochka), an over-the-top Romantic gambler, bully, and teller of tall tales (Nozdryov). As Chichikov interviews each of them for his project, he holds up a mirror – making sure that his own face is nowhere reflected. The final portrait, of the miser Plyushkin and his neglected polluted estate, presents us with a sort of black hole, where goods move directly from the storehouse to the dump, where greed rots everything and returns it to a state of nature.

After the ruin of Plyushkin, the road stops. Chichikov lingers in town, nursing a slight cold, and now that he has stopped traveling, words about him begin to gather and stick. Ominous rumors circulate about his identity: is he a ravisher of maidens, perhaps Napoleon in disguise, perhaps even the Antichrist? By the time he bursts out of the story, Chichikov has become so encrusted with ludicrous pseudo-identities that his actual biography – if we believe the form in which Gogol provides it in the final chapter – is somehow dissatisfying, intolerably drab.

The moment of Chichikov's escape takes place in some indescribable realm. Deflated, disgraced, he is in his carriage heading out of town. Suddenly the carriage becomes a troika, flying up and down hillocks:

> Chichikov merely kept smiling, jouncing a little on his leather cushion, for he loved fast driving. And what Russian doesn't love fast driving? How should his soul, which yearns to go off into a whirl, to go off on a fling, to say on occasion: "Devil take it all!" – how should his soul fail to love it? Is it not a thing to be loved, when one can sense in it something exaltedly wondrous? Some unseen power, it seems, has caught you up on its wing, and you're flying yourself, and all other things are flying . . .[27]

The authentic new hero has become movement itself, the boundless Russian space into which Chichikov escapes, bleak, dingy, dispersed – as Nabokov writes, "Russia as Gogol saw Russia" (p. 107). Nabokov then adds that for Gogol, Russia was "a peculiar landscape, a special atmosphere, a symbol, a long, long road." The bursting-out along this road need not be strictly linear; both geographically and stylistically, it can be a zigzag or a swirl. Digressions, hyperbolic metaphors and broken idioms can twist in a moment's time from the grotesque to the pious, from the pious to the insane. Whatever principles govern the brilliantly excessive verbiage of Gogol's prose, they represent the opposite of Pushkin's, which were, we recall, "precision, brevity, ideas and more ideas." "The prose of Pushkin is three-dimensional," Nabokov says crisply; "that of Gogol is four-dimensional, at least" (p. 145).

What can be said in summary of these two very different worlds and legacies, Pushkin's and Gogol's? Pushkin certainly knew anguish and the impulse to escape. But part of being an aristocrat meant avoiding plots based on comic "impersonations upward" by people of low rank. His own "poor clerk" Evgeny from *The Bronze Horseman* is singularly indifferent to his rank and craves a modest life, even though he is of noble ancestry. Pushkin bestows honor and self-respect everywhere, on all deserving parties, on runaway monks and renegade Cossacks. When he does play with rank, he prefers the aristocratic and Shakespearean device of "impersonation downward" – such as in the final Belkin Tale, "Lady into Peasant," where a gentry maiden dresses up (or better, down) as a peasant girl in order to catch the attention (and then love) of her otherwise inaccessible gentry bridegroom. After Onegin turns down her proposal of love, Tatyana Larina is willing to become a princess but in no way prefers that status to her earlier, simpler rural life.

Gogol does not do genteel pastoral masquerades of this sort. His material is more voluble, patchy, and vulnerable. It takes the form of the miserable private madness of poor Poprishchin in *Diary of a Madman* – who looks around, sees a vacancy, and chooses to be the King of Spain – or the pretenses of a Chichikov and Khlestakov, who also "pretend upward" but so flamboyantly and publicly that eventually they are driven out of town, or fly out of it. The pastoral is also of little use to Dostoevsky, except as a 'Golden Age' recalled in childhood or projected into a utopian dream. The first realm of Gogol's that Dostoevsky will appropriate is the painful, embarrassed world of the ambitious poor clerk who insists that he cannot be the person he knows he really is – but unlike Gogol's timid little men, these characters will find some other person, or some theory, to blame for it.

In fact, so brilliantly did Dostoevsky apply his new devices of psychological prose to Gogol's flattened world that Gogol himself was somewhat eclipsed.[28] In part this was due to Gogol's confusing ideological profile: his final published book, *Selected Passages from a Correspondence with Friends* (1847) was a humorless and politically reactionary treatise, poorly received by the critics. In part the eclipse was due to tsarist copyright, which, after Gogol's death in 1852, reverted for fifty years to his mother and four sisters. They were inexperienced in publishing and failed to promote or distribute new editions of his work. This matter was rectified only with the centennial of Gogol's birth in 1909, and in the 1920–30s Gogol at last began to receive successors worthy of him.

Pushkin's posthumous life is another story. Beginning in the mid-1850s, he became an idol and a myth. Both Dostoevsky and Tolstoy cultivated a special relationship with Russia's premiere poet. In 1880, at the unveiling of a statue to the poet in Moscow, Dostoevsky delivered a speech declaring Pushkin a national prophet, the savior and beacon of his people, and his fictive heroes a force for moral good – in terms that would have stunned the poet, but that electrified the audience. Tolstoy, in every way Pushkin's equal as an aristocrat, was not present at the ceremony (Turgenev had invited him to speak but Tolstoy politely declined; he disapproved of jubilees, for others and for himself). Tolstoy was the first major Russian writer not to pass through the Romantic school. "Read *The Captain's Daughter*," the 25-year-old Tolstoy jotted down in his diary on October 31, 1853. "Alas, I must admit that Pushkin's prose is now old-fashioned – not in its language, but in its manner of exposition. Now, quite rightly, in the new school of literature, interest in the details of feeling is taking the place of interest in the events themselves. Pushkin's stories are somehow bare."[29] As regards "details of feeling," Tolstoy will indeed have no rival. But the "bareness" of Pushkin's prose remained for him a constant inspiration. Twenty years later, Tolstoy would stumble across an abandoned prose fragment by Pushkin and credit it, together with the Belkin Tales, for providing him with the courage to begin *Anna Karenina*.

Chapter 6

Realisms: Dostoevsky, Tolstoy, Chekhov

1825–55:   Reign of Emperor Nicholas I
1850:   Dostoevsky begins term of hard labor in Siberia
1854–55:   Tolstoy, age twenty-seven, serves as lieutenant during Siege of
              Sevastopol in Crimean War
1855–81:   Reign of Emperor Alexander II
1861–64:   Great Reforms: liberation of serfs, introduction of jury system,
              military reforms, first use of word "glasnost" for officially sponsored
              lessening of censorship
1878–80:   Tolstoy begins his public opposition to the state, church, and military
              institutions of his time
1881:   Death of Dostoevsky at age sixty
1881:   Alexander II, the "Liberator Tsar," assassinated by terrorist bomb
1888:   Chekhov receives Pushkin Prize
1891–92:   Disastrous famine in Central Russia and Ukraine
1894:   Nicholas II crowned (will reign until 1917)
1901:   Tolstoy excommunicated from Russian Orthodox Church
1904:   Chekhov dies of tuberculosis at age forty-four
1910:   Tolstoy dies at age eighty-two

At some point between 1845 and 1855, the Russian nineteenth century breaks in two. This watershed was real not only in the judgment of later literary historians ("Romanticism" before that time, "Realism" after it); contemporaries also acutely felt the discontinuity. Political, social, and military markers were overt. In 1848, revolutionary uprisings throughout Europe caused panic among the imperial censors and internal police, recalling Catherine II's reaction to the Terror in France in the early 1790s. In 1856, a humiliating defeat in the Crimean War finally convinced ruling circles of the need for modernization, railroads, and a mobile labor force. The new tsar Alexander II, succeeding the reactionary Nicholas I in 1855, committed to wide-ranging reforms.

Within the alienated creative elite, cultural evolution was more gradual. Since the 1830s, literature had been out of the hands of poets in aristocratic salons or the imperial court and increasingly the business of entrepreneurial booksellers and journalists. This new commercial class saw its most lucrative markets not in poetry but in prose – and especially in the long serialized novel, indispensable for retaining and satisfying subscribers with installments stretching (if possible) over years.

Russia's two major cities were developing different cultural mythologies, each of which would prove exceptionally durable. As an alternative to "bureaucratic, cynical, pleasure-seeking" St. Petersburg, the ancient but newly rebuilt city of Moscow came into its own – "young, idealistic, inspired, philosophical," identified with Russocentric or Slavophile beliefs and influenced by German Romanticism.[1] Non-noble background was no longer an obstacle to literary activity, as it had been to the critic Vissarion Belinsky (1811–48), a doctor's son and autodidact whose passionate, opinionated, highly influential screeds on the Russian writers of his day unerringly selected the most gifted. Writers and critics now met in "circles" and constituted an intelligentsia, a mixed class based on education and ideological commitment rather than birth or government rank. At last, in the 1860s, the cultural traffic between East and West became two-way. Upper-class Russians still spoke and read West European languages – but not as reliably as before. More important than the fading out of multilingualism at home, however, was the fact that some Western European countries began to consider Russian literary products worthy of translation into their own languages. In part because of the lengthy residence in France of the urbane, highly respected Ivan Turgenev, Russia began to be seen as a place that might contribute to the European literary canon.

This diversification, democratization, and Europeanization of Russian literature coincided with the beginning of Russia's serious revolutionary movement. All great writers took a stand toward it or featured fictional heroes from it. Russia's first political dissidents were dreamers and closeted debaters. Without practical experience and with no political responsibility, this idealistic and ineffectual generation became known as the "fathers," the "people of the [eighteen]-forties." On the far side of the mid-century divide, their sons and daughters became radical populist activists, the so-called "people of the sixties." Their goals and tactics varied: some were peaceful educators, others went abroad to Geneva or Paris, still others threw bombs. By century's end, the number of Marxists and internationalists had grown dramatically. Around these polemics and political sympathies a new literary tradition was constructed. Famous Romantic-era heroes (Onegin, Pechorin, Chichikov, Akaky Akakievich) were reclassified in civic categories, into "superfluous heroes" for upper-class protagonists and "naturalist," pathetic portraits for the urban poor. Neither Pushkin nor Gogol would have understood literary creativity catalogued in this way.

With a brief aside on poetry in an age of prose, this chapter is limited to the work of three titans: Dostoevsky, Tolstoy, and Chekhov. Our strategy will be to take themes and genres familiar from the Romantic era – issues of rank, honor, embarrassment, comedies of self-improvement, the "love story" and "death story" – and suggest how they continue to live inside new literary worlds and answer to new realities. In the previous chapter, for example, we saw that the duel of honor, a central ritual of self-respect and the cause of death for two great writers, survived into the Realist period largely in parodied forms. (This is not to say, however, that Realist-era authors were immune to its appeal in their own lives. In May 1861, Tolstoy venomously provoked a quarrel with the placid Turgenev, his elder by ten years, over a private matter – the latter man's education of his illegitimate daughter – and challenged Turgenev to a duel with pistols. Friends intervened and the confrontation was averted.) Perhaps because it was so often parodied, dueling retained some literary currency. Other canonized Romantic themes were not so much parodied as pried open, examined from the inside, and given a deeper consciousness.

Consider, as a test case, Gogol's Petersburg stories of urban poverty and humiliation. His narrators look in on the story from the outside with some glee, moving the sufferer rather quickly to his denouement. Akaky Akakievich falls ill and dies within a page, Poprishchin is committed to a madhouse in half-a-dozen diary entries after which we can assume he dies there – or at least falls silent. Following in Gogol's footsteps, Dostoevsky takes the same clerk but postpones the end, endows him with more self-awareness and pride, and cuts off the escape. Madness must be lived through at length, and dying people talk right down to the finish line. Since Dostoevsky's clerks are not just alone but terribly lonely, they seek wherever possible to turn their inner torment into an addressed dialogue. Thus – to take only the pre-exile fiction – Dostoevsky first reworks Poprishchin's clerkly confessions as an epistolary novel (*Poor Folk*, 1846); then as a transcript of schizophrenia, with several sides of a single personality in erratic, edgy communication with one another (*The Double*, 1846); finally as a dream-fantasy addressed equally to the reader and to a possibly dreamed-up love object (*White Nights*, 1848). As these lengthy painful exercises unfold, the hero's humiliation, embarrassment, and need to hide from himself become so great that his consciousness must "burst out" into some sort of freedom – but not as Gogol's heroes do, not one-way, disappearing down the street. In Dostoevsky, bursts or explosions are contained within the narrative, as "scandal," and they tend only to confuse the survivors. They resolve nothing. Bursting out into the freedom to commit murder – Raskolnikov's route – is an impulse we begin to understand only after the whole length of *Crime and*

Punishment. This "will to murder" is refined in the later novels, where rebellion can assume exclusively intellectual forms.

One aspect of Gogol's storytelling remains constant for Dostoevsky's art from start to finish, resurfacing in the Symbolist novel. This is the suspicion that authorship itself is the product of demonic pride – and thus a cunning, evasive, unreliable narrator is the most appropriate vehicle for it.[2] When "doubles" appear to the tormented heroes in Dostoevsky's mature work (most famously, Ivan Karamazov's petty devil), they infuriate and terrorize their interlocutors not by threats of eternal fire and brimstone, but by reminding them of their earlier words, ideas, or creations, which – however wise or clever they seemed at the time – now embarrass them. The devil straps our old stories to our back and won't let us outgrow them. "I forbid you to speak of 'The Grand Inquisitor,' Ivan exclaimed [to his apparition], blushing all over with shame."[3]

What about Tolstoy? Although also a great master at portraying social anguish and public shame, in his deepest concerns Tolstoy starts and ends elsewhere. Of more significance to him than exposure and censure by others (for Tolstoy always rushed to censure himself first) was honor. His definition of the term was not Pushkin's – Tolstoy respected different codes, and he related "honor" more directly to "honesty" as he understood that quality – but it was well within the Pushkinian tradition. For Tolstoy too there was a violent component to honor, the obligation to face hostile fire and sudden death. But Tolstoy takes honor out of the duel and places it on the battlefield. War remained centrally important to him, even after his crisis and conversion of the early 1880s, when he began to advocate exclusively non-violent modes of resisting evil, including conscientious objection to military service. Near the end of his life, this committed pacifist was still working on his Chechen novel *Hadji Murad* (1904–07), which ends in an epic orgy of slaughter astonishing in its inevitability and purity. The torso of the besieged Hadji Murad is slowly filling up with bullets, but "his strong body continued the thing that he had commenced."[4] This "thing" was the act of dying, which was beyond pain, feeling, desire, and judgment. When a soldier took his dagger to the head of Hadji Murad, stretched out on the ground, it seemed that "someone was striking him with a hammer and he could not understand who was doing it or why. That was his last consciousness of any connexion with his body. He felt nothing more and his enemies kicked and hacked at what had no longer anything in common with him" (p. 667).

In the death of this brave warrior we witness the creation of a Tolstoyan "double," not by a psyche splitting in two (as in Dostoevsky), but by a body being severed from the spirit. The death of Hadji Murad is a lapidary Tolstoyan moment. During this brief and narrow passage, two perspectives emerge in what had been one coordinated human being. But who precisely is the "he" / "him" referred to in the above passage? By the end of the dying, the kicked and hacked corpse has "nothing in common with him." So "he" still exists. But where? Is Hadji Murad "dead"? Nowhere in his fictive or theoretical writings does Tolstoy insist on an afterlife, only on "light," and he adamantly rejects taking any miracles in the Gospels literally, especially the Resurrection. Such delicate, God-like maneuverings by Tolstoy around the life–death boundary are not unique to his war scenes, of course. The culminating moments of "The Death of Ivan Ilyich" and the flickering final seconds of Anna Karenina perishing under a train produce similar distancings and doubled perspectives. But for all that he excelled at sickness and suicide, Tolstoy returned again and again to the behavior of men under fire as a recurrent marker of courage and honorableness. One cannot imagine Dostoevsky doing war stories – even though the most formative moment of his own life was a scaffold experience, where certain death, he believed, was three minutes away.

Biographies of events, and biographies that are quests for the Word

As a framework for these and other paradoxes in the fiction of Russia's two greatest novelists, it is helpful to keep in mind their biographies. These celebrated lives qualify as novels in their own right – and in the minds of some, as legend or saints' lives. Both writers drew deeply on their own experience for their art. Both grew into the role of national prophet and participated in their own mythologization. Each had a "break" in his literary career.

For Dostoevsky (1821–81), the break was traumatic, geographical, and coerced from the outside. In 1849 he was arrested for illicit political activity and condemned to death by firing squad – a sentence that was commuted at the last minute to four years' hard labor in Siberia followed by six years' duty as a garrison soldier. Between 1850 and 1859, which coincided with the more general "break" in the Russian nineteenth century, Dostoevsky lived a life apart from his nation's literature and society. In Siberia he experienced a re-conversion to Russian Orthodoxy as well as the onset of chronic epilepsy, so severe that he referred to his attacks as "little deaths." In 1860 Dostoevsky returned, much changed, to a much changed homeland. Although he had written startlingly innovative works before his arrest, most notably *Poor Folk* and *The Double* (both 1846), his name was largely forgotten. He had to create himself anew.

This was not an easy task, and Dostoevsky had few means of support. In 1865, at age forty-four, Dostoevsky fled Russia to write and evade his creditors (he had taken on his deceased brother's debts); he gambled everything away. After marrying his stenographer in 1867, he remained abroad for four more years, fleeing debtors' prison. Of their four cherished children, two died: their first, Sonya, as an infant in 1868, and ten years later the youngest, Alyosha, of epilepsy at age three. Through all these evictions, migrations, compulsions, crises and tragedies of his post-prison life, Dostoevsky wrote constantly and with great discipline: every night, from eleven o'clock to five in the morning, by candlelight, sustained by tea and cigarettes. In Petersburg, Dresden, then the Russian provinces, he steadily produced and then serially published his four great novels: *Crime and Punishment* (1866), *The Idiot* (1868), *Demons* (1872), and *The Brothers Karamazov* (1880). Not until the mid-1870s did Dostoevsky, already famous, enjoy anything like financial security. Even then, husband and wife continued scrupulously to observe the same ascetic work ritual. The writer had a passion for order and cleanliness. Their daughter Lyubov recalls never seeing her father in slippers or dressing-gown at home, only in starched collars and a tie. Stains on his clothing prevented him from concentrating.[5]

Dostoevsky's whole external biography, in fact, can be seen as a series of unexpected "little deaths" followed by disciplined resurrections, from night to morning. These tribulations were imposed, by and large, by external agents and conditions: by a police state in 1849, by nagging poverty, and by his own dysfunctional body, which flung him down and required him to rise on his own. To tell the story of this life, it is enough to point to its events. Dostoevsky did this himself. Working as editor and journalist during the 1870s, he was known to display – like stigmata – the scars from his leg fetters and insist that they gave him the right to speak on behalf of the suffering Russian people. And yet for all the traces of victimization in his life, Dostoevsky never tolerated theories (or lawyers, or juries) that blame a crime on the environment. Criminals are free and make choices. Responsibility accrues and repentance is required. Among Dostoevsky's many complaints against socialism, both the secular utopian sort and its demonic apotheosis in Ivan Karamazov's "Grand Inquisitor," was its promise to replace this radical freedom with material and mental security. Hence one of Dostoevsky's great paradoxes: the healthy, free mind demands continual destabilization and doubt if it is to exercise acts of faith, but our deeds are stable, answerable, and belong to us alone. In his *Diary of a Writer*, issued sporadically beginning in 1873 to a rapt readership, Dostoevsky mixed creative fiction with personal memoir and (often reactionary) political commentary on current events, delivered in the comically unreliable voice of a Gogolian narrator. Dostoevsky the novelist remained a newspaper man.

Tolstoy's temperament and experiences were different. So was the "break" in his life. It was triggered by observation and moral outrage rather than by punitive acts against his person, and was coerced, as it were, from the *in*side. Tolstoy's long life (1828–1910) also became the stuff of myth – but not because of its events. On the surface, it was the privileged high-born biography of its time. Born a wealthy count on the large Tolstoy estate of Yasnaya Polyana, near Tula, he lost his mother at age two (probably the definitive shock of his life). He dropped out of a provincial university at age eighteen, caroused, gambled, womanized, compulsively recorded these lapses in his diary and vowed to reform, joined the army and saw action at Sevastopol during the Crimean War (spring 1855), visited Petersburg, toured Western Europe (to pay homage to his beloved Rousseau), caroused, gambled, womanized, all the while reading voraciously in four languages. In 1851, Tolstoy began to write up quasi-autobiographical accounts of his childhood, his wanderings abroad, and his military experiences. In 1862, at age thirty-four, he married, settled down at Yasnaya Polyana, started a family, and began to write in earnest. Like Dostoevsky, he was blessed with a devoted wife who became his indispensable secretary and household manager. Unlike Dostoevsky, Tolstoy turned away from his wife after his spiritual conversion: she came to represent for him the vanity of fame as well as the persistence of the "animal principle," and he resented his continuing desire for both. For forty-eight years, Tolstoy lived and worked at Yasnaya Polyana. Five of the couple's thirteen children died in infancy or early childhood. But overall his was a secure, prosperous, healthy, fertile, productive life. Nothing punitive was imposed on it from the outside; it was a life without sacrificial events or material want. A natural aristocrat and patriarch, Tolstoy did what he wanted to do. He appeared to take for granted the pleasures and pitfalls of abundance: an excess of vigor, wealth, appetite, children, freedom, words. This man to whom everything had been given created an event by taking something away.

Indeed, taking away and giving up could bring only positive gains. To Tolstoy's uncompromisingly logical mind with its belief in Rousseau's doctrine of natural good, evil was acquired, unnatural, a byproduct of bad contracts or bad habits. Evil might well disappear once we shed the habits and material burdens that sustain it. As always, Tolstoy began with himself. His own formal "break" with the world of privilege came in 1880, at age fifty-one, at the peak of his fame. He marked it by a highly publicized *Confession* in which he discredited, one by one, each of the earlier phases in his quest for the meaning of life: self-perfection, pedagogy, fame, family, belief in progress, science, faith through the Church. The break was not as severe as it seemed, however. Tolstoy's gift had always been for a radical estrangement from what others claimed to live by. He had never been comfortable with his era, his rank, his society, his self, and the pleasure he received from writing had always struck him as illicit. Renouncing both *War and Peace* and *Anna Karenina* as "counterfeit art," he declared the mission of his final thirty years to be moral philosophy – of a thunderous sort. Beginning in the early 1880s, treatises went forth from Yasnaya Polyana attacking the major institutions of imperial Russia: state, military, Church, the aristocracy as a class, the Table of Ranks, private property, schools, Western ideas of progress. Tolstoy became a pacifist and vegetarian. His ideal was "Christian anarchism," into which he eventually incorporated some Buddhist precepts: non-participation in evil, the cultivation of loving habits toward all living things, a restraint of appetites, a simple life of manual labor close to the soil, and no obligations except to one's own conscience. Tolstoy distrusted the idea of "news" – which, in his view, was merely a distraction from one's own spiritual growth – and he disliked the fadmongery of "current events." He was pursuing the eternal. Tolstoy was not a newspaper man.

Yet by some curious twist of fate, Tolstoy's quest to simplify human nature and return us to nature coincided with the worldwide graphic revolution. Dostoevsky (d. 1881) had been his own agent and handler. The printed word was his medium. Tolstoy, living three decades longer, became the world's first multimedia celebrity – and he was handled by others. Not only photographers but cartoonists and newspaper columnists pursued him, or better stalked him, through telegraph, wax cylinder, color photo, newsreel, film. The "wealthy Count dressing up as a peasant" was mercilessly satirized in the public domain.[6] But the media assisted Tolstoy too. Even while parodying his image, it spread his word. This mattered, because Tolstoy did not like to travel or to speak publicly from podiums, as Dostoevsky had loved to do; he preferred to receive guests at home, one on one. As Yasnaya Polyana became a place of pilgrimage for "Tolstoyans" from around the world, access to the great man was increasingly controlled by his wife, children, and domestic staff. Some Tolstoyans were arrested and imprisoned for their beliefs; others were exiled. Beyond his excommunication by the Church in 1901, however, Tolstoy, to his anguish, was not touched by the arm of the state. For the final twenty-five years of his life Tolstoy was kept under police surveillance, but neither Tsar Alexander III (r. 1881–94) nor Nicholas II (r. 1894–1917) was foolish enough to add a martyr's crown to his glory.

At century's end, Maksim Gorky (1868–1936) came to know both the aging Tolstoy and the ailing Chekhov in the Crimea. In a complex tribute to the older writer composed after Tolstoy's flight from Yasnaya Polyana and final illness, Gorky wrote: "I have always been repelled by that stubborn and despotic urge of his to turn the life of Count Lev Nikolaevich Tolstoy into the saintly Life of our

Blessed boyar Lev."[7] It would have sanctified his wisdom and made it irresistible, equal to those leg-iron scars that lent such authority to Dostoevsky's word. But as a radical activist devoted to social reform, Gorky saw only part of the truth. Dostoevsky had been tied to his time; his scars were historically determined and thus inevitably dated. Tolstoy's relatively "empty," unpersecuted life freed him up to become a carrier for ideas valid for all people of all times. And this is what Tolstoy craved. The one section of *The Brothers Karamazov* that Tolstoy admired (his bedside reading during the last month of his life) was Book Six, "The Russian Monk," Alyosha's compilation of peak life-moments and homilies from his mentor, the Elder Zosima.

The two men chose never to meet, but much lore circulated about their opinions of each other. Dostoevsky deplored Tolstoy's tendency to write "landlord novels" set in an historical period irrelevant to the teeming present. Gorky recalls Tolstoy saying that Dostoevsky lacked the courage to create healthy heroes; indeed, he "didn't like healthy people. He was convinced that since he himself was sick, the whole world must be sick." "It's odd that so many people read him," Tolstoy later remarked. "I can't understand why. It's difficult and futile – all those Idiots, Adolescents, Raskolnikovs, and the rest, things aren't like that, it's all much simpler, more understandable."[8] After Dostoevsky's death in 1881, Tolstoy wept. But nevertheless he wrote soon after to their common friend, Nikolai Strakhov: "one cannot place on a pedestal for the instruction of posterity a man who was all struggle."[9] These two biographical trajectories – Dostoevsky's labor-camp martyrdom and return to life, and Tolstoy's pure trans-historical moral outrage – are the most influential literary variants of a "righteous person" [*pravednik*] in the Russian literary canon.

Anton Chekhov (1860–1904), with one-half Tolstoy's life span to work with, matured as a writer in the all-but-blinding aura of both great novelists. Although he had a marked "Tolstoyan period," Chekhov took a different path. For him, bigness of form and excessive energy in articulating an idea – or in carrying out an idea – already bordered on the fraudulent. Bodies, voices, ideas, and intentions in Chekhov's world are more quickly exhausted. Pretensions to pan-humanity (Tolstoy) or to messianic struggle (Dostoevsky) were to him equally flawed. In Chekhov's life, the most important extra-literary events were training as a doctor, traveling to the penal colony on Sakhalin Island north of Japan in 1890, and dying, for fifteen years, of tuberculosis. An urbane, confident, ironical man, he remarked in 1894, in a letter to his friend Aleksei Suvorin, that he had cooled toward Tolstoy: "Reason and justice tell me that there is more love for mankind in electricity and steam than there is in chastity and abstaining from meat."[10] Chekhov did not seek to propagate a Word. But no writer could ignore the legacy of Russia's two massive novelists.

Time-spaces (Dostoevsky and Tolstoy)

The Tolstoy/Dostoevsky parallel lives can also help us grasp the organization and value-hierarchies of their respective literary worlds. Very early, during Tolstoy's lifetime, readers sensed that these two worlds were incompatible. In 1902, the Symbolist poet and critic Dmitry Merezhkovsky published a lengthy comparative study in which he called Dostoevsky a "seer of the spirit" (a poet of faith and mystic revelation) and Tolstoy a "seer of the flesh" (a singer of corporeality and unclouded vision). In 1929, in what proved to be another tenacious opposition, Mikhail Bakhtin defined Dostoevsky as "dialogic" or polyphonic (character-centered) and Tolstoy as "monologic" (author-centered).[11] The dialogic writer emphasizes horizontal relations and dispersed, centrifugal, competitive points of view; the monologist, in contrast, stresses the vertical, the centripetal, the absolute. Since there is some measure of truth to these broad binary generalizations as they relate to our two novelists, we expand on them here.

Dostoevsky's most memorable heroes are depicted in an unstable or borderline phase of their lives. This brief slice of their life is under great pressure. The heroes are being tested at an extreme "threshold" moment; one can almost see the outline of the scaffold behind them, that moment in late December 1849 when Dostoevsky, at age twenty-eight, was led out by drumroll to the Semyonovsky parade ground already dressed in his shroud. We meet Raskolnikov on the brink of committing a murder. Myshkin is in a pre-epileptic state for much of *The Idiot*. Three of the (perhaps) four Karamazov brothers are at their father's throat from the first family reunion in the monastery up to (and beyond) the parricide. Most Dostoevskian heroines live on the brink of hysteria. The Underground Man is liminal in a more metaphysical sense: he never gets off the threshold – eventually an editor must cut him off – because he refuses to let any definitions of himself coalesce. Such contrariness, he thinks, guarantees his freedom. This high energy under maximum pressure can erupt at any moment into tragedy or comedy, for Dostoevsky, like Gogol, is an irrepressibly comic writer. Significantly, in a routine Dostoevskian scene this energy tends to build and then to erupt. It does not leak out slowly or fuel its characters with a steady, stabilizing flame.

Dostoevsky favors built-up, congested environments: a prison barracks, a tenement building, houses strung out along a street. Spatial thresholds – windows, door-jams, corridors, fences, stairways, and landings – are prominent in this architecture. The plot leaps forward at moments of tense eye-to-eye contact over a threshold, as when Raskolnikov, in a panic, commits two murders just inside the door, or when the jealous Rogozhin pulls a knife on Prince Myshkin, the Idiot, at the top of the stairs. For Dostoevsky, truths are released in crisis time. In the calmer, more coherent and linear time-space of the criminal trial, such as the lengthy legal procedure during which Dmitry Karamazov is found guilty of parricide, truths are bungled or lost. At the end of *The Double*, Golyadkin is committed to a madhouse by the very double he has himself conjured up as his successful fantasy self. Before this ghastly final stop, Golyadkin's lookalike toady delivers him to his doctor's house, where suddenly a high-ranking dignitary appears in an armchair at the top of the landing. "The front door opened with a crash . . . Sick with horror, he looked back. The whole of the brightly-lit staircase was thick with people. Inquisitive eyes were watching him from all sides. . . . Our hero gave a scream, and clutched his head. Alas! He had felt this coming for a long time!"[12] The passage of time merely reveals what was always true.

Around the edges of a Dostoevskian townscape, nature can be oppressive. Petersburg is a city of dirty slush, rain, unbearable heat, but its weather is always symbolically marked. Nature can also seem magical, as it does to the Dreamer wandering the streets during *White Nights*, or in the image of "sticky green leaves in the spring" that intoxicate Ivan Karamazov. Dostoevsky can mesmerize with glimpses of the natural or non-urban world. The placid Siberian steppe as seen from Raskolnikov's hard-labor camp in the Epilogue of *Crime and Punishment* is one such moment, preparing us for the hero's rebirth; other moments are nostalgic, such as the utopian vision of a Garden in the "Dream of a Ridiculous Man" (1876). But these spaces are always only glimpsed. The hero or heroine cannot enter them in a practical way or work in them. They are either transitory or hopelessly lost in time, either past or future. Nature does not exist on its own, under the open sky.

In Dostoevsky's typically explosive, "built" environment, natural and biological cycles are muted. Over time, families tend to break down. Except for the occasional unsatisfying snack in a pub, discussion over cognac, or scandal at a funeral feast, Dostoevsky's characters do not sit down to regular meals, nor do they sleep normal hours, go out to work, or observe fixed schedules. If a child is born, it dies within hours or weeks. Men and women often rush, but to nowhere in particular, simply beyond the boundaries of the story. This abruptness and disorder is only partly explained by poverty. Energy is not spent on maintenance or on routine material things. (In *The Idiot*, the robust lunches of cheese, honey, and cutlets enjoyed by the three "tall, blooming, sturdy" daughters of General Epanchin, who "took no pains to conceal their appetites" and were in no hurry to get married (Part I, ch. 4), are comically presented – a tribute to Gogol in Dostoevsky's world.) Crisis events give rise to a huge amount of talk, but never small talk; all parties are well read, intellectually curious, articulate even when drunk, and keen to debate topics in ethical philosophy. The pace can be frenetic – these huge novels are short on clock time, lasting from a few days to a few months – but there is always time to tell one more story.

Dostoevsky's novels are immediate, *talking* texts: how something is told, and by whom, are key. As with Gogol, one senses a narrator who, out of ineptitude, caprice, or malice, can willingly distort or withhold the story. This is not the playfulness of Pushkin's digressions and plot-suspensions in the Belkin Tales, which are simply and honorably erotic (designed to prolong pleasure), nor is it Gogol's focus on humiliation and embarrassment. In Dostoevsky there is a darker envelope: a keen knowledge of the criminal mind, with its pride that combines boastfulness, indifference to repentance, acceptance of one's sinfulness, and taboo. Lying and liars are everywhere very important.[13] Many of Dostoevsky's exuberant concealments mix buffoonery with more than a little meanness, for his narrators want to be storytellers themselves and know the power it brings. A narrator can begin embodied, as a neighbor or onlooker reporting (unreliably) on what he sees or hears, and then fade out or evolve into something else as soon as the reader's trust has been won.[14] We find ourselves thrown into a world of ideas and rumors that demands our direct participation and judgment, since information is not being filtered through a single omniscient consciousness.

This is Bakhtin's main point about Dostoevsky as novelist. Dostoevsky endows his heroes – including his negative ones – with so much independence, mobility of perspective, uncertainty of motive, and potent storytelling skill that readers, wishing to know what is going on, bypass the author/narrator and respond directly to the heroes. This ability to sustain the illusion of autonomous consciousnesses inside a fictional world both qualifies that fiction as "Realism" (for it replicates the way real people live, each on their own, into an open future) and represents an ideal far beyond the ambitions of most "Realistic" authors. For the autonomy of fictive characters *is* an illusion. Their lines are fixed; they were created toward an end. Dostoevsky, a teacher and a prophet no less than Tolstoy, had a point of view on the world and a passionate value system that he desired us to take seriously. He wanted us to admire the meekness and loyalty of Sonya Marmeladova and despise that calculating blackmailer, vulgar capitalist and *poshlyak*, Pyotr Petrovich Luzhin. He wanted us to reject the Grand Inquisitor's rationale for a paternalistic socialism based on "miracle, mystery, and authority" and embrace instead the free inequality promised by Christ and spelled out in the teachings of the elder Zosima. Dostoevsky was no relativist. But he was a radical pluralist and personalist, fastidious in presenting the fullest possible case for every option directly out of the mouth of the protagonist who believes in it.

This strategy, we should note, does no one any favors. Being so aware of oneself can be painful and paralyzing. The Underground Man is the first to realize that he is crippled, made ridiculous, and encouraged in his cruelty by his "hyper-consciousness," which anticipates responses to himself and refutes them in advance. But such is the logical paradox. In that most terrible of satires on the abuse of our freedom to construct a self, Dostoevsky's trapped underground voice reasons thus:

> The final end, gentlemen: better to do nothing! Better conscious inertia!
> And so, long live the underground! Though I did say I envy the normal
> man to the point of uttermost bile, still I do not want to be him on those
> conditions in which I see him (though, all the same, I shall not stop
> envying him . . .) But here too, I'm lying . . .
>
> (*Notes from Underground*, Part One, XI)

The inevitable "uttermost bile" that results from such radical indeterminacy fueled Maksim Gorky's lifelong resistance to Dostoevsky, both on his own behalf and in the name of the new Soviet state. One could not build anything durable in the presence of that dialectic. What is more, the dialectic admits of no anchoring of the self in a supra-personal framework. "The time has come to attack Dostoevskyism all along the line," Gorky wrote in 1933. "I should prefer that the civilized world were unified not by Dostoevsky, but by Pushkin."[15] Gorky's juxtaposition of these two writers is intriguing. If freedom for Pushkin is the right to stand one's ground and act as a man of public honor, then freedom for Dostoevsky is an individual's right to choose, capriciously or soberly, in the presence of partial knowledge. This principle will not unify the world. Since freedom is the goal and since Dostoevsky allows truths to be multiple, a high priority in his prose is always to increase the number of available perspectives and to complicate all possible resonances of the spoken word. Then truths can test one another at their points of intersection.

The time-space of Tolstoy's novels differs from Dostoevsky's in almost every way. Tolstoy, of course, is no stranger to tragedy and crisis, nor even to the most Dostoevsky-style crisis of all, murder. (Two famous Tolstoyan narratives from 1889, "The Kreutzer Sonata" and "The Devil," both involve the killing of a woman out of jealousy.) But he handles the cause and aftermath of such crises differently. In his 1890 treatise, "Why Do People Stupefy Themselves?", Tolstoy remarks in passing that Dostoevsky's Raskolnikov did not kill the old pawnbroker with an axe on the day of the murder but had been killing her for months, lying feverishly and resentfully on his couch in his garret, making the possibility of that murder a habit of his mind. Tolstoy sensed that with Dostoevsky, for all that he multiplies perspectives on events and filters them through gossipy untrustworthy narrators, a tragic act (when it finally comes to pass) tests not a person but an *idea*. Does Raskolnikov have the right to kill the old pawnbroker? Does Dmitry or Ivan Karamazov have the right to wish their father dead? In what does freedom consist (the Underground Man provokes us to ask), if not in my right to disappoint your calculations and act "not like a piano key or an organ stop" but according to my own whim? Such tests contrast starkly with Tolstoy's understanding of human character. Tolstoyan personalities do not represent ideas – in fact, they do not represent any single question that can be put to the test. Tolstoy was explicit about this in his drafts for a preface to *War and Peace*: he could not force his characters to act or talk in a way that would "prove or clarify some kind of idea or series of ideas."[16] People, he believed, do not act out of an idea (more likely they will slap an idea on a deed or an appetite after the fact, to dignify it); they act out of a bundle of good and bad habits, some conscious, but most not.

In the great Tolstoyan novels before 1880, the ability to assume and then to shed many different ideas while remaining open to a variety of life situations is the defining mark of a successful hero. A great deal of talk goes on in these novels too, but, unlike Dostoevsky's astonishingly "casual" conversations on cosmic matters, much Tolstoyan talk is "small." Tolstoy greatly values observation and practical skills – knowing how things work in a hands-on way – but he does not tolerate much abstract philosophy from his heroes. He mercilessly exposes academics and book-writing intellectuals (like Levin's half-brother Koznyshev in *Anna Karenina*, who throughout the full length of the novel labors over a book that then receives feeble, miserable reviews), and he pities theoreticians of war (like General Pfühl in *War and Peace*) who think that a battle unfolds like a "plan."[17] In Tolstoy, a person's identity is most secure when it is most flexible, that is, when *not* fastened down to a single coherent unfolding idea.

Recalling our Chapter 2 on heroes and plots, we might say that Tolstoy doesn't do "types," just as he doesn't do (and doesn't believe in) formal institutions. The closest his ideal hero comes to one of our categories might be the Fool – not of the holy variety, to be sure, but the bumbling, well-meaning fool, honest where honesty has no place, awkward in society and continually ridiculed by society for his eccentric ways. Pierre Bezukhov and Konstantin Levin are both questing fools in this sense, continually surprised by themselves, and Tolstoy richly rewards them for it.

We might make a corollary observation. Tolstoy mistrusted "official authority": policemen, military recruiters, tax collectors, the arm of the law, the word of the monarch. He felt that official power could *only* corrupt. In contrast to Tolstoy, Dostoevsky is remarkably kind to policemen and other people who wield power. As a rule, they are merciful and generous to sufferers. Porfiry

Petrovich, a police investigator, is a key instrument of Raskolnikov's salvation, and by the end of the novel almost functions as his spiritual foster father and confessor. The police officers on the Petersburg streets of *Crime and Punishment* are attentive, compassionate professionals, concerned to protect young girls from abuse and to prevent suicides. Makar Devushkin, timid impoverished clerk of Dostoevsky's earliest "Gogolian variation," *Poor Folk*, repeats Akaky Akakievich's humiliating scene in front of his department chief but with this important difference: where Gogol's downtrodden clerk receives a bawling out that leads to his death, Devushkin's boss, seeing his underling's shabbiness and misery, slips him a 100-ruble note. Given Dostoevsky's own poverty and experience with punitive institutions – and Tolstoy's inexperience with both – this difference is worth pondering.

Tolstoy's reluctance to work with types is related to the high value he puts on gradual, minute-by-minute effort and change. Idleness, anger, "lying on the couch for months" not so much thinking about that specific pawnbroker as simply not taking oneself in hand to act in a positive way (as Raskolnikov's best friend Razumikhin acts; he is, for Dostoevsky's palette, a very Tolstoyan hero): these were the errors that led Raskolnikov to murder, and that will lead Pozdnyshev to murder his innocent wife in "The Kreutzer Sonata." Tolstoy's novels center squarely on the conviction that we act not out of our ideas but out of our bodies. And if ideas have logical consequences, then bodies have needs. Since these needs arise out of our most basic anxieties and hungers, we all recognize them and share them. We build structures to contain them so that our consciousness and energies can be freed up for other tasks. In Tolstoy's patriarchal, work-oriented, hearth- and agrarian-centered worldview, marriage should be one such structure. Closely connected to marriage is habit. Indeed, for Tolstoy, the most satisfying type of love was not romantic-erotic or melodramatic – selfish states that were bound to collapse – but habitual kindness, attentive to the other's tiny, ongoing idiosyncratic needs, what he called "active" love.

Tolstoy, perhaps unfairly, did not see enough of this stable, finely differentiated love in the Dostoevskian landscape, love that feared crises rather than flared up eagerly during them. In a related complaint, Tolstoy also professed surprise at Dostoevsky's "careless," and in his view often monotonous, narrative style. The charge might appear odd, given the brilliant diversity and manifest excitement of a Dostoevskian hero's high-pitched life. But Tolstoy's own fictive scenarios suggest that he considered crisis and hysteria in themselves monotonous, homogenizing behavioral states. For the duration of this unnatural condition, people tend to sound and act alike, regardless of what might have triggered the blow-up. For Tolstoy, only stable forms of living and interacting can create genuine heterogeneity. In his late treatise *What Is Art?*, Tolstoy went as far as to call literature that appealed to our logical faculties or stimulated our intellectual curiosity "counterfeit art." He suspected (again, perhaps unfairly) that the most passionate and intimate relationship experienced by a Dostoevskian hero was with his idea, not with another human being. For Tolstoy, a big self-justifying idea is like a big crisis, a big crime, or a big scandal: it isn't true, it tells you very little about what's going on, and it won't last.

In 1877, Dostoevsky published a two-part review of *Anna Karenina* in his journal-newspaper *Diary of a Writer*.[18] He dwelt most appreciatively on the scene of spiritual reconciliation between the humiliated lover Vronsky and the deceived but resurrected husband Karenin, which takes place at Anna's bedside after the birth of her daughter and on the brink of her anticipated death (Part IV, chs. 17–23). The scene has every mark of a Dostoevskian epiphany: a crisis followed by a threshold moment, when – as Dostoevsky put it – "the transgressors and enemies are suddenly transformed into higher beings." Dostoevsky had no sympathy at all for Anna's tragic end, which he considered the triumph of evil, a "gloomy and terrible picture of the full degeneration of a human spirit." This curiously truncated review of the novel, like Dostoevsky's equally curious Pushkin Speech delivered three years later, provides little insight into the subject under review but a great deal of insight into Dostoevsky. The genius of Tolstoyan psychology lies not in the peaks but in the slopes. Crucial to watch is how he brings a hero or heroine down *off* a crisis moment. Only when Anna is again healthy, back into her routine life and needs, does she realize what she has become for real. Then the tragedy starts, for she sees the falseness of the crisis state (her all-but-certain death from puerperal fever) and her inability to sustain its noble-minded, feverish theatricality. Anna wants and loves Vronsky for the long term. She slips back into this desire, and therein resides her truth. She cannot arrange her life so that "having Vronsky" is a habitual, invisible, secure part of her daily routine. This might be degeneration, but is it evil? At this juncture we see clearly the mechanisms – habit on the one side, epiphany on the other – that run a Tolstoyan versus a Dostoevskian world.

Wherein lies the special texture of Tolstoyan reality? Above all, it feels slower and more "filled-in." We tend to see it before we hear it talking. Even in violent descriptions of war, human gestures seem somehow more ordinary, on a continuum with everyday life. Given the chance, they will slip back to civilian norms – as happens to the astonished Nikolai Rostov during his first battle, noticing the blue eyes of the young French soldier he was on the verge of bayoneting. Nature in Tolstoy is not primarily symbolic, as the Petersburg climate is

for Dostoevsky, but at all times it is thickly present. Simple bliss at one's physical surroundings can cause characters to shout with joy (the lengthy pastoral
insert on the Rostov family fox hunt in *War and Peace* is the sublime example).
The beauty and pure, stubborn cyclicity of natural processes is for Tolstoy a
standard that adult human intervention can only pollute. His final novel *Resurrection*, in which he exposes and condemns every purported "civilizing" human
institution, opens with a lyrical passage:

> Although men in hundreds of thousands had tried their hardest to
> disfigure that little corner of the earth where they had crowded
> themselves together, paving the ground with stones so that nothing could
> grow, weeding out every blade of vegetation, filling the air with fumes of
> coal and gas, cutting down the trees and driving away every beast and
> every bird – spring, however, was still spring, even in the town.[19]

Tolstoy doesn't like cities. All Tolstoyan narratives have a stern moral geog-
raphy. Life in the countryside is healthiest. Messy and profligate Moscow, that
"big village," was tolerated by Tolstoy (his own large family had a town house
there); but he loathed rank-obsessed, military-bureaucratic Petersburg. Of
course Pushkin, Gogol, and Dostoevsky also did not like Petersburg – but
they were fascinated by the place and understood the vitality of its myth and
the infectiousness of its atmosphere. Tolstoy was simply physically disgusted.
Worthy people fall sick in cities and recuperate outside them.

Nature, for Tolstoy, is necessity. He respects it. And nature cannot be rushed.
Cities, and the suspicious railroads that connect cities to one another, create
the illusion that human goods can be packaged by strangers and rushed from
one place to the next. Convictions, like families, are born and mature slowly,
on the basis of repeated contact. In Tolstoy's novels we see people making jam,
gathering honey, sewing dresses for balls, slowly giving birth (each contraction)
and slowly dying (each spasm) – in what is more a direct presentation than a
telling. When Tolstoy compares Moscow on the brink of Napoleon's entry to
a "dying hive" (*War and Peace*, Book Three, Part III, ch. 20), it is immediately
clear to any beekeeper that the author has not only read about beehives but
has himself rummaged around inside them. In this Tolstoy resembles his own
fictional peasant hero Platon Karataev, prisoner of war in 1812 and jack-of-
all-trades; he has *been there* and learned to do almost everything he describes.
Perhaps for this reason he does not insert a mocking narrator between the reader
and an event, nor is he concerned with multiplying or obfuscating points of
view on this event.

Tolstoy does not banish doubt or self-criticism. In that area Tolstoy is easily
Dostoevsky's equal. He offers us a vast, variegated panorama of confusions,

uncertainties, and entrapments. But with Tolstoy, sooner or later we sense that all the critics and doubters are, as it were, in the same doubt together. Consider the end of his late, great tale "Master and Man" (1895). A wealthy merchant freezes to death in a blizzard and saves the life of his workman Nikita with the warmth of his own dying body. We then learn that Nikita, "more sorry than glad to have survived," lived another twenty years, forgave his wife her infidelity, was relieved to release his son from the burden of feeding him – and (here is the stirring final line) "whether he is better or worse off there where he awoke after his death, whether he was disappointed or found there what he expected, we shall all soon learn."[20] In Dostoevsky, there is no sense that we shall ever all learn the same thing, even after death. Nor is such assurance required.

This Dostoevskian point of faith is illustrated well in one scene from the greatest twentieth-century product of the Gogol–Dostoevsky line in Russian literature, Mikhail Bulgakov's novel *The Master and Margarita*. Satan, here in the guise of a professor of black magic called Woland, has turned up in Moscow during the 1930s and is hosting his annual ball. Among the summoned guests is the severed head of one unfortunate materialist-atheist, former chairman of the Soviet Writers' Union, who was decapitated by a streetcar in the novel's opening pages. Woland assures this poor torsoless creature, whose eyes blink in terror, that the theory he had postulated – that when a head is severed, life ceases – is both "incisive and sound," but that

> "one theory is as good as another. There is even a theory that says that to each man it will be given according to his beliefs. May it be so! You are departing into nonbeing, and from the goblet into which you are being transformed, I will have the pleasure of drinking a toast to life everlasting!"[21]

In the Dostoevsky line, there is simply no single vantage point from which, as Tolstoy put it with such lapidary assurance, "we shall all soon learn." In the radical freedom that Dostoevsky will not relinquish, each of us might *become* our own belief. Not only is the end unknown, so is the path – and these paths are decidedly plural. Even that, however, cannot be known. We are not all in the same doubt. Very possibly this suspicion that dispersal and heterogeneity are natural, not freakish, led Dostoevsky to value above all things the striving for human communion. The self is not saved by a reformed splinter of its own self; it needs a genuine other consciousness.

Tolstoy was never wholly convinced of this need. In fact, in his writings on the far side of his "break," noticeably in "The Death of Ivan Ilyich" (1886), the opposite appears to be the case: growing into one's own courage and wisdom means precisely *out*growing the need for another person, who will sooner distract or seduce you from your path than help you to pursue it honorably. The fact that Ivan Ilyich's wife, daughter or son might have needed *him* during his lengthy and painful dying, that he might owe them some gratitude or sympathy and might even benefit from reaching out to them, seems not to have occurred to this terminally sick, self-pitying man (with the exception of several seconds when he notices that his son has been weeping). The horror of this dying is made clear, but Tolstoy nowhere suggests that his isolation is avoidable or his egocentrism abnormal. The only dialogue that matters is between Ivan Ilyich and his own death, which becomes his private enlightenment. The validating mark is always the hero's own solitary "I." Bakhtin noted this trait early in his 1924–25 lectures on Tolstoy, long before he had worked out the dialogic–monologic distinction, remarking that all of Tolstoy's work could be distributed between two categories, "how I am for others" (which for Tolstoy was the fraudulent realm of culture) and "how I am for myself" (which was always lonely and alone).[22] Bakhtin found such a binary, with the "I" its automatic point of reference, uncongenial and unnecessarily desperate. Many who prefer Dostoevsky to Tolstoy – and it is routine to prefer one or the other – consider this solipsistic relation that Tolstoy appears to foster a far more serious ethical flaw than the exclusionary intimacy Dostoevsky sets up between a person and his idea.

Of course Tolstoy valued acts of loving. But in his mature years, what he valued more and more was love that streamed out uninterruptedly from the "I" – regardless of what might trigger it and how it might be received. Where, or upon whom, that love landed was of secondary importance. Tolstoy doesn't do doubles, at least not demonic ones; one suspects that his lonely, questing positive heroes do not need the company of another person sufficiently to undertake the agony of conjuring one up. Like true fools, while looking after themselves they will stumble on to what they need. Pierre Bezukhov bumbles his way around to Natasha Rostova, a most unlikely match; Tolstoy makes certain that Kitty remains unmarried long enough for his favored Levin to get over his injured pride and bumble his way back to her. Meanwhile, if his fictional creations need a friend, Tolstoy himself will be that "friendly other." First he shows the reader what happens, then he tells us what the characters think about what happened, then he tells us what the author thinks about what the characters do and think. A typical Tolstoyan description of an event is multilayered – but contrary to the presentation of a Dostoevskian event, each Tolstoyan layer tends to reinforce the same perspective rather than to relativize or undermine it. One scene from *Anna Karenina*, a strong example of this strategy, will illustrate the deep difference in narrative guidance between the stalwart Tolstoy and the sly, more "loopholed" Dostoevsky line.

Count Vronsky makes a surprise visit to Anna on the day of the steeplechase (Part II, ch. 22). While waiting on the veranda for her son Seryozha to return from his walk, Anna informs Vronsky of her pregnancy. We are told that the presence of Seryozha was always an embarrassment to the two lovers, invoking in them the feeling that a sailor might have after glancing at his compass and confirming that he had indeed strayed from the proper course – but the sailor, Tolstoy hastens to add, was unable to stop, because to stop would mean to acknowledge that he was lost. This observation then receives a further gloss: "This child with his naïve outlook on life was the compass which showed them the degree of their departure from what they knew but did not want to know."[23]

These three confirmations (or redundancies) effectively plug up the meaning of the scene. In Tolstoy's view, this is not a bad thing. For the task of responsible art lies not in its ability to multiply fictions, positions, or voices (that was Dostoevsky's passion), but to justify why this particular fiction is true from all sides. This does not mean that truth is simple (or that behaving truthfully is easy or simple). Nor does it mean that experience can be transmitted in generalized terms. In his individualizing, sequencing, and pacing of tiny shifts of emotion, Tolstoy has no equal. But infinitely diverse experiences can, and must, reveal compatible eternal truths.

In his late treatise *What Is Art?* (1898), Tolstoy made explicit this paradoxical recipe. Individuals are endlessly varied and mutable on the outside, but at one with each other within. Politics, economics, intellectual ideas – indeed, all human institutions – are capable solely of dividing us, exhausting us, and masking our innate brotherhood; only art can uncover a unity beneath our natural variety. Thus art cannot be a "profession," a specialized language, or a product in thrall to a market. It rarely succeeds in its duties when exhibited or staged. Art is authentic, Tolstoy insisted, when author, narrator, performer, and spectator-reader are all united in one fused spiritual experience, "infected" with the same emotion that had seized the artist during the act of creation. To this end, spontaneous folk songs and well-timed jokes are more likely to qualify as true art than are symphonies and novels. If no such flush of "oneness" comes about, either the artwork is counterfeit, or else it can be shown that we are "not in our right mind" – drugged, drunk, duped by the sloth of upper-class life, stupefied or overstimulated by cigars, caffeine, lust. Part of Tolstoy's extraordinary faith in the body, which qualifies him as a "seer of the flesh," is his insistence that all "cleansed" bodies are basically alike and will respond in kindred ways. Like that sailor in the scene from *Anna Karenina*, each of us "carries the same compass" – which is conscience. We can pollute ourselves and thus blur our vision, we can turn away from the compass or even deny that such an instrument exists, but such actions affect neither the truth of the compass nor the orienting poles of the objective world. Like his senior contemporary Karl Marx and his junior contemporary Sigmund Freud, Tolstoy had created a theory that, maddeningly, could not be proved false: if you disagreed with it, either you were displaying your false (polluted, stupefied) consciousness, or you were involuntarily repressing the truth.

Tolstoy's *What Is Art?* caused a scandal. Resistance to it helped launch a new aesthetics that preached the autonomy of art and free rights to aesthetic expression, with the more multivalent and mystical Dostoevsky as its patron saint. This Symbolist-Age aesthetics would inspire Russian letters until the Bolsheviks succeeded in stamping it out at home and driving it abroad. But Tolstoy's moralizing, "communalizing" convictions about the proper functioning of art were quite familiar to Russian literary thought. Karamzin had espoused the same ideal of spontaneous "co-feeling" through his Sentimentalist short story "Poor Liza" in the 1790s. In the Soviet period, Tolstoyan Sentimentalist-style aesthetics were officially revived – and practiced with fervor, even by those who were dissidents to the regime, such as Aleksandr Solzhenitsyn.

If Bulgakov's *Master and Margarita* is the twentieth-century pinnacle of the Dostoevsky line, then the "Tolstoy line" culminates in Solzhenitsyn's *Cancer Ward* (1968). The novel is saturated with references to Tolstoy and to the vanities of the dying body (Ivan Ilyich's fatal disease was probably cancer, which in Tolstoy's time was undiagnosable). Its touchstone Chapter 8, titled "What Do People Live By?" after one of Tolstoy's most famous cautionary tales, passes that question through a wide spectrum of patients, ranking them morally by their response. The major heroes – the two doctors and Oleg Kostoglotov, the author's alter ego – implement Tolstoy's most precious ascetic ideal: they purify themselves by giving something up. Tempted by others, they choose to remain solitary. By the end of the novel, Doctor Lyudmila Dontsova, the oncologist, most likely has cancer herself. Vera Gangart, a surgeon, lost her fiancé in the war and proudly remains faithful to him. The patient Kostoglotov, whose cancer is successfully arrested, has a chance to pursue both Vera and (more explicitly) the nurse Zoya, but he rejects both women in favor of returning alone to his place of exile. In an insightful passage of Tolstoyan wisdom, Kostoglotov laments the fate of the ex-convict who is freed from labor camp to fend for himself, praising instead the liberating effect of banishment. "He [the banished man] had not sought to come here, and no one could drive him away," Kostoglotov reasons. "He knew he was following the only path open to him, and this gave him courage."[24]

This ideal of the delimited path, which bestowed on the penitent a freedom *from*, is characteristic of Tolstoy's scenarios of spiritual maturation. In the Russian mind it aligned him with the Eastern Orthodox virtue of "emptying out" (*kenosis*). Tolstoy could never empty himself out enough, however; his critics did not forgive him his high birth, title, and wealth, and he never forgave himself for failing to divest wholly of this birthright. The more he tried to shed those privileges, the more he was accused of hypocrisy. His acquisitive and media-driven era could only be unkind to a man of his inclinations. An earlier Greek precedent for Tolstoy might be the ancient Cynics (fourth century BCE), who did not perceive self-limitation to be perverse self-denial or sacrifice, but simply the means to happiness.[25] Cynics ignored public opinion, disdained politics, rejected private property and commercial networks, denied the validity of the polis or state – positions that Tolstoy adapted, and blended with primitive Christianity. Cynics also considered "schools" bogus and quoting earlier books as an authority useless, even harmful. Individual reason or intuition should be able to arrive at all necessary truths on its own. In any event, the sole necessary knowledge for Tolstoy (and for the Cynics) was "how to live."

Dostoevsky and books

Dostoevsky was devoted to the printed word, and so are his fictional characters. Several strategies exist for "replaying the words of a book." Dostoevsky was adept at them all. The author can take an earlier literary character and re-run his plot, but only after endowing the character with more consciousness and thus with more intricate conflicts. Such is Dostoevsky's technique in *The Double* (1846), which portrays a madman not according to the usual author–reader contract – that is, with the madness present as a written trace – but in a far less stable form. The model for Dostoevsky's tale, Gogol's *Diary* [or *Notes*] *of a Madman* (1835), had chosen for its strategy the externalized written trace, accessible as a document from the outside, which establishes a reassuring distance between reader and madman. Dostoevsky replays the slide into insanity from the inside, before any transcript of it could be made. With schizophrenia, this is not an easy task. We watch, or hear, the consciousness of Golyadkin break in two, as one side of his humiliated persona tries to assure the other side that everything he does is "normal, quite all right" (visiting his doctor, forcing his way into a party uninvited, or simply waiting on the trash-filled landing for the right moment to enter, knowing it will cause a scandal and in denial about that knowledge). Finally, one side of this persona actually materializes, breaks off into a body, and evolves from Golyadkin's companion into his rival and betrayer.

Hovering over these split, frightened, defensive voices is a narrator with access to all three perspectives – but only erratically. That access might be an illusion as well. The reader cannot know, just as Golyadkin's mind cannot know, the reliability of any source. Although the beginning and end of the story remain Gogol's, the madman's experience in between is thicker and scarier. The reader no longer merely observes a single disintegrating consciousness but participates in it, and must work hard to ascertain who is speaking, and from where. This technique, which grew out of an apprenticeship to Gogol, became Dostoevsky's signature narrative style.

Another strategy for replaying a book occurs in Dostoevsky's maiden work, *Poor Folk*. The poor clerk of this epistolary novel, Makar Devushkin, receives from Varenka, his female correspondent and platonic love interest, two stories to read: Pushkin's "Stationmaster" (one of the Belkin Tales) and Gogol's "Overcoat." He misreads both – which is Dostoevsky's device for deepening our understanding of the hero. Devushkin, an aspiring writer in the Age of Realism, has no concept of fiction. He loves the Pushkin story because he identifies with (and sympathizes with) Dunya's father, the embittered old man who takes to drink after losing his daughter to the dashing Minsky. But Devushkin is scandalized by "The Overcoat." Clearly it had been written by someone who had spied on *him*, in all his poverty and misery. "I can no longer live in peace in my little corner," Devushkin complains. Who knows what other people will "worm their way into my nest, to spy out how I'm living … whether I have boots and how they've been soled, what I eat, what I drink, what I copy out."[26] As their exchange of letters proceeds, however, this untalented reader Devushkin, who eventually loses his Varenka to her earlier seducer, actually learns how to see and to write. His literary tastes, initially appalling (trashy steamy potboilers and parodies of Gogol's Ukrainian tales), improve dramatically. His final letters to Varenka describe the lives and deaths in his tenement house with discreet compassion. Then she departs. His real life lost out to their epistolary novel.

The darkness of this theme expands as Dostoevsky's talent matures. Both *White Nights* and *Notes from Underground* feature a hero – or anti-hero – of contemporary consciousness cobbled together out of literary bits and pieces. In the longer novels, this "underground" tension between "writing down an event in order to be honest to it" and "writing down an event so that others can read it as a piece of literature" produces the false confession. These documents are intended by their confessing authors to lend dignity to their lives, over which they have lost control. Most of them fail. Midway through *The Idiot*, at Prince Myshkin's birthday party at Pavlovsk, the eighteen-year-old Ippolit, in and out of hysteria and dying of consumption, reads out loud to a reluctant gathering his just-authored "Essential Explanation" that is to preface his suicide at dawn (Part III, chs. 4–7). The document crams into one breathless sequence all his convictions, experiences, personal outrage, dreams – the final testament by which he wished to be remembered. And everything is a fiasco: the audience guffaws at it, the pistol misfires, and Ippolit dies without fanfare, in the margins, almost unnoticed further on in the novel.

The Demons [mistranslated as *The Possessed*] contains an equivalently "false" and failed document, a chapter censored from the first publication of the novel: "Stavrogin's Confession." In it the blighted hero confesses, among other ugly incidents, his violation of a fourteen-year-old girl and her subsequent suicide by hanging. As Stavrogin informs his confessor, Bishop Tikhon, this statement is to be printed up in 300 copies and distributed. Tikhon, something of a holy fool, begs his visitor not to broadcast his sins but to atone in some other less boastful way. Stung to the quick, Stavrogin accuses him – as the fictional Devushkin had accused the Gogol who authored "The Overcoat" – of spying on him, prying into his soul. This contradictory gesture of desiring publicity and yet resenting it as an abuse of privacy is part of Russian literature's rich assimilation of Rousseau's *Confessions*. Dostoevsky understood it as the book writer's permanent lure. "Writing something up" and "making my own what another has written" were for him always primal acts, demonically attractive.

A poor clerk like Devushkin fretting over his look-alike in "The Stationmaster" or "The Overcoat" is a form of affectionate parody. Other sorts of Dostoevskian interventions, not in secular books but in the Book – the Christian Bible – were closer to blasphemy. One such is the Grand Inquisitor's recasting of the Three Temptations of Christ in the Wilderness (Matthew 4:1–11) in *The Brothers Karamazov*, where the Catholic Church is shown to be serving Satan. Dostoevsky embeds that extraordinary monologue in several layers of "relativizing" text. In the inner narrative frame, Christ receives the Inquisitor's tirade silently and bestows upon the old man a kiss (the kiss of forgiveness? the kiss of Judas?). Alyosha bestows an equivalent kiss on his brother in the outer frame. And Ivan, who recites the tale, dismisses the entire literary effort as an "absurd thing" – even though, he insists, every author should have at least one listener. But the force and eloquence of this blasphemous replay of the Gospels was such that Dostoevsky himself despaired of creating an image of the Elder Zosima that could compete with the rhetoric of the Grand Inquisitor.

Such embeddings and re-accentings of prior literary texts were not of special urgency to Leo Tolstoy. He distrusted equally both the original and its subsequent wrappings.

Tolstoy and doing without words

Tolstoy hoped that the media revolution would not only advertise his own moral message, but also make all verbal art more honest. In August 1908, on his eightieth birthday, he was interviewed about the cinema. Of course this new technology will be exploited by businessmen – "where are there not businessmen?", Tolstoy remarked – but films were wonderful: responsive, infectious, and so much more flexible to write for than the stage, which was "a halter choking the throat of the dramatist." "You will see that this little clicking contraption with its revolving handle will make a revolution in our life – in the life of writers," he insisted. "The cinema has divined the mystery of motion, and that is greatness."[27] At the end of his life, the world's most famous wordsmith and enemy of technology contemplated writing a screenplay. He foresaw in the art of (still silent) film a chance for images to live forever, sacrificing none of their wholeness, visibility, or mobility: one answer, perhaps, to the insult of death. Significantly, it was capturing the motion that mattered. Tolstoy leapt at the possibility of communication that reduced the need for uttered words.

For just because a writer is a superb craftsman with his chosen material – in this case, words – does not mean that he need trust or respect the morality of his medium. Tolstoy often found himself in this dilemma. His despair was not that of the Romantic or Symbolist poet who lamented that inspiration was always so divine and execution so tedious. Tolstoy was just as suspicious of poetic inspiration (in his view, a markedly indulgent form of intoxication) as he eventually became of meat, liquor, grand opera, and sexual arousal. What appalled Tolstoy was second-hand experience, and from that perspective his relation to books is fascinating. One of the best read and most learned men of his age, Tolstoy detected falsehood in almost all formal systems of education. He was a compulsive diarist and a superb letter-writer. But early on, Tolstoy wished to express what he felt to be true more directly, from the point of view of nature itself.

His major challenge in this matter of uncovering life's truth was not competition with earlier worldly writers (Gogol or Pushkin) but the very fact, or indignity, of having to pass human experience through the word at all. Language was too convention-driven, the act of writing too prideful, the act of reading too passive. Dostoevsky worked variations (and at times vicious parodies) on earlier writers or plots to whom he was indebted. Chekhov in the early 1880s wrote dozens of slight but amusing parodies of earlier literary styles from Karamzin to Gogol to Turgenev. Tolstoy, however, rarely took on other writers in his fiction. Why add another obfuscating layer of words? In Chapter 10 of his 1852 tale "The Raid," he remarks on the relationship between Russian courage and French phrase-making on the battlefield. When a man "feels within himself the capacity to perform a great deed, no talk of any kind is needed."[28] Tolstoy had always been eager to shock us out of being a mere audience: not only to other writers, but equally to the products of his own writing self.

A startling example comes in Tolstoy's 1855 Crimean War story, "Sevastopol in December," designed as a "tour" addressed to the reader-"tourist" in the second person.[29] Here you see a pile of coal, over there frozen manure, the carcass of a horse, now notice this whizzing cannonball, a cart full of corpses, a gorgeous sunrise, an amputation clinic, and although your first impression is disagreeable, look more closely, for "the truth is altogether different." But of course looking more closely into his story will never equal being there. Gradually this truth (a complex one) becomes clear to the reader, as we are drawn in to the suffering and heroism of the scene. Once drawn in, we begin to feel guilty for being mere observers via the printed word, whereas the war is being fought by participants whose bodies are dying. It is testimony to Tolstoy's art in these Sevastopol sketches that the tsar wept at the courage and patriotism he saw displayed there, whereas other readers consider them among the most damning anti-war literature ever written. Later, in a famous episode in *War and Peace* (Book Three, Part II, chs. 31–32), Tolstoy will fill in all the steps of this incriminating process. His topic is again the (literal) theatre of war: Pierre Bezukhov, in a crisp civilian swallow-tail coat and white top hat, "goes to watch" the Battle of Borodino at what soon becomes one of its bloodiest sites, the Rayevsky Redoubt. He emerges unharmed, but horrified, from the mud and carnage.

Chekhov will use the same second-person ethical "wake-up" device of the guided tour in his grim parable "Ward Number Six" (1892), in order to introduce his reader to the lunatic wing – or prison – of a corrupt provincial hospital. "If you do not mind being stung by nettles," suggests the narrator, "let us go along the narrow path . . ." The inmate Ivan Gromov (who suffers from persecution mania) and Doctor Ragin (the good-natured but slothful medical man who negligently committed Gromov to the ward years earlier) are intellectual opponents of Dostoevskian intensity. Both incline toward philosophy. Quite by accident, the doctor rediscovers his patient and begins visiting him, for he is "the most interesting person in town." Citing the Cynic Diogenes, Ragin rationalizes his inability to intervene against evil deeds. Gromov, disgusted, responds with a defense of activism. The story ends as it must: Ragin's medical staff diagnoses him as ill (that is, imprisons him in the ward) together with his patient; Ragin dies of a stroke on the first evening spent locked inside a reality that he had not bothered to register or resist while he was free. Both Gromov and Ragin had been passionate readers of books. And remarkable about both the bookish Pierre Bezukhov and the bookish Doctor Ragin – healthy, thoughtful, free men – is the extreme slowness of their waking-up to the difference between reading a book, and being there. "Ward Number Six" is often taken as Chekhov's criticism of Tolstoy's doctrine of non-violent resistance to evil.

Doubtless it is that – but it also sounds a chord of recurrent Tolstoyan concern. How can reading, as a habit of the body and mind, be made less pleasant, less easy, more a goad to action?

It is characteristic of this "Tolstoyan" story of Chekhov's, and of Tolstoy himself, that the very process of reading is targeted for attention rather than the content of the work being read or witnessed. Dostoevsky tells you straight out that Devushkin is reading Pushkin and Gogol (and precisely which stories); immediately a dialogue starts up between works of literature. But Tolstoy scholars are still debating the identity of the unnamed English novel that Anna Karenina is reading on the train back to St. Petersburg after meeting Vronsky in Moscow, and also – to shift to the performing arts – the identity of the unnamed opera that Natasha watches in *War and Peace*, which primes her to be seduced by Anatole Kuragin. (There is no consensus on the novel, although it seems to be by Trollope; the most recent hypothesis on the opera is Giacomo Meyerbeer's *Robert Le Diable*.)[30] What concerns Tolstoy is not the text, not its specific characters, plots, or ideas, but the physiological effect on the human body of the physically passive but often arousing activities of reading, watching, and experiencing art.

The finest example of this concern is Tolstoy's late story "The Kreutzer Sonata" (1889). Not music itself, but remembering how his wife had created such music with the violinist "for no practical reason" is what enflames the jealous husband Pozdnyshev, both against his wife and against Beethoven. Pozdnyshev considers himself a "madman," and the courtroom that tried him for murdering his wife concurred with the criminal, bestowing a verdict of temporary insanity. But as with all of Tolstoy's fools and social outcasts – quite distinct from the Gogol–Dostoevsky line of madmen, who are not used in this way – a truth is transmitted through them that is intended to wake up the rest of comfortable humanity. Tolstoy stood behind many of Pozdnyshev's maddest views. The powerful art of music, like the powerful art of the word, should be deployed only in the service of brotherhood. At the very least, it must not draw attention to itself as art, and whatever emotions it arouses must be usefully discharged, attached to a desired action. If a funeral, then a lament; if a battle, then fife and drum. Since the salon provides no proper moral conduit for channeling the energy released by art – just small talk and sherbet – how could there not be infidelity, jealousy, murder?

Best of all is to show people doing without words altogether. Responsive glances from a loving face will do the necessary work. The most famous of these word-free scenes in Tolstoy, the courtship between Kitty and Levin in *Anna Karenina* (Part IV, ch. 13) is based on Tolstoy's own magical experience proposing marriage to Sofya Andreyevna Behrs in 1862. Kitty and Levin meet unexpectedly at a dinner party at the Oblonskys in Moscow. Timing is all. By now she has recovered from her rejection by Vronsky; Levin too has recovered from the insult of her initial rejection of him. Through glances and gestures, Kitty and Levin forgive each other and already trust in each other's love. The actual marriage proposal is conveyed through a parlor game, *secrétaire*, in which the players must guess out sentences and replies solely from the initial letters of words. Kitty and Levin guess out a great deal, grabbing the chalk from one another, but at a certain point "a darkening came over him from happiness. He simply could not pick out the words she had in mind; but in her lovely eyes shining with happiness he understood everything he needed to know" (p. 398).

An equivalently famous episode in *Crime and Punishment* – when the hero and heroine realize their love and commit to each other – might help to focus, albeit in extreme form, the difference between a Dostoevskian dependence on the Book as mediator, and a Tolstoyan striving to reach the realm of the authentic without having to rely on words. That "love story" comes about in three installments, Raskolnikov's three visits to Sonya Marmeladova in Parts IV (ch. 4), V (ch. 4), and VI (ch. 8) of the novel. The grounds for this love are laid in their first meeting. Raskolnikov seeks out Sonya in her quarters. Bewildered at her faith in God amid such moral filth, he concludes she is a holy fool (and fears that in her company he will become one too). He demands that she read to him the account of the Rising of Lazarus, but rummaging around in the Gospels he can't find the passage. Sonya sternly reprimands him, takes the Bible, locates the page, but does not need to read it: she need only recite. She has *become* its narrative. After the Lazarus story is over Sonya closes the book, at which moment Raskolnikov promises to come to her the next day and tell her who killed Lizaveta. Of this pivotal scene Dostoevsky writes that the candle was flickering out, "casting a dim light in this destitute room upon the murderer and the harlot strangely come together over the reading of the eternal book" (IV, ch. 4, p. 328). Everything about this scene speaks of a Dostoevskian epiphany. In Dostoevsky, knowledge is communal and symbolic.

In Tolstoy, as in Pushkin, "understanding what one needs to know" depends not on accessing or citing a verbal narrative, but on proper maturation. Lay down the right habits or structures in the individual, and wisdom will come at the right time – even without words. This knowledge cannot be forced by merely "talking it out," with oneself or another person. The most terrible example of that hopeless strategy is Anna Karenina's lengthy "monologue" to herself before her suicide (Part VII, chs. 26–31). By this point in the novel, Anna's heightened consciousness rivals the Underground Man's in its alertness to its own perversity. She makes impossible demands on Vronsky and impossibly contradictory demands on herself (unwilling to give up society, son, or lover, she is aware that no structure exists capable of containing them all). She will punish Vronsky for that fact, not for the infidelity of which she accuses him even as she knows her suspicions are unfounded. Everyone she sees on that fatal ride to the train station is reduced to mean-spirited caricature. She is not in delirium – that is the terror of the passage – but she understands her needy self with absolute clarity and does not wish to entertain any other opinion about it: "my love grows ever more passionate and self-centered, and his keeps fading and fading . . ." (p. 763). Only at the final moment of her life does the candle flare up "by which she had been reading that book filled with anxieties, deceptions, grief, and evil" (p. 768). In addition to lies and grief, that book might have contained truth – but Tolstoy, here as with the dying Ivan Ilyich, gives his questing heroes access to it only at the final irreversible moment, after the wretched pattern of their lives has claimed its due.

Anna's awful death prompts one additional contrast between Dostoevsky and Tolstoy: how best to come to terms with one's guilt. In a Tolstoyan world, which is intensely concerned that each autonomous "I" improve its behavior, the worst possible habit I can acquire is to insist on my helplessness and inability to initiate, on my own, some small betterment in my life. In a Dostoevskian world, relying on oneself is no special virtue – but the "I" does have obligations. Here, the worst habit for any character is to say that someone else is guilty. Best always is to insist that "*I* am guilty," I am responsible to all. The guilty Dostoevskian "I" is not Tolstoy's, however, and herein lies the meat of the comparison. Even if technically you are innocent – as Dmitry Karamazov is innocent of parricide, and as his brother Ivan is innocent – admit your guilt anyway, take responsibility. Let someone else say (as Alyosha says to his brothers): "It wasn't you." For Dostoevsky, it is the task of *others* to absolve you of your worst suspicions; it is not for you to reason it out and absolve yourself. The more wary, stubborn, guilt-ridden Tolstoyan personality does not invite others inside to share the burden or negotiate the terms. In this difference we see the core of Tolstoy's radical and brave individualism, and Dostoevsky's radical and brave dialogism.

Poets and novelists (Dostoevsky and Nekrasov)

The controversial opposition above, between single-voiced (or individualistic) monologism and multivoiced (other-dependent) dialogism, we owe to Mikhail Bakhtin – who assigned Tolstoy, his less loved example, to one side of the divide and Dostoevsky to the other. But Bakhtin initiated an even more controversial binary in his writings of the 1930s, between novels and poetry.[31] True novels, he argued, strive toward polyphonic fullness, with competing voices that address one another horizontally, and they are "Copernican" to the extent that the author is displaced from the center of the fictive universe (novels are open, translatable, and thrive on alien input). Purely "poetic style," in contrast, tends toward the single-voiced and unitary, locating its idealized, silent, or solipsistic addressee along a vertical axis (poetry talks to itself in a static utopian language, associated by Bakhtin with a "Ptolemaic" worldview that demands affirmation and identity, not dialogue). Bakhtin's novel–poetry distinction is striking, but crude and (unless qualified) easily refuted. Our partial refutation of it here will permit us to touch briefly upon the fate and variety of poetry during the age of the great Russian novel (1850s–80s), through an episode in the work of Dostoevsky.

Dostoevsky, arch-novelist and polyphonist, remained throughout his life a Romantic realist. Although he did not write poetry himself, he was temperamentally attuned to the vigorous civic verse being practiced by Nikolai Nekrasov (1821–78), journalist and leading poet of the "Realist school." Poetry did not disappear at the end of the Golden Age, with the deaths of Pushkin and Lermontov. But it changed its status and venue. The radical wing of Russia's fledgling institution of literary criticism declared poetry no longer the voice of the gods but (at best) a rhythmically effective means of communicating social ills. When the aristocratic salon gave way to the bookseller's market, lower-brow poetic genres began to flourish: satires, street ballads, urban romances, opera libretti, and folk-based narrative poetry (often in authentic dialect, with shocking rhythms and images) describing the lot of the Russian peasant. Nekrasov excelled in the last of these genres, both while a struggling student and later as a publisher. In 1846, Nekrasov acquired the journal *The Contemporary*, founded by Pushkin ten years earlier, and transformed it into a forum for civic poetry so critical of Russian social reality that the journal was closed by government decree in 1866. Nekrasov promptly purchased another journal and became its editor-in-chief. But startling images in his poems from the 1850s published in *The Contemporary* had already found their way into Dostoevsky's *Crime and Punishment*.

Nekrasov, like Dostoevsky, was a newspaper man. He was also a pioneer in poetic – and *lyrical* – expressions of those plotless observations and ruminations that by the 1850s had become a common feature in "news around town" columns of the Russian periodical press. In 1859, Nekrasov published his lengthy narrative poem *On the Weather* [*O pogode*], whose first part is subtitled "Street Impressions." In tone and literary device it resembles the first of

Tolstoy's Sevastopol stories, in which the reader is taken on a "tour" of a city under active bombardment as if it were a museum (or a guidebook). Nekrasov's images from this poem end up not in Tolstoy, however, but in Dostoevsky, at the moral center of Raskolnikov's graphic dream of the beating, and then brutal murder, of an exhausted mare.

Nekrasov's narrator in *On the Weather* strolls through the town, taking in the sounds and sights, each one more cruel than the other. Before sundown he comes upon a crippled mare [*loshad'-kaleka*] dragging an impossibly heavy load. She staggers; her driver grabs a log: "(the knout, it seems, isn't enough) – / And he set to beating her, beating her!" The mare sinks back, legs splayed, "sighed deeply / And gazed . . . (as people gaze, / Succumbing to unjust attacks)." The driver beats her across the back, the sides, "across her weeping, gentle eyes." Throughout this ghastly scene the narrator gazes at the tortured horse, grows angry and then depressed. "And shouldn't I intercede for her?" he asks himself mournfully. "Nowadays it's all the fashion to sympathize, / We'd have nothing against helping you, / A mute victim of the people, – / But we cannot even help ourselves!"[32] In the end the narrator-voyeur does nothing. The wretched mare rallies and sets off jerkily down the street, rewarded for her efforts by more blows. When Rodion Raskolnikov dreams this scene in the novel, it is the passivity of Nekrasov's spectator-poet (duplicated in his own cautious father, who assures his son "it's not our business") that impels the young boy to rush to the dying mare and kiss her bleeding eyes. Little Rodya will not "sympathize and do nothing." He *will* "help himself" – by murdering the pawnbroker and thereby righting injustice. That solution too proves to be a disaster. Neither Dostoevsky later nor Nekrasov in this poem offers an easy exit from this moral paralysis. But Nekrasov does demonstrate that poetry, even the most fragile lyric, is fully capable of carrying a civic burden and obligating the reader to respond to it. In 1856, he published in *The Contemporary* an eight-line poem that would also resonate with *Crime and Punishment* a decade later: "Yesterday, a bit after five / I walked out on Haymarket Square; / A woman was being beaten with the knout, / A young peasant woman. / No sound came forth from her chest, / only the whip whistled, playing . . . / And I said to the Muse: 'Behold! / Your sister!'" To insist, as Nekrasov does, that a violated woman is sister to the Muse would have been alien to the poetics of Pushkin and Lermontov but was well within the realm of the great moral Realists, Dostoevsky and Tolstoy. It provides an appropriate transition to Chekhov. As a seer, Chekhov was both of the spirit and of the flesh. As a writer he was far less obsessed with mortality, very possibly because he was forced – both professionally as a medical man and on the testimony of his own organism – to confront it far earlier.

Anton Chekhov: lesser expectations, smaller forms

Chekhov's relations with Dostoevsky were not profound. He referred to him rarely in his letters, ironically in his works, and had to force himself to finish *Crime and Punishment* (by age forty, he promised himself, he would get to the end; he did, and he was not impressed). Tolstoy, however, was an abiding presence in Chekhov's life. The two writers were on very friendly terms. Beginning in the late 1890s, both were obliged to winter in the Crimea for health reasons, although Chekhov, thirty years younger, was by far the sicker man. Chekhov's "Tolstoyan period" began in the mid-1880s, when he was twenty-five, and lasted for ten years. As Chekhov wrote to his friend Aleksei Suvorin, he had been swept up by Tolstoy's immense energy and intellect, his authority, by his "very reasonableness, and no doubt a species of hypnotism peculiar to him."[33] The "reasonableness" or common sense of Tolstoy's prose – its reliance on sober observation, logical clarity, and its subtle depiction of nuanced emotional states – offered special benefits to a young writer like Chekhov, who specialized in short forms. Before the 1880s, the short story had been largely a Sentimental or Romantic genre: nostalgic, conventionalized, felt to be a relic or fragment from an earlier era. Literary seriousness meant the big serialized novel, a cutting edge acknowledged by all writers. Even short-story masterpieces, such as Turgenev's *Sportsman's Sketches* (1852), were gathered together and sequenced by their author into a cycle. Realism was descriptive, full of ideas, fearless in its psychological probing, and long.

To be sure, the novel did have some competition. In the 1850s, the ethnographic "sketch" [*ocherk*] and newspaper *feuilleton* [from Fr. "leaf" or "sheet of paper," usually street news or gossip by a roving observer or *flâneur*] emerged as favored short forms for recording everyday life, both urban and rural. Each featured a chatty, mobile first-person narrator whose job it was to report on the local terrain. Both the "sketch" and the "leaf" grew out of periodical print genres, the gossip column and the theatre- or special-interest section of newspapers, which were widespread in the popular press that was Chekhov's literary apprenticeship. Dostoevsky extended this form far beyond a stroll around the city. His *Notes from Underground* (1864), which grew out of the intent to write a hostile review of Chernyshevsky's *What is to be Done?*, became philosophical satire once Dostoevsky turned over the story to an irritable, first-person voice filtered through a well-read urban columnist, trapped for some reason in a dark garret where the only newsworthy item he could report on was himself.

Chekhov was obliged to support himself by his pen and early became a master of the chatty topical sketch. In his hundreds of commissioned stories he parodied almost every style and genre that Russian literature had known. In his "Death of a Clerk," a comic rewriting of Gogol's "Overcoat," a titular councilor inadvertently sneezes on a general during an opera performance at a provincial theatre and, unable to persuade the general to take his apology seriously, dies (literally) of shame.[34] Such cameo parodies were supplanted in the mid-1880s by his first mature work, the spatial tone-poem "Steppe," published in a serious literary journal when Chekhov was twenty-eight. After 1888, he rapidly acquired the perspective and intonation peculiar to him, one far more lyrical than parodic or chatty. Chekhov is lyrical not in the way of most lyric poets, however, but in a distinctly "clinical" way; as a medical doctor. How Chekhov looked at the follies of the body, and to what extent he felt an author had the right to intervene, diagnose, systematize, and pass judgment on those follies, will be our focus in this final section.

Tolstoy cast a long shadow on Chekhov's generation. But not all of the mature Tolstoy struck Chekhov as reasonable – especially his theories on sexuality and illness, of obvious interest to a doctor. Together with Russia and much of Europe, Chekhov read "The Kreutzer Sonata" in 1889 and followed the ensuing scandal. In various supplemental tracts to that story, Tolstoy argued that women instinctively dislike the carnal relation, that intercourse while pregnant or nursing causes hysteria, and that celibacy within marriage would guarantee the physical and spiritual health of both parties. In response, Chekhov complained to his friend Aleksei Pleshcheyev in February 1894 that Tolstoy "out of sheer stubbornness has never taken the time to read two or three pamphlets written by specialists." Chekhov was correct: Tolstoy had no use for specialists. Gorky reports Tolstoy saying of Chekhov that his profession spoiled him. "If he hadn't been a doctor he would have written still better" ("Memoirs," p. 71). In Tolstoy's view, a clinical approach to the human condition could only blur its duties. In 1897, Tolstoy remarked that Chekhov was highly gifted but "writes like a decadent and impressionist, in the broad sense of the term." In the winter of 1900, Tolstoy took in a performance of a Chekhov play at the Moscow Art Theatre and wrote in his diary (January 27): "Went to see *Uncle Vanya* and was shocked." What shocked him he doesn't say, but we might speculate.

The play provides no moral resolution. There is also no cumulative action, motion, or lessons learned. The old professor and his young wife Elena arrive at the beginning and depart at the end. The presence of this provocative couple throughout four acts inspires one unsuccessful declaration of love, one unsuccessful suicide, one unsuccessful seduction; in fact, "everyone in this play is a loser."[35] The closest thing to a "deed" is the professor's fantastic proposal to sell his daughter Sonya's estate on terms advantageous to him in his retirement. Comically impotent moments are highlighted by references to literary classics.

In Act III, the professor launches his self-serving plan by quoting the mayor's opening line from Gogol's famous play: "Gentlemen, I have invited you here to announce that we are about to be visited by a government inspector." The joke falls flat. Later in that same explosive scene, Sonya's uncle Vanya, enraged, shouts at the old professor: "My life's ruined. I'm gifted, intelligent, courageous. If I'd had a normal life I might have been a Schopenhauer or a Dostoevsky. But I'm talking nonsense, I'm going mad . . ." Indeed, Tolstoy would not like this sort of comedy. And Dostoevsky – for whom madness was metaphysical and symbolic – would not have understood it either. Chekhov's four great dramas and over six hundred short stories represent an ambitious, calculated descent from the didactic comedy of earlier centuries and from the heights of the Great Russian Novel as well. We will view this descent through two lenses: illness, and the *Anna Karenina* plot.

Like Dostoevsky, Chekhov was ill for much of his creative life with an incurable disease. Unlike Dostoevsky, who chose to see in his own chronic epilepsy some visionary potential or symbol (while remaining objective enough to give his disease both to a scoundrel, Smerdyakov, and to a righteous man, Prince Myshkin), Chekhov did not make a special point of trying out his consumption on his fictive characters. When he does, as in "The Black Monk" (1894), the result is distanced and chilly: the morally flawed and hallucinating hero dies in a rush of blood from the throat, presided over by an apparition of the sinister monk. But no judgment is passed on the unhappy hero.

Tolstoy despised doctors, and in this area he never missed a chance to pass judgment. He never allows his heroes to be cured by medical professionals. Freed from French captivity (which had, characteristically, disciplined his body and improved his health), Pierre Bezukhov falls ill for three months, "but despite their treatment – with bloodletting and various medicines – he recovered" (*War and Peace*, Book Four, Part IV, ch. 12, p. 1228). Doctors summoned in Tolstoy's novels are useless, harmful, usually charlatans – and when examining a young girl, always lascivious charlatans. For Tolstoy, the body is a serious matter, a source of joy and our singular means to appreciate nature. But its owner is obliged to monitor it constantly, because the "animal principle" will struggle against the higher purposes of the soul. No amount of "scientific treatment" imposed upon the body from outside will cure it. The frailer, more physically vulnerable Dostoevsky needed and respected doctors, granting them considerable professional competence. But in Dostoevsky's fiction, as in Tolstoy's, illness is often metaphorical, melodramatic, graphically shocking. Chekhov strikes a more sober and objective note. His work features a large number of doctors, and among them – this is a new note for Russian literature – illness can be almost comic.

Chekhov saw what medical people can hardly avoid seeing: that possessing a mortal body means sooner or later something will go wrong with it – it will make a fool of itself, sicken, and die. Cancer and consumption follow their own rules, of course. But the same treatment, or the same accident, can have no effect on one organism, awful consequences on another, curative effects on a third. The body is not obliged to explain itself. Thus the body cannot be conceived as a moral unit. Medical records are neither shocking nor symbolically meaningful. They are records of an organism's rise and fall. Pain, too, is simply there; it buys nothing and redeems nothing. In what is probably the most famous passage in all of Chekhov, from his short masterpiece "Lady with a Pet Dog" (1899), we are shown how this moral blankness can actually be recruited for human well-being and hope. Gurov and Anna Sergeyevna are sitting on the beach at dawn and listening to the "monotonous muffled noise of the sea":

> It had made that noise down below when neither Yalta nor Oreanda existed; it was making that noise now, and would continue to make that noise in that same hushed and indifferent way when we are no longer here. And in that permanence, in that complete indifference to the life and death of each one of us, is perhaps concealed a guarantee of our eternal salvation, a guarantee of the constant movement of life on earth and of endless perfection.[36]

In Chekhov, then, pain, illness, and dying are tragic in a clinical and local sense only, not in a moral sense. Death is not punitive, and survival is more a matter of good fortune or timing than of ethical absolutes. Two stories are exemplary in this regard, among the darkest in the canon. In each, one detects a doctor's trained eye, and a doctor's tactful, tolerant commiseration that does not pretend to know what it cannot know.

The short story "Enemies" (1887) opens five minutes after Kirilov, a district doctor, has lost his only child, a boy of six, to diphtheria. His wife is stretched out in despair over the dead body; the doctor's hands are burnt with carbolic acid, the standard disinfectant for this contagious disease. At that moment a neighboring landowner knocks, in a panic, to summon the doctor: his wife has just fallen dangerously ill; can the doctor come? Kirilov says no, he is in mourning. The distraught man persists; finally the doctor, in a stupor, climbs into his carriage, and upon arrival at the man's manor house it is discovered that the wife had feigned illness to run off with her lover, their house guest. Both doctor and client are stunned. This farce allows each to give furious vent to his individual grief. "Never in their lives," Chekhov writes, "had they uttered so much that was unjust, cruel, and absurd. The unhappy are egotistic, spiteful, unjust, cruel, and less capable of understanding each other than fools. Unhappiness does not bring people together but draws them apart . . ."[37] In this story there is no philosophy, no attempt at transcendence, no defense of the nobility of suffering. Dostoevsky and Tolstoy would have tried to provide both. Most Chekhovian characters lack the energy for such transformations.

The second story does present an epiphany, but it is a clinical one – and also stained with carbolic acid. This is "The Name-day Party" (1888), narrated from the perspective of a woman seven months pregnant. Throughout the tedious day, corseted in to conceal her condition, the wife watches her attractive husband act the charming host to young girls while she, exhausted, obliged to be gracious to unwanted guests, resents both him and his reluctance to confide his troubles to her. Name-days – the Russian equivalent of birthdays, celebrated not on your birth date but on the official day of the saint after which you were named – were important family events and full-day celebratory affairs. It is an ordinary stressed day in the obligatory social life of a marriage. But it ends with premature labor, an operation, death of the infant, an unknown number of blank days and nights, the despair of the husband, and for the wife, a "mistiness in the brain from chloroform" and "dull indifference to life." The husband weeps by the window and wrings his hands: "Olya! Why didn't we take thought for our child?"

But there had been no reason to take special thought. At the end of this bleak story, no specific person or event is to blame. It was a ghastly accident. Chekhov is astute at presenting the frivolities and insincerities of both social and family life, and the name-day party was indeed a strain. But neither corsets nor social conventions were necessarily lethal to an unborn child. If the doctors treating Olya discovered why her body had suddenly broken down and miscarried, Chekhov doesn't tell us. He cannot and will not do what Tolstoy does in "The Death of Ivan Ilyich" written two years earlier, which is to condemn everything the suffering hero had lived by – that entire round of legal and social duties that made up the life of the condemned judge, Ivan Ilyich – in order to justify the ghastly accident (cancer) that led to his death. No narrator has the right to reconstitute moral causality with such assurance and pass final judgment. About this matter Chekhov felt very strongly: he even wrote "A Tedious Story" (1889), his counter-version of a "bad death," in response to Tolstoy's didactic Ivan Ilyich.

On this matter of radical contingency and tragic accident, Chekhov would have considered Dostoevsky even less of a precedent. The symbolic move made at the end of *The Brothers Karamazov*, where Alyosha gathers all grieving parties together on a note of rejoicing and reaffirmation after Ilyusha Snegiryov's death, is not available in Chekhov's world. A better lesson from the lives and deaths of children, perhaps, can be found in mid-career Tolstoy: the fate of Petya Rostov in *War and Peace*. A life lovingly nurtured for seven years over a thousand pages is cut down by a random bullet in a single paragraph. It is a terrible shock in fiction, a shock of real-life proportions, to lose so casually a person we have come to know well. Getting to know a character can be a challenge in the short narrative form. In the newspaper sketches Chekhov wrote for a living in the early 1880s, he was often limited to a per-story length of one hundred lines. In very short compass, how might a writer deepen and thicken an environment so that meaningful choice, genuine accident, and the wisdom (or folly) of other lives can be experienced through it?

One means for adding dimensions to a work of slender compass is to evoke earlier, familiar literary worlds and fictive characters. The young Dostoevsky did this brilliantly with Gogol, and Chekhov often avails himself of this strategy. But mere isolated interjections tend to be ironic or unkind. In *The Duel*, for example, Layevsky is reminded of Anna Karenina's dislike of her husband's ears at just the moment when the white neck and curls of his own mistress are getting on his nerves. Such passing references make their point – both about Anna and about Layevsky's lazy use of literary images for self-justification – but overall, Chekhov seeks to communicate on a plane more durable than ridicule. He wishes to examine other ways of adjusting to reality. For Chekhov is not so much a "realist" as he is an *accepter of reality*. His much discussed "comedic" quality probably originates here. Thus he gives us the genuine tragic accidents – "Enemies," "The Name-day Party," tragedies of the failure to heal or cure – and then the false tragedies, which are in fact comedic. These are situations felt as tragic by their indolent or self-pitying participants who cannot (or will not) act to change their situation, although they are free to do so. From Chekhov's correspondence, we know that he considered such laziness to be a major vice of his age, and if his dramas were indeed the comedies he called them, it was because they built their plots out of this vice. Chekhov might have been drawn to recast *Anna Karenina* in just this direction, because the one thing that this tragic Tolstoyan heroine refused to do was to adjust to the reality that her own actions had brought about. By the 1880s, *Anna Karenina* was already an "infidelity stereotype." The briefest reference to a plot detail (black unruly curls, meeting a future lover at a ball, squinting or screwing up one's eyes when lying to oneself, prominent jutting ears, trains, or simply the name "Anna") invokes the whole. Chekhov rewrote that whole several times, each time in a different key.

In the 1886 story "A Calamity," a young woman with a sluggish, preoccupied husband is being courted passionately by a neighboring lawyer, Ilyin. He is ashamed of his behavior but attractive to her because of it. Trains are prominent in the story – some train whistle is always interrupting his entreaties – but not as a tragic motif. The story ends as the heroine is rushing out the door to a tryst with the persistent and lovesick Ilyin; her husband wasn't interested in hearing about her temptation, her daughter suddenly struck her as phlegmatic. The young wife is disgusted at her own duplicity, appetite, and ordinariness (to that extent she is still an "Anna"). But to balance those self-recriminating Tolstoyan moments, she is also curious, excited, and willing. Chekhov does not dismiss the seriousness and validity of lust. Like a doctor he gently probes its dynamics. The heroine will learn some sort of lesson from this "Calamity," but it will not be a tragic one.

The same non-tragic message, albeit in a cynical key, underlies "Anna on the Neck" (1895). Anna Petrovna, eighteen-year-old beauty from a poor family married against her will to a pompous middle-aged bureaucrat, quickly perceives that her husband values her solely as a social asset and stepping stone to higher rank, the Order of St. Anna. This husband is no unexciting but inoffensive Aleksei Karenin; he is a direct descendant of Dostoevsky's Luzhin. But Chekhov's Anna cannot get out of the marriage in time, as Dunya Raskolnikova did, and must adjust to her new reality. After she succeeds in pleasing the appropriate "Excellency" at a gala ball, she calls her husband a blockhead to his face and more honest relations between them are established. Her infidelities become her own business. And she is no longer visited by her nightmare, that a "storm cloud or locomotive was moving in on her to crush her."

In "About Love" (1898), the third rewrite of the novel, Chekhov is already parodying Tolstoy in a deeper, more spiritually satisfying way. Rather than merely supply alternative erotic and cynical contexts for the *Anna* plot, Chekhov now rematches entire Tolstoyan characters. "About Love" is the final story in Chekhov's *Little Trilogy*. Its narrator, Pavel Konstantinovich Alyokhin, closely resembles Tolstoy's Konstantin Levin: a loner, an intellectual turned farmer with a high sense of honor and a habit of severe self-criticism. The love story he relates to his friends concerns his unconsummated passion for Anna Alekseyevna, wife of his good friend, and he frames it with his confession, years later, that the failure to consummate this passion was probably a mistake. Chekhov's variant bears all the marks of a clinical tragedy as he understood that genre: a tragedy of accident and timing. A Levin and a Kitty fall in love – both of them decent, proper people committed to responsible behavior – but they fall in love after the woman has married someone else. This is the plot that could easily have occurred in *Anna Karenina*, but Tolstoy makes sure it will not. He safely removes his attractive Kitty and disillusioned Levin from circulation until the wound caused by their mutual "accident of timing" – her rejection of his initial proposal, his pout over it – could heal on both sides. These two author's pets are granted immunity, which means, a plot "timed" in their favor. Chekhov will have none of that.

Alyokhin and his Anna Alekseyevna are in love. But being neither Anna Kareninas nor Vronskys, not possessing the selfishness or the heroic initiating power required to launch the *Anna* plot, they continue over several years to "do the right thing," which is to do nothing. Irritations and tensions between them increase, to their mutual distress. What energy there is, the would-be lovers spend on kindness and on respecting prior commitments, but both sense its falseness. By their decency and model self-discipline they are, of course, spared Anna's and Vronsky's terrible denouement. But Chekhov will not close on that pellucid moral. "About Love" still ends on a train scene. The reader must decide whether it is a victory or a defeat. In the coach, saying farewell, the two finally confess their love. Relating the story years later, Alyokhin concludes:

> "I realized that when you love someone, your reasoning about that love should be based on what is supreme, on something that is more important than happiness or unhappiness, sin or virtue in the way that they are usually understood, otherwise it is not worth reasoning at all."[38]

What might that supreme thing be, that replaces all reasoning? Chekhov does not say. Although the title of his story echoes Tolstoy's imperious position-papers from his final two decades – "About War," "About Religion," "About Relations between the Sexes," "About Life," – a less Tolstoyan final verdict, unsettling in its openness, could hardly be imagined for a story about extra-marital love.

A year later came the most famous Anna story in all of Chekhov, "Lady with a Pet Dog" (1899). Here too we have our share of trains and theatres. But this is a genuine love story, one of the world's greatest, in which Chekhov mixes Tolstoyan prototypes, and at times Tolstoyan diction, to achieve a new perspective on adultery and adult responsibility. Dmitry Gurov, from whose perspective the tale is told, resembles a Vronsky, or perhaps an Oblonsky; Anna Sergeyevna, whom he meets in Yalta, is a timid, inexperienced Kitty. But there is an important difference: neither Gurov nor Anna Sergeyevna is free. Both have Karenin-like spouses: Gurov's wife is a bluestocking intellectual, Anna Sergeyevna's husband a "flunkey" who serves in some provincial office. The first half of the story is written in the voice zone of a Stiva Oblonsky, from a light philandering position. Anna Sergeyevna's departure on a train back north at the end of the story's Chapter 2 concludes that type of infidelity plot, the "successful one-time affair" that hurts no one and leaves no scars. But then the second half of the story takes both hero and heroine by surprise. It begins to resemble the expansive mid-parts of Tolstoy's novel, where the reader realizes, with excitement and growing dread, that (however absurd it seemed at first) the love between our two adulterers is real. The fact that Vronsky might be a frivolous military officer unworthy of a person of Anna's caliber, or that Anna is trying to have it all in a society where she will be lucky to have even a part, is completely unimportant; they simply love each other, as Tolstoy amply demonstrates. And love works changes. Vronsky becomes stronger, better, more self-critical. Likewise with Chekhov's Gurov: he becomes dissatisfied with his Moscow life. He can't forget Yalta. He tracks down Anna Sergeyevna in the city of S., after which she begins to visit him in Moscow. The "supreme thing that replaced all reasoning" now sits at the center of their lives. A rhythm is established that reflects a deep, and deepening, fidelity. The story ends on the verb "*nachinaetsia*," "beginning": they both felt that "the most complex and difficult part was only just beginning."[39]

At issue here is not only that Anna Sergeyevna, however unhappy, will not commit suicide. The key to the change that Chekhov works on a Tolstoyan worldview – and, I believe, on a Dostoevskian worldview as well – can be found at the story's end, in Gurov's meditations en route to the hotel where Anna is waiting for him. He is explaining to his daughter how thunderstorms work. At the same time he is marveling at the inevitability of a human being having a "double life." There is nothing pathological about this doubling. That we can act in the world *not* as we are "in reality" is, for Gurov, a very good thing. Our public life, "which was visible to everybody who needed to know about it, but was full of conditional truth and conditional deceit" (p. 181), was balanced by a private life, which was hidden from others and in which we are sincere. Doubleness is not duplicity. It is precisely the sincerity of what is hidden that makes tolerance so necessary and moral condemnation so difficult. "And he judged others to be like himself, not believing what he saw, and always supposing that each person's real and most interesting life took place beneath a shroud of secrecy, as if under the veil of night. Every individual existence is a mystery . . ." (p. 181).

This entire meditation, with its binary structure and frequent repetitions, recalls Tolstoy's style. But its moral is purely Chekhovian. Ideally for Tolstoy, there is always an integration between inner and outer. Before a spiritual epiphany can occur, the false life must be brought into line with the true life. The Tolstoyan self strives toward wholeness, even if the moment does not and cannot last. There should be nothing to hide – which is one reason why the Tolstoyan narrator grants himself such extraordinary access to his heroes' inner lives.

The Chekhovian self is more modestly constituted. Its credo is not self-perfection and self-completion, but some other thing, perhaps acceptance of the "indifferent noise of the sea" that, according to some strange impersonal contract, promises us salvation. Chekhov's truths, if he has truths, are not punitive, not public, and not symbolic. Tolstoy could not agree to this. The inadequate, makeshift, purely private and secret structures that sustain true human relations in Chekhov's most luminous stories could not, for Tolstoy, be an acceptable moral resolution. So Tolstoy was to some extent correct when, in 1897, he remarked that Chekhov "wrote like an impressionist." He was wholly incorrect to suggest that Chekhov wrote like a Decadent.

By the turn of the century, "getting out from under Tolstoy," explicitly and implicitly, was a major task for the new generation of Russian writers and artists. This "seer of the flesh" seemed far too cramped and archaic. Writers looked to Pushkin, Dostoevsky, and Chekhov for guidance. Many of them celebrated precisely what Tolstoy despised: mixed-art extravaganzas, opera, the potential of St. Petersburg as a cultural icon. But what they insisted upon most earnestly was mystery at the core of a narrative and of a self.

Chapter 7

Symbolist and Modernist world-building: three cities, three novels, and the Devil

1904–05:	*Russo-Japanese War, ending in Russian defeat*
1905:	*The "first Russian revolution" (general strike, establishment of State Duma)*
1914–17:	*Great War with Germany and Austria (later called World War I)*
1914:	*Zamyatin, a naval engineer, in England supervising the construction of Russian icebreakers*
1917 (spring):	*Strikes, war losses, and corruption at court force abdication of Romanovs; installation of Provisional Government*
1917 (fall)	*Bolshevik seizure of power in Petrograd (St. Petersburg)*
1918–21:	*Civil War between Reds, Greens (peasants), and Whites (tsarist forces)*
1921:	*New Economic Policy (NEP) partially restores capitalism at retail level*
1925:	*Bulgakov begins eleven-year association with Moscow Art Theatre*
1927:	*Closing down of private publishing houses*
1931:	*Zamyatin emigrates from USSR*
1931–33:	*Collectivization and resultant famine claims 1 million lives*
1934:	*Death of Bely at age fifty-four*
1936–38:	*The "Great Terror" (two million Soviet citizens repressed)*
1937:	*Death of Zamyatin of heart disease at age fifty-three*
1940:	*Death of Bulgakov at age forty-nine, blind from uremia, after dictating final draft of "The Master and Margarita" (first publ. 1966)*

In 1893, eight years before publishing his magisterial study "L. Tolstoy and Dostoevsky," the Symbolist critic Dmitry Merezhkovsky (1865–1941) wrote a curious essay titled "On Reasons for the Decline of Contemporary Russian Literature, and on its New Tendencies."[1] It is often taken to mark the end of the Age of the Novel and the beginning of the Symbolist era. In this essay, Merezhkovsky discusses the arrival in Europe of Impressionism, an artistic movement – he approvingly notes – that cared more about mystical content and a heightened use of the poetic symbol than about art's responsibility to socioeconomic problems. Russian literature too had experienced the split in European nineteenth-century culture between a materialist-scientific worldview and an idealist one. But Merezhkovsky then insists that the master Russian prose writers – Tolstoy, Turgenev, Dostoevsky, Ivan Goncharov (1812–91, author of *Oblomov*) – are in fact idealists, although Russia's militant radical critics refused to recognize it. With the exception of the ascetic pamphlets being produced by the aging Tolstoy – who "would take the pipe away from a bachelor, the jug of wine away from a worker, thereby further narrowing and darkening a man's life that was already sufficiently narrow and dark" – the works of these novelists are permeated with symbols, a mystical concern for other worlds, and a quest for the beautiful in art. If (he concluded) we now sense there has been a "decline," it is because literary spokesmen have shouted "utility," critical realism, and sociopolitical relevance for so long that free artistic inspiration no longer seems sufficient.

Merezhkovsky, a herald of the later Symbolists, had lost patience with literary strategies devised to create the "illusion of reality." No writer of genius, he felt, could be motivated by so meager a desire. Since the 1880s, the market for poetry had been growing. In fact, the abundance of poetic talent in this pre-World War I generation encouraged later critics to apply retroactively the label "Silver Age" to these decades, invoking as benchmark the glorious "Golden Age" of Pushkin and fabricating between the two eras a direct spiritual bond. This revived passion for non-representational poetic worlds did not occur in a vacuum. Interest in spiritualism, ghosts, séances, exorcism, folk taboo, and the ethnography of religious cults had flourished throughout the Age of Realism as a vigorous minor line investigating "Homo Mysticus."[2] By century's end, curiosity about metaphysical and visionary experience had become a legitimate topic of study in learned circles. The founding, in 1885, of the Moscow Psychological Society at Moscow University fed a resurgence of interest in Kant and German Romantic philosophy.[3] Professors and philosophers openly identified themselves as "idealists" – but this did not imply reclusive mystics or ivory-tower intellectuals. Idealists argued passionately in the public arena against the reigning tenets of positivism (the theory, made famous by Auguste Comte [1798–1857], that valid knowledge is received solely through sense experience) and on behalf of the autonomy of philosophy, professionalization in all disciplines, and non-reductive approaches to the human being. Spiritual life had reemerged as a serious competitor among public ideologies promising to restore human dignity. Several events in particular were key for the three Modernist writers whose novels are the focus of this chapter.

The fin de siècle: Solovyov, Nietzsche, Einstein, Pavlov's dogs, political terrorism

Between 1877 and 1881, Russia's first great speculative philosopher, Vladimir Solovyov (1853–1900) delivered a series of spellbinding lectures in St. Petersburg on what he called "Divine Humanity" or "Godmanhood."[4] The audience included both a skeptical Tolstoy and an enthusiastic Dostoevsky, who was Solovyov's good friend. The first lecture was devoted to Russia's need for "positive [or affirmative] religion," understood as the striving toward an absolute or ideal principle, which was the opposite of materialist positivism. "Contemporary religion is a pitiful thing," Solovyov declared. Reduced to a ritual, "a personal mood, a personal taste," it was no longer able to inspire or unite humanity. Several candidates had been put forward to fill the void, but all had proven inadequate: the institution of the Church, the ideals of socialism, the French Revolution, empirical science. Christian faith provided one part of the solution, by affirming the unconditional significance of each individual in the eyes of God. But secular humanism must complement this faith and converge with it.

A second factor in this religious renaissance, and seemingly at cross purposes to it, was the profound impact on Russian culture of Friedrich Nietzsche. Debts here were varied and vast. The ideas of the "super-human," a radical reassessment of all values, and a "will to power" that could bestow health, dignity, and autonomy on creative artists naturally appealed to the tiny trapped Russian intelligentsia. The debt was to some extent reciprocal. In 1888, Nietzsche had remarked that the Dostoevskian underground "contained the most valuable psychological material known to him" – suggesting that the German philosopher was prone to take seriously metaphysical worldviews that Dostoevsky subjected to cruel satire; the novelist's doubts were congenial to Nietzsche, the Christian epiphanies were not. Still, turn-of-the-century Russians found much to admire in Nietzschean thought. Symbolist journals like *Mir iskusstva* [The World of Art] translated broad swaths of Nietzsche's prose. Especially popular were the ideas of Zarathustra as proud artist-leader, the social misfit as above society (not superfluous to it), and an "existential renewal and vital mythic vision" that would replace utilitarian moral criticism.[5]

The first generation of Russian Symbolism coincided with a renaissance of interest in Classical Greece and Rome, and to this group the most vital mythic vision revealed by Nietzsche was the myth of Dionysus. In that vision, the life force is simultaneously destructive and creative, cyclical, rebellious, ecstatic, at times nihilistic, but always transformative. The end point of Russian Dionysianism was a "new man." For some, this coveted figure coincided with the Second Coming of Christ; for others, with a charismatic leader of the masses or a neo-Romantic cult of the poet as quasi-divine prophet. The poetic variant was especially attractive, since it integrates Dionysian inspiration with the Apollonian ideals of restraint, sobriety, and disciplined form. In this spirit, Merezhkovsky wrote an essay for the 1899 Pushkin Centennial claiming that this most perfect of poets was precisely "the Russian solution to the tragedy of dualism dramatized by Nietzsche and symbolized by the Apollonian–Dionysian polarity" – the genius who could bridge spirit and flesh, art and life, East and West.[6] Unsurprisingly, Leo Tolstoy vigorously condemned the Nietzsche cult (which he encountered in vulgarized form and which he vulgarized further). In January 1900, the same month *Uncle Vanya* so shocked him at the Moscow Art Theatre, Tolstoy wrote with some irritation in his diary that Chekhov's short story "Lady with a Pet Dog" was "all Nietzsche," adding: "Previously people who hadn't evolved for themselves a clear philosophy of life, one that could distinguish good and evil, used to seek anxiously; now they think they are beyond good and evil, but they remain on this side, that is, they are almost animals."[7]

A final factor jolting Russian art out of the mimetic-Realist groove was Einstein's revolution in the physics of time and space. The theory of relativity, made public in 1905, augmented Newtonian laws of energy, mass, and momentum with the innovative postulates that time could dilate, length could contract, and the "reality" of time and space depend upon the perspective, distance, and velocity of the observer. These ideas affected not only science; they also stunned and fascinated creative artists working in all media. In Russia, Einstein was invoked to legitimize multiple and local points of view, individual initiative, and fantastic theories for restructuring life and abolishing death. That consummate physicist fed into longstanding Russian debates over the freedom of the soul against the dead determinism of matter. Readers of *The Brothers Karamazov* might recall how Dmitry, already in prison, rails against the mechanistic theories of the French physiologist Claude Bernard: is it possible, Dmitry frets, that it's all "nerves in the brain," and "that's why I'm able to think, . . . and not because I have a soul?" (Book Eleven, ch. 4, p. 589). In 1880, Dostoevsky had been defending human freedom against the empiricist tradition in Russian science, which investigated behavior modification through manipulation of external stimuli. The mystical Symbolists continued Dostoevsky's polemic against the tyranny of visible matter. By 1904, the lines were drawn: one year before Einstein announced his theory, Ivan Pavlov was awarded the Nobel Prize in Physiology for his clinical research on digestive processes. The fame of Pavlovian mechanistic reflexology peaked just before World War I.

To this confluence of philosophy, science, physiology and metaphysics we must add two crises of a different sort: the outbreak of the 1905 Revolution on the ruins of Russia's humiliating defeat in the Russo-Japanese War, and an intensification of political terrorism. After decades of isolated terrorist acts against the government – which some in the artistic avant-garde applauded, but most deplored – revolutionary violence against officials suddenly rose steeply.[8] There were 9,000 targeted casualties throughout the country between 1905 and 1907. Terrorist attacks and banditry became so common that they were no longer featured individually in the newspapers but listed in special sections devoted to that day's assassinations and "expropriations." The type of terrorist also changed. In the nineteenth century (except in the fictive visions of Dostoevsky, who foresaw everything at its most ecstatic and terrible), an aura of self-sacrificing asceticism still surrounded such violent acts, as if they were the work of a righteous person, a *pravednik*. The four assassins of Tsar Alexander II, hanged in 1881, enjoyed this status. The twentieth century saw an influx into the terrorist ranks of cynical, profiteering, pleasure-seeking and criminal types. Their perfect representative was the double agent who extorts equally from both sides. This perverse climate was exacerbated by certain elite fin de siècle fashions: for suicide, sexual experimentation, opium, and alcoholism as a path to higher truth. To Tolstoy this was all the most revolting decadence, the result of a craze for losing control of one's body. To others, however, the "Dionysian" element in Russian consciousness and society seemed at last to be breaking forth on its own, releasing otherwise inaccessible energy. This zone, both horrifying and thrilling, expanded to embrace the entire country during the next two decades: world war, revolution, civil war.

In 1923, Evgeny Zamyatin, a naval engineer, wrote an essay summing up the effects on Russian Modernism of Nietzsche's Dionysianism, Einstein's relativity, and the campaigns against the "illusion of realism." He titled it "On Literature, Revolution, Entropy, and Other Matters." His opening question was: "Ask point blank: 'What is revolution?'" His answer:

> Revolution is everywhere, in everything . . . A literature that is alive . . . is a sailor sent aloft: from the masthead he can see foundering ships, icebergs, and maelstroms still invisible from the deck.
>
> In a storm, you must have a man aloft. Today we are in the midst of a storm . . . Only yesterday a writer could calmly stroll along the deck, clicking his Kodak (a genre scene); but who will want to look at landscapes and genre scenes when the world is listing at a forty-five-degree angle, the green maws are gaping, the hull is creaking? . . . Let yesterday's cart creak along the well-paved highways . . . What we need today are automobiles, airplanes, flickering, flight, dots, dashes, seconds.[9]

Zamyatin's "sailor aloft in the storm" could not differ more profoundly from Tolstoy's sailor with a compass in *Anna Karenina*, who points out to adulterers their singular, cart-drawn course.

Modernist time-spaces and their modes of disruption

Our sampling of the Symbolist–Modernist period will be organized around three great novels (and in passing, some poetry) associated with two myth-laden cities. The first novel, set in the imperial capital, is Andrei Bely's *Petersburg* (1916–22). The second, set in Moscow, is Mikhail Bulgakov's *The Master and Margarita* (1928–40). The third, Evgeny Zamyatin's *We* (1921), unfolds in the fantastic glass metropolis of OneState in the twenty-sixth century – and might be said to distribute, in concentrated and exaggerated form on opposite sides of the Green Wall, the myths of those two archetypical Russian cities. These three novels did not "influence" one another. Only one, *Petersburg*, was published in Russian during its author's lifetime. *We* appeared abroad in the 1920s first in English and then in Czech; it was published in Russia in its original Russian only in 1988. Bulgakov finished *The Master and Margarita* during the dark Stalinist years; he could not have imagined its publication in the USSR as he knew it. The novel first appeared, posthumously and heavily censored, in the thaw year 1966.

Although these three works belong to different stylistic traditions, intriguing comparisons can be made. Each novel disorients and disrupts the flow of the narrative, to achieve the "estrangement" and displacement so important to the texture of post-Realist prose. Bely's Symbolist novel *Petersburg* is a productive starting point, for it combines arcane theories of cognition with a hallucinating Dionysian subconscious. For Bely, the very act of naming creates a primary aural reality, a "third world" of sound that enables the poet to access previously non-existent realms.[10] Complicating these ambitions in *Petersburg*, however, is the narrator's deflating, endearing irony, which unexpectedly humanizes the plot at crucial moments and turns it into something approaching comedy – a signature technique of the Gogol–Dostoevsky line. The plot of *Petersburg* can even be seen as a variant on the political conspiracies of *Demons* (a novel that at one point obsessed Bely) with a nod to the parricide in *The Brothers Karamazov*. The time is the revolutionary year 1905. The philosophy student Nikolai Apollonovich Ableukhov has made a rash promise to a splinter terrorist group to assassinate his own father, Apollon Apollonovich, a senator of high rank. Horrified when he is actually summoned to plant a bomb in his father's house, the son tries to decline, but he is compromised by a double agent. So the son sets the mechanism; the bomb, hidden in a sardine tin, starts to tick.

Apollon Apollonovich wanders in to his son's study and removes the curious tin to his own room. The son is frantic. At the end of the novel the bomb explodes, but no one is killed.

This anticlimax with the sardine tin is emblematic. Every time one of the novel's heroes entertains a "creative disguise" or a show of power, something goes wrong: ordinary suspenders flash forth from under a red domino costume; the targeted senator retires from his ministry in humiliated confusion and is reconciled with his unfaithful wife precisely when his death is supposed to be a meaningful political statement; and in a subplot, a minor officer tries to hang himself in disgrace but the plaster cracks, the ceiling falls in, the noose won't hold. Apocalypse and strong closure are everywhere prepared for during these agitated revolutionary days, but they default to more shabby, compassionate, everyday outcomes. The result is a strange landscape: Bely's "third world" of transformative word-symbols almost peaks at several points but then unceremoniously peters out. In this aspect, the events of the novel recall Chekhov's *The Duel*, where the bumbling intervention of some well-meaning comic figure deflates the word-games poised to kill the antagonists.

This pulsation between tragedy and farce, and between a rational and an intuitive response to the world, is essential to the novel's rhythm. Bely held that the excellence of an artwork was proportional to its kinship with music. Music is structured emotional flow; the "world of appearances" (that is, palpable, fixed form) is always a constraint on that flow, on our free experiencing through time.[11] The author-poet, who works in a medium located halfway between the poles of architecture and music, must balance the claims of space and time. The scenes in *Petersburg* are chopped and short. Scraps of dialogue appear without a framing context, with ellipses and free-standing punctuation that suggest more an intonation than a communication. Against the unstoppable ticking of the bomb, verbal symbols float and then suddenly disrupt. In a conspiracy novel where double agents, drunkenness, hallucination, and concealed threats play so potent a role, such disruption inevitably has demonic overtones. But the process is also potentially divine, and the apocalypse barely averted cannot be reduced to mere idle cerebral play.

Zamyatin wrote his Modernist novel not under the aegis of Symbolism but under the star of Einstein's relativity. Zamyatin too is in the Gogol–Dostoevskian tradition of storytelling, in which fictional characters go out of their mind together with portions of the narration containing them. The concern that so occupied Bely, however – the transfiguration of the self through verbal art – is different in Zamyatin. The son of an Orthodox priest, Zamyatin made rich use of biblical subtexts in *We* – ranging from Adam and Eve's

Fall in the book of Genesis to Dostoevsky's Grand Inquisitor, who castigates Christ for his reluctance to work the miracles required to guarantee humanity its material security.[12] Despite these motifs, Zamyatin was a wholly secular writer, and skeptical as regards divine or mystical allegory. Although authority is everywhere in OneState, neither miracle nor mystery has a place. The world of *We* is a post-Edenic blueprint, and to drive this point home Zamyatin plays openly, even mechanically, with alphabets and prefixes.

All citizens ("numbers") of OneState are named with an initial letter plus a numerical digit. Males begin with consonants (the hero is D-503), females with vowels (O-90, I-330). D-, the novel's Adam, is a mathematician by profession, and his prefix is written in Cyrillic, Д, a letter derived from the Greek delta, also the mathematical symbol for change. The novel's Eve, the seductress I-330, is named not with the Russian equivalent of this vowel, И, but with the Latin 'I': the English first-person singular pronoun, the dangerous unit that has broken away from the "We." The double-agent doctor who is in league with I-330 also carries a Latin prefix, S- (snake, G. *Schlange*, Fr. *serpent*), not the less slinky Cyrillic equivalent, C. But the lesson to be learned from these cunningly named heroes and their biblical subtexts is not one of salvation, and certainly not of sexual guilt. Zamyatin was curious in a scientific, "Einsteinian" way about the growth of consciousness out of a multiplication or fragmentation of human perspectives. Thus his novel tells a different cautionary tale than Bely's.

Zamyatin constructed his *We* as a series of diary entries that read like an experiment in mechanics. Stretches of narrative are punctuated by the visual play of sharp-edged or intersecting surfaces, panoramic shots followed by abrupt close-ups. Fragments, splinters, emissions and cracks have an ominous texture to them ("A knife. A blood-red bite." "A microscopic bubble of saliva appeared on his lips and burst"). Material objects and human organisms are chopped up, inventoried, and juxtaposed to one another from various points of view. These episodes list at a forty-five degree angle and flash by as if glimpsed from a speeding car. About the day of the liquefaction of a dissident poet:

> Cube Square. Sixty-six powerful concentric rings: the stands. And sixty-six rows: quiet faces like lamps, with eyes reflecting the shining heavens, or maybe the shining of OneState. Blood-red flowers: women's lips.[13]

As long as D-503 remains a loyal subject of OneState, he perceives three-dimensionality, depth, and the capacity to absorb and project personal desire – what the doctors diagnose as the birth of a "soul" – as illness and imminent death. Forty diary entries (his forty days in the Wilderness) chronicle his metamorphosis from an obedient servant of impersonal reason into a grasping, loving, rebellious singularity, a process that D-503 both craves and bitterly resents. The beautiful I-330, midwife to the birth of his soul, is a member of the *Mephi*, a sect named after Goethe's demonic tempter Mephistopheles, which flourishes beyond the Green Wall enclosing the City.

His soul expanding, D-503 watches with horror as his diary, begun as a dutiful and devout propaganda piece for the missionary spaceship of which he is First Builder, transforms itself into a treasonous document. There is nowhere to tuck it away; its pages, increasingly full of anguish and doubt, are discovered on his glass desk through the glass walls of his room and become incriminating evidence. After the rebellion of the *Mephi* fails, D-503 is seized and lobotomized. His final diary entry, #40, resumes in the voice of a bland, collective "normalcy." Impassively recorded there is the spectacle of his beloved I-330 being interrogated – tortured by suffocation – under the Glass Bell.

This closing scene especially has resonated throughout twentieth-century anti-totalitarian literature. In discussing his 1948 novel *1984*, George Orwell acknowledged a debt to his Russian predecessor. In both novels, the betrayed female beloved (Julia or I-330) is tortured, or set up to be tortured, in front of the collapsed male hero-victim (Winston Smith or D-530) who has been broken on the wheel of their love. Orwell's novel, however, is an anti-utopia precisely because the shabbiness, fraudulence, and doublethink of Ingsoc are clear to all from the start. Life in Oceania's capital London, with its Ministries of Peace, Plenty, Truth, and Love, is utopia with its signs reversed, a city pasted all over with exuberant untruths in the spirit of Swiftian satire. Zamyatin's *We* is the more dynamic and unsettling genre of dystopia: a *dysfunctional* utopia, the purportedly perfect city, at first applauded by an insider, which in the course of the novel turns into a nightmarish prison because a soul has matured and rebelled inside it.

Petersburg recreates Dostoevskian themes of parricide and political conspiracy; *We*, in contrast, the coldly satiric sides of *Notes from Underground*. In that dark place, we recall, Dostoevsky's anti-hero speaks mockingly of a rationalist utopia, a dwelling-place made entirely of glass (the "Crystal Palace"), where transparency has become a way of life. No one has anything to hide (or anything to envy) because each person's needs are mathematically calculated in advance and efficiently satisfied. Thus happiness is as possible and unambiguous as "twice two equals four." This Crystal Palace becomes the world incarnated in Zamyatin's OneState, which the Underground Man, a committed irrationalist, would immediately recognize as "not life, gentlemen, but the beginning of death."[14]

Dostoevsky's paradoxical Underground provides only one subtext to the dynamics of *We*, however. For further clues, we must turn to Zamyatin's early journalism. In 1918, Zamyatin published his first polemical essay, "Scythians?" The Scythians, a fierce nomadic tribe that left Central Asia in the eighth century BCE for the Don and Dnieper rivers, were adopted as a symbol during the revolutionary years by several avant-garde Russian writers to celebrate maximalism, spontaneity, absolute independence of spirit, and "eternal readiness to revolt." This was the Dionysian impulse, writ large on the political canvas of the day. Zamyatin's essay criticizes a recent anthology of "Scythian" writings for its insufficiently principled rebelliousness. "The Scythian is an eternal nomad," Zamyatin writes:

> He is alive only in the wild, free gallop, only in the open steppe . . . Christ victorious in practical terms is the grand inquisitor . . . The true Scythian will smell from a mile away the odor of dwellings, the odor of cabbage soup, the odor of the priest in his purple cassock . . . and will hasten into the steppe, to freedom.[15]

Several years later, Zamyatin structured *We* around this mesmerizing "Scythian" binary of entropy versus energy, authoritarian stasis versus unfettered (and even purposeless) motion. Dostoevsky had applied similarly rigid polarities to his trap of the Underground: on one side, deterministic reason and the smug material security of the Crystal Palace; on the other, irrational spontaneity and perpetual doubt. But Dostoevsky is maximally distant from the revolutionary romantic celebrated by Bolshevik-era admirers of the Scythians. In *Notes from Underground*, he satirizes the irrationalist option as severely as he censures its opposite. Dostoevsky's abject anti-hero is indeed a rebel. Every word, argument, and recollected event in the Underground Man's monologue, however, makes it clear that he is interested not in freedom but in power (over others, and over his right to define his own purpose). He knows better than anyone else how few are the exits from that controlling passion. Zamyatin's *We*, although it was written in a Nietzschean era, is a brighter satire, almost a utopian satire, celebrating everything that does not require any firm point of support or point of rest. It is also, after a fashion, a love story. But nothing resembling a free or responsive personality could ever evolve on either side of its Green Wall. Nor was the presentation of such a life-option part of Zamyatin's intent.

Bulgakov's *Master and Margarita* belongs to a different era and tradition, and – for all its demonology – is a genuine hybrid. Its time-space is divided equally between secular and sacred realms. It too is a love story, although grounded in modesty and reduced expectation rather than in Scythian rebellion or excess, and one that *does* end, perhaps even triumphantly, on a point of rest. The plot weaves together three familiar stories, albeit with unfamiliar, altered names. The first is the visit of the Devil (here called Woland, professor of black magic) to a major city (here Moscow) during a springtime full moon, to find a hostess for his annual ball. The second is the Faustian contract between this devil and a bereaved person (here Margarita), who bargains her soul in hopes of locating her disappeared beloved (the Master, a novelist out of favor with Stalinist literary bureaucrats). The third is the crucifixion of Christ (here called Yeshua) in Jerusalem (here Yershalaim), told as a detective story – in places a secret-police story – scattered in four installments throughout the Moscow narrative. The two cities are frequently superimposed on one another, Moscow's towers and turrets signaling the city's status as the "New Jerusalem," with violent events in one prefiguring similar violence in the other.

Such double-tiered, "palimpsest" narration need not in itself be disorienting. What startles the reader is Bulgakov's chronotopic play, that is, the fact that miracles, madness and magic do not occur in the environments where we would most expect them. The Moscow chapters are crammed with supernatural happenings, devils (sublime and petty), vampires, witches, hallucinations, carnival trickery, and yet are set in a familiar city full of recognizable streets, buildings, Soviet-style communal apartments, famous landmarks, as well as real people and events out of the Stalinist 1930s. This invasion of the comic-diabolical into everyday activities – professional meetings, tram rides, visits to the theatre or grocery store – recalls much more the texture of Gogol than of Dostoevsky, who doesn't really have an "everyday." Bulgakov's use of this device in the Moscow chapters functions in part as political allegory. As the Terror gained momentum after 1936, innocent people were disappearing as if by witchcraft, their apartments sealed and their names effaced from public record.

If Moscow is the humdrum demonic, what of the Jerusalem chapters? They constitute a genuine historical novel – perhaps even a "novelized history." Bulgakov was a meticulous researcher, and in the early drafts of his novel he footnoted sources for the scenes describing Yeshua's arrest, Pontius Pilate's migraine and political cowardice, the machinations of the High Priests, the anguish of Judas, and the stations of the Cross from the perspective of a tormented disciple. Of course, in the official judgment of atheistic Moscow in the 1930s, these New Testament chapters would have to be declared a "fiction." Inside the chapters, however, we would expect to find some evidence, intonational or visual, of the miracles that animated the disciples and sustained their faith. This is not the case. Regardless of who relates the crucifixion – and the installments are respectively related orally by the Devil, dreamt by a Muscovite poet, and read silently by Margarita as part of the Master's novel – all narrators are identical in their sobriety, authority, majestic high-Realist secular style, and compassionate psychological detail with no trace of miracle. The Jerusalem chapters are clearly all the same book – the Master's novel – regardless of who delivers it, or when, or how. Such a confluence of realistic diction in *all* segments of this inserted drama, whether uttered, dreamt, or read silently to oneself, lends an aura of pre-verbal authenticity to Christ's Passion. It also suggests a conviction dear to the Symbolist era: that the true artist has an intuitive perception of Truth, superseding eyewitness accounts left us in the Gospels. The realness of such a vision is not dependent on any local narrative conventions or approximations.

Thus we might say that the boldest "estrangement from reality" in *The Master and Margarita* is not the magic – that is, not the fact that black cats can walk upright and talk, that Margarita becomes a witch and flies around on a broomstick, that Woland dispatches a drunken theatre bureaucrat to Yalta in five seconds, or that Muscovites turn up in the marsh of a Siberian river with dancing mermaids at full moon. Such character types and episodes are completely routine and rule-abiding within the conventions of the genre from which they come: a Ukrainian folk tale as Gogol might write it up, or a Faust drama. The jolt comes when the reader realizes that the "illusion of reality" in those supremely realistic Jerusalem chapters has not been designed to "*feel* or *look* real" according to the usual fictional contract, where readers suspend their disbelief in order to enter into the fictive world. Those chapters simply *are* real. Or rather, they are as close as a work of verbal art can come to that condition, construed as a window on to an *un*constructed prior fact. The names of people and places in the Jerusalem chapters are not the familiar canonized names of the Gospel accounts but what people and places were called back then, in their own time. They are not aware of their own symbolic significance. These scenes do not know that they are being read.

At one point the Master, terrified he will be arrested for the crime of writing about Jesus in an atheist state, burns his novel. Woland hands the book back to its author intact with the comment that "manuscripts don't burn." But *why* a manuscript doesn't burn is of key importance. It is not only because the Prince of Darkness is there to retrieve it from the flames, his natural element and thus under his control, and not only because the artistic Word is immortal. Bulgakov suggests something more radical. The Master has not so much created as re-created reality, preserving truth and then releasing it through his novel. For this reason, even he cannot get rid of the document, which is a portal.

Such a Modernist project, which presumes the existence of other worlds to which poets have privileged access, recalls Bely's *Petersburg*. But Bulgakov's reasons are quite different from Bely's Faustian search for knowledge in the dual worlds of Symbolism, or Zamyatin's celebration of the Dionysian impulse in the *Mephi* beyond the Green Wall. Bely disrupts the "Realist contract" through rhythmic word-symbols. Zamyatin slices visual images along multiple planes to invade and break down familiar worlds. Bulgakov adopts the Tolstoyan strategy of making a story even more truth-bearing if it can be shown to *do without words* – that is, if it can avoid the indignity of being dependent on one speaker's limited perspective. Woland introduces this theme in the opening scene.

Mikhail Berlioz, editor, atheist, and head of the Writers' Union, meets the "strange professor" at Patriarch's Pond in Moscow. Berlioz and his poet-friend are suspicious of this foreign-looking fellow, especially when the three get into a debate about the historicity of Jesus Christ. Suddenly the professor whispers to them: "Keep in mind that Jesus did exist":

> "You know, Professor," answered Berlioz with a forced smile, "we respect your great knowledge, but we happen to have a different point of view regarding that issue."
> "No points of view are necessary," replied the strange professor. "He simply existed, that's all there is to it."
> "But surely some proof is required," began Berlioz.
> "No, no proof is required," answered the professor.[16]

At this point the professor's foreign accent "somehow disappears," and the first installment of this true story flows out from behind the text. Bulgakov had originally planned his novel as a "Gospel According to the Devil." This Devil, a sad, thoughtful figure, remains the novel's wisest, most authoritative source of knowledge, the coordinator of its various planes, and – like Zamyatin's *Mephi* – an uneasy ally of the Good. Both sets of events, Woland in Moscow and Pontius Pilate in Jerusalem, take place from Wednesday through Saturday night of the vernal full moon (Passover Week). Only in the final minutes of the final night do all levels of the novel unite on the same plane, in a triumphantly ahistorical timelessness. It is a time-space that Tolstoy always dreamed of. Every earthly creature had been in the same doubt, and now they can all be in the same truth. The author does not have to prove or persuade with the illusion of reality. He simply draws back the veil.

Bulgakov's first biographer suggested that the idea for a "Gospel According to Woland" might even have come to Bulgakov from Tolstoy, who, after his "break" in the 1880s, "rewrote the Gospels to make them more logical and coherent."[17] Bulgakov, the son of a professor of theology at the Kievan Academy, was well versed in religious controversies and texts. He also deeply loved Leo Tolstoy. In the 1880s and 1890s, in pursuit of a faith that was compatible with reason, Tolstoy had produced his own version of the Gospels, deleting all the supernatural prompts. Bulgakov eliminates the same miraculous layers and legends from the Master's novel. The truth does not need them.

Bulgakov's Satan figure, Woland, thus emerges as a fascinating bridge figure between our two great nineteenth-century philosopher-novelists. As we saw in the preceding chapter, which introduced Woland conversing with Berlioz's severed head at Satan's Ball, this devil is firmly in the Dostoevsky line of "multiple valid truths." Individuals (in this case, the Moscow public) are allowed to live – and die – by their own professed beliefs. To be sure, most of these beliefs are shoddy, and Woland's devilish Gogolian retinue forces their hypocrisy to the surface. A more profound debt is owed to that clownish devil who turns up in *The Brothers Karamazov*, hallucinated by the middle brother, Ivan. Ivan's devil defends his existence on earth as a guarantee that there would continue to be events, absurdities, human suffering, for "otherwise everything would turn into an endless prayer service," tedious and undifferentiated.[18] Woland defends himself with the same argument, when challenged at the end of the novel by his detractors from the Christian side. "What would your good do if evil didn't exist," he retorts to Matthew the Levite, "and what would the world look like if all the shadows disappeared?" (ch. 24, p. 305).

For all his debts to Dostoevsky and Gogol, however, Bulgakov's Satan also realizes an authorial fantasy very precious to Tolstoy: the ethically ideal relation between an author and a reader. Except when he is the mouthpiece for an installment of Christ's Passion, Woland is a taciturn man. This is appropriate. He shows rather than tells. Woland might have originated in Ivan Karamazov's devil. But in Bulgakov he is sobered up, transformed from a chattering buffoon into a seer, and serves both the Gogol–Dostoevsky and the Tolstoy line.

City myths: Petersburg, Moscow, OneState

What is the Petersburg Myth, and how does Bely's novel named after that city contribute to it? This question was formalized as a research area in the mid-1980s, when Yury Lotman and his fellow semioticians turned their attention to the "Petersburg text" as exemplary of the cultural symbolism of cities.[19] With Russian space in mind, they drew up several robust distinctions. First, the city as a demarcated site could stand in one of two relationships to the undeveloped territory surrounding it. Either it could spread out to absorb and personify its surroundings – such was the historical experience of Rome – or it could become the antithesis of that surrounding space, perceived to be in an antagonistic relation to the wilderness it ruled. In the former "absorptive" model, the city becomes a symbol for the organic core of the universe. No matter where on the map the city is actually located, it feels like the "center," a nested place. Such concentric cities are static and eternal, often situated on hills, and believed to mediate between heaven and earth. Examples are Jerusalem, Rome, and Moscow. (There is logic to Moscow's two epithets, "New Jerusalem" and "Third Rome.") Opposed to such concentric cities are eccentric ones, often situated on the threatened edges of empires, built as outposts on seized or conquered land. Born in violence, eccentric cities frequently have apocalyptic myths attached to their ends. They seem "willed" and inorganic, driven by crisis and subject to floods, earthquakes, and aggressive invasions. When they win, they become symbolic of a victory of mind over matter, but when they lose they spread doom, rumors of the Antichrist, and reinforce the principle that surrounding nature is hostile to human habitation and will always do battle with it.

Lisbon and Alexandria are two of the world's great, doomed "edge cities," but for Russia, the prototype is St. Petersburg. This city of stone was founded in 1703 by a fiat of Peter the Great as a military beachhead on a stoneless, uninhabited watery inlet. Built by conscripted labor, it fostered portents of catastrophe and death – especially by floodings and sinkings – from its earliest years. But also (and somewhat counterintuitively), its very artificiality and abrupt genesis came to represent rational utopia, the grandeur of imperial will. As one legend relates, since the swamp sucked everything in, Peter forged the city in the air and then laid it gently down on the soft earth. An airborne artificial city can do without a foundation, without organic history from the bottom up. In similar manner, the myth of Petersburg began not on the solid ground of lived experience but in literature and oral legend – which then fed into its history and in fact created that history.

Petersburg was illusory, phantasmagorical, a stage set. Gender ratios and demographics added to the sense of artifice. Petersburg exploded in size and population during the nineteenth century (whereas Napoleon's invasion and burning, plus cholera epidemics, checked the growth of Moscow). Owing to so many military personnel, males outnumbered females in Petersburg by almost three to one, and this high number of wifeless men assured a huge population of prostitutes and attendant diseases.[20] Masquerades, uniforms, military and civilian ranks – all forms that cover up and standardize the body – were the norm. In the early Bolshevik years, the fashion for public spectacles that reenacted historical scenes as street theatre further blurred the distinction between an actual event and its stylization for posterity. Outside those rituals, masks, and tightly fitting costumes was chaos: invisibility and the abyss.

In this startling set of images from urban semiotics, we see the outline of a Nietzschean dichotomy. Petersburg is an unstable, apocalyptic city of Dionysian energies, barely contained by an Apollonian crust of rock and granite. This tension sits like a coiled spring at the center of Bely's *Petersburg*. Its first chapter contains a section, "Squares, Parallelepipeds, Cubes," in which the senator Apollon Apollonovich – a man "born for solitary confinement," modeled on the real-life obscurantist Procurator of the Holy Synod Konstantin Pobedonostsev (1827–1907) – rushes out to work through the fog along rectilinear streets in the black cube of his carriage; "proportionality and symmetry soothed the senator's nerves."[21] The Dionysian revolution creeps in, however, in the form of conspiracy, his son's red silk domino, the ticking of the bomb, and the ominous rising waters of the Neva.

Gogol, Dostoevsky, and Bely provided the myth with its pedigree in prose, but Pushkin the poet is its founder. His 1833 narrative poem *The Bronze Horseman*, part ode and part personal tragedy, is based on the devastating flood of November 7, 1824, in which the Neva River rose six feet above street level in a single hour and claimed hundreds of lives. The poem opens on Peter the Great envisaging his great city rising from the wilderness. It closes on the corpse of a poor government clerk, Evgeny, driven mad after losing his sweetheart to the flood. The bereaved clerk had dared to shake his fist at the statue of Peter on Senate Square, which clattered down off its pedestal and chased its puny challenger around the city. The flood was nature's vengeance against the very idea of building a city in such a wild unnatural place, but the imperial city could withstand it; the defeat and death of the poor clerk by the statue of Peter became a symbol of this double-pronged attack against the helpless, unheroic little man by outraged nature and merciless autocrat. Pushkin's 1829 notebooks contain a startling sketch of the statue – without its rider. The specter of the Riderless Horse has haunted Russians ever since: the Bronze Horseman was death-dealing, certainly, but where would their country gallop without a powerful despot in the saddle?

In Petersburg, power erupts unexpectedly and punitively: the emperor, the river, a conspiracy, a sudden frost. These eruptions cause personal losses that can drive residents out of their minds. But before that moment, there is a flash of insight more profound than anything that could have evolved in a gentler way. During one of the extended drunken hallucinations in Bely's *Petersburg*, the Bronze Horseman descends once again from his pedestal and pays a visit to the revolutionary terrorist Dudkin. Glowing white hot, the statue of Peter "pours into his veins in metals" the resolve necessary to murder the double agent (ch. 6, p. 214). Such is the fate of consciousness in this odd urban site, which the Underground Man calls, at the beginning of his *Notes*, "the most abstract and premeditated city in the world": it progresses by flashes, leaps, and fevers. And it dies without descendents; only the words of the myth remain.

If the "Bronze Horseman" launches the imperial nineteenth-century Petersburg Myth, then *The Twelve*, by the Symbolist poet Aleksandr Blok (1880– 1921), inaugurates the Soviet era. This long narrative poem, composed in three weeks in January 1918, is set in the howling winds and snowdrifts of the revolutionary capital. Twelve Red Guards are patrolling the city, firing into the darkness. One of them, Petka, catches sight of his former girlfriend Katya on a sledge with her new (and wealthier) beau. Petka fires his rifle at them – she is killed, the new lover gets away, and whatever temporary remorse the murderer feels is mocked out of him by his comrades.

Throughout the poem, Blok imitates or partially quotes snatches of folk song, popular spiritual verse, Bolshevik slogans, staccato-like curses, robber and gypsy songs, urban romances. In his lectures on Russian literature from the mid-1920s, Bakhtin had curious things to say about the multivoiced, decentered quality of speech in Blok's *Twelve*.[22] "The poem is unified around the theme of revolution," he notes.

> But any justification of *The Twelve* can only be that of a drunken soul, nailed to the countertop of a pub, the justification of a jester [*shut*] …
> Here Blok is a pure Romantic: he who is fastened down to some definitive thing will not seek anything; he who has nothing can acquire everything. God loves those who are not fastened down by anything, who have nothing. The absence of positive qualities places them closer to God, makes them heralds of the Divine.

Bakhtin's musings here help explain the end of the poem, which surprised the poet himself. A starving dog trails behind the twelve guards. A blood-red banner precedes them. And invisible in the snowstorm, invulnerable to bullets, "In a white wreath of roses – / Up ahead, Jesus Christ." This idea of invisible transcendence, exemplified by a dozen rowdy soldiers being led by a force in which they themselves do not believe, was glossed by Blok in an essay he wrote during that same month of January 1918, titled "The Intelligentsia and Revolution." He noted that "the great Russian artists – Pushkin, Gogol, Dostoevsky, Tolstoy – were immersed in gloom" but had endured it because they believed in the light and knew the light. Now the Russian people are bolder. They believe simply in life, in "doing everything themselves," in "awaiting the unexpected" and believing "not in what exists but in what ought to exist," now that the Russian people, "like Ivan the Fool, has jumped down off its sleeping-ledge."[23] A new hero was born out of the Nietzschean binary between Dionysus and Apollo: the Bolshevik recruit as trigger-happy unholy fool.

One recent study of physical Petersburg opens on the observation that its middle spaces are few.[24] Surprisingly, perhaps, for the official proletarian capital of the world, industrial spaces like factories were not welcomed into the literary myth but exiled to its margins (either to the outskirts of the city, or to the Urals and the south). In Petersburg stories proper, the copy clerk Akaky Akakievich and his pre-industrial quill pen are recycled up through the twentieth century. Huge urban castle-fortresses, once the luxury residences of aristocrats and the royal family but now decaying, subdivided tenement houses, suggest anything but a modernizing "window to the West," which was the ideal city of the Petrine Imperial Project. In this time-space, urban rumor is always frenetic. A Petersburg text foregrounds Gogol's truth (which Dostoevsky then made a point of honor): that once uttered, any story will almost inevitably circulate, incorporate new and usually nastier elements, and become gossip or slander serving the interests or pathologies of its most recent speaker (the urge to re-speak out of one's own perspective being universal). Such runaway, randomly multiplied words are arguably the collective hero of Bely's *Petersburg*. The old senator has always assumed that words generate reality. However, in the midst of the "Dionysian" crises of 1905, the senator suddenly realizes that he controls and creates nothing at all with his words: "History has changed. The ancient myths are not believed, and Apollon Apollonovich is not the god Apollo. He is a civil servant" (ch. 7, p. 231). After the general strike began, although he continued to sit in his office and "order after order promptly sped off into the darkness of the provinces . . . he felt himself a skeleton from which Russia had fallen away" (p. 232). This flesh-and-blood Russia, the "darkness of the provinces" over which he had no control, was anti-Petersburg. Most of this vital untracked space is rural, forest, or steppe. But if it has an urban image at all, it is Moscow.

What is the Moscow Myth, and how does Bulgakov's *Master and Margarita* contribute to it? Gogol was among the first to point out, in 1836, the symbolic importance of Petersburg being masculine gender in Russian (it ends in a consonant), and Moscow [Moskva], with its -*a*- ending, feminine. The roundness of the city center, its confluence on several inland trade routes, its bulbous domes and bulging cacophonous bells, the concentric circles spiraling out from the Kremlin and the fact that it was, until 1812, largely a city of wood, have all helped to connect the city with a womb: all-encompassing and organic. If Petersburg poets like Blok found themes of bleakness, abandonment, the arbitrary violence of power and blinding white snow compatible with the energy of their revolutionary city, Moscow was a retreat. It looked back, not forward; inward, not beyond. After Marina Tsvetaeva (1892–1941) introduced her fellow poet Osip Mandelstam to Moscow in 1916, taking him on tours of ancient churches and cemeteries and persuading him that Russian history was as worthy of his pen as ancient Greece or medieval France, Mandelstam's cosmopolitan poetry broadened its scope to include Russian architecture, history, and fate.[25] Tsvetaeva herself wrote a cycle of poems in spring and summer 1916, "Verses about Moscow," that self-consciously juxtaposed the two cities as male–female, imperial–provincial, prideful–humiliated, the seat of power versus the ringing bells of faith. Its fifth poem declares:

> But higher than you, tsars, are the bells.
> As long as they thunder forth out of the sky-blue depths –
> Moscow's primacy is indisputable.
> – And the entire forty times forty churches
> Laughs at the arrogance of tsars!

In two brilliantly mocking poems from her 1931 cycle "Verses to Pushkin," Tsvetaeva portrays her great predecessor's relationship to Petersburg as that of rebellious poetic genius against the arrogant Tsar Nicholas I – "butcher, censor, poeticide." Moscow was a messy city, not in official uniform, and thus her virtues were more than skin deep.

Inwardness, warmth, darkness, and moistness – the qualities of fertile soil – are central to the myth of Moscow as a regenerative site. It was in Mother Moscow (restored as Russia's capital in 1918) that the first underground metro system was constructed in the Soviet state between 1931 and 1935, an enormous showcase task.[26] To compensate for a scarcity of skilled technicians and a rushed timetable, the government resorted to prison labor bolstered by cults of heroic sacrifice and youthful enthusiasm. The "metro-builder" became a new national hero, an unprecedented type of frontiersman who would conquer the underworld much as arctic explorers conquered the North Pole and cosmonauts would later conquer outer space. The underground stations – at unheard-of depths of twenty to thirty meters, designed to double as bomb shelters – were to resemble palaces, radiant with light. Taming the damp, at times recalcitrant earth for the metro project became Moscow's equivalent to taming the floodwaters of the Neva for the Petersburg Myth.

Moscow, first mentioned in the Kievan chronicles in 1147, is three times as old as Petersburg. But the myth feels somehow younger, more diffuse, greener, and – one might say – more promiscuous. Moscow's huge city houses were old, wooden, walled in with shabby fences behind which their owners cultivated large vegetable gardens, after the manner of the Russian village. People lived not in the streets, cafés, or paved squares, but at home. Unlike Petersburg, full of bureaucrats and military personnel, Moscow has been traditionally associated with tradesmen, families, and children.

A good introduction to the Moscow Myth was provided after the 1997 celebration of the city's 850th birthday by the cultural historian Svetlana Boym, an eyewitness to the festivities.[27] Boym claims that the myth of the city was consolidated during that jubilee year as never before in its history. In a series of mass spectacles aided by the latest technology, Russian tradition was reinvented alongside a nostalgic tribute to Soviet grand style. The tradition invoked was dual: Moscow as the Third Rome, and Moscow as the Big Village. In the first myth, initiated by a seventeenth-century monk more as a warning against abuse of power than as glorious prophecy, Moscow was declared the heir to both Christian Rome and Byzantium, an image of heavenly Jerusalem. She was to be the final Rome; "a fourth there shall not be."

The "Big Village" myth was equally fraught. Moscow's mayor since 1992, Yury Luzhkov (who, we recall from Chapter 3, sponsored the reconstruction of Christ the Savior Cathedral in the early 1990s) has a passion for monumentalization. Not any monument will do, however: only those in accord with a healthy, regenerative, slightly childlike and naïve vision of the city. Neither the imperial façades of Petersburg nor the unhappy post-communist work of memory and grief is appropriate for the refurbished Moscow Myth. A serviceable common language was found, however, in the cozy, intimate characters from rural Russian folklore, in a mix of commercialism with the cartoon, church bells with pagan ritual. This sense of Moscow as both wonder tale and Christian terminus is central to Bulgakov's *Master and Margarita*. The three cities mentioned by Lotman as prime examples of the embedded, concentric city – Jerusalem, Rome, and Moscow – are precisely the sites, actual or implied, of this novel. But Bulgakov is a complex contributor to the Moscow Myth. He stitches in a great deal that is associated with Petersburg, most noticeably from Gogol.

As prosewriter and playwright, Bulgakov was permeated by Gogolian texts. In 1924, he published the story "Diaboliad," where a Soviet version of Gogol's poor clerk Akaky Akakievich goes mad after the manner of Dostoevsky's Golyadkin in *The Double*. That same year he wrote "The Adventures of Chichikov," a dream-poem in ten entries, in which the hero of Gogol's *Dead Souls* turns up in Soviet Moscow during the free-enterprise heyday of the New Economic Policy (NEP). There he finds all the familiar scoundrels alive and well, cheating the state and defrauding the public, and he finds himself a cozy berth too, only to end having his belly slit open by Soviet officials to extract swallowed diamonds.[28] Two of Bulgakov's most famous novellas show Gogolian demonology already "Muscovized" – that is, reoriented toward fertility, botched reincarnations, and the production of biological as opposed to mechanical monsters. When body parts come off in a Gogol Petersburg tale (recall "The Nose"), they strut around the city as incarnated Rank, identifiable not by the face (if there is a face) but by the official shape of the button. When living bodies are rearranged in Bulgakov, they either proliferate out of control or – to the horror of all – become human beings.

Like Chekhov, Bulgakov was trained as a medical doctor. He understood and respected physiology. The first of his science fiction – or science-gone-wrong – tales, *The Fatal Eggs* (1925), tells the story of a Moscow zoologist's discovery of a fantastically potent red ray that, when directed at living tissue, causes it to grow exponentially in size and viciousness. When the state requisitions this ray to increase chicken-egg production, a minor bureaucratic accident intervenes: instead of chicken eggs, reptile eggs are radiated, and when they hatch, Soviet Russia is devastated by man-eating dinosaurs. An untimely frost in August kills them off. The second novella, *Heart of a Dog*, again combines science and reproduction, but more on the model of Frankenstein's monster than H. G. Wells's *Food of the Gods*. Also written in 1925, this manuscript was confiscated (together with Bulgakov's diaries) in a secret-police search of the writer's apartment in 1926, and first appeared in Russia only in the glasnost year 1987. Its plotline resembles *The Fatal Eggs*. Another scientist-professor, this time a surgeon, specializes in human rejuvenation via an implantation of youthful sexual organs. But his private passion is more ambitious: to create a New Man. He succeeds in transplanting the pituitary gland and testes of a recently deceased criminal into a mongrel dog. The dog turns into a human being with criminal habits but a canine psyche, the exemplary proletarian, who eventually hints to his aristocratic creator that he is preparing to denounce him to the authorities. Before any harm is done, however, this hybrid humanoid beast is re-operated into a dog. It is no accident that Woland, the enabling hero of *The Master and Margarita*, is also a professor, albeit of black magic, not body parts. The area of experimentation has now moved from reptiles through the human-canine body to the human soul. This is an appropriate sequence for the biologically inflected myth of Holy Moscow.

Along the lines of these early Gogolian exercises, in his *Master and Margarita* Bulgakov casts an entire layer of madcap demonic events in the comic, petty-devil zone. But there are important, Moscow-oriented differences. Bulgakov's madness resides in the fictive characters alone. It does not infect the voice, vision, or sobriety of his narration or his narrator, who reports on gossips and rumors but never, or almost never, is dissolved in them. He addresses the reader from a congenial, authoritative distance, as might a responsible historian or an epic poet. Ethically, *The Master and Margarita* is a traditional humanist novel, with domestic tranquility as its final reward. Its hero and heroine, rescued by Woland from the Stalinist capital but not qualifying as martyrs who might live in the Light, end up crossing a moss-covered bridge to their new home. It is set (we are led to believe) in some quiet rural corner under blossoming cherry trees, in eternally recurring Moscow time.

Can there be a myth of the future? If so, how does Zamyatin's OneState distribute, on either side of its Green Wall, the mythical essence of Russia's two major cities? One way of reading the novel *We* in the context of the Russian literary tradition is to see it as a distilling chamber for several prominent tendencies, or anxieties, associated with the literature of each capital.

The overwhelming binary remains city versus country, the urban factory versus the rural village or steppe. Inside OneState, the architectural principle of Petersburg reigns, albeit grossly exaggerated and essentialized: the triumph of the grid, square, box, the regimented "life in uniform" with its respect for reflecting surfaces, external rank, and standardized norms. It is one of Zamyatin's masterful twists on the Petersburg tradition to represent the birth of D-503's individuated consciousness (the birth of an "I" out of a "We," recounted in entry 16) as the softening up of a mirror. Throughout the Gogol–Dostoevsky line, the anguish of a hero's isolation, humiliation, and descent into madness is portrayed with the help of mirrors. These poor clerks gaze at themselves, are revolted by what they see reflected in that flat surface, deny that it exists, fantasize a substitute – and as a sign of their madness, a Double emerges. D-503 too resists his own reflection. He has been happy. But his soul flares up anyway. As the doctor explains to his bewildered patient (p. 87):

> Take a flat plane, a surface, take this mirror, for instance. And the two of us are on this surface, see, and we squint our eyes against the sun . . . But just imagine now that some fire has softened this impenetrable surface and nothing skims along the top of it any longer – everything penetrates into it, inside, into that mirror world . . . The plane has taken on mass, body, the world, and it's all inside the mirror, inside you . . . And, you understand, the cold mirror reflects, throws back, while this absorbs, and the trace left by everything lasts forever.

This is a Moscow moment, absorptive, dark, and (once begun) unstoppable, when some living impulse "takes root" inside. In Gogol's and Dostoevsky's Petersburg, mirrors are flat and doubling – a sign of insanity. Inside OneState, a "softened" surface is criminalized. But it is a sign of budding sanity.

If inside OneState is the regimented city, then outside is the Big Village. This image, too, is exaggerated. Exiles from the city don't need houses at all; homes have reverted to the trees out of which they were built. Separating the city of OneState from the forested wilderness is the glass Green Wall. The point of passage is the "Ancient House" – one of those ramshackle wooden homes tucked away down Moscow streets and alleys – presided over by a decrepit old woman who is all wrinkles and smiles, a Baba Yaga in league with the Mephi, able to control the boundary between life and death. Spiritually, I-330 is one of her daughters. Of course Zamyatin, a builder himself, is not advocating the Outside as anything like productive freedom. D-503 describes his visit beyond the Wall as a Dionysian nightmare: "It's as if they set off a bomb in my head and all around, piled in a heap, are open mouths, wings, screams, leaves, words, stones...I couldn't move, because I wasn't standing on a surface, but something disgustingly soft, yielding, alive, green, springy" (pp. 148–49).

The naked humanoids in this fantastic place are covered with glossy fur. They bask in the sun, drink wines, nibble fruit. Much in this wilderness partakes of the Moscow mythic cluster of values: fertility, an abundance of food and drink, natural rhythms and cycles, the sense that the ground underfoot is black earth, not stony pavement. Moscow is what survives when the utopian planners fail and the machines blow themselves up. Within her domain, life is supported at any cost and corporeal reality is never sacrificed for mathematics or a mere disembodied idea. At the last minute, I-330 arranges to slip O-90, pregnant illegally with D-503's child, beyond the Wall to give birth. There, amid the moss and the screeching of birds, the child will be permitted to live.

Twenty-first century Russia has already worked huge changes on these city myths, which in time will register on the new literary canon of the post-communist era. In 2003, St. Petersburg celebrated its 300th birthday with a massive facelift of all architectural and sculptural monuments and an immersion in its canonical city texts. But partly for this reason, Petersburg, Pushkin's celebrated "window to the West" and Russia's City of the Revolution, feels more than ever like a museum, a nostalgic site. Revolution has become an old idea. What is new is where the money and markets now are, which is Moscow in its post-Village phase. This globalized "city of the future," bristling with anti-Western rhetoric but oriented toward the capitalist corporation, scrubbed clean of its most painful historical events or packaging them as "tours" and theme parks, is planning an ambitious International Business Center, "Moskva-City," of glass skyscrapers and gleaming pedestrian bridges to the west and southwest of the historic center.[29] With the razing of the gargantuan Rossiya hotel, a monolith from the Soviet 1960s that overlooked St. Basil's Cathedral, the

Kremlin itself will be incorporated into a vast, slick new mall with majestic vistas, porticoes, and arcaded façades. The plans indicate no turrets or onion domes.[30] It remains to be seen if any aspects of the older, more organic and black-soil traditions of the Moscow Myth can survive this onslaught of high technology and commercialization.

These single-city novels by Bely, Zamyatin, and Bulgakov, together with the loosely defined urban myths generated by each, provide a bridge to our next chapter, which will cover some of the same years (1920s–50s) from the perspective of a more politically approved ideology, socialist realism. In early Leninist terminology, the geographical opposition of "city" (proletariat) versus "countryside" (peasant) was often expressed in terms of "consciousness" versus "spontaneity." Consciousness in this Marxist sense meant not individual creativity, inspiration, or (as it often did for Dostoevsky) the freedom of personal will and the responsibility of choice, but was applied more narrowly, to mean an awareness of the dialectical shape of history and the inevitable victory of the proletariat. Opposed to this party-minded awareness was "spontaneity": people reacting anarchically, instinctively, out of their immediate anger or blind need, peasants burning manor houses or peasant-soldier recruits deserting the Imperialist War of 1914–17, voting for peace with their feet. Both energies, Lenin knew, were essential for revolution. But which energy would control and exploit the other? Hundreds of early Bolshevik-era novels were constructed around this dichotomy. Many believed that a symbiotic relation between these two forces was possible, at the level of the individual body as well as the body politic.

Russian Futurists, Constructivists, Cosmists, Nietzschean god-builders, and other immensely creative revolutionary visionaries desired to turn the body into something healthy, expressive, coordinated, and free.[31] The Bolshevik 1920s were an era of genuine lyricism about the possibility of the machine to liberate human labor and everyday life, not into inhuman regimentation or totalitarianism but into a kind of disciplined rhythmic dance. The enemy was not the Crystal Palace or OneState, which no one had ever seen, but the chaotic filthy sweatshop and the germ-laden tenement, which were everywhere.[32] Ready to sweep the old factory and slum away were the ideals of efficiency, hygiene, and technological beauty. In the aesthetic sphere, Vsevolod Meyerhold (1874–1940) trained his acting company in "biomechanics," a course in athletics and bodily self-discipline that incorporated eurhythmics, labor-efficiency studies, stylized use of gesture, and even the reflexology of Pavlov's laboratories toward the ideal of a standardized, externalized, and thus democratized expression of emotion. In the 1930s, this theatricalization of the body would be regimented into sports parades, mass physical culture extravaganzas, and military exercises.

The relationship between Modernist aesthetics and the most destructive totalitarian regimes of twentieth-century Europe – Fascism and Stalinism – has long been in dispute. On the Russian front, one transition can be found in the closing sentences of Leon Trotsky's *Literature and Revolution*, published in 1924. It is an eloquent and enlightened Marxist treatise, in which Futurists, Russian Formalist critics, and budding proletarian art are all discussed, their positive and negative aspects weighed. Trotsky, although no friend of Modernism, acknowledged the artistic avant-garde as a potential ally in building the new world. He did not, of course, exempt its members from the "consciousness" versus "spontaneity" dialectic: "We stepped in to the Revolution," he insists, "while Futurism fell into it."[33] But "mysticism" and "Romanticism" of the old Symbolist and nineteenth-century sorts are declared altogether incompatible with the Revolution.

Then Trotsky ends his treatise on a vision so mystically romantic that it recalls an utterance from Zamyatin's D-503 in his most true-believing phase, before the birth of his doubting soul. "Man will make it his purpose to master his own feelings, to raise his instincts to the heights of consciousness, to make them transparent . . . to create a higher biologic type, or, if you please, a superman," Trotsky wrote (p. 256):

> Social construction and psycho-physical self-education will become two aspects of one and the same process . . . Man will become immeasurably stronger, wiser, and subtler; his body will become more harmonized, his movements more rhythmic, his voice more musical. The forms of life will become dynamically dramatic. The average human type will rise to the heights of an Aristotle, a Goethe, a Marx. And above this ridge, new peaks will rise.

Trotsky was expelled from the Soviet Union in 1929 and murdered in Mexico on Stalin's orders in 1940. But the utopian sentiments expressed in those final lines continued to inspire, guide, and torment writers throughout the Stalinist years.

Chapter 8

The Stalin years: socialist realism, anti-fascist fairy tales, wilderness

1921:	*Victory of Bolsheviks in Civil War; imposition of one-party rule*
1921:	*New Economic Policy (NEP) (some private enterprise restored in service sector and limited free market)*
1921–28:	*Maksim Gorky in exile in Italy*
1924:	*Death of Lenin*
1928:	*Joseph Stalin, General-Secretary of the Party, launches first Five-Year Plan*
1929:	*Expulsion of Trotsky from the Soviet Union*
1930:	*10 million peasants forcibly collectivized during two winter months*
1931:	*Beginning of terror-famine in Ukraine*
1932:	*Creation of Union of Soviet Writers and doctrine of socialist realism*
1934:	*First Congress of Union of Soviet Writers*
1937–38:	*The Great Terror*
1941:	*Hitler invades the USSR*
1945:	*World War II ends with full victory for USSR*
1948:	*Party crackdown on creative elite*
1953:	*Death of Stalin*

It is always difficult to reconstruct the appeal or the relevance of a losing side. All that remains are the products, without the living, electrifying myths or manipulated audiences that sustained them. The Stalinist period of the Russian literary tradition (1928–53) is one such massively discredited enterprise. Politically, economically, militarily, culturally, the Soviet Union was a "command state": governed by decrees from above and profoundly unliberal in its professed ideals.

This chapter limits itself to the literary side of the Stalinist experiment. Appalling violence, waste, caprice and lies disfigured those years, but boldness and a thrilling enthusiasm illuminated them as well. We tend to forget how very bad Western capitalism looked in the 1930s and 1940s, with its worldwide depression, unchecked military aggression, abominable race relations – and thus how courageous and appealing many found the Soviet insistence on an entirely new basis for literary and political culture, a fresh slate of heroes and plots. Our starting point will be 1934, the First Congress of the Union of Soviet Writers. That Congress declared the doctrine of "socialist realism," formulated two years earlier, as the official (and sole) successor to the Russian literary tradition as we have presented it so far in this book. In his opening speech, the recently repatriated Maksim Gorky, president of the Writers' Union, surveyed that tradition and found it seriously flawed, especially in two widespread nineteenth-century movements he proceeded to classify as unacceptably bourgeois: "the old romanticism" and "critical realism." To help us grasp Gorky's plea for a clean literary slate for Russia, and to better orient us in the resulting ideological terrain, we must first clear away two enduring Western misconceptions – two bad binary oppositions – about artistic creativity in the Stalinist period.

First is the familiar opposition of "collaborator" versus "martyr." This convenient yet dysfunctional Cold War binary divides up the residents of a totalitarian society into two camps: conformists or dissidents, the triumphantly self-righteous or the suffering victim – which was itself a Romantic cliché that Gorky deplored. Most people, including artists, are neither. They simply survive, balancing daily the benefits and costs of being useful, "normal" citizens in their society. This means taking a stand at some points, lying low at others, and constantly devising compromises to protect one's comfort, dignity, work, and family. Moreover, during these years the collaborator often *became* the martyr, rewarded one day and pilloried the next. Such a carrot-and-stick, two-steps-forward-one-step-back method proved to be one of the shrewdest psychological levers of Stalinism. In a system run not by market mechanisms but by patronage plus terror, it was hardly worth "commanding" or terrorizing minor talent. But this policy of seduction and rejection complicated any easy model of "Poet versus Tsar." Thus the famous ritual humiliations: pampering Shostakovich, then publicly shaming him in 1936, then reincorporating him into Soviet music; banning Bulgakov's work and then (after a personal phone call from Stalin in April 1929) partially reinstating him in the Moscow Art Theatre. Mikhail Zoshchenko (1895–1958), an immensely successful satirist in the 1920s, was singled out for savage attack, together with the preeminent poet Anna Akhmatova, to mark the onset of a new repressive party line in the arts in 1946. The martyrdom of these writers was all the more precious to the Party when there was collaboration, or at least acquiescence, on either side of it.

The second bad or inadequate binary pits "free" against "unfree" art. Liberal or open societies usually insist on the right of creative artists to be political or apolitical as it suits them. In this regard, Stalinism grotesquely narrowed the sphere of the private: every personal act was potentially political. This politicized dimension was not necessarily punitive or imposed. Recent work on

Stalin-era diaries suggests that "forging an identity," for a young Soviet citizen, was not the individualizing process familiar in the West (or in Tolstoy), with its goal of a unique voice free from societal constraint. More likely it was the reverse, a striving for the transcendence of the personal: "a Communist should make himself permanently at home in a heroic universe by means of uninterrupted, sustained ideological thinking and acting" and should understand failure as a matter of one's "personal deviations from a mandated norm."[1] This model recalls the saint's life, which a human subject internalizes and "grows into" as into an ideal prototype. Such self-fashioning complemented a more general shift toward active monitoring of creative acts. To the negative censorship familiar from tsarist Russia (deleting what could *not* be said) was added a new layer of positive censorship (dictating what *must* be said). This peremptory guidance was transmitted through a *sotsial'nyi zakaz* or "social command".

The Soviet state had another carrot, however, which in the minds of many creative artists worked to offset the constant intimidation, control of culture by thugs and hacks, and silencing of the disobedient. This was the fact that the state and Party were committed to sponsoring serious art – and, at the same time, to ensuring that a large spectrum of artistic media and genres were considered "serious." As part of the Leninist cultural revolution of the early 1920s, lavishly financed outreach programs in the popular arts reached mass audiences. Factory workers were organized into brigades and bussed to theatre performances; crews of writers and musicians were dispatched to factories to explain operatic plots and teach workers how to write poetry. Such aggressively proletarian programs were discontinued in the 1930s. By that time artists no longer explained their craft; their craft was explained to them by censorship and repertory boards. But traces of this cultural populism remained. Musical theatre and film were valued as moral education, not only as entertainment, and the nation's most gifted artists produced magnificent scenarios, propaganda canvases, and musical scores on commission.

As state violence became more capricious and widespread in the upper ruling circles, public campaigns intensified for "culturedness" [*kul'turnost'*] at the local level. Culturedness drives, beginning in the mid-1920s, covered not only literary and visual education – the domain of writers and filmmakers – but also personal behavior, mental attitude, health and hygiene. Lenin's wife Nadezhda Krupskaya is on record saying that to persuade workers to wash their hands would be a revolutionary step forward. Much attention was paid to the proper use of sexual energy, where "spontaneity" could easily be unproductive unless harnessed for society's benefit and regulated by the norms of *kul'turnost'*. Although the Party resisted laying down strict rules in this realm, Leninist pamphlets explained to Soviet youth the most seemly, efficient means for dealing with the functional necessity of intercourse. A brisk public debate developed over the best ways to avoid sexual arousal ("Never drink alcohol . . . Upon waking, stand up at once . . . Urinate before going to bed . . . Flirtation, courtship and coquetry should not enter into sexual relations . . . There should be no jealousy").[2] In 1927–28, as part of this high-profile debate, Vsevolod Meyerhold defended to Party skeptics his staging of Sergei Tretyakov's play *I Want a Child*, about the conception and production of a healthy Soviet child by a no-nonsense communist woman who refuses to endure the indignities of Dionysian libido. Meyerhold advocated turning its strange love-free plot into a public discussion, bringing the audience on stage for improvised dialogue in the spirit of *commedia dell'arte*.

With this agenda in the moral and physiological sphere, conflicts of state interest were inevitable. Some high-ranking Bolsheviks, who promoted a healthy and harmonious body for the New Soviet Man, advocated the prohibition of all alcohol – but in 1927 Stalin (following his tsarist predecessors) instituted a state monopoly on vodka, justifying it as an indispensable revenue source for Russia's industrialization.[3] These clean-living campaigns might strike us now as naïvely high-minded, but such priorities appealed powerfully to many artists, as much for Tolstoyan reasons (subduing our "animal" side) as for political ones. Many took pride in the fact that in communist Russia, "healthy art for the people" was not obliged to cater to a Hollywood market mentality aimed at pleasing the crowd at any price, nor (at the other extreme) to an arrogantly isolated, incomprehensible avant-garde. Indeed if need be the tastes of both elite and mass audiences could be ignored, since the official success or failure of a work was judged "scientifically," before its publication or performance, by Party committees. Serious art in Russia meant serious social engagement toward a positive goal, determined in a collectively "conscious" – not an independently "spontaneous" – manner. Consciousness, once achieved, was always unified, goal-directed, and stable: a second-order simplicity.

Collaborator versus dissident, free versus unfree: such categories are too rigid to be useful. From the perspective of Russia's most gifted creators, it is possible that the maximally criminal aspect of Stalinist cultural policy might turn out to be not its cruelty, wastefulness, utopian or dictated aspects – although those qualities certainly applied – but the fact that it was so arbitrary and discontinuous. Party-line shifts were abrupt, unpredictable, justified by coded or meaningless phrases. Even those who wanted to cooperate (a far more compassionate verb than the sinister "collaborate") could never be sure how to go about it. This arbitrariness – defined here as a demand that does not need to justify itself – is called in Russian *proizvol*. Live under it long enough, and the result (at best) is indifference, a quick default to irony, loss of creative initiative, and at worst, paralyzing fear.

Faced with this reality, some writers (and the editors and publishers who vetted their work) began to practice "the genre of silence" – a phrase coined by Isaak Babel in self-defense at the 1934 Writers' Congress. During the most dangerous periods, the entire culture-producing apparatus could grind to a halt. In more flexible years, Babel and other great artists (among them Mikhail Bulgakov and Boris Pasternak) worked in literary fields less ideologically regimented than creative writing: translation, adaptations for stage, screenplays, literary scholarship or textology, literature for children. In a bureaucracy this vast, it was easy not to know precisely how one fit in to the "system," or why one was cast out. Why was Pasternak not arrested in 1938–40? (a miracle). Was some lower-level rival, not the Party or party line, responsible for denouncing Shostakovich's work in 1936? (he thought so). Some creative artists, of course, were unwaveringly proud to be part of the social command. But artists of the highest talent could not be put repeatedly in a position where they trusted neither the inner rules that governed their own creative imagination, nor the outer rules that governed the society of which they were a part.

Massive literacy campaigns, begun in the early 1920s, created millions of new readers, both among the rural population of European Russia and (in newly devised alphabets) among those peoples or tribes in Siberia that previously had no written language. Approved authors and books had unimaginably large print runs. Newly re-canonized and cleansed, classic Russian writers flooded the country in millions of copies, especially during their centennials (Tolstoy in 1928, Pushkin in 1937). Thus cultural expansion and cultural contraction occurred together. Alongside the gradual curtailment of foreign travel for ordinary citizens came the disappearance of foreign (European) language instruction in the schools. Only specialists received this training; the ordinary Russian reader encountered the outside world through carefully controlled translations. Russian high culture – which for two hundred years, through all degrees and severities of censorship, had been among the most polyglot in Europe – became officially monolingual. This narrowing, in conjunction with the closing down of churches and religious education, resulted in the new Soviet reader's unprecedented reliance on the state and Party for intellectual and spiritual guidance.

Throughout the 1920s, a profusion of literary groups competed for readers. For most of them, the devastated economy and paper shortage ruled out anything like the "thick journal" of nineteenth-century fame, but relations between these groups were nevertheless articulate, shrill, and saturated with ideology. Proletkult ("Proletarian Culture") was founded during the Civil War, on the slogans of class struggle. In 1923 the Futurist-inspired LEF ("Left Front of Literature") was attacked by the more militant "On Guard" and "October" groups, which had no patience with formally innovative poetry even when it supported the Bolshevik cause. Peasant writers and proletarian writers each had their own national organizations. Some insisted on the author's right to be political in an individually chosen way (excluding, of course, the option of opposition to Bolshevik rule); Trotsky labeled these non-aligned but non-hostile writers *poputchiki*, "fellow travelers" of the Revolution, and recommended that they be tolerated. In 1925, the Central Committee of the Communist Party formally resolved that it would not commit itself to support any particular literary school.

By the mid-1920s, a certain "normalization" had set in. One index of stability was Maksim Gorky's decision in 1927 to return to Russia from Sorrento, Italy, after seven years of self-imposed exile. Such returns into the lap of Stalinism would be repeated by other great Russian creative artists, including the composer Sergei Prokofiev in 1936 and the poet Marina Tsvetaeva in 1939. A world-famous and well-traveled writer before the Revolution, Gorky had exiled himself once before, 1906–13, to the Italian island of Capri. There he befriended Lenin and other visionary revolutionaries. But his relations with Lenin became tense, and at times bitter, during the Revolution, especially over repressions of the cultural elite. By temperament Gorky was more a revolutionary humanist than a Bolshevik (he was not a Party member). His humanitarian activity on behalf of threatened writers embarrassed the more iron-fisted of the Bolsheviks. But Gorky, an autodidact from a working-class family with no formal schooling after the age of eleven (and with no "suspicious" foreign languages at all despite his several sojourns abroad), had achieved the Soviet-era equivalent of the status that Count Leo Tolstoy enjoyed under the Old Regime. Ties with Lenin, together with his fame and reputation for moral goodness, made him a difficult man to silence. Lenin himself pressed a second voluntary exile on Gorky in 1921, "for reasons of his health."

The regime trumpeted Gorky's return as a political and cultural triumph, rewarding him with fabulous gifts. He received a former millionaire's mansion as his Moscow residence, an estate in the Crimea, an unlimited bank account (although Gorky cared little about money), and the honor of having towns, streets, schools and factories named after him while he was still alive. At the same time, police surveillance over Gorky (sustained at modest levels during the exile years through members of his own household) significantly increased. Surely Gorky's monolinguality heightened his willingness to return; unlike the quatralingual Prokofiev or Tsvetaeva, Gorky carried Russia within him wherever he was and could make for himself no other verbal home. It seems that he accepted the chairmanship of the Writers' Union in 1932 with the intent of saving lives, as he had done in 1919–21. But deeper affinities to emerging Stalinist norms must have played a role as well: his unquenchable idealism, his intolerance for truths that depress and deplete, and his preference for hope (which Gorky saw as a form of creativity) over the harmful facts of the present.

The stabilization of literary politics in the mid-1920s turned out to be more apparent than real: the spectrum was shifting. One early harbinger of the change had been the so-called "philosophers' steamship" in 1922, the deportation to Western Europe of Russia's prominent idealist philosophers and religious thinkers (with no right of return). This gifted group lent prestige and visibility to the Russian emigration until the end of World War II. Philosophy permitted to remain active on Soviet soil increasingly came to share the tenets of dialectical materialism – or, as it was popularly known, "diamat." This worldview became part of the (willing or unwilling) mental equipment of all Soviet citizens, who were required to take academic courses in the discipline at all levels of their education. Dialectical materialism could be resisted, amended, and parodied (as Bulgakov does brilliantly on several levels in his novel *The Master and Margarita*), but only privately. Combined with socialist realism, the presumptions of "diamat" made possible the optimism, self-confidence, and energetic but oddly flattened psychology of generations of state-approved Stalin-era "positive heroes."[4]

Dialectical materialism might be laid out simply as follows. All reality, in its essence, is material. Matter is objective and primary. But matter is not *dead*; Marx insisted that motion is an essential quality of all matter, and by this he meant not mere mechanical motion but a vital impulse, a tension inherent in the material world. Since the psyche that receives this vital material is initially blank and has no independent existence, reality is fully knowable. The knowing subject must act on matter so as to release the energy in it. In this sense, subjects are both born into their world and become the responsible makers of it. But a subject is not authorized to act or think in a wholly autonomous way, as in Romantic or Idealist theories of cognition, because the material world, to a large extent, determines the subject. This circular conditioning takes place through "social being," of which the subject can be more or less aware. In this imported "Western" doctrine of dialectical materialism we already glimpse certain tenets compatible with Russian folk and Orthodox views of the world: a reverence for matter and its transfiguration, the primacy of the communal whole over the individual specimen. Not by chance did many great twentieth-century Russian religious philosophers experience in their youth a passionate Marxist phase.

Dialectical materialism has other aspects less compatible with a religious worldview, however. Although all material nature forms an interconnected whole, there is nothing absolute or eternal in that whole. Development is not the result of a uniform evolutionary process but is punctuated with periods of cataclysm: qualitatively different, revolutionary change. All change is the result of a conflict between opposing tendencies, which in principle can be resolved temporarily in a new synthesis. During the Stalinist years, what it means to know, act, and succeed within the confines of such a doctrine had a profound effect on the psychological motivation of literary heroes, as well as on the shape of the plot in which they moved.

What was socialist realism?

In April 1932, by official decree, all independent writers' organizations were dissolved and replaced by a single Union of Soviet Writers. The word "union" [*soyuz*] in the Soviet context has nothing in common with employees' "unions" in the West (trade unions and the like), which exist to defend the rights of worker-clients against employers. In the USSR, no such rights formally existed; also, there were no private employers, nor were there neutral courts to adjudicate conflicting claims. "Creative unions" were conduits for social commands. Novels, poems, poster art, and symphonies were perceived as cultural products that could be put to work for the good of socialist society, just as pig iron, an industrial product, was put to work. This does not mean that the unions were monolithic or unmindful of the needs of their respective artistic disciplines. But only in its bosom could one live professionally by one's art.

Stalin called Soviet writers "engineers of the soul." To be recognized as a writer – and thus to be officially employed (a non-trivial obligation in a state with anti-parasite laws) – one had to do more than write and submit one's work. One had to be a member of the Union. Since the Writers' Union had a financial division (*Litfond*) in addition to an organizational bureaucracy (*Orgbyuro*), it functioned both as literary agent and as ideological monitor. In reward for compliance and high productivity, the Union provided its members with royalties, commissions, access to vacation resorts operated by cultural agencies, quality living quarters, forums for discussion of their work, and foreign travel (under certain conditions: that the writer be engaged in an approved study of a foreign culture, be willing to serve as propagandist for Soviet art, be available to file reports for the security police, and have family members who could be left behind as hostages). Soon after its founding, the Writers' Union, in collaboration with the Communist Party's Central Committee, worked out its literary policy, a vital part of Stalin's second Five-Year Plan (1933–37) that was to enact Soviet Russia's official transition to a classless society. The ideological charge to writers was "socialist realism," defined in the statutes as "demanding of the artist the truthful, historically concrete representation of reality in its revolutionary development."

The weirdly abstract nature of that definition was first explicated for a Western audience in 1959, by an insider, Andrei Sinyavsky – that same writer who, as an émigré two decades later, would publish his Sorbonne lectures on Ivan the Fool. In his essay "What Is Socialist Realism," published under the pseudonym Abram Tertz, Sinyavsky explained that the doctrine seems odd to outsiders because the concept of "revolutionary development" has nothing to do with any visible or palpable reality. The "socialist realist" writer is neither realist in the old way – he does not attempt to describe "what exists," as did Tolstoy or Chekhov – nor is he socialist in an overtly political fashion, oriented toward today's struggles. This new type of writer hardly sees the present. What *is* seen, Sinyavsky remarks with some irony, is "Purpose with a capital P."[5] Focus steadfastly on this Purpose, and your consciousness will be transformed. However fleetingly, you will see the future goal manifest in the messy and mediocre present. Skeptics laugh at these ardent true believers, Sinyavsky admits, just as the urbane pagan Romans laughed at (and crucified) the early Christians. But the nineteenth century, with its doubts and quests – "soft, shriveled, feminine, melancholy" – was a disaster from the perspective of Purpose. Sinyavsky concludes his essay by suggesting that twentieth-century socialist realism is actually closer to neoclassicism, a favored carrier for the ideological certainty and patronage art of the eighteenth century.

Sinyavsky's tone in this 1959 essay is caustically provocative, as befits a Purpose that had grown decrepit and cynical over a quarter century. But Sinyavsky faithfully repeats many of the points Gorky made in 1934, even though Gorky uses the phrase "socialist realist" only once. For its time and place, Gorky's speech was astonishingly cosmopolitan. Much of it is devoted to the history of world literature, and how Soviet Russia might enrich that history by overhauling its repertory of heroes and plots. We consider only two of his most influential positions: his blistering critique of "bourgeois literature," and his hopes for a new Russian alternative to it.

Throughout his 1934 speech, after the manner of so many Russian critics from Belinsky to Bakhtin, Gorky projects onto the world at large what are essentially native Russian values: traditional folk worldviews, prejudices against mercantile activity, Russified Marxist truisms. He begins by confirming that labor, the spoken word (incantations, spells), and a "materialist mode of thought" lay at the base of all primitive cultures.[6] He then insists that "when the history of culture is written by Marxists, we shall see that *the bourgeoisie's role in the process of cultural creativity has been grossly exaggerated"* (p. 233, Gorky's emphasis). Especially repellant to Gorky is the fact that the heroes of bourgeois literature are all "swindlers, thieves, murderers, and detectives" – the detective novel being an idle game between propertied capitalists, the "favorite spiritual repast of satiated people in Europe" (p. 238) – devoid of plots that could engage or inspire the working class that actually produces the wealth. In addition to crooks and the detective who stalks them, the nineteenth century showcased the "superfluous person." This empty and Purposeless individual had been featured in both lines of progressive European literature familiar in Russia: "critical realism" and its softer, more ecstatic precursor, "revolutionary romanticism." The former "-ism" saw clearly the ills of society but offered no constructive alternative to them; the latter did not see at all.

What should the new Soviet person strive to see? This person should not dwell on the dark or perverse sides of human nature. Those are "survivals," relics, reality not in its "revolutionary development" but reality stuck motionless somewhere far back on the path. Access to the "truthful, historically concrete representation of reality" depends on one's Party-disciplined eye picking out the proper details on which to focus, and ascertaining where, on the ladder to the future, they belong. Truth in this context might be compared to an energy field surrounding and infusing the subject; immersed in the proper class or collective milieu, any person could become "conscious" and begin to see. Under the new regime, literature was no longer primarily a record of self-expression, and not even "a form of passive ideological reflection, but an active, 'healthy,' controlled ideological instrument, not a mirror any more but a weapon."[7] History could be hastened along by attitude alone, an energy resource that never runs out – even when a population is devastated by every conceivable type of war, famine, economic collapse, personal loss, and grief.

Four socialist realist principles eventually governed what a conscious subject, inside and outside the fictional text, is privileged to see.[8] *Partiinost'*, "party-mindedness," decrees that every artistic act is also a political act. The source of all authoritative knowledge is the Party. *Ideinost'*, "idea-mindedness," is specifically topical: the "idea" of the artwork should embody the current high-priority party slogan (reconstructing a ruined factory, abolishing drunkenness, building the Moscow metro, destroying the fascist enemy). *Klassovost'*, "class-mindedness," both acknowledges the social-class origin of art and obliges it to further the struggle of the proletariat. *Narodnost'*, "people- or folk-mindedness," requires art to be accessible and appealing to the masses by drawing on their traditions, language, melodies, rhythms, and values. Since the Soviet Union was a multinational state, *narodnost'* authorized considerable cultural diversity (within, of course, a framework of ideological uniformity). In practice this meant that folk songs, legends, colorful costumes and superstitions, local peasant and tribal rituals were allowed their own expression, even their own national language, and could coexist alongside the more "consciously" proletarian plots of hydroelectric dams, cement factories, and metros. But like historical facts inside a patriotic history play during the Romantic era, "authenticity" here was ornamental, sentimental, pre-packaged, and essentially powerless.

The third principle in this quartet, class-mindedness, became less important after 1936, when the new Soviet Constitution declared that the USSR had become a classless society and thus all class antagonism was officially ended. Such conflictlessness made it difficult for fiction writers to find, from within the domestic population, villains, rogues, or any negative principles out of which to construct plots. A new genre appeared: the "optimistic tragedy." This manic optimism affected writers personally as well as creatively. Mikhail Zoshchenko (1895–1958), perhaps the greatest prose satirist of the 1920s and like so many comics and clowns a clinical depressive, wondered why, if reality could be manipulated and human bodies and natures reforged through attitude alone, he was such a failure at it. In the 1930s, Zoshchenko began writing deeply auto-therapeutic texts, such as *Youth Restored* (1933), in which he attempted to "engineer" his own physical and psychic health.[9] In 1943, in a strange work of "literary research" titled *Before Sunrise*, this troubled writer attempted to reason himself out of his phobias using a combination of Pavlovian reflexology and Sigmund Freud. Although the choice of Zoshchenko as one scapegoat for the post-war crackdown on writers in 1946 certainly exemplified *proizvol*, the punishment was probably not without justification in Zoshchenko's own guilt-ridden mind.

Socialist realism, like every other party line in Stalinist Russia, was never a fixed formula, and certainly not in the 1930s. En route to cleansing Russia of her superfluous heroes and depraved plots, quite a bit of humor and self-criticism remained. Language satire was one vital site for it. Much as eighteenth-century playwrights, including the Empress Catherine II herself, had satirized awkward and ill-learned Frenchifying among the upwardly mobile rural gentry, so the garbled Soviet-speak of the new, barely literate peasants-turned-officials, full of acronyms and poorly digested Bolshevik slogans, was ridiculed by masters of oral narrative or *skaz* (Mikhail Zoshchenko was one such master; Isaak Babel another). Several years before his suicide in 1930, the poet-playwright Vladimir Mayakovsky had parodied this jargon through the brilliant jingles and slick commercial street talk that formed the aural backdrop to his futuristic farce, *The Bedbug*. Dysfunctional or substandard speech – a product of the imperfect, and thus potentially sympathetic human face – is naturally individualizing. The right to integrate such disoriented language into art was an indispensable safety valve in a society that otherwise demanded ever more conformity and obedience.

Satire and criticism were tolerated, even welcomed, if the target of the satire was a corrupt official or a "NEPman," one of the small entrepreneurs who flourished between 1921 and 1927. (Bulgakov's "Adventures of Chichikov" from the mid-1920s follows this approved formula.) The vast expansion of government bureaucracy had provided many berths for swindlers; both state and reader benefited by having this fact made public. The most beloved hero in this vein, however, was thoroughly unruly and seemingly of no benefit to anyone but himself. This was the con man and imposter Ostap Bender, heir to Gogol's Khlestakov, created by a pair of comic journalist-novelists known by their pen names Ilf and Petrov (Ilya Fainzelberg, 1897–1937 / Evgeny Kataev, 1903–42). They published two famous novels about this trickster, *The Twelve Chairs* (1928) and *The Golden Calf* (1931), at the start of the Stalinist cultural takeover – and each became an immediate bestseller.[10] Throughout the darkest years, Soviet readers continued to respond to these novels rapturously, with a mix of indignation, envy, and unfeigned admiration. Ostap Bender became the shadow comic double to those more single-minded heroes who frantically, devotedly built socialism in the serious novels of the time.

Outright mockery of the heroic task of socialist construction was not permissible. If authors desired to provide an alternative or ambivalent perspective on the state-building or state-defending events of the 1930s and 1940s, the literary means had to be indirect. The three exemplary prose works for this chapter, two novels and one play, were selected with this problem in mind. The basic plotline of each (parodied to various degrees) reflects the simplified types and roles canonical for the era. A positive, politically conscious hero who furthers the Purpose is confronted by an "enemy" – which can be either a person or a concept, usually faceless, always heartless. A third indispensable actor is the "masses": hungry, responsive, confused, in need of leadership and an "idea." This cast of characters invariably seems flattened and two-dimensional when compared with the peaks of nineteenth-century psychological prose. Its "simplified" quality can inspire us, irritate us, amuse us or depress us, depending on the genre in which the characters are embedded and the attitude we bring to the Purpose being pursued.

Only one of our three exemplars is canonically socialist realist. The other two hover around the periphery of that doctrine, build off its needs, mouth its words, envy or parody its self-confidence, and expose its impossible pretensions. Fyodor Gladkov's *Cement* (1925) was one of several party-minded novels

(Gorky's 1906 *Mother* was another) to be declared a prototypical socialist realist work retroactively, that is, after the doctrine became official policy in 1934. In return for this honor, Gladkov was obliged to rewrite his novel several times in accordance with changing party-mindedness. The plot of *Cement* is original to the Soviet experiment and constructed in defiance of the Western novelistic canon; its driving force is not money, fame, self-expression, erotic or family love, but economic production. Our second exemplar, Evgeny Shvarts's dramatized "fairy tales for adults" and especially his *Dragon* (1943), rely on familiarity and old-fashionedness, not originality and industrialization. Shvarts created a distinctively self-conscious, quasi-ironic tone for the stage that did, after a fashion, follow Gorky's 1934 behest to writers to exploit the "profound, striking, artistically perfect types of hero created by folklore." Andrei Platonov, our final exemplar, is the greatest writer of the three. He would have liked to be a "fellow-traveler." But that category of writer had disappeared by 1931 – when Stalin himself purportedly read Platonov's short story "For Future Use" "Vprok" and wrote in the margins: "Talented, but a son-of-a-bitch" [*talantlivo, no svoloch*]. Platonov was classified a "kulak writer" and relegated to the opposition.

Cement and construction (Fyodor Gladkov)

Fyodor Gladkov (1883–1958), a self-made writer from a family of poor Old Believer peasants, became a Marxist early in life and was helped by Gorky toward a literary career. "Lermontov, Dostoevsky and Tolstoy intoxicated me," Gladkov wrote in an autobiographical note. "Pushkin and Gogol left me cold."[11] *Cement* tells the story of the reconstruction of a ruined factory under the leadership of one of its workers, Gleb Chumalov. Returning from the fronts of the Civil War (1918–21), Gleb finds the cement factory in ruins and its workers pilfering, squabbling, and demoralized. His wife Dasha, now liberated from hearth and marriage, heads the Women's Section of the Party. Their hut is neglected, their daughter Nyurka now lives in a children's home. Everything around him is estranged and paralyzed. But Gleb is a *bogatyr*, an epic hero.[12] Once recovered from his initial shock, he radiates energy and restlessness.

Gladkov's fondness for Dostoevsky (and his indifference to Pushkin) leaves its trace in the extraordinarily lush hyperbole of his prose and its heightened emotional aura. His world is one of uninterrupted crisis time and precarious threshold space. Characters are constantly grinding their teeth, clenching their fists, gasping, frothing, flailing their arms. Maximalism is the norm. When Gleb recruits the old-regime engineer Kleist to the factory's cause, he promises him 5,000 workmen, all the material he wants, his word of honor to shoot any saboteurs on the spot, if only he will complete a task that should take a month within four days (p. 116). Kleist is skeptical at first, but then won over. "Heroism means doing the impossible," Gleb remarks to his female comrade Polya (p. 55), who tosses her curly head in agreement – in this novel, men and women flirt via such phrases. Gladkov taps into Nature's wanton energy as well, with nourishing and intoxicating metaphors that we can almost taste, as in the opening lines of the novel: "Behind the roofs and angles of the factory the sea foamed like boiling milk in the flashing sunlight. And the air, between the mountains and the sea, was fiery and lustrous as wine" (p. 1).

The ruined factory is always at the center of our vision. Inside this structure, however, the production of cement is intermittent at best. Production starts up halfway through the novel but is immediately interrupted by armed attacks from anti-Bolshevik forces in the surrounding mountains (tsarist Whites, anarchist-peasant Greens, hostile Cossacks). Mostly the factory is the site of party meetings. Unlike the "boiling milk of the sea" and the lustrous wine-like open air, indoors everything is tobacco smoke, screaming, tramping, rush, filth. Notwithstanding this local ecology, however, Gladkov's novel introduces a new chord in the Russian literary canon: the positive presentation of bureaucratic work. To be sure, bureaucrats can always ossify into self-serving scoundrels, and Gleb is forever threatening to line them up and shoot them. The image of the bullying (and lecherous) Party boss was censored variously in different editions of the novel. But overall, Gladkov presents the stern, leather-jacketed, bronze-faced committee chairmen and security police, who answer to "higher organs" and authorize inhumanly cruel measures, as necessary, positive repositories of consciousness.

Thus the novel *Cement* modifies a longstanding Russian literary tradition that presents bureaucratic activity as pathetic, corrupt, mad, or worthless: the pen-pushing clerks or venal officials in Gogol (Akaky Akakievich, the major who tries to bribe Khlestakov), the schizophrenic functionaries in Dostoevsky (Golyadkin), the irrelevant or ineffectual state ministers in Tolstoy (Aleksei Karenin), the doddering reactionary senator in Bely (Apollon Apollonovich). In Gladkov and socialist realism generally, a man – or woman – can answer to a committee or take part in a task force and not be ridiculed for it. In fact, this is the proper route. Look first to institutions and only later to the specific needs of individuals. Genuine agency resides in Party and collective doctrine, not in the personal story.

This new positive role for committee work went hand in hand with an enhanced role for the secular book. In a novel otherwise obsessively taken up with deeds and deadlines ("do it on time or be shot"), the seemingly passive act of reading is an important marker of virtue for Dasha, the novel's most positive heroine. Amid disintegrating households, ailing children, and ripening treason, she spends hours at her undusted desk, struggling to grasp the truths contained in a Marxist-Leninist textbook. The lessons are learned. Early in the novel, soon after Gleb's return, the couple visits their daughter Nyurka in the children's home. When the matron – whom Dasha suspects of stealing from the children – remarks that "Your Nyurochka is such a lovely little girl," Dasha tenses up: Stop that, she says, "they're all equal here, and they all ought to be lovely" (p. 39). While Gleb is away at party headquarters and Dasha is otherwise occupied, Nyurka dies from malnourishment; she "flickers out" in the children's home. Her mother, we are told, is in anguish but steels herself to conceal it from others. Never do we see that she regrets her decision to abandon her present child for the sake of the equitable flourishing of future life.

Gleb has an equally tensed moment, but for him it is formative. He has been home only a few days and is campaigning to be elected head of the Factory Committee. His most persuasive qualifications are his Civil War stigmata. He has looked death in the face and – he tells the meeting – "I'm as tough as Koshchey the Deathless" (p. 67). Do you need proof? He tears off his tunic and shirt. By the light of the oil-lamp (recalling the vessels placed before holy icons) the assembled voters see: wherever he touches his chest, side, and neck, "purple, pallid scars" show forth. " 'Shall I take down my trousers?' " he then shouts. " 'I'm wearing the same sort of decorations lower down . . . Choose me for this job!' " None of the workers dares to approach Gleb. "They looked at his naked body, all knotted and scarred. Dismayed and shocked by his words, they steamed with sweat and were silent, glued to their seats" (p. 68).

Significantly, Gleb's war wounds are all on the surface. He seems to have suffered no lasting internal damage, and this anatomical diagnosis has some metaphorical weight. Being wounded did not cause Gleb to doubt, but only hardened his resolve. The crisis time, threshold tension, and theatrical bodily display in this novel recall a scene out of Dostoevsky – minus, of course, the genius, richness of ideas, and unreliable or ironic narrator – but in the Dostoevskian novel, crucifixion and resurrection imagery must always serve the inside of the person, not the surface. The depthlessness in socialist realist characters cannot ultimately be explained by the techniques of the psychological novel. They require a different framework, perhaps one more akin to the simpler forms of epic.

Boris Gasparov has put forth the following hypothesis to explain the socialist realist innovation in character construction.[13] The classic psychological novel is built on continuity. Events in it are internalized, remembered, brooded over, recovered in a crooked way, partially confronted or evaded. The illusion of depth in each character derives from this sense of uninterrupted development combined with inner incompleteness – for at any given moment, the hero is multidirectional. Doubts coexist with convictions. The Modernist novel, in contrast, overtly experiments with *non*-continuity: abrupt breaks, hallucinations, glimpses, slices. Juxtaposition and contrast matter more to it than the development of character. Since socialist realism emerged as a deliberate, even militant alternative to Modernism, it is not surprising that psychology returns. As we saw in *Cement*, the spectrum of emotions is broad and the vigor of their expression almost embarrassing. What strikes one as depthless and thin, however, is the unnatural linearity, segmentation, and "one-wayness" of the emotions expressed. There are powerful displays of hatred, jealousy, love, grief – but only in a row, one at a time. Dasha grieves intensely over the death of her daughter, but her grief passes and does not impede her future Party work. Badin, the leather-jacketed chairman, enters Polya's room and rapes her; she is upset about it for one night, his womanizing makes everyone uncomfortable, but it too passes without any lasting consequence, neither straining him nor traumatizing his targets. (It bothered the Stalinist censor, however, when official policy shifted toward conventional "family values" in the mid-1930s; Gladkov was required to tone down Badin's libido.) Gleb is devastated by the loss of his wife and home – but a few lines later he is joking with a neighbor woman and then is delirious with joy at the opening of the factory. Transitions are never a problem, Gasparov points out, and each character, at any given time, is whole. The inner struggle of a personality to answer for a contradictory, side-by-side layering and backsliding of deeds, emotions, responses, is not part of the hero's task.

There is also a Tolstoyan moment in the closing scene of the final chapter, titled "A Thrust into the Future" – Tolstoyan not in style, but in idea. The factory is again working. The dedication ceremony is under way, brass bands playing, the speaker's platform vibrating, Gleb is "pale and glazed," his face convulsed. Gleb does manage to utter some slogans, but the novel ends entirely focused on the mute mass deed. As deeds go, a cement factory would hardly have interested the sage of Yasnaya Polyana – although he would have approved the transcendence of sexual love and the escape from the trap of the biological family. But the reopening of the factory is *not* in fact the deed being celebrated. The primary product is not material, but psychological and sentimental. Just as in Tolstoy's theory of art, what is being celebrated is not the artifact – a novel, a symphony, a cement factory – but the change of spirit in the producer and the receiver of the artifact. This change in attitude is made possible through "revolutionary romanticism": the insistence on seeing and acting on a singular, united sense of the good.[14] Cement is a byproduct. Tolstoy would agree with these priorities. It is significant that throughout the Stalinist period, the quest for a "Red Tolstoy" continued. Appropriately trimmed and packaged, his legacy was not incompatible with many versions of socialist realism. A "Red Dostoevsky" or "Red Chekhov" is inconceivable.

The Dragon and destruction (Evgeny Shvarts)

With its lack of irony and its advocacy of a straightforward Purpose, socialist realism (if judged by Enlightenment criteria) seems to infantilize its partici-pants. For skeptics, this is one reason why children's literature enjoyed such high status under communism. But more substantial reasons exist for the high priority placed on writing fiction for the young. Intense interest in the proper upbringing of the "New Soviet Child" (Gorky founded the first post-revolutionary magazine for children in 1919) reinforced Russia's distinguished research record in developmental child psychology. Writing for children attracted brilliant literary talents who were also shrewd child psychologists – most notably the poets Samuil Marshak (1887–1964) and Korney Chukovsky (1882–1969), both protégés of Gorky – as well as avant-garde poets and prose writers interested in Modernist, Formalist techniques of "estrangement." But children's literature was always a haven. The "world from the view of the child" is an ancient mode of protest against servility and convention, from the Andersen tale of "The Emperor's New Clothes" to the response of the childish Natasha Rostova to an opera performance in *War and Peace*. Fantastic and eccentric visions too whimsical or provocative to pass the grown-up censorship were often tolerated as a category of childish imagination.

Like Nikolai Gogol, Evgeny Shvarts (1896–1958), son of a provincial doctor, was active in amateur theatricals as a child and displayed a great gift of mimicry. In the early 1920s, Shvarts arrived in post-Civil War Petrograd, where he asso-ciated with Surrealist, Absurdist, and Futurist poets; by the end of the decade he was working for children's literary magazines and the Leningrad Children's Theatre. In 1933 he was invited by the Experimental Workshop of the Leningrad Music Hall to create a "Soviet fairy tale."[15] His first attempt, a satire against obstructionist bureaucrats, already exhibited his trademark deadpan tone. His basic recipe mixed everyday routine with the fantastic; concretely realizing metaphors (the bureaucrat really *is* a bloodsucking vampire; the cleaning lady *is* a good fairy, with a certain quota of miracles to perform each quarter) and committing itself, by hook or crook, to the happy end.

Shvarts had a talent for performing the brief, incongruous, manic-dramatic anecdote. He was famous for his jingles and madcap improvisations (a nervous tremor in his hands made it impossible for him to speak from notes). He managed to ply his trade throughout the worst Stalinist years. The fairy-tale format provided optimism without the ambitious bombast of the production novel; moreover, since villains were essential to the folk tale, evil could be portrayed close up even after class antagonism had been formally dissolved by the 1936 Constitution. Shvarts was not repressed, but his best work – a dozen plays in all – either never made it to opening night, or else played once and then were abruptly withdrawn. Only posthumously did his plays enter permanent repertory.

The depthless and detached narration of the folkteller's art would seem to work against its successful dramatization. But Shvarts, at home in the avant-garde from his early Petrograd years, overcomes this handicap by estranging the fairy tale from itself – making it, in its dramatic form, "self-aware." Characters comment to one another on their own fixed function in the plot, which provides them with the security of distance and a certain solace. The most comic and most politicized of Shvarts's plays to speak out in this way is his 1943 classic, *The Dragon [Drakon]: A Fairytale in Three Acts*.

The Dragon was first published as an anti-fascist pamphlet in 500 copies. In it, Shvarts wove together the legend of Sir Lancelot and the Dragon, by the French founder of the literary fairy tale, Charles Perrault (1628–1703), with motifs from European folk-tale repertory transposed to a vaguely Teutonic environment. A kingdom is ruled by a changeling dragon-wizard, his corrupt Bürgermeister [Mayor] and his crony son Heinrich. The Dragon demands a new girl every year. This year's girl, Elsa, is a pragmatist, as is her long-collaborating father. Both have reconciled themselves to the upcoming sacrifice. There are many good reasons to do so, which Elsa's friends and family enumerate in Act I: the Dragon, after all, hasn't been defeated for 400 years; "he's a brilliant strategist and great tactician"; "he got rid of the gypsies for us"; "as long as he's here, no other dragon dares touch us"; "The only way to be free of dragons is to have one of your own."[16] But then an errant knight and professional rescuer of maidens, one Lancelot (a mix of St. George and a Russian *bogatyr*), arrives in town to take him on. The Dragon, although a braggart, is tired of his toadies. He takes Lancelot into his confidence. "I've made these people cripples," he tells the young man. "The human spirit is very hardy. Cut a man's body in half and he croaks. But break his spirit and he'll eat out of your hand . . ." (p. 173).

Lancelot is unimpressed by the Dragon's argument. After all, most of the people he liberates, in story after story and kingdom after kingdom, advise him against such heroics. His task is not only to save the maiden but to wake up the bewitched, collaborating town, to bring it to new consciousness, however quixotic – or holy-foolish – the gesture. Shvarts's characters are cool and flat, surprised at nothing, like "real" fairy-tale folk. Lancelot courts Elsa as Bulat the Brave courted Vasilisa for the Tsarevich: matter of factly, without exaggerated desire or anxiety. He reminds her that neither of them has much freedom within the genre; he has to fight the Dragon, she will have to love him for it. The "animal tale" is also present in this play – a genre whose task is to expose specifically human folly. A plain-speaking, truth-telling cat, disgusted at the town's cowardice, teams up with a donkey serving a group of craftsmen with *skomorokh*-style professions: musical instrument-makers, weavers, and hatters who produce magic carpets and invisible caps. This group of Russian tricksters are the play's subversives, the nucleus of the resistance.

The Mayor and his son Heinrich reproach Lancelot. Call off this challenge, don't fret our dear old Drag, things were quiet here and the Dragon was busy purging our enemies, so who invited you? They bribe Lancelot to withdraw. But the conventions must be observed; "professional villains and heroes" have their obligations, the battle in the sky must begin. Although Lancelot is mortally wounded, he lops off all three of the Dragon's heads. The town takes note. The Mayor, startled, commands the townspeople not to believe their own eyes but only the official communiqué. Eyewitnesses can be mistaken until the course of history is properly understood.

Act III, set one year later, pits the innocence of the fairy tale, with its mandatory transformations and happy ending, against more acerbic types of folk-tale narrative: animal tales and tales of everyday life. In the last two, we recall, the most sinister path is usually the most sensible, and nothing need work out for the heroes at all. Which type of folk tale will this turn out to be? The Mayor is now President, Heinrich is Mayor, and history has been rewritten. It is now officially the President who killed the Dragon – that's his new epithet, Dragon-Slayer – and all his enemies are in prison. He is about to marry Elsa. But something has changed. The letter "L" keeps turning up on walls. The animals and fish can't be forced to talk. Elsa's father can't be bribed with a 153-room apartment with a view. And Elsa, during the wedding ceremony, says "no." The gathered functionaries discount her errant remark, but at that moment Lancelot materializes, greets the crowd, and marches the villains off to prison. The President and his Mayor son make feeble excuses but do not resist. Every rogue and villain in this play knows who he is. Then the returning hero surveys the townsfolk and announces to his Elsa that they must work to "kill the dragon in each of them" – tedious yet necessary work, he says, "more fine-grained than embroidery." As in Pushkin's historical romance *The Captain's Daughter* and other political catastrophes resolved by fairytale techniques – even as far back as the submerged city of Kitezh before the Mongol horde – the righteous are saved at the last minute by a miracle that no one has any right to expect. But mercifully the genre requires it.

The Dragon was written at a dark time. Shvarts's native Leningrad, with a population of almost 3 million, had been blockaded by Nazi troops since September 1941, in what was to become a 900-day siege. Throughout December of that extremely cold winter, with daily bombardment and without fuel, water, heat, or rations, 3,000 people starved to death daily. Shvarts and his wife refused to leave the city. Grown terribly thin but still working as a firefighter, he agreed to be evacuated only in December 1941, when he was almost certain to die of starvation. In reluctant exile from the besieged city, he wrote a play about the Leningrad Blockade titled *One Night*; like the rest of his work, its language was that of a stylized, "self-aware" fairy tale. A Moscow-based committee rejected it for performance. Although the committee members had not themselves experienced Leningrad under siege, they were under orders to minimize the image of that city's suffering. A year later Shvarts wrote *The Dragon*, having been evacuated even further, to Dushanbe (then Stalinabad, Soviet Tajikistan). In August 1944, Akimov's theatre in Petersburg ran *The Dragon* for one night and the play then disappeared from repertory. Like *One Night*, its courage was judged insufficiently patriotic and single-voiced.

The Dragon (and Shvarts's legacy more generally) has been understood in many ways, as anti-Hitler, anti-Stalin, anti-Soviet, anti-bourgeoisie, pro-proletariat, even pro-religious. This broad range suggests the astonishing versatility of folklore genres in times of crisis. For all its author's unimpeachable patriotism, the play could not be reduced to a one-dimensional formula. In this stylized meta-fairy tale – and nowhere more so than in the cowardly collapse of all villains at the end, which suggests that evil is a sham – one senses a trace of eighteenth-century neoclassical "corrective comedy," where virtue takes its triumph for granted and vice, once exposed, literally has no language with which to defend itself. But Shvarts's Prince-Charming end still sounds sly and double-voiced.

In the final act, Elsa's father, who for the first time in his life has just resisted a bribe and thus ceased (for the moment) to collaborate, says to the President: "Stop tormenting us. I've learned how to think, and that is tormenting enough." The moment is stunning. Shvarts's play builds on a long line of Russian fictions that portray the breaking-out of an individual consciousness from the benumbed or terrorized collective, often unwillingly, sometimes as a fool, sometimes as a martyr and a hero – but invariably as a person who is "learning to think." Always there is a wound and a sense of loss. We recall D-503 from Zamyatin's *We*: his growing horror at his specificity, at "feeling himself" separate, since (he persuades himself) "*We* comes from God, *I* from the Devil" (Entry 22). Cast in the folk tale rather than the Modernist mode, however, such threshold breakaway moments will tolerate no hyperbole or hysterics. The testing and magical transformation of heroes in a fairy tale must be described mechanically, dispassionately, as something inevitable regardless of personal fears or preferences. In *The Dragon* that tone is scrupulously preserved. For the villains, it justifies their naked cynicism. For the mortal (but always revivable) hero Lancelot, who has been freeing people against their will for a very long time, it is all in a day's work. For the helpers and the sought-after reward (Elsa), it registers as the triumph of good – but a depleted good. The story is not over when the Princess is won. Lancelot's leisurely announcement of the small, tedious everyday tasks yet to come signals the couple's exit from fairy-tale mode. It also helps explain Shvarts's remark that his favorite author was Chekhov. As in "Lady with a Pet Dog," a happy ending means that the hard work is just beginning.

The discomfort over Shvarts continued into the post-Stalinist and then post-communist periods. Akimov's Comedy Theatre in Moscow revived *The Dragon* at the end of May, 1962, to cautious reviews. In December of that year, Khrushchev signaled the end of the cultural thaw with his crude outburst against Modernist art at the Manezh exhibit. In the spreading cultural freeze, Akimov's theatre was charged with "ideological ambiguity." The director defended his dramatic repertory as both "socialist realist" and true to "idea-mindedness" [*ideinost'*]. *The Dragon* hung on until the end of the season (May 1963), with certain lines deleted – but the censors were nervous about deletions, which, in a well-known playtext, only drew attention to the gaps. In 2005, reviews were also mixed (although for different reasons), when Shvarts's screenplay *Goodbye, Cinderella!* was revived by Anatoly Praudin in his St. Petersburg experimental theatre. The retelling had no Prince and no Ball; all that had been simply a dream. "No, spectator," the commentator ended her review. "It's time to grow up."[17]

Andrei Platonov and suspension

Shvarts was not a dissident. But his techniques of "estrangement," his mastery of folk narration, and his belief in the correctives of a child's quick and healthy wit were effective responses to rigid party-mindedness. Many such strategies were devised by survivors whose lives and works fell somewhere between the extremes of "collaborator" and "martyr." Among great writers in this category, the life and works of Andrei Platonov (1899–1951) are the most haunting.

Platonov departs from our other exemplary writers in having no special city. He is associated with open spaces: wilderness, steppe, desert, tumbleweed, the wandering of lost people or tribes through exotic Siberian and Asian-Russian locales. Activity in that wide-open space is contemplative rather than aggressive; it does not know the frenetic pace of the production or construction novel. But Platonov was not a "peasant writer" with nostalgia for the pre-industrial village or patriarchal homestead – not, in other words, like Russia's most famous twentieth-century Slavophile, Aleksandr Solzhenitsyn. Platonov was part of the new Russia. He knew machines and admired them. In his world, however, the human body is the furthest possible thing from a machine.

Born in the south of Russia into a poor metalworker's family, Platonov, the eldest son, trained as a metalworker and hired himself out to build electric stations. After the Revolution he found work as a specialist in land reclamation in central Russia, where he gained first-hand knowledge of the terrible famine in rural areas during the early 1920s. In the mid-thirties, after Stalin's savage drive to collectivize the peasantry, he made a trip to Turkmenistan in Soviet Central Asia, where the poverty, drought, and suffering had yet to find its chronicler. Throughout these years he wrote steadily: ten novellas, a hundred stories, four plays, six film scenarios, and dozens of critical articles.

Platonov began publishing seriously in 1927, although in small editions. His heroes and plots were out of step with the time: dreamers and drop-outs at grandiose but unrealized construction projects. When, in 1931, Stalin happened to read a short story of Platonov's that struck him as sympathetic to the rich peasants (called kulaks or "fists") then being deprived of their lands and goods, the author found himself almost unemployable. In 1938, his only son, age fifteen, was charged with counter-revolutionary conspiracy and sentenced to ten years' hard labor in a far northern camp. Through the intervention of Mikhail Sholokhov (1905–84), Party-approved author of *The Quiet Don*, Platonov secured his son's release in 1940, but the boy was already dying of tuberculosis. During World War II, Platonov worked as a war correspondent, and after he was wounded was again briefly published. By 1946, he was back on the blacklist – this time for a singularly beautiful short story, "The Homecoming," about a soldier returning from the front to his now-unfamiliar family, a plot Stalin considered "anti-Soviet." From then on, Platonov eked out a living by rewriting folk tales in a mandated pro-Stalinist spirit until his death at age fifty-two, from tuberculosis contracted while nursing his son. Out of this very ordinary, very terrible Soviet-era writer's biography, we will consider only one work, the 1929–30 novel *The Foundation Pit* [*Kotlovan*], the first and greatest philosophical commentary on the structure, language, energy level, and party-mindedness of Gladkov's 1925 production novel *Cement*.

The production of cement, like the destruction of the fascist enemy, is a straightforward material task. Platonov's position on "matter" is far more potent and strange. Socialist realist works presume that the material world can be shaped for the better. There will always be sabotage, fresh destruction, violence, waste, decay, natural disasters – *Cement* is full of these – but the energy that new generations can apply against this "entropy" or anarchy is not questioned. The great ally in this struggle is the industrial machine. Platonov does not reject this faith. In his autobiography he remarked that from his youth he had loved steam engines, shrill whistles, sweaty work, and that there was a link (he didn't know exactly what) between burdocks in the field, electricity, locomotives, and earthquakes. But unlike the construction novel, where this energy passes from animate to inanimate entities (from human muscles, always tensed and hot, to the pulleys that will haul fuel to the factory or bags of cement out of it), in Platonov the flow is more often reversed. Far from being concentrated or accelerated, the energy of human beings escapes and dissipates in open space. Even people eager to work on behalf of a Purpose rapidly cool down. Or as Platonov puts it in his 1938 Turkmenistan novella *Dzhan*: "Men live because they're born, not by truth or by intelligence, and while the heart goes on beating it scatters and spreads their despair and finally destroys itself, losing its substance in patience and in work."[18]

Platonov's two great themes are the persistence of inert matter and the weariness of the working body. In *The Foundation Pit*, both of these "gravitational pulls" prevail over human life. The very language of the narrator is thick, languid, rich in associations, weighed down. We learn in the opening paragraph that the protagonist Voshchev is an outcast, expelled from the machine factory because of his "tendency to stop and think," which interrupted the general pace of work.[19] A traditional Russian wanderer, an ascetic and a seeker, he has also absorbed the new Soviet builder's cosmic ambitions: he "could no longer strive and walk along the road without knowing the exact construction of the whole world and what a man must seek in it" (p. 7). Voshchev wanders onto the construction site of an "All-Proletarian Home" and enlists to dig its foundation. As utopian hopes for the Home increase among the weary workers, so must they increase the depth and dimensions of the foundation pit in order to support this structure, further exhausting their strength. Among other items, their excavations reveal a hundred coffins that had been stockpiled by a nearby village. The second half of the novel recounts violent bizarre episodes from the collectivization of peasants, ending on the death of Nastya, an orphaned little girl, the mascot and muse of the builders. They bury her deep down in the pit, almost in solid rock, so the earth can no longer harm her.

The Foundation Pit has been called a parody of the "Five-Year Plan novel" – novels that celebrate the accomplishments of a planned economy – and the parallels, or inversions, of the Stalinist industrial-production narrative are startlingly evident.[20] Both *The Foundation Pit* and *Cement* depict building projects in the wilderness. The cast of characters in both includes party activists, labor enthusiasts, an old-regime specialist recruited to socialist labor, and a small martyred girl. Violence against class enemies is routine. Both feature "materialist" heroes in the sense of people who believe in the defining power of matter: Voshchev and the two Chumalovs. But there the similarities end. The cement factory rises and the All-Proletarian House sinks. That opposing movement along a single axis partakes of a larger, more disturbing difference in the economy of the two sites, which concerns the relationship between material things, energy flow, and language. In this novel, Platonov offers his alternative to the dynamic of "consciousness" versus "spontaneity" that underpins the official socialist realist worldview. We consider here only two episodes, common to both novels: an "expropriation scene," and the death of a young child.

In Chapter 11 of *Cement*, a Party detachment arrives in town to strip the local bourgeois households of their surplus, round them up with their miserable bundles, and lecture them on the new state of affairs. "You've been living in palaces," says Gleb, "now try huts for a while!" (p. 185). For all the grimness of the event, the scene radiates energy: the communist worker Lukhava strides up to the homeless families, his hair "fluttering like black flames"; "with flaming face, Polia ran up to Gleb" (p. 185). At the very moment of inventory, however, the Whites and Greens join forces and attack the factory. The Reds call an emergency meeting. Motion gives way to more motion. In this whirling knot of events, wealth is grabbed, redistributed, robbed, for a short time even produced – and in all these transactions we sense the dialectic so important to Maksim Gorky in his 1934 speech: in the New Russia, there will be no more superfluous people. Even the capitalists in their comfortable homes can be a source of goods, just as Engineer Kleist is a source of technical knowledge. Matter – energized through machines, guided by ideology, seized by revolutionaries and redistributed by committee – can transform life. The dialogues in *Cement* abound with slogans that promote the continuity between human and mechanical bodies. "Idleness and jabbering!" the engineer Brynza shouts to Gleb at the beginning of the factory reclamation project. "These are machines, and machines are not words; they're hands and eyes!" (p. 17).

The death of Nyurka, the Chumalovs' daughter, works another variant on the same task, that of "steeling" the body and controlling emotions. Part of the "revolutionary romanticism" of Gladkov's novel lies in its patches of very old-style sentimental pathos. Nyurka's life is "flickering out." Every morning and evening Dasha stops by to see her, but "the child had become all bones, and the skin on her face was yellow and rumpled like an old woman's" (p. 243). Ideologically, the mother has gone forward: she is the New Soviet Woman and activist, her red headscarf flashes as she strides down the village path. The child, the new generation, has stayed behind. When Dasha asks Nyurka if she feels any pain or wants anything, the child answers: "I want to stay with you, so that you'd never go away – and always be near . . . and some grapes . . . near you, and grapes" (p. 245). After this exchange, Dasha leaves the Home, flings herself down on the grass, and sobs – but goes back to work. The child was her "life's sacrifice"; we are told the loss was unbearable, but she bears it. She will not grab up Nyurka, feed her, or refuse to part from her. We do not see the actual death; it's not clear that Dasha was present for it. When Gleb gets back from his meeting, Dasha tells him that "Nyurka is no more" with eyes full of tears. But the first subsection of the next chapter (ch. 16) is titled: "Our Hearts Must Be of Stone."

Let us now consider equivalent scenes in *The Foundation Pit*. Compared with a genuine construction novel, the expropriation of the kulaks in Platonov is accomplished with a bare minimum of infrastructure and machines: no tractors, few visible tools, hardly even any weapons. The kulaks have slaughtered their livestock rather than allow it to be requisitioned. Under such conditions there should be a feast. But nourishment from those animals seems to be impossible: "Having liquidated the last of their steaming live inventory, the peasants began to eat meat . . . During that brief time, eating meat was like Communion. Nobody wanted to eat, but it was necessary to hide the flesh of the butchered family beasts inside one's body and save it there from socialization" (pp. 100–01).

Some peasants grew bloated, some vomited, and those who let their livestock be collectivized "lay down in their empty coffins" and made their homes in them, "feeling sheltered and at rest." The expropriating Bolsheviks employ a tame bear to sniff out hoarded food. But edible food is not to be seen; the entire episode is swarming with flies from these carcasses, which seem more alive than their peasant owners. The kulaks too are exhausted. The bear pokes at them with its paw, the requisitioners prod or smack or push them over, and when they die their bodies are simply stacked up. The passage from life to death is scarcely perceptible. One peasant asks his horse if it wants to join the collective farm. "'So you've died?'" he says, getting no response (p. 100). But then we read that "the horse's life was still intact – it merely shrank in distant poverty, broke up into continually smaller particles, and could not weary itself out."

The kulaks are dispatched on a raft down the river, after which the peasants on the *kolkhoz* [collective farm] celebrate the successful expropriation with a party. Singing weakly and stomping heavily, the peasants start up a strange dance. To get them to stop, to rest, they must be tackled by the local cripple and tumbled to the ground. Immediately they fall silent like mummies. The entire sequence echoes one of the most famous grotesque "dance scenes" in Russian literature, Gogol's wedding party at the end of his 1831 Ukrainian tale "Sorochinsky Fair." "People whose sullen faces seem incapable of smiling stamped their feet and shook their shoulders in time to the music," Gogol writes of their drunken swaying. A group of old women is singled out: "Blind to all around them and quite incapable of sensing either compassion or innocent delight, these old hags were propelled by the sheer power of drink into a movement that was faintly human, like lifeless machines set in motion by a mechanic . . ."[21] Such a Gogolian dynamic, poised between animate and inanimate bodies and moving indifferently between them, appears to govern "blind matter" in a triumphantly socialist village as well. The cumulative effect of these entropic scenes in Platonov is mesmerizing and suggests that his materialism was of an entirely original, non-dialectical sort. Such a message was not welcome during the Stalinist era of heroic achievements. Matter, Platonov suggests, is not so easy to mobilize or to control, nor can mere words energize it. Energy flows slower through it than we suppose and cannot be stored reliably in it. The focus of this truth is the death of the orphaned girl Nastya.

Recall how Nyurka had clung to her mother and begged for love and for grapes, speaking like an ordinary little girl, without ideology. Nastya, living in a novel written five years later, is another sort of being, sunk immeasurably deeper into the Stalinist period of re-education and transformation. Her mother dies early in the book, after which Nastya announces to her adoptive collective that at first she "didn't want to get born," she was afraid her mother would be a bourgeois, but "as soon as Lenin came, I came too" (p. 62). She goes to school and learns to chant and to compose letters, one of which she sends to her protector: "Liquidate the kulak as a class," she writes. "Regards to the poor kolkhoz, but not to the kulaks" (p. 84). Instead of signing her name on a document, she signs a hammer and sickle (p. 119). All these childish gestures are somehow both comic and awful. When Nastya dies one night of a chill, the minuscule remaining energy of the pit-diggers dissipates. For she was the forward-looking emancipated one, already living in the future; the adults were the emotional relics, held back by matter and weariness, hoping to learn from her example. If Nyurka's death in *Cement* is the price exacted for her parents' collective idealism, then Nastya's death in *The Foundation Pit* is no longer a meaningful communal sacrifice, only a private elegy.

The "right to the lyric" in an Age of Iron

If judged by Gorky's 1934 speech, socialist realism in literature would appear to be a doctrine designed for the longer forms of prose. Lyric poetry, with its personal addressee, contemplative texture, attention to subtle shifts of emotional state, and intense respect for privacy, could hardly recommend itself in this era of large, heroic narrative forms. But in fact, the smaller poetic forms flourished, although the official function they filled was not that of the Golden or "Silver" Age. The lyric was respected as efficient, earnest, truthful, euphonic speech. When overtly non-political, it was free to be sentimental. A vigorous campaign for the "right to the lyric" was mounted in the mid- to late 1930s, which peaked around three jubilee celebrations: the 100th anniversary of Pushkin's death in 1937, the 150th of Byron's birth in 1938, and the 125th of Lermontov's birth in 1939.[22] A socialist realist climate took naturally to hyperbole and heroic extremes. The huge event of World War II, its "aboveground" moral simplicity, to a certain extent clarified and unified public poetry. The most exquisite lyric cycle of the Stalin years, however, could not be made public: the "Requiem" of Anna Akhmatova (1889–1966), inspired by her son's arrest, written in 1935–43 but not published in its entirety in Russia until 1987. This sequence of ten short, compact, painfully concrete poems, framed (or insulated) by a preface, dedication, prologue, and epilogue, begins with the poet waiting in a prison queue, promising to give voice to the Terror, and ends with that same woman cast in bronze by the banks of the Neva. The cycle passes through every lyric register, from denial through lament, protest, folk ditty, chant, and elegy. In the penultimate poem, "Crucifixion," we see Mary silent near the Cross that bears her dead Son, with Magdalene sobbing and the Disciple turned to stone – but the Mother stands apart, "no one dared look at her." At the deepest reaches of dissidence and grief, one is beyond being watched or seen. We recall in Blok's *Twelve* the image of Jesus Christ, garlanded by white roses but invisible in the storm, leading the Red Guards to some unknown (yet possibly blessed) destination. The end point of this twentieth-century Russian journey can be sensed in Akhmatova's Golgotha tableau.

One final image might be added to this poetic sequence on sacrifice and appropriate vision, from "Hamlet," the first of the "Poems of Yury Zhivago" appended to Pasternak's great novel of the Revolution, *Doctor Zhivago* (1957). The applause is over; Hamlet is about to walk out on stage. He knows his lines and his fate. Both the "murkiness of night" and "thousands of binoculars" are focused on him. He is "willing to play this role" – he is an actor, he has no choice – but "another drama is now taking place. / For now, release me." And so Hamlet's plea: "If you can, Abba, Father, let this cup pass me by." Shakespeare's tragic hero as Christ figure in this poem has its own huge subtext in Pasternak's life. It peaks during the Terror, the very years that Akhmatova was composing her "Requiem," and is linked with the poet's reverence for Meyerhold, and especially for that great director's conviction that every canonical literary work should be adapted freely to the stage in the spirit of its present-day contemporary audience. Early in 1939 Meyerhold, already shamed in the press and deprived of his theatre but still at liberty, commissioned Pasternak to prepare a new translation of Shakespeare's tragedy for staging at the Pushkin Theatre in Leningrad.[23] Pasternak produced the translation but Meyerhold never read it: in June of that year the director was arrested, and several months later, executed. Pasternak expected his own arrest. It never came. Throughout this period he sustained himself by *Hamlet*; twelve versions of his translation remain. Indeed, "another drama was going on."

In the early, ambitious Bolshevik years there were spirited debates over "crises" in all inherited literary genres. In 1922 Osip Mandelstam, one of the century's very great lyric poets, predicted the end of the novel. The European novel, he wrote, had been perfected over an immensely long period of time as "the art form designed to interest the reader in the fate of the individual." Its two identifying features, "biography transformed into a plot" and "psychological motivation," require a "special sense of time," developmental and continuous. That sense, Mandelstam insisted, has been lost. Personal psychological motifs are now impotent; individual action has become abrupt, disconnected, and cruel. "The future development of the novel will be no less than the history of the atomization of biography as a form of personal existence," he predicted. "We shall witness the catastrophic collapse of biography."[24]

To be sure, Mandelstam was wrong about the novel. But Mandelstam's musings in the 1920s are instructive in light of our three exemplary Stalin-era writers. Their fictional worlds are very much a product of the ideology of their time – which, among other savageries, did indeed further the "atomization of [individual] biography" in a ghastly literary sense. Gladkov, Shvarts, and Platonov represent very different ways of accommodating the Stalinist experiment as Maksim Gorky laid it out in 1934 at the First Writers' Congress. All were to some extent "believers." Gladkov created a master socialist realist narrative to celebrate the experiment, in earnest and single-voiced fashion. Shvarts produced ironic, double-voiced but also strangely inspirational fairy tales that required a miracle to bring off their happy ending. Platonov suspended the experiment, ran it in slow motion almost below the voice barrier, and was barely heard in his own time. After Stalin's death in 1953 and the first Thaw in 1956, a broader and more public coming to terms began.

Chapter 9

Coming to terms and seeking new terms: from the first Thaw (1956) to the end of the millennium

1953:	*Death of Stalin*
1954:	*Thaw: Second Congress of Union of Soviet Writers*
1956:	*20th Party Congress, Khrushchev's "secret speech" on Stalin's crimes*
1956:	*Rebellions in Hungary and Poland against Soviet rule*
1958:	*Freeze: Pasternak awarded the Nobel Prize (and is required to renounce it)*
1961:	*Thaw: Stalin's body removed from mausoleum on Red Square*
1963–66:	*Freeze: Arrests of Joseph Brodsky, Andrei Sinyavsky, and Yuly Daniel (1966)*
1968:	*Brezhnev orders invasion of Czechoslovakia to end "Prague Spring"*
1970:	*Solzhenitsyn awarded the Nobel Prize (and accepts it)*
1974:	*Solzhenitsyn deported from USSR*
1987:	*Glasnost (open-ended thaw) begun by Mikhail Gorbachev*
1989:	*Fall of the Berlin Wall*
1991:	*Putsch against Gorbachev fails; abolition of state censorship; Yeltsin becomes president*
1994:	*Solzhenitsyn returns to Russia*
2004:	*B. Akunin's detective novels pass the 8 million mark in Russian sales*

The first half of the twentieth century in Russian literature can be surveyed in terms of its successive doctrines: Symbolism, Futurism, Acmeism, socialist realism. The second half has conventionally been linked with changes in temperature. The journalist and novelist Ilya Ehrenburg (1891–1967) provided the impetus for the "seasonal" metaphor with his minor but immensely influential post-Stalinist novella, *The Thaw* (1954). The image is reassuring. A thaw [*ottepel'*] suggests that culture has not wholly died out nor lost touch with its past – however frozen, exhausted, or lifeless the surface might appear. Spores hide latent under the ice and snow, ready to be warmed back to life as soon as another cycle begins. A lengthy period between a freeze and a thaw, when die-off is not cataclysmic but prohibitions and taboos proliferate (as under Leonid Brezhnev, in office 1964–82), came to be known as a "stagnation" [*zastoi*].

The Thaw that opened out into a meltdown, initiated by Mikhail Gorbachev (in office 1985–91), became famous around the world as glasnost, literally "openness" or "the right to public voice."

Thaws were erratic and unreliable. At the peak of the first Thaw in 1956, Aleksandr Fadeyev (b. 1901), competent novelist and dutiful head of the Union of Soviet Writers from 1939 to 1954, felt the ice shifting and shot himself. Even before Stalin's death, writers began to call for "sincerity" and "honesty" in literature (tentatively, timidly, with a pureness of heart that is now hard to believe). These pioneers discovered, to their astonishment, that they were not expelled from the Writers' Union or arrested for their outspokenness. Since this premiere post-Stalinist Thaw (1954–56) raised issues repeated in later freezings and meltings right up to the final collapse of communism, a brief look at some of its landmarks will help place our exemplary texts and writers.[1]

This first Thaw was bracketed by two institutional sensations: the Second Congress of Soviet Writers, called in 1954 after a twenty-year hiatus, and the Twentieth Party Congress of 1956, where Khrushchev first officially criticized aspects of Stalinist policy, albeit during a secret session. To be sure, neither Congress publicly entertained the possibility that all of communism – or even all "guidance from above" – was a bad thing for writers, any more than Catherine the Great, satirizing the abuses of her regime from the safety of her imperial court, had entertained the possibility that serfdom should be abolished or that her autocracy should become less absolute. But this semi-official exposure of state crimes emboldened the liberal critics. The gains of this initial Thaw fall into four categories: rehabilitations of repressed writers, renewed contact with the outside world, newly permitted literary heroes and plots, and an internal criticism of socialist realism itself.

Posthumous rehabilitation, which cleared for public mention and re-publication many writers who had been put to death or silenced, could be disorienting. Often no reasons were given for the initial repression, nor for the sudden return of the victims to official life. Names restored to the Russian canon included Babel, Bulgakov, Platonov, Zoshchenko (who had four more years to live), and Meyerhold – although the fates of these artists had varied widely, from mere reprimand by Stalin-era bureaucrats to the most brutal murder. Zamyatin remained under taboo. National pride could at last be openly registered for the fact that Ivan Bunin (1870–1953), friend of Chekhov, Tolstoy, and Gorky and émigré since 1919, had won a Nobel Prize in Literature in 1933. Also restored to life was Fyodor Dostoevsky. He was not wholly snuffed out during the Stalin era, of course, but unlike the magnificently manipulated and co-opted Tolstoy, Dostoevsky had been under a dark cloud since his massive discrediting by Gorky even before the Revolution. His greatest works had been weeded out of libraries and banned from school reading lists. In 1955, Dostoevsky was officially recognized as a "great classic Russian writer" and his collected works reissued to mark the seventy-fifth anniversary of his death.

It became somewhat easier for Russians to see, and be seen by, the outside world. More translations into Russian appeared, many of them on the pages of the newly founded journal *Foreign Literature*. Russian readers began to get a taste of non-Russian writers other than those judged to be "progressive" or communist fellow-travelers. Famous émigrés were invited back to visit their birthplace. Among these celebrants were the linguist Roman Jakobson in 1956 and the composer Igor Stravinsky in 1962, both of whom had departed for the West in the 1920s. It was proof of life before the freeze. Each was rapturously received by Russian audiences.

Encouraged by the indifference, or disgust, shown toward the Soviet literary establishment by its more sophisticated colleagues in Eastern bloc countries, some Russian writers began to question the very idea of a single authoritative definition for what literature should do. Initial discussions about socialist realism were guarded and painful. All the "-mindednesses" proclaimed in 1934 (party-, idea-, class-, people-) now seemed tainted. Perhaps writers did not need a "basic method" or a unified goal at all? But the best Russian writers – and their critics, the public intellectuals who wrote about literary art – had always served some higher thing. It was part of their professional definition, that which set Russian literature apart from the rest of the world. Usually this service had been rendered to a collective abstraction: the Russian God, Russian historical destiny, the Russian Word, the People, the good of the nation, the international proletariat, humanity's moral improvement, a Higher Beauty. Neither self-expression nor market demand seemed a satisfactory substitute. If a socialist realist definition of literary purpose was no longer adequate, should it not yield to some other, more worthy priority?

Moreover, socialist realism, however weird and harsh by Western standards, was Russia's own invention. With that doctrine in place, she did not have to compete. She was blazing a different path. Reformist calls for more "variety" in plot or character development sounded suspiciously like a defense of those decadent bourgeois novels that Gorky had exhorted Soviet writers to discard. Those novels were still the sop and opiate of the Western world, inclining their readerships to value private life over public duty, illicit love over fidelity, pleasures over economic productivity, doubt and weak closure over faith in the future, and an obsessive curiosity about the darker human impulses. Of course in literature one wanted to hear "confessions rather than sermons" – as one bold essay put it in 1953 – but what was to keep those confessions from becoming the cruel, indulgent ramblings of an Underground Man? Or worse? To be sure, dialectical materialism and "reality in its revolutionary development" were dry slogans when hacks and toadies applied them to art, but they were more than political opportunism. They implied that human beings could improve themselves by taking the high road. No one at the Writers' Congress doubted the enormous benefits of the Thaw for "freedom *from*": from arbitrary violence against writers, from a corrupt bureaucracy, from a moronic social command. But about "freedom *to*," there was no consensus. From inside the profession, these troubled debates concerned not only "Stalinism versus freedom" (that simplistic and persistent binary) but also "Marxist-Leninist humanism" versus triviality, self-indulgence, and despair.

The virulent campaign directed against Boris Pasternak over the Nobel Prize in Literature is one index of the tension and confusion. When Pasternak received the prize in 1958 for his novel *Doctor Zhivago* (an Italian edition had appeared the previous year, followed soon by the English), he was vilified in the press and at official meetings nationwide as a traitor, philistine, and "decadent formalist" – even though very few Soviets had read the novel, which was still unpublished in Russian. The Bolshevik Revolution is portrayed in that novel for what it was, a political coup rather than a mass uprising, and Strelnikov (the husband of Zhivago's beloved, Lara) destroys peasant villages out of military necessity. But arguably more serious than these political indiscretions is the novel's literary texture, its unapologetic alliance of poetry, medical healing, and erotic love. Russia's suffering becomes background to a personal love story – actually, several love stories – whose resolution always seemed more pressing than any social or moral task. The ease with which this complex philosophical novel was reduced to a sultry, silly, but tuneful and picturesque Hollywood box-office hit (David Lean's 1965 *Doctor Zhivago*, starring Omar Sharif and Julie Christie) is confirmation of its "Western"-friendly plot, if judged by the perspective of party-minded Russian literature at mid-century. Even today, Russians despise the American film as unworthy of their great novelist-poet. In 2006, a Russian television serial based on the novel was produced that polemically targeted that Hollywood bowdlerization.

Pasternak was compelled to renounce the Nobel Prize. If he had left the country to receive it, he would not have been allowed back in. Other international prizes (Venice Film Festival, Cannes) were tolerated, but Soviet authorities bristled about Stockholm. The uneasy relationship between Russian writers and that coveted prize has helped shape the foreign footprint of the Russian canon. Since the founding of the Nobel prizes in 1901, five Russians have won the award for Literature, three of them while on Russian soil. (That Leo Tolstoy, the world's most famous writer, was still alive during the first nine years of the award and not selected for it was a scandal – although the bard of Yasnaya Polyana would surely not have accepted: he craved repression, not one more award, and the idea of literary honor linked to, and financed by, the discoverer of dynamite could only have struck the pacifist Tolstoy as obscene.) The three "Soviet-based" laureates are Boris Pasternak (1958), Mikhail Sholokhov (1965, for his war epic *The Quiet Don* written a quarter-century earlier, 1928–40), and Aleksandr Solzhenitsyn (1970). All awards were political. Even Sholokhov, who had served the Stalinist literary establishment impeccably, was known for his intercessions on behalf of writers. In a spectacular speech at the 1956 Twentieth Party Congress, Sholokhov shamed the Union that had nourished him, remarking on the "huge piles of gray trash" that buried the handful of intelligent books produced over the past several decades – and noting that the Union contained almost four thousand members but this size was deceptive, because among them were so many "dead souls."

Of Russian Nobel laureates, the most heroic in productivity, longevity, and resistance has been Solzhenitsyn. He will be this chapter's first, "Tolstoyan" anchor for its survey of the post-Stalinist literary field. Our second and contrasting anchor will be the most "Dostoevskian" of the women prose writers of the next generation, Lyudmila Petrushevskaya (b. 1938). The third section of this chapter, devoted to three younger prose writers of the post-communist period already well established in English translation, makes no attempt at anchoring or synthesis – only at sampling the rich variety out of which a twenty-first-century literary canon will emerge.

The intelligentsia and the camps (Solzhenitsyn)

Solzhenitsyn is a master of several prison-camp genres, each informed by his privileged position as an intellectual reduced to the ranks of the unfree. *One Day in the Life of Ivan Denisovich*, published in 1962 and a milepost for the new Thaw, was one type of testimony: modest, private, Chekhovian, a single bricklayer's survival from dawn to dusk. Prisoner Shukhov's one day is drawn from Solzhenitsyn's own experience in 1951 in the Siberian camp of Ekibastuz, a vast complex established exclusively for "politicals." But the events of the day are filtered through a far simpler mind. Self-pity and bitterness in this pungent oral diary are minimal. Although the canonical prototype of Siberian hard labor is Dostoevsky's life and prison memoirs, a deeper subtext for Ivan Denisovich's relatively successful day might be Platon Karatayev, prisoner of war, Tolstoy's ideal of a reconciliation with one's fate through resourcefulness and simple manual labor.

Stalinist practice had grotesquely distorted this Tolstoyan motif, with the willing (or recruited) support of the literary establishment. In 1934, Gorky and thirty-five other prominent writers published a festive volume celebrating the completion of the 140-mile Belomor [White Sea] Canal in the far north. The Belomor project had been directed by engineers arrested for this purpose and built by slave labor, as a model for "re-forging" the social renegade into the New Soviet Citizen through corrective physical labor. Its brutal construction plan, which assigned prison crews the task of chipping with primitive tools through solid granite, cost 100,000 lives and resulted in a waterway too shallow to be of commercial value. Ivan Denisovich was not being "reforged." Nor does his author focus on the perverse details of that far less harrowing one day. Solzhenitsyn later remarked that his intent was not to document his own despair, which was very real, but "something more frightening – the gray routine year after year when you forget that the only life you have on earth is destroyed."[2] The "gray routine" of this day nevertheless knew its share of modest success and triumph. That restrained tone surely contributed to the story's publishability in 1962. Solzhenitsyn's older friend and fellow witness Varlam Shalamov (1907–82) saw the Gulag inferno in less quotidian fashion. His collection of *Kolyma Tales*, smuggled out to the West in the early 1970s and drawing on seventeen years in various labor camps between 1929 and 1954, is a sardonic, horrific corrective to Solzhenitsyn's more heroic-ascetic focus on individual moral growth. Shalamov's camps contain lepers who pass unnoticed as maimed war invalids and prisoners whose "workday" includes logging a mountainside that, eroded by the wind, suddenly reveals a "mass prisoners' grave, a stone pit stuffed full of undecayed corpses from 1938" – for in far-north frozen Kolyma, "bodies are not given over to earth, but to stone."[3]

Solzhenitsyn's two quasi-autobiographical novels, *The First Circle* (1964) and *The Cancer Ward* (1968), explore other sides of the Tolstoyan legacy: the morality of science collaborating with evil; and the imperative to die well, with circumscribed desires. These great novels in the style of conventional nineteenth-century psychological realism stand apart from Solzhenitsyn's most ambitious genre hybrid, the massive *Gulag Archipelago* (1973–75), subtitled "an experiment in literary investigation." That subtitle deserves attention. Its "investigatory" dimension was meant to expose Gorky's "disgraceful book on the White Sea Canal, which was the first in Russian literature to glorify slave labor."[4] The "literary" aspect refers, first of all, to the mass of personal narratives woven into the three volumes – but also, one suspects, to the status of Solzhenitsyn's sources. For the safety of their tellers, these orally transmitted horror stories had to remain anonymous. Nevertheless, Solzhenitsyn challenges us to consider all this unverifiable testimony as non-fiction.

The cumulative effect of this strategy is a nightmarish myth spread out along the archipelago of camps – leaping from island to island. Its impact is more powerful than any footnoted facts could ever be, because we know we have access to only a small part of a larger, untellable or lost story. Awe grows as signatures and agents are withheld. This device serves both political and literary ends. It was first perfected by Gogol for his *Dead Souls* in a comic vein, albeit laced with dread; the same dynamic lends weight, authority, and terror to the ominous rumors circulating through Bely's *Petersburg*.

A surprising number of Gogolian moments dot the three *Gulag* volumes. Among the most grotesque is an episode in Volume I (69–70): no year, no place, referenced only as "told me by N. G – ko." At the end of a district Party conference, a tribute to Comrade Stalin provokes stormy applause. Three, four, five minutes of clapping ensue. But since secret police line the hall, no one wants to be the first to stop, or even to appear to be slowing down. Eight, nine, ten minutes pass. The presiding chairman, a recent replacement for a just-arrested man, doesn't dare to desist in full view of all. Finally the director of the local paper factory, a decent and strong-minded man, simply sits down. The exhausted hall immediately falls silent. The director is arrested that night. The specific pretext for the arrest didn't matter; under a system of "economic crimes," every producer could be criminalized for something. What the system targeted was not so much criminals as unfearful, autonomous people. The clapping episode was one of a thousand preemptive ways to weed them out.

Autobiographical novels, memoirs, and "experiments in literary investigation" were means for coming to terms with a political past that could not yet be openly documented or talked about. They were written "for the drawer" or slipped abroad for publication, waiting for the right time. Russia's literary canon, however, was effectively timeless, internalized in each reader and ever ready for quotation. Solzhenitsyn's debts to this canon are reflected in his Nobel Prize speech of 1970. Thematically that speech is permeated by allusions to Dostoevsky – from the 1872 novel *Demons* as an anticipation of Stalinism, to Dostoevsky's enigmatic comment that "beauty will save the world," to a narrowly construed Russo-centrism. But the mission that the Nobel speech laid out for literature was deeply Tolstoyan. Only what is Good and True can also be Beautiful, a justification for aesthetic activity straight out of Tolstoy's 1898 *What Is Art?* People belong to such different worlds, Solzhenitsyn argues; the cultural standards of measurement are so diverse that no mere "newscast" can transmit another's suffering. We might be aroused to anger or curiosity, but we will remain voyeurs. Only the experience of art can communicate the full force of truth across the barriers of nationality and generation. Politics, philosophy, official history, radios, newsreels can (and do) lie with elegance and impunity, but a lie in art will immediately be sensed as false. It will not survive. "In the struggle with lies, art has always triumphed," Solzhenitsyn insists. "Age-old violence will topple in defeat." Thus the writer must not despair but must recommit to the moral struggle, where he is now more necessary than ever. "One word of truth shall outweigh the whole world."[5]

In his subsequent two decades of exile with his family in Cavendish, Vermont, sheltering his three sons from American consumer culture and writing without cease, Solzhenitsyn hardened and universalized his roster of rejections, very much in the style of the later Tolstoy. In 1992, on the brink of the collapse of the Soviet experiment, the prose writer and journalist Tatyana Tolstaya wrote a review of Solzhenitsyn's just published *Rebuilding Russia: Reflections and Tentative Proposals*. She spoke of the myth of his Vermont fence. To émigrés and to Russians on the "mainland" (the USSR), she remarked, this isolated exile had become a "quasi-mythological figure":

> Indeed, he was transformed into an archetype from Russian folklore, into one of those immortal, omnipotent, and often ornery old people who lives in a distant, inaccessible place, on an island or a glass mountain or an impenetrable forest, once-upon-a-time-in-a-far-off-kingdom ... rather like the ancient characters Koshchei the Deathless or Grandfather Know-all or Baba Yaga, a powerful old crone who lives in a forest behind a pike fence decorated with human skulls ... In Russia it was claimed that the fence around the Solzhenitsyn estate was high and impenetrable, topped with barbed-wire snares, like a labor camp.[6]

The Solzhenitsyn fence had nothing to do with Baba Yaga's hut on chicken legs or with the Gulag, of course; it was a modest wire structure to keep out the deer. But the extravagance of the Solzhenitsyn myth, well into an era when such modes of protest seem crankish, utopian, and outdated, speaks to its historical potency.

In January 1993, one year before his return to Russia, Solzhenitsyn was awarded the National Art Club's medal of honor for literature. His wife accepted the award in his name; his son Ignat read a translation of his acceptance speech (a buffered arrangement also reminiscent of the Tolstoy household). The speech was titled "The Relentless Cult of Novelty and How It Wrecked the Century." It sums up this eclectic "Tolstoyan" mode of assessing the Russian tradition.

At fault, Solzhenitsyn insists, was a pursuit of novelty and "avant-gardism" at all cost. After the "general coma of all culture" that had marked Russia's "seventy-year-long ice age" of communism, "under whose heavy glacial cover one could barely discern the secret heartbeat of a handful of great poets and writers," Russians "are crawling out, though barely alive":

> However, some writers have emerged who appreciate the removal of censorship and the new, unlimited artistic freedom mostly in one sense: for allowing uninhibited "self-expression" . . . [Rather than seek eternal values,] many young writers have given in to the more accessible path of pessimistic relativism. Yes, they say, Communist doctrines were a great lie; but then again, absolute truths do not exist anyhow, and trying to find them is pointless . . . Before, [this revolt against culture] burst upon us with the fanfares and gaudy flags of "futurism"; today, the term "post-modernism" is applied.[7]

Solzhenitsyn is indeed no fan of the future or the post-. A bitter opponent of socialist realism in its coercive and formulaic guise, he nevertheless endorses something of that doctrine in its ideal ecstatic form, as did Leo Tolstoy. Solzhenitsyn's writing too can be humorless and morally inflexible, with a self-righteous narrator who takes pride in the ways Russia cannot integrate into the fast-moving consumer cultures of the rest of the world. Such a worldview is easily caricatured. In 1987, the satirist Vladimir Voinovich (b. 1932), several years into forced exile in Germany, published his "anti-anti-utopia" *Moscow 2042*. In this comic projection, the rusting, dysfunctional Moscow of the future, surrounded by three concentric walls or "Rings of Hostility" (Filial, Fraternal, Enemy) and fueling itself by extracting energy from human excrement, is visited by one Sim Simych Karnavalov. Sim is the Solzhenitsyn figure, returned to a country that no longer has the patience for him. "I thought I'd known everything about Sim, but there proved to be a good deal of substance that I didn't know," the narrator writes in Part V, in a chapter titled "New Word on Sim." "It turns out that, during my absence in the twentieth century, he had torn himself away from *The Greater Zone* long enough to dash off four slabs of memoirs entitled SIM."[8] In his own time, the octogenarian Tolstoy had been lampooned in similar fashion, for his disbelief in material progress and for the rigidity of his refusal to depart from the "confessional mode" – that is, from his own Truth as revealed to his own mind through his personal biography. Tolstoy died a nay-sayer and rebel against state, organized religion, and all political movements. The final decade of Solzhenitsyn's life might be displaying a different pattern.

Solzhenitsyn's dissenting voice, first heard in 1962 with *One Day in the Life of Ivan Denisovich*, still rings out in 2007, at age eighty-eight (most controversial in recent years has been his homegrown history of Russian–Jewish relations published in 2001 as *Two Hundred Years Together*). Over Solzhenitsyn's half-century of polemical resistance, the enemy has shifted. Atheistic, expansionist communism and the rapacious imperial West remain his focal realms of evil, as both have been unresponsive to his call for "Repentance and Self-Limitation in the Life of Nations."[9] But the conservative authoritarian nationalism of President Vladimir Putin, former KGB operative, has agreed with Solzhenitsyn. In several well-televised home visits, the President sought the writer's counsel. Generously subsidized by a state-owned bank, the first Russian-language Complete Works of Solzhenitsyn (thirty volumes by 2010, the first three published in 2006) are under way in Moscow. In June 2007, Solzhenitsyn was awarded a state prize for outstanding achievement in the humanities. Putin emphasized that "several steps being taken today are in keeping with what Solzhenitsyn wrote."[10] This renaissance of Russia's most celebrated living dissident on the "state side" of the reigning ideology has provoked caustic debate. When the authorized *Solzhenitsyn Reader: New and Essential Writings* appeared in 2006, edited by two distinguished American professors teaching at Christian colleges, both the *Reader* (and its subject) were criticized as duplicitous.[11]

Solzhenitsyn despised Stalinism while depending on its unrelieved awfulness to organize his heroes and plots. But the power and uncompromising moral texture of his mid-career novels transcend political witnessing. Tolstoyan worlds lie just below the surface of all his writings, played out in intricate variations. Consider only one detail in *Cancer Ward*. The Tolstoyan provocation is from *War and Peace*: Vera Rostova and her philistine husband Berg, decorating their apartment while Napoleon's troops loot Moscow in 1812. Solzhenitsyn's variation on the type is the vulgar, grasping materialist of the communist New Class, Pavel Rusanov, who believes that "after forty years a man and his just deserts can be judged by his apartment . . . Live well, and you think correctly. As Gorky said, a healthy spirit in a healthy body."[12] That's the cartoon. But again like Tolstoy, Solzhenitsyn diversifies his positive heroes against the stereotype. He doles out cancer to communists who are not repellant – who are attractive, idealistic, unafraid to die – and to young girls who are utterly non-political. All of them are slated to lose the organ (vocal cords, stomach, breast) they value the most, the bodily part they had thought they lived by. And even this sacrifice will not necessarily save them. Solzhenitsyn is dry-eyed and epic enough to show us good people who strive and fail. What he will never tolerate is a life devoid of quests for moral self-improvement. In him, the Tolstoyan vein of the Russian prose tradition reaches its natural apex: the monologic *pravednik* confronting a monologic evil.

Beginning in the 1970s and then at galloping pace since 1991, it became clear to emerging generations of Russian writers that both truth and evil were frag-mented far beyond the point where a single psychology or single sinful target could organize them. Focus turned to modes of protest more subtly transgres-sive and imitative, more in the spirit of Pushkin's ripped-off button at Nicholas I's imperial court. The *Gulag* story of the paper-factory director, arrested after being the first to stop clapping for Stalin, was supplemented by other applause scenarios more likely to result in survival. (The poet Yevgeny Yevtushenko relates in his memoirs, for example, how Dmitry Shostakovich, obliged to be present at Khrushchev's pep talks to the "creative intelligentsia" in the early 1960s, grabbed his notebook and assiduously scribbled in it every time the hall burst into applause, creating the impression that he was "writing down all these great thoughts . . . Thank God [the composer confided to the poet], everyone can see that my hands are busy."[13]) In communism's waning years, pretensions to know the shape of history – or even the shape of a single story or a single intent – were impatiently dismissed. Bombastic gestures became ludi-crous. There was a thrilling attention to the peripheral dialect, the wandering detail, the eccentric gesture. Where the true-believing center had been, or had pretended to be, there was a void.

In this new climate, the Tolstoyan pole of post-Stalinist writing met its rival in a revived, more dialogic and ironical Dostoevskian pole. What seemed to appeal most was Dostoevsky's apocalyptically dark side, a cynicism that endorsed nei-ther the spiritual generosity of the positive characters (Sonya, Alyosha, the Elder Zosima) nor Bakhtin's celebrated polyphony, which detected in Dostoevsky the optimistic unfinalizability of all utterances. The new Dostoevsky was a dead-ended Muse. Solzhenitsyn, in the terms laid down in his 1993 National Arts Club speech, would recognize in this newly fashionable desperate literature the "pessimistic relativism" inseparable, in his view, from postmodernism. These dark intonations pervade the work of Lyudmila Petrushevskaya.

The Underground Woman (Petrushevskaya)

Women in Russian literature, and Russian women as writers of literature, have not been a focus of the present book. A brief sketch of the legacy might therefore be useful. The Swiss author Madame de Staël (1766–1817) and French novelist and feminist George Sand (1804–76) were both avidly read in nineteenth-century Russia, as elsewhere on the continent. But Russian authors and readers alike were soon captivated by two domestically produced ideal types: woman as Muse (Pushkin's Tatyana Larina) and woman as religiously inflected "savior" of a sinning man (Dostoevsky's Sonya Marmeladova). To some extent both became restrictive models, a fate hinted at by the title of one pioneering book that confronts this tradition head on, *Terrible Perfection: Women in Russian Literature*.[14] Tolstoy broke with both models in his *Anna Karenina* (1879), arguably the first great Russian heroine in a title role who existed and suffered for her own sake, not as an index to lessons being learned by a man.

In the 1920s, the era of Gladkov's *Cement*, a new paradigm emerges. Without a doubt Dasha Chumalova fails as the parent of an immediately present and needy child. But we should not ignore the fact that she succeeds, and was designed to succeed, as the mouthpiece for a radically new, more self-respecting sort of male–female love. Our horror at Nyurka's starvation in the Children's Home, while her mother attends political meetings and studies Marxism-Leninism, overshadows the final word that Dasha utters in the novel. She has just gathered her pillow and bundle and informed Gleb that the pre-tense of living together as husband and wife is over. Gleb is still raging, as he had been in the opening chapters: first at her withdrawal, now at her betrayal of him with Comrade Badin. He calls Badin a "worthless scoundrel" who has "gobbled up" both his wife and comrade Polya (p. 308) – and fingers his pistol. On this score, his "consciousness" has made no gains against "spontaneity." But with sex as with everything else merely personal (except, temporarily, her daughter's death), Dasha remains calm. "Love will always be love, Gleb, but it requires a new form," she tells her husband. "I shall come to you, go on, my darling . . . We shall find each other again. But bound by other ties, Gleb?"

By the mid-1930s, the conservative Stalinist revolution firmly placed "family values" front and center. Although women had been liberated full-time into the urban workforce ever since the 1920s, in their socialist realist dimension they were increasingly depicted nursing babies in the sunlight or harvesting grain with scythes or tractors. World War II exacerbated the tensions inherent in those dual roles as robust, relaxed mother and economic producer. When so many men did not come home, women stayed on as engineers, doctors, fac-tory workers, sharpshooters and machine-gunners. They became the "positive heroines" in literary plots that still tended to feature feeble, drunken, incon-stant, and superfluous men. The Russian super-heroine does everything. She is both surgeon and street-sweeper. Heavy physical labor has long been part of her lot, and female sobriety and longevity an economic necessity. As one impatient female voice put it in the 1980s, "national disgrace" comes not when women are idle trophy wives at home but when they are out shoveling icy snow-drifts and pouring asphalt "that is then pressed by a steamroller driven by a man."[15]

By the 1970s, women's voices were louder and ranged more widely. One of the most astute belongs to Lyudmila Petrushevskaya (b. 1938), playwright, poet, and prose writer, whose own devastated childhood in children's homes, on the edges of war and surrounded by the Terror, shapes her dark vision and style.[16] Hers is a Dostoevskian "underground" voice, lodged inside a first-person perspective that thoroughly distrusts the natural world as well as other human beings. One of Petrushevskaya's best stories, "Our Crowd" ["Svoi krug," lit. "One's own circle"] (written 1979, publ. 1988) opens on the words of the Underground Man, slightly modified but in the same arrogant, abject stream of consciousness: "I'm a hard harsh person, always with a smile on my full rosy lips and a sneer for everyone . . . I'm very smart. What I don't understand just doesn't exist."[17]

There is this important difference, however. Dostoevsky's Underground Man is to such an extent a shade, an abstract philosophy, that his ailments, inner-organ complaints, and toothaches are all sensed to be metaphysical, which is to say, not sensed at all. When he tells us that "he thinks his liver is diseased" but he's not going to doctors – to hell with doctors – we appreciate this information more as an ideological position than a medical problem. The first-person narrator of "Our Crowd" does not just speak of disease but appears to be dying from it (probably some severe form of diabetes, as we learn in an offhand way): "in a single winter I'd lost both parents, with mother dying of the same kidney disease that some time ago had begun to show up in me and which starts with blindness" (p. 14). The plot of this story, punctuated by random violence and left unexplained to those who most need to know it (if their sympathy is to be aroused), is her attempt to find among her friends a surrogate mother for her soon-to-be-orphaned son.

Petrushevskaya's universe is grim and unsentimental. It is also strongly anti-Tolstoyan, in its rejection of all benign, coordinating narrative authority and all hope for a spark or leap of communication between human beings. For reasons quite different from those of Evgeny Shvarts, she has a passion for the fairy tale and has written several collections for adults. In her hands it becomes a mechanical, faceless, morally blank genre. Her experimental plays, very popular in the 1970s, were produced by amateur student theatre groups before any official journal dared publish her prose (the Lenin Komsomol Theatre caused a sensation with *Three Girls in Blue*, her redo of Chekhov's *Three Sisters*, in 1985). In Petrushevskaya's anatomical materialism, bodies are not transfigured. They routinely vomit, urinate, sweat, and bleed. But these bodies are not mere vehicles for substance abuse or casual suffering; they are symbolic of damage done to the spirit.[18]

In Petrushevskaya's most ambitious piece of prose, *The Time: Night* (1992), the depth of this damage is made clear, as is her status as "pessimistic relativist." The Underground, a valueless dead end, is always pessimistic and relativistic. But being a woman and mother appears to worsen the conditions and raise the costs. The heroine of *The Time: Night* is a mediocre poet and hack journalist, Anna Adrianovna, who seeks an identity by surrounding herself with literary quotations. She worships her "namesake," the great poet Anna Akhmatova, boasts of her girlish thinness (so like Akhmatova in her youth), and more than once hints at her desire to write herself into the suffering Mother at the Foot of the Cross that crowns the magnificent poetic cycle, "Requiem." Her negative role models are taken from Tolstoy. As caregiver for her grandson Tima, dropped on her when her daughter's shotgun marriage fell apart, she remarks:

> Of course she [her daughter Alyona] never lets on who she's living with or whether she's got a man at all; all she does when she comes here is weep. It was *Anna Karenina* all over again, the lost mother reunited with her son – and me of course in the role of Karenin.[19]

Of Russia's many reworked "Anna stories," Anna Adrianovna is the most awful. If Chekhov in the 1890s had provided clinical and lyrical variants on the characters in Tolstoy's great novel, pushing their plots up into the light of day, Petrushevskaya in the late Soviet period remains deep in the Underground. This feminized Underground is marked by certain features that Dostoevsky's hero, or anti-hero, did not have to face. Apart from his brief contacts with Liza, the Underground Man hurts most of all himself – and Liza, after his final insult to her, will not come back. She understands that he has no capacity for sustained mutual relations of any sort. Underground women can hurt themselves too, of course, but given the range of their family duties (and cramped living quarters) in the Soviet context, usually they hurt others first, and far more effectively. These others are often children. And the adults come back.

Anna Adrianovna is matriarch of an apartment in which her entire dysfunctional family is "registered." (In the Soviet era, the state provided its legally employed citizens with living quarters and regulated the square meters available to each resident.) Among those registered in this space are Anna's mother (later moved to a psychiatric ward and then to a mental hospital), her son Andrei (just back from two years in prison and still pursued by his criminal buddies), her daughter Alyona (who, after off-loading Tima, produces two more illegitimate children in the course of the novel). Petrushevskaya obscures chronology and events, providing few external markers to help orient the reader; the time is simply night, when Anna Adrianovna writes it all up. What never changes, however, regardless of season, is the lack of space, food, and privacy. Locks are always being changed, doors slammed or pried open, and sooner or later some mouth, usually male, will turn up and eat the fridge empty. Or steal money. Anna begs bread, soup, and candy from her hosts and employers to feed her grandson, neglecting (she tells us) her own needs. She considers herself a martyr and tries to win our support.

As always in an Underground, the speaking voice is defensive, boastful, consumed by self-hate fused with self-love, and embattled. But again our heroine differs from the resident of Dostoevsky's parent text. The original Underground Man's existence is static. Half of his "confession" is a recollection of events already many years past. The entire document is enclosed, closed off, with its crises already well rehearsed and stylized. This is one reason why a "philosophy" can be so easily extracted from the *Notes*. As so often is the case in Dostoevsky, life is used to illustrate an idea. Petrushevskaya gives us no abstract philosophy as such. Real people are still trying to live down there.

Of all the interactions in this stressed three-room apartment, the relation between mother and daughter is the most complexly double-voiced, allowing us some relief from Anna's strident grip on the narrative. Lengthy direct dialogues and several embedded texts inspire our trust: Alyona's naïve diary of sexual initiation and subsequent humiliations, found and read by her mother who intersperses her own mocking comments, and then a strange entry written by Anna in the voice of her daughter (based on one of their hysterical exchanges). "That's the scene I wrote," Anna announces petulantly in her own voice; "fully self-critical, completely objective, though why on earth you might well ask" (p. 94). In some stretches of text, it is utterly unclear which side of Anna's voice to believe; they seem to coexist in perfect, if hostile, balance. This situation is routine in Dostoevsky's Underground, of course, where a single voice divides against itself. In Petrushevskaya, whole scenes divide, scrambling and compromising the speakers. Alyona has just called her mother, hinting that she's very ill. Who will take care of her baby daughter, Alyona whimpers, now that another child is due to be born in two weeks (Anna didn't know):

> . . . what the whole conversation amounted to was this: Mummy, help me, hoist just one more burden on your back, you've always come to my rescue before, rescue me now – But daughter, I haven't the strength to love yet another creature, I'd be betraying the boy, he couldn't take it . . . – But what am I to do, Mum? – Nothing, I can't do any more to help, I've given everything, my darling, all the money I have, my darling, my sunshine – I'm going to die, Mum, it's terrible . . .   (pp. 99–100)

Dostoevsky's Underground Man could never have sustained such piercing, other-directed utterances from another voice center. He saw to it that no one needed him.

In Anna's accounts, especially her rewrites of the constant vicious family squabbling, she is the heroine and sole provider. Reasons to sympathize with her certainly exist, although undercut by her own self-importance and pre-emptive irony. Aspiring writers – we know this from Dostoevsky – cannot be trusted. It is interesting that Western critics of *The Time: Night* overwhelmingly distrust Anna and consider her abusive, dishonest, and manipulative, whereas Russian readings can be quite compassionate. In one 2005 guide to contemporary literature for high school students, Anna is classified as a tragic figure, an "aging, poverty-stricken poetess" burdened by a criminal son, a depraved daughter, a senile mother, a sick grandson, and here she is a working woman, doing her best, alone and lonely – in a word, Petrushevskaya (says the female author of the guide) gives us nothing at all like playful postmodernism, only "harsh realism."[20]

One day Anna comes home to find that her daughter, unhinged by their last fight, has taken all her children away. The apartment is deserted. At last Anna is completely alone and needed by no one: the authentic enabling condition for the Underground has arrived. At this point the manuscript breaks off. Doubtless Anna Adrianovna, as she falls silent, recalls the second poem in Akhmatova's "Requiem," a tiny lyric of four couplets, the last two of which read: "This woman is sick, / This woman is alone, / Husband in the grave, son in prison, / Pray for me." *The Time: Night* is submitted to a publishing house anonymously by the daughter Alyona, and appears to be posthumous. But if this Anna, following her Tolstoyan prototype, has committed suicide in order to punish those who have ceased to need her, that story is discreetly in the margins.

In the vastly expanded pool of Russian literary plots by and about women, *The Time: Night* stands out not only because it is written so graphically on the body, where a great deal of the drama of female life is focused. Equally important, women are allowed to be tested and to fail on what was traditionally male terrain (honor, creativity, supporting a family), making use of men's excuses. Anna Adrianovna doesn't have a man of her own in sight, to save or to ruin, and she does not perish out of disappointed (or jealous, or unrequited) love – that powerful but narrow and hopelessly clichéd plot. Is she a tragic figure, a superfluous one, a duplicitous one, perhaps even a comedy villain? As with all first-person narration under the star of Dostoevsky, no single answer suffices. But we can speak to the games being played. The interminable Underground identity game – "Here I am. But don't pin me down. The real me is over here" – is to a certain extent endorsed by Dostoevsky. He cares that human beings not be manipulated or denied their freedom of choice. "Anna" might even be the conventional nomination for this burden of the flesh. In 1990, Viktor Erofeyev's three-page story, "Anna's Body," appeared in an anthology of glasnost-era writings.[21] The plot takes place mostly in bed, alone, during one of her nightmares, amid cigarettes and cognac, lamenting her lost youth and the lovers who had jilted her. Various parts of that body had been going out of control for some time: "Sometimes Anna felt that she was Anna Karenina, sometimes – Anna Akhmatova, sometimes just an Anna on the neck." At the end of her reverie she turned off the light, "passed her dry tongue over her lips, and, as in an old fairy tale, gobbled up the man she loved."

Viktor Erofeyev (b. 1947, not to be confused with Venedikt Erofeyev, 1933–88, author of the phantasmagoric *Moscow to the End of the Line*) is a skilled male practitioner of "women's prose." It is no accident that his Anna in Bed eats her men, like some latter-day Baba Yaga. In Erofeyev's novel *Russian Beauty* (1990), the high-class prostitute Irina Tarakanova, in search of true love, moves to Moscow, compromises a wide circle of Russian dissidents, then forms a mystical union with an elderly man whose child she conceives after he is already deceased. Hailed as both a "Russian Molly Bloom" and a "Russian Moll Flanders," Erofeyev's sex-queen also recalls a more local prototype updated to psychedelic dimensions: Martona, the "debauched woman" of Chulkov's 1770 *Comely Cook*.

In 1990, the year he published *Russian Beauty*, Erofeyev announced the death of socialist realism and the liberation of the Russian author from all socio-moral strictures, in a landmark essay titled "A Wake for Russian Literature." Five years later, in his "Russia's *Fleurs du mal*," he called for a new, unsentimental literature of evil to re-complicate the simplistic psychology of the Soviet period. Post-communist freedom had arrived, and postmodernism could not be far behind. Or perhaps the sequence should be reversed? Mikhail Epstein has argued that postmodernism was *born* in Russia, in the Russia of the Brezhnev stagnation – post-Stalinist, but still within the rhetorical force field of socialist realism.[22] In that unfree, unreal place, full of ruins and scrap-heaps of an official faith system, postmodernism possessed a vigor beyond the wildest dreams of academic theorists in the West.

We are only several decades into this unraveling process and cannot yet know which of the recent generations of writers and works will endure. Soviet communism's twilight years yielded several precocious candidates. One is *Pushkin House* (completed 1971, published in Russia 1989) by Andrei Bitov (b. 1937), a piece of "delayed literature" and a carnivalesque "post-mortem on the tradition" that ends up – very much in the Russian manner – confirming the tradition. *Pushkin House* has been read in a wide variety of ways, from a liberal-humanist condemnation of Stalinist oppression (and thus in the Solzhenitsyn line of self-critique, a confession from educated society forced to face up to the camps) through a more absurdist and blankly postmodernist fantasy.[23]

Bitov explores a theme much beloved in Russian literature, that of warring "Fathers and Sons," in the context of an "evil Stalin" plot. A young literary scholar discovers that his father (a famous academic) had denounced his own father (an even more famous academic) during the height of the Stalinist purges, building a career on those paternal ashes. The grandson's attempt to get to know his grandfather – who, it so happens, is not dead as assumed but unexpectedly rehabilitated – is a disaster. The old man, turned cynical and alcoholic in the camps, resents his rehabilitation, because it made a mess of his attempt to give shape and meaning to his fate: "The regime is the regime. Had I been in their place, I would have put myself away."[24] Not only was his life ruined; his martyrdom too had been interrupted. The old man disdains his grandson as a fop whose knowledge of life is nil, who doesn't even know that he doesn't know, who thinks he can work with life the way he works with his favorite books.

Indeed, that is the fantasy fueling *Pushkin House* the Book. Bitov labels his sections, chapters, and episodes with famous titles (or garbled parodies) from the Russian classics: *Fathers and Sons, A Hero of our Time, The Fatalist, The Duel, The Shot*, "The Humble [or Poor] Horseman" [*Bednyi vsadnik* instead of *Mednyi vsadnik*, Pushkin's "Bronze Horseman"] and "Bronze People" [*Mednye lyudi* instead of *Bednye lyudi*, the "Poor Folk" of Dostoevsky fame]. No literary parallel quite works, of course, so the hero has a chance to gloss each of them with scholarly commentary, partly for real and partly farce. The Pushkin House is an authentic research institute in Petersburg. It is also the site of the novel's final caper, in which the hero generates his own rival and double. On the eve of the fiftieth anniversary of the Revolution, these two rivals get into a fistfight that degenerates into a duel in which the hero is killed – but not before the two of them trash priceless documents in the Museum of the Pushkin House. Cursorily brought back to life, the anxious scholar hurries to replace the destroyed items with forgeries. But no one notices the difference.

Confusion between the real and the fake ends up as indifference to the distinction: the perfect postmodernist scenario of a simulacrum without an original. Bitov's *Pushkin House* is an early statement of this condition, written for insiders, contained within research libraries and museums. The next generation of genuinely post-communist writers breaks out of that House. Of our three exemplary prose writers, Vladimir Sorokin (b. 1955), Viktor Pelevin (b. 1962), and Boris Akunin (b. 1956), the last two especially have managed to accomplish that difficult and necessary deed: bridging the distance between high and low readerships.

Three ways for writers to treat matter: eating it, transcending it, cracking its codes (Sorokin, Pelevin, Akunin)

Under the old regime(s), state control of culture pursued a two-pronged ideal. The first was to subsidize high-minded, healthy, politically conformist literature; the second, to prevent the publication or circulation of literature that was low-minded or morally corrupt. Readers who rejected state guidance in these matters availed themselves of *samizdat* ("self-published," illegally circulating manuscripts), *tamizdat* (works published "over there" in the West and smuggled in), *magnitizdat* (illicit popular music smuggled in, recorded on tape or X-ray plates), and radio wavelengths beyond the range of state monitoring. Guidance in this "illegal" or unsponsored side of culture was provided by cult artists, poets, guitar bards, filmmakers, and select dissidents admired as the conscience of the nation. Since "unsponsored" meant free of censorship and thus more honest, many writers and their readers came to assume that unofficial cultural products were necessarily of high artistic quality.

The post-1991 literary market broke down that assumption. It began with a glut of the new. Once censorship lifted, a mass of texts appeared all at once: native "delayed" works (written decades earlier, like Bitov's *Pushkin House* or Petrushevskaya's plays and stories), translations of ancient religious tracts, formerly forbidden or bowdlerized works from the world market (the Marquis de Sade, Nabokov, sex manuals), and warehouses of films never cleared for release. These cultural statements, some produced a thousand years ago and others yesterday, appeared in no special order and often without any frame or context. It was unclear to which "reality" – or which transitory strip of reality – they referred. Banned philosophical classics (Freud, Nietzsche) were brought back. And new explanatory systems devised by Western theorists (Derrida, Foucault, Baudrillad) rapidly received their translation into Russian, resulting in an overlay of enticing, provocative foreign categories transliterated but poorly integrated. The situation recalled the culture shocks of Peter the Great's reign, when teams of official translators labored to find non-existent Russian "equivalents" for German, French, and English concepts – and later, the linguistic fervor of the 1790s, when Karamzin "injected" into written and spoken Russian currently fashionable French modes of expression. The initial phases of a new glasnost are often felt as abrupt, artificial, polluting, and violently imposed. Several émigré writers, including Solzhenitsyn before and after his return to Russia in 1994, made passionate pleas to restore the authority of the "thick journals" that had once carried high literary culture. But subscriptions plummeted. By the mid-1990s, with the legalization of multiple political parties, Dostoevsky was recruited and celebrated by Russian neo-fascists as an anti-Semite (replacing his earlier, "dissident" image as a Christian mystic). Tolstoy, sanitized and officially canonized since 1928, was declared anathema in 1994 by several reactionary chauvinistic parties for his criticism of Holy Russia, the Emperor, and the Orthodox Church. Calls even went out to young people to resist Tolstoy's corrupting, unpatriotic teachings.[25]

A large number of new heroes and plots emerged, created by writers for whom Stalin and World War II were fully historical events, over before they were born. If they were parodists, these writers addressed a tradition that they had absorbed as a "relic," not experienced in their own lives. Among the most controversial of these "workers with relics" has been the visual and verbal Moscow conceptualist artist Vladimir Sorokin (b. 1955), master at the metaphysics of disgust.[26] Trained as an engineer at the Moscow Institute of Oil and Gas, Sorokin worked throughout the 1980s as a graphic artist and book illustrator. His stories were banned. In 1985, the Paris publishing house Syntaxis brought out his comic romance *The Queue* [*Ochered'*], several hundred pages of random snatches of dialogue overheard in line (including an attendance roll call of 720 names), spun out of the socialist-economy shortage-of-everything cliché: if you see a line in the street, immediately join it, even if no one can tell you what is being sold up front. The English translator of *The Queue* aptly likens the narrative to "a musical score . . . for some bizarre street symphony."[27] We never find out what the line was for. But the hero befriends the saleswoman who had engineered the queue and ends up satisfied and happy – in the final chapters, several dozen "dialogic" pages are devoted to the monosyllabic sighs and moans of lovemaking. More scandalous than this mildly dissident, naughty spoof has been Sorokin's mature work and its "bipartite style."[28] A trivially banal "model" text (household, landscape, routine conversation) is abruptly interrupted by a stretch of "killer" text from the mouths of the same speakers – shockingly violent, obscene, or incomprehensible images or words – only to have the banal model stereotype resume its course, unruffled. Unlike the classic "mad" or schizophrenic heroes in the Gogol–Dostoevsky line, who degenerate as their narrative proceeds inexorably to its denouement, Sorokin's characters are sane and insane simultaneously. They can reclaim their surface conformity even after their monstrous subcutaneous life is revealed. According to this psychology, we do not develop or decay in any linear manner but simply display ourselves at different levels.

Another key strategy for Sorokin is to peel back the clean, wholesome, and self-satisfied veneer of late-Soviet-era socialist realism and, in the deadpan spirit of Gogol, turn its ideas into food. Sorokin "realizes" metaphors. In one of his more startling stories, "Sergei Andreyevich" (1992), a star pupil listens dazzled to his high school teacher's platitudes on a class field trip and then, coming across the teacher's excrement lying in greasy coils in the grass, proceeds to eat it, greedily and reverently. But "eating it" can also be less ecstatic, a duty expected (or in the Soviet context, vaguely required) of each honest citizen. Early in his huge, eight-part novel *The Norm* (written during the bleakest years of the Stagnation, 1979–84, published 1994), we realize that the dark, moist, pre-packaged "ration" that everyone carries around, nibbles at, scrambles up into omelets or dissolves into cocoa is human feces. For some reason, people are not allowed to forgo eating their daily norm. In an episode recalling Gogol's "The Nose" (the opening scene where the barber, who has just found a human nose in his breakfast roll, surreptitiously tries to drop it in a Petersburg canal but is prevented by a police inspector), one Kuperman tries to toss his norm into the Moscow River. It won't sink. Two conscientious young people see it floating on the surface and alert the police.[29]

Sorokin won a National Booker award in 2001. In 2002, he achieved international visibility when the Putin-inspired youth movement "Moving Together" attempted to imprison him (unsuccessfully) on a pornography charge. Article 242 of the Russian criminal code was brought against the 1999 novel *Blue Lard* (which features, among other improprieties, sodomy between clones of Khrushchev and Stalin). But Sorokin insists he is not a political writer and that his interests are purely analytical and aesthetic. In an interview from June 2007, in response to a question about the current state of Russian literature, Sorokin remarked:

> It's complicated. But it's been complicated for a long time – Russian
> literature, that is. It's an international brand. Like Russian vodka or
> Kalashnikov. In front of us passed the Mesozoic or Paleozoic nineteenth
> or twentieth centuries, where such extravagant animals lived. Everything
> was trampled down and eaten up by them. And here we are, on this field
> trampled down by Tolstoy and Dostoevsky, by Bulgakov, Shalamov and
> Platonov, and we're trying to create something new . . . But in general,
> there shouldn't be many good writers.[30]

Like Petrushevskaya from an earlier generation, in turning his lens on the body with its undignified products, Sorokin forces us to see how the spirit is trapped in matter. In his 2002 novel *Ice* [*Lyod*], about a millenarian sect in search of its secret members, the 23,000 "True People" are revealed only when struck on the chest with an ice hammer and forced to utter their real names. These awakened ones are carriers of the primeval Light, which will return to the Cosmos as soon as matter (death giving birth to death) is dissolved. Sorokin's primary concern is everywhere to disentangle language from the body, to lay bare the workings of each, and to resist one being casually or thoughtlessly reproduced by the other.

Our second exemplary post-Soviet writer, Viktor Pelevin (b. 1962), also toys with Stalinist ruins and also denies any political intent. But he is not, in the brutal corporeal way we have just sampled, a "materialist." Like the mystical Symbolists of the 1910s–20s, Pelevin builds his works "on the windowsill" between different worlds.[31] His technique is one of constantly switching perspectives, back and forth across both sides of the sill. He resists writing on specifically "Russian subject matter"; in fact, he says, subject matter as such does not exist.[32] He doesn't care for Sorokin and considers postmodernism overall to be "like eating the flesh of a dead culture." Influenced by the philosopher Nicolas Berdyaev and the Symbolist poet Aleksandr Blok, Pelevin has pursued a single question, to which the politics of post-communism contributes only tangentially: what is reality, and where must one stand to gain access to it? He gives the reader very few clues, and none at all from his personal biography.[33] Contrary to the heroic Dostoevsky–Tolstoy–Solzhenitsyn model, where one's life openly nourishes one's art, Pelevin cultivates the image of a mystic recluse: rarely appearing in public, disappearing for long stretches of time (often to Tibet), and almost never granting interviews (only contradictory press statements). One suspects that this is the sort of biographical image Gogol would have cultivated, had he the means, managerial skill, and technology.

Pelevin's first route to "reality" was science fiction. But he goes further than Gogol in "The Nose" or Bulgakov in *Heart of a Dog*. Both those masters of the grotesque remain within the realm of the human, or at least of the animate. One early Pelevin story, "The Life and Adventures of Shed Number XII" (1991), concerns the coming to consciousness of a storage shed, a delicate process dependent upon its contents (bicycles or barrels of brine). When the bikes are moved out and the pickle-barrels take over, the shed commits suicide. Like Akaky Akakievich, the shed returns to haunt its owner, in the form of a spectral bicycle. Pelevin's oscillation between equally valid, utterly different worlds is more clinical than uncanny. His 1994 novel *The Life of Insects*, populated by mosquitoes, dung beetles, flying ants, and moths, has been compared with Kafka's "Metamorphosis," but the analogy is inexact. Kafka's Gregor Samsa wakes up one morning as a beetle and remains one until his miserable death.

Pelevin manages to show us a bloodsucking mosquito who is at the same time a New Russian businessman, back and forth in the same scene and even from the same balcony – and a sexy housefly Natasha who flirts, sunbathes, and sips a drink full-size, only seconds before ending up as a speck on restaurant flypaper.

Pelevin's work has been described as a "satirico-philosophical fantasy" as well as a "mix of super-science fiction and harsh realism."[34] In Chapter 1 we briefly mentioned the hero of Pelevin's first novel *Omon Ra* (1992), Omon Krivomazov ["Crooked-smear"], who thinks he is training as a cosmonaut. He has enrolled in the Meresyev Flying School, named after Aleksei Meresyev, the legendary World War II pilot who continued to fly sorties after having lost both his legs in combat (a deed immortalized in Boris Polevoy's socialist realist classic *Story of a Real Man* [1946] and in Prokofiev's opera of the same name [1948]). Omon's flight instructor welcomes the entering class by recalling Meresyev's heroism: "after losing his legs, he didn't lose heart, he rose up again on artificial legs and soared into the sky like Icarus to strike at the Nazi scum! . . . and we will make Real Men of you too in the shortest possible time."[35] Indeed: the school's initiation ritual for each new trainee involves amputating the feet (or legs: the Russian word *noga* refers to both foot and leg, so it is unclear how far up the surgery extends). The reference to Icarus is apt. Like Platonov's *Foundation Pit*, the higher the deception soars, the more subterranean and awful the reality. The Soviet space program is being run by cripples and trick cameras from the Moscow Metro – the pride of Stalinist construction, built partly by slave labor, here revealed as a shabby, deceptive, muddy maze of tunnels.

Life and death in their physiological dimension are not easily distinguishable in Pelevin's later work. A devoted Buddhist, Pelevin gives us one lucid Eastern parable, *The Yellow Arrow* (1993), in which a sealed train carrying a cross section of late communist society is heading toward a ruined bridge. The hero, who manages to crawl up to the roof of a train car and look around (passengers are allowed to do this, but most aren't interested), suddenly "wakes up." This interrupts the Chain of Being. The train stops, time stops, bubbles are suspended in a glass of liquid; he gets off and walks into a dusty unmarked wilderness.

The most complex intersection that Pelevin makes with the Russian literary tradition is his 1996 novel *Chapayev and Emptiness* (1996, first appearing in English as *The Clay Machine Gun*, then retitled *Buddha's Little Finger*). It links Dostoevsky's *Crime and Punishment*, a bit of Bulgakov's *Master and Margarita*, the 1919–21 Civil War, Stalinist-era heroism and kitsch, Eastern mysticism (real and bogus), and the venerable tradition of alternative truths accessible only in the madhouse. The hero, Peter Emptiness [Pyotr Pustota] is, as far as we can tell, a suspect writer trying to avoid arrest. He lives simultaneously in two times,

Moscow of the 1990s and the post-revolutionary Civil War circa 1919. Pyotr's first assignment as a recruit of the Bolshevik secret police is to raid (read: shoot the audience in) a Symbolist café, where some poets are putting on a little play called "Raskolnikov and Marmeladov" in the style of Chekhov's *Seagull*. One of those famous poets, Valery Bryusov, asks Pyotr if he's found time yet to read Blok's *The Twelve*. Pyotr says yes – but "What is Christ doing walking in front of the patrol? Does Blok perhaps wish to crucify the revolution?"[36] Pyotr wakes up from that politically fraught nightmare in an asylum for the insane. As with the Master's weirdly engineered fate in Bulgakov's novel, however, this asylum is no torture chamber; it is a modern clinic equipped with the most humane drugs and cutting-edge cures, including dream therapy.

As the novel progresses, an Eastern element begins to displace the Dostoevskian. During further dreams in the asylum, Pyotr becomes a disciple of Vasily Chapayev (1887–1919), peasant commander for the Red Army on the southern Ural front. Structurally, the Chapayev legend functions for Pelevin somewhat as the Jerusalem chapters and Yeshua/Jesus do for Bulgakov in that equally layered novel. The historical Chapayev, cut down in battle, was revered as a secular martyr of the Revolution and became part of its holy writ, a Stalinist icon adapted for stage, screen, and opera. But Pelevin returns Chapayev to his true guise as Buddhist seer. By the end of the novel, on the edge of discovering "inner Mongolia," all matter is about to pass away.

Chapayev and Emptiness is a seriocomic pastiche of Russian fantasies about space: upper, lower, outer, across, the unmappable Eurasian frontier and physical volume that does not have to obey the laws of Western materialism. It is, in its way, a postmodernist sunken city of Kitezh. Inevitably, Pelevin's project has been associated with Marshall McLuhan's media extravaganzas and with the French theorist of simulacra and simulations, Jean Baudrillard. But as one astute student of the current literary scene has observed, "Pelevin is interested not in the transformation of reality into simulacra but rather in the reverse process: the birth of reality out of simulacra. This strategy is the polar opposite of the major postulates of postmodernist philosophy."[37]

Pelevin's quasi-parodic mysticism and skill at bringing low philosophically highbrow plots have made him a bestseller, with a growing reputation outside Russia. However, both Pelevin's Buddhism for the masses and Sorokin's alleged pornography were eclipsed in the first years of the twenty-first century by the runaway impact of the most prolific practitioner of Russia's fastest-growing genre, the *detektiv* or detective novel: the Moscow-based, Georgian-Jewish B.[oris] Akunin, pen name of Grigory Chkhartishvili (b. 1958). (The "Bakunin" connection in this pen name is clear; less evident, perhaps, is that

Akunin means "villain" in Japanese). Akunin is creator of a cycle of historical mystery novels around the detective Erast Fandorin, all set in the "terrorist" portion of the nineteenth century (1870s–1905). This Fandorin is as clean-living, energetic, disciplined, and self-reliant as the Sorokin hero is befouled and the Pelevin hero is multi-temporal. Fandorin is also a commentary and corrective update to our roster of Russian nineteenth-century heroes, beginning with the poor government clerk.

We first meet Fandorin in the opening novel of the series, *Azazel'* (1998, translated as *The Winter Queen*). An eighteen-year-old civil servant of the fourteenth class (collegiate registrar), he is scraping away with his quill pen, orphaned after his father died bankrupt in the railroad boom-and-bust of the 1870s. But young Fandorin is no Akaky Akakievich. He has been raised to speak European languages and is in fact something of a dandy, like Eugene Onegin; one-third of his meager first-month salary is spent on a whalebone corset for men (the "Lord Byron") of American make. More astonishingly, Fandorin has chosen to clerk not for some pompous, vacuous Petersburg "Your Excellency," but for the Moscow Criminal Investigation Commission. His superiors are well-meaning men, but – true to their Moscow temperament – somewhat lazy and self-indulgent. Fandorin, in equal part disciplined and intuitive, combines the best of both capital cities. His bosses are perfectly willing to send this ambitious young fellow out to follow leads that interrupt their lunch hour.

Like a Dostoevskian protagonist (Raskolnikov, Stavrogin, Alyosha Karamazov) designed to prolong the reader's curiosity, Fandorin is a pleasure to look at: "long girlish eyelashes," "a most comely youth with black hair . . . and blue eyes . . . rather tall, with a pale complexion and a confounded, ineradicable ruddy bloom on his cheeks."[38] This combination of naïve energy and blooming health is the Alyosha side of Dostoevsky's good-looking men, neither Raskol-nikov's fevers nor the sinister, strikingly beautiful mask of Stavrogin. What is more, Fandorin is squarely on the sleuthing and justice-bearing end of the murder mystery, not on the crime-committing or gothic end. Following long-standing Russian convention, Fandorin is spared having to deal with criminal sex and its hideous exfoliations.[39] In this new post-communist positive hero, Goodness, Beauty, Truth, and wholesome bashfulness come together.

Erast Fandorin is a harbinger of Russia's smooth new cosmopolitanism. Reborn for the international market, it is retrofitted to Dostoevsky's turbulent final decade (from the troubled aftermath of the Great Reforms to the assassination of the Liberator tsar). Akunin skillfully taps into multiple reader-ships. Detective-novel buffs smile at the steady flow of affectionate parodies of Sherlock Holmes; history buffs marvel at the accuracy of detail, whether in England, Persia, or the Suez Canal. Akunin's stories integrate Russia's first telephone, first terrorist bomb delivered by post to a civilian target, and the earliest imports of American gadgets – Remington typewriters and exercise trikes. But the Russian reader is probably most struck by the mass of familiar literary reminiscences with moral valences reversed. Tsarist epaulettes, the Table of Ranks, imperial wars, and the Third Section (secret police) were all symbolic markers hostile to the great nineteenth-century writers from Pushkin to Tolstoy. Here they appear unambiguously as forces for good. From the perspective of a patriotic civil servant like Fandorin, these old myths take on new life.

The Winter Queen, for example, is framed by Karamzin's "Poor Liza." Our new Erast meets his lovely seventeen-year-old Elizaveta while investigating the novel's first mysterious suicide. When the two are being married in the final chapter (preparations for which reproduce Levin's wedding-day bumblings and delays from *Anna Karenina*), the bride whispers to her bridegroom: "Poor Liza has decided not to drown herself and to get married instead" (p. 235). By the end of the day she has been blown up by a terrorist bomb. Inside these two bookended poles of the resolutely death-dealing "Poor Liza" plot, Erast confronts a multitude of other nineteenth-century literary "quotations." He stumbles upon a portrait of a wondrous beauty ("A. B.") lifted directly from the Nastasya Filippovna of Dostoevsky's *Idiot* (p. 18), and later turns up at a soirée run by the same enchantress, with the same cruel games and cash bids for her favors. One adorer, Count Ippolit Zurov, is a survivor from the Romantic era of Pushkin, Lermontov, and Gogol: he presides over a gambling scandal involving a Jack (rather than a Queen) of Spades, then passes through a Pechorin moment en route to a Nozdryov phase (the compulsive swapper and gambler from Gogol's *Dead Souls*). Zurov resurfaces in the London slums as pure Rogozhin, Nastasya Filippovna's jealous suitor, and true to his Dostoevskian prototype eventually carries off his A. B. (or perhaps shoots her). The multipurpose Romantic hero Zurov saves the life of Fandorin, who has been tricked by a buffoonish double agent named Porfiry, subjected to graveyard apparitions out of Gogol's Ukrainian horror tales, and almost drowned and blown up on the banks of the Thames. But this new, upright and unsentimentalist Erast is not beholden to any of the classic Russian literary heroes who surround him, threaten him, or pluck him from certain death. They are part of his adventure plot, but he is not obligated by theirs. He has one goal: to serve the Russian Empire with honor by following his own counsel and by sticking with a case until it is solved. His superiors – even those who turn out to be double agents, and whom he must then annihilate – immediately sense his integrity. "Speak up!" his chief insists during one of their early talks. "I recognize no difference in rank where work is concerned!" (p. 79). We might say that the plot of *The Winter Queen* turns on a utopian vision – or more accurately, a conspiracy – that is the mirror opposite of Dostoevsky's Grand Inquisitor: an inspired pedagogue aims to infiltrate the incompetent, corrupt governments of the world with something like philosopher-kings, and to that end she raises thousands of young men and women "with a sense of their own dignity" and "possessing the freedom to choose" (p. 230).

Mystery novels are not all that Akunin produces. He has a postmodernist side as well. Like Petrushevskaya, he has tried his hand "rewriting" (or co-writing) a Chekhov play. She did a variation on *Three Sisters*; he, a playscript published in 2000 as A. Chekhov / B. Akunin, *The Seagull. A Comedy and its Continuation.*[40] Chekhov's original play, we recall, closes on the off-stage suicide of Treplev, failed writer and a failure in love. Akunin transforms this suicide into a murder and the "comedy" into a detective drama. Dr. Dorn locks all the suspects in one room and conducts the investigation – during which time no character can be shown not to have killed Treplev. Under such pressure, characters reveal their most selfish, bitter sides and Chekhov's vulnerable, often whimsical dramatic dialogues turn grotesque.

The mystery novels, not the spoofs, are the global bestsellers. Akunin has been heralded as the creator of a "Slavic Sherlock Holmes" and a "Russian Ian Fleming." Naïvely but intriguingly, some politically conservative commentators in the West see in Erast Fandorin a new type of positive, proto-capitalist hero on post-Soviet soil. All Russia's previous heroes (so this argument goes) were discredited by the fall of communism: the starry-eyed dissident-to-the-death extremist, the slovenly nihilist, the nay-saying anarchist, the Bolshevik activist negligent of family and faith. The new Akunin-style detective, we are told, is a person who, in the tradition of sober disciplined Chekhov and the Calvinists, draws up rules only for himself – and follows those rules.[41]

Akunin has a readership in the many millions. Whether his spic-and-span, code-cracking detective Fandorin is taken for a role model among post-communist entrepreneurs, or becomes simply a Russian contribution to the world's repertory of private detectives, remains to be seen. Chkhartishvili himself – a professional linguist and translator from the Japanese in addition to being Boris Akunin – has confessed that with his bashful, brave detective he had consciously aimed to fill the space in Russian bookstores between serious literature and trash. In an interview from 2004 he left a revealing testimony about the genesis of his Fandorin:

> When I was a kid there was never a Russian literary character whom I could imitate. I was either Sherlock Holmes or d'Artagnan or some other bloody foreigner. You cannot pretend when you are 11 or 12 that you are a hero of Turgenev. What would you do? Sob? Complain? I

approached this problem in a scientific way. I grafted a bit from every protagonist in Russian literature whom I admire. I took 10 per cent of Andrei Bolkonsky [from *War and Peace*], 10 per cent of Prince Myshkin [*The Idiot*], 10 per cent of Lermontov's Pechorin [from *Hero of our Time*]. Then I added a recipe of my own design, mixed and stirred. At the beginning he looked like Frankenstein, a homunculus. Then miraculously he came to life . . .[42]

What do Prince Bolkonsky, Prince Myshkin, and Grigory Pechorin have in common that Akunin might have admired? Those three nineteenth-century Russian heroes are all aristocratic and to varying degrees disdainful or eccentric; they are attractive to women but flout society's expectations; and (for very different reasons) each is fundamentally indifferent to the turmoil or suffering he causes in others. Their private lives are often shrouded from view; their public persona is invariably enigmatic and compelling. Each novel in the Fandorin series is dedicated "to the Nineteenth Century, when literature was great, the belief in progress boundless, and crimes were committed and solved with elegance and taste."[43] If only as the post-socialist ego ideal for a readership still uncertain how to come to terms with the twentieth century, Erast Fandorin is worth watching: a resplendent new Russian Hero for our Time.

Solzhenitsyn was not correct about postmodernism, of course: by no means is it always nihilistic or pessimistic. But he is certainly correct that Russian experiments in this realm are not to be reduced to a single moral standard. Nor will postmodernist authors, or their successors, relinquish their right to laugh at horror and annihilate it with their own playful devices. One efficient example of such postmodernist resistance is a poem by the recently deceased (d. 2007) Moscow Conceptualist Dmitry Prigov, "Dialogue No. 5." This piece of quasi-doggerel short verse, Prigov's favorite subversive form, is a contribution to the "Poet versus Tsar" theme in Russian literature, here cast as a conversation between Prigov and Stalin.[44]

To prepare for Prigov's 46-line composition, let us recall the conversation between the fifteenth-century holy fool, Michael of Klopsko, and the monastery superior, discussed in Chapter 3. The Blessed Michael turns up at the monastery gate. The superior questions him; but instead of answering, this *yurodivy* repeats the question or throws it back at his interrogator unchanged. Prigov maneuvers his august interlocutor in a similarly holy-foolish manner. Stalin begins by shouting self-serving slogans, which Prigov dutifully repeats. Midway through, piling up self-congratulatory epithets, Stalin asks: "What else is Stalin?" to which the poet responds with a subservient echo: "What else?" "The six great letters!"

Stalin retorts. "And how would it be if we left one letter off?" asks Prigov. "How would it be?" repeats Stalin, drawn inexorably into the mirror-imaging poetic logic of the exchange. "It would be Talin!" Prigov shouts back. Now his interlocutor is labeled Talin. "Talin!" Stalin shouts. And from then on down to nothing, the dictator is undone by the poet:

Prigov	And if we left another off?
Talin	Another?
Prigov	It would be Alin.
Alin	It would be Alin!
Prigov	And if we left another off?
Alin	Another?
Prigov	It would be Lin.
Lin	It would be Lin!

Finally Stalin is prompted to remove the single remaining letter N – and there the poem stops. There is no one left to answer; the tyrant has literally, letter by letter, dissolved. In Prigov's postmodernist exercise, power is tricked into dismantling itself by very traditional means. The Poet, feigning foolishness, sets up the framework, poses the enticing question, and controls the final creative – or annihilating – Word.

There are many ways for "one word of truth to outweigh the whole world." True to the Tolstoy line, Solzhenitsyn prefers this truth to be uttered right-eously, single-voicedly, with the intonations of a preacher or prophet. Prigov, who belonged to the Gogol–Dostoevsky line, relies on double-voiced cunning and carnival dismemberment to reveal that truthful word. Both approaches are dependent on a vast reservoir of inherited literary images and values – espe-cially, one could argue, from the Sentimentalist tradition, more durable on Russian soil than either the analytical or the cynical. From Karamzin through Dostoevsky's redeemed sinners, Tolstoy's idea of art, socialist realism, Solzhen-itsyn, even Pelevin's quasi-parodic mystic fusion of East and West, painful or isolating complexity resolves itself through emotion and communion. The contemporary Russian avant-garde does not campaign for a "blank slate" or "fresh start" – one of the more intoxicating fantasies from the revolutionary 1910s and 1920s. That fantasy is over. The critic Vladimir Kataev concludes his book *Playing with Shards: The Fate of the Russian Classic in the Era of the Postmodern* (2002) with a relatively sanguine prognosis. Postmodernist writers are partial to "secondariness" and "citationality" in constructing their texts, he admits, but the classics have been neither encapsulated nor mummified by these strategies.[45] In the early years of Bolshevik rule, the avant-garde Zamyatin also predicted the demise of literature, the poverty of present-day writers. But these are cyclical complaints, Kataev assures his readers (p. 228), and never come true:

> In their campaign against petrified language clichés, the postmodernists can be compared with wolves, the sanitary workers of the forest, who fulfill the honorable and necessary task of eating refuse and eliminating the weak so that the fittest remain, ensuring that life continues. But to consider – as the admirers of Sorokin do – that from now on one must write only the way he writes or not write at all, this would be like insisting that out of all the animals of the forest, only wolves should remain. Fortunately, nature permits nothing of the sort.

"Postmodernism today should be understood as a sort of pause, an intermission in the development of literature and culture," Kataev advises (p. 231). "In general it might seem that literature has been completely crushed by the aggressiveness of other forms of information transfer. But as long as literature is alive, any development taking place in it – however endlessly distant from traditions it might appear – one way or another, ultimately returns to the classics." This sentiment was given lapidary formulation by Mikhail Bakhtin, in the 1940s, during twentieth-century Russia's darkest years. In a fragment devoted to Gogol's laughter that has lost none of its relevance to the present century, Bakhtin wrote, "Only memory, not forgetfulness, can go forward."[46]

Notes

Introduction

1 Michael Wachtel, *The Cambridge Introduction to Russian Poetry* (Cambridge: Cambridge University Press, 2004), p. ix.
2 Prince D. S. Mirsky, *Pushkin* (London: Routledge, 1926), p. 239.
3 This understanding of literary tradition is eloquently argued in Michael Wachtel, *The Development of Russian Verse: Meter and its Meanings* (Cambridge: Cambridge University Press, 1998), especially in his "Afterword: The Meaning of Form," pp. 239–59.
4 Milan Kundera, "Die Weltliteratur", *New Yorker* (January 8, 2007), 28–35, quote on p. 30.
5 This observation was made by the linguist Roman Jakobson (1896–1982) while editing some Czech versions of Pushkin in the late 1930s. See Jakobson, "Poetry of Grammar and Grammar of Poetry" [1960], in *Language and Literature*, ed. Krystyna Pomorska and Stephen Rudy (Cambridge, MA: Harvard University Press, 1987), pp. 121–44, especially 121–22.
6 "Some Words about War and Peace" [1868], in Leo Tolstoy, *War and Peace*, ed. George Gibian, Norton Critical Edition, 2nd edn. (New York: Norton, 1996), p. 1090.
7 Jeffrey Brooks, *When Russia Learned to Read: Literacy and Popular Literature, 1861–1917* (Princeton: Princeton University Press, 1985). Between the emancipation of the serfs in 1861 and the Bolshevik Revolution in 1917, the most popular works on the market were detective serials, melodrama, and adventure thrillers.
8 The term "negative identity" comes from Lev Gudkov's collection of essays (1997–2002) *Negativnaia identichnost'* (Moscow: Novoe literaturnoe obozrenie, 2004); especially pp. 282–84.

1 Models, readers, three Russian Ideas

1 "*Krome chteniya, idti bylo nekuda*"; Fyodor Dostoevsky, *Notes from Underground*, trans. Richard Pevear and Larissa Volokhonsky (New York: Knopf, 1993), Part II, ch. 1, p. 48.

2 In *Delo* 10 (October 1870), as cited in Charles A. Moser, *Esthetics as Nightmare: Russian Literary Theory 1855–1870* (Princeton: Princeton University Press, 1989), p. 29.

3 The reference occurs in *Crime and Punishment*, Part IV, ch. 5, where Porfiry Petrovich mentions General Mack surrendering at Ulm (a crucial episode in *War and Peace*, Book One, Part II, ch. 3).

4 This underexplored area is currently being researched by Kathleen Parthé; see her "Civic Speech in the Absence of Civil Society," European Association for Urban History, Stockholm Conference (2006).

5 Viktor Shklovsky, "Art as Device," *Theory of Prose*, trans. Benjamin Sher (Normal, IL: Dalkey Archive, 2000), p. 5.

6 Amy Mandelker, "Lotman's Other: Estrangement and Ethics in *Culture and Explosion*," in *Lotman and Cultural Studies: Encounters and Extensions*, ed. Andreas Schönle (Madison: University of Wisconsin Press, 2006), p. 63.

7 Nicolas Berdyaev, *The Russian Idea* [1947] (Boston: Beacon Press, 1962), especially ch. 10, pp. 252–55.

8 Wendy Helleman, ed., *The Russian Idea: In Search of a New Identity* (Bloomington, IN: Slavica, 2004).

9 Thomas Seifrid, *The Word Made Self: Russian Writings on Language 1860–1930* (Ithaca: Cornell University Press, 2005), p. 3.

10 Kathleen F. Parthé, *Russia's Dangerous Texts* (New Haven: Yale University Press, 2004), pp. 2–23.

11 Andrew Baruch Wachtel, *Remaining Relevant after Communism: The Role of the Writer in Eastern Europe* (Chicago: University of Chicago Press, 2006), p. 12.

12 Prince D. S. Mirsky, *A History of Russian Literature*, ed. Francis J. Whitfield (Evanston, IL: Northwestern University Press, 1999), p. 4.

13 Parthé, *Russia's Dangerous Texts*, pp. 24–28.

14 Marshall T. Poe, *The Russian Moment in World History* (Princeton: Princeton University Press, 2003). Poe argues that it was not the "Mongol Yoke" that barbarized Russia, but rather her proximity to savagely aggressive European states, with their cutting-edge weaponry.

15 Mikhail Epstein, "Russo-Soviet Topoi," in *The Landscape of Stalinism: The Art and Ideology of Soviet Space*, ed. Evgeny Dobrenko and Eric Naiman (Seattle: University of Washington Press, 2003), pp. 277–306, esp. 278.

16 Mikhail Vasil'evich Il'in, "Words and Meanings: On the Rule of Destiny. The Russian Idea," in *The Russian Idea*, ed. Wendy Helleman, pp. 33–55, esp. 37 and 40–41.

17 Alexander Pushkin, *A Journey to Arzrum*, trans. Birgitta Ingemanson (Ann Arbor, MI: Ardis, 1974), p. 51.

18 Mikhail Veller, "Khochu v Parizh" [I Want to Go to Paris], as discussed in Alexei Yurchak, *Everything Was Forever Until It Was No More: The Last Soviet Generation* (Princeton: Princeton University Press, 2005), p. 159.

19 Yuri M. Lotman, "Symbolic Spaces. 1. Geographical Space in Russian Medieval Texts," *Universe of the Mind: A Semiotic Theory of Culture*, trans. Ann Shukman (Bloomington: Indiana University Press, 1990), pp. 171–77.

20 Ksana Blank, "The Invisible City of Kitezh as an Alternative 'New Jerusalem'," in *New Jerusalems. The Translation of Sacred Spaces in Christian Culture. Materials from the International Symposium*, ed. Alexey Lidov (Moscow: Indrik, 2006), pp. 169–71.

21 For more on these distinctions, see Pavel Florensky, "Spiritual Sobriety and the Iconic Face," *Iconostasis*, trans. Donald Sheehan and Olga Andrejev (Crestwood, NJ: St. Vladimir's Seminary Press, 1996), pp. 44–59. Florensky (1882–1937) was an Orthodox priest, poet, mathematician, chemist, and theorist of art.

22 S. G. Bocharov, "Vokrug 'Nosa'" [1988], *Siuzhety russkoi literatury* (Moscow: Yazyki russkoi kul'tury, 1999), pp. 98–120. Bocharov summarizes and expands here his earlier 1985 essay "The Riddle of 'The Nose' and the Secret of the Face."

23 See Nancy Ries, *Russian Talk: Culture and Conversation during Perestroika* (Ithaca: Cornell University Press, 1997), and Dale Pesmen, *Russia and Soul* (Ithaca: Cornell University Press, 2000).

24 Boris Gasparov, *Five Operas and a Symphony: Words and Music in Russian Culture* (New Haven: Yale University Press, 2005), pp. xiii–22.

2 Heroes and their plots

1 Simon Franklin, "Nostalgia for Hell: Russian Literary Demonism and Orthodox Tradition," in *Russian Literature and its Demons*, ed. Pamela Davidson (New York: Berghahn Books, 2000), p. 33.

2 Kathleen F. Parthé, *Russia's Dangerous Texts* (New Haven: Yale University Press, 2004), p. 133.

3 Margaret Ziolkowski, *Hagiography and Modern Russian Literature* (Princeton: Princeton University Press, 1988), pp. 14–17.

4 Marcia A. Morris, *Saints and Revolutionaries: The Ascetic Hero in Russian Literature* (Albany: SUNY Press, 1993).

5 Katerina Clark, *The Soviet Novel: History as Ritual*, 3rd edn. (Bloomington: Indiana University Press, 2000), p. 55.

6 See Ewa M. Thompson, "The Archetype of the Fool in Russian Literature," *Canadian Slavonic Papers* 15.3 (Autumn 1973): 245–73.

7 A. Sinyavskii, *Ivan-Durak. Ocherk russkoi narodnoi very* (Paris: Syntaxis, 1991), pp. 34–44.

8 Russell Zguta, *Russian Minstrels: A History of the Skomorokhi* (Philadelphia: University of Pennsylvania Press, 1978), pp. 25–31.

9 For this Russian connection, see J. Douglas Clayton, *Pierrot in Petrograd: Commedia dell'Arte / Balagan in Twentieth-Century Russian Theatre and Drama* (Montreal:

McGill-Queen's University Press, 1993); and Catriona Kelly, *Petrushka: The Russian Carnival Puppet Theatre* (Cambridge: Cambridge University Press, 1990).

10 Faith Wigzell, "The Russian Folk Devil and his Literary Reflections," in *Russian Literature and its Demons*, ed. Pamela Davidson (New York: Berghahn Books, 2000), pp. 59–86, esp. 68.

11 John Givens, *Prodigal Son: Vasilii Shukshin in Soviet Russian Culture* (Evanston, IL: Northwestern University Press, 2000), chs. 4 and 5, esp. p. 59.

12 Helena Goscilo, "Madwomen with Attics: The Crazy Creatrix and the Procreative *Iurodivaia*," in *Madness and the Mad in Russian Culture*, ed. Angela Brintlinger and Ilya Vinitsky (University of Toronto Press, 2007), pp. 226–41, esp. 233.

13 Svetlana Vasilenko, "Little Fool," trans. Elena Prokhorova, in *Shamara and Other Stories*, ed. Helena Goscilo (Evanston, IL: Northwestern University Press, 2000), p. 241.

14 See the section on *mit'ki* in Alexei Yurchak, "Dead Irony: Necroaesthetics, 'Stiob,' and the *Anekdot*," ch. 7, *Everything Was Forever Until It Was No More: The Late Soviet Generation* (Princeton: Princeton University Press, 2005), esp. p. 239.

15 For a good introduction to these larger "geo-literary concerns" see ch. 1 of Paul M. Austin, *The Exotic Prisoner in Russian Romanticism* (New York: Peter Lang, 1997), pp. 12–51.

16 "Frol Skobeev, the Rogue," in *Medieval Russia's Epics, Chronicles, and Tales*, ed. Serge A. Zenkovsky (New York: Dutton, 1963), pp. 474–86, quote on p. 484. This indispensable and well-annotated anthology is the source of all pre-Petrine texts discussed in this volume.

17 Marcia A. Morris, *The Literature of Roguery in Seventeenth- and Eighteenth-Century Russia* (Evanston, IL: Northwestern University Press, 2000). Morris devotes a chapter to each of these four types.

18 Nakobov provides for both *poshlost'* and *poshlyak* a marvelous phonic and semantic analysis during his discussion of Chichikov, hero of *Dead Souls*, in Vladimir Nabokov, *Nikolai Gogol* (New York: New Directions, 1944), pp. 63–71.

19 Simeon Polotsky: "The Merchant Class," in *Medieval Russia's Epics*, ed. Zenkovsky, pp. 518–19.

20 For a lucid survey of these (and other) pre-Byronic European heroes, see Peter L. Thorslev Jr., *The Byronic Hero: Types and Prototypes* (Minneapolis: University of Minnesota Press, 1962), pp. 52–61.

21 For a survey of the Gothic tradition as Russian writers assimilated it (largely from the British), see Mark S. Simpson, *The Russian Gothic Novel and its British Antecedents* (Ann Arbor, MI: Slavica, 1983); for its later democratization, see Jeffrey Brooks, *When Russia Learned to Read: Literacy and Popular Literature, 1861–1917* (Princeton: Princeton University Press, 1985), pp. 183–213.

22 This thesis is developed in Ellen B. Chances, *Conformity's Children: An Approach To The Superfluous Man in Russian Literature* (Columbus, OH: Slavica, 1978).

23 My survey here is indebted to Molly W. Wesling, *Napoleon in Russian Cultural Mythology* (New York: Peter Lang, 2001).

24 Letter from Turgenev to the poet Afanasy Fet, April 6, 1862, cited here from the Norton Critical Edition of Ivan Turgenev, *Fathers and Sons*, trans. and ed. Michael R. Katz (New York: Norton, 1994), p. 174.

25 For a discussion of Maksim Gorky's views on Dostoevsky, see Vladimir Seduro, *Dostoyevski in Russian Literary Criticism 1846–1956* (New York: Octagon Books, 1969), pp. 83–93.

3 Traditional narratives

1 Isabel de Madariaga, *Ivan the Terrible* (New Haven: Yale University Press, 2005), p. 155.

2 For a lucid introduction, see Dmitry S. Likhachev [Likhachov], dean of Russian medievalists, especially his "Religion: Russian Orthodoxy," in *The Cambridge Companion to Modern Russian Culture*, ed. Nicholas Rzhevsky (Cambridge: Cambridge University Press, 1998), pp. 38–56; and Dmitry Likhachov, *The Great Heritage: The Classical Literature of Old Rus* (Moscow: Progress, 1981), especially "The First Seven Hundred Years of Russian Literature," pp. 7–31.

3 With the exception of the folk tales and the folk epic *Ilya Muromets*, all texts discussed in this chapter (plus other vital genres such as chronicles, sermons, laments, and historical tales) can be found in Serge Zenkovsky, ed., *Medieval Russia's Epics, Chronicles, and Tales* (New York: Dutton, 1963). Referred to in body of text as Z.

4 The best introduction to "dual faith" remains George P. Fedotov, *The Russian Religious Mind: Kievan Christianity, the 10th to the 13th Centuries* (Belmont, MA: Nordland, 1975), chs. 1, 2, and 4.

5 Simon Franklin, "Nostalgia for Hell: Russian Demonism and Orthodox Tradition," in *Russian Literature and its Demons*, ed. Pamela Davidson (New York: Berghahn Books, 2000), pp. 31–58, esp. 40.

6 Faith Wigzell, "The Russian Folk Devil and His Literary Reflections," in *Russian Literature and its Demons*, ed. Pamela Davidson (New York: Berghahn Books, 2000), pp. 59–86, esp. 67.

7 For a pathbreaking study of Russian paganism and early Christianity from the perspective of their female traits, see Joanna Hubbs, *Mother Russia: The Feminine Myth in Russian Culture* (Bloomington: Indiana University Press, 1988), especially ch. 3 on Mother Earth.

8 Katerina Clark, "Three Auxiliary Patterns of Ritual Sacrifice," ch. 8, *The Soviet Novel: History as Ritual*, 3rd edn. (Bloomington: Indiana University Press), pp. 178–82.

9 John Garrard and Carol Garrard, *Faith and Patriotism in the New Russia: From Party to Patriarch* (Princeton: Princeton University Press, forthcoming), especially ch. 6, "A Faith-Based Army."

10 Max Lüthi, *The European Folktale: Form and Nature*, trans. John D. Niles (Philadelphia: Institute for the Study of Human Issues, 1982), p. 85.

11 Tolstoy to N. N. Strakhov, March 22/25, 1872, in *Tolstoy's Letters*, ed. and trans. R. F. Christian, vol. I: *1828–1879* (New York: Charles Scribner's Sons, 1978), p. 244.

12 Her traits are exhaustively catalogued in Andreas Johns, *Baba Yaga: The Ambiguous Mother and Witch of the Russian Folktale* (New York: Peter Lang, 2004), esp. chs. 1 and 5.

13 For the *bylina*, see Victor Terras, *A History of Russian Literature* (New Haven: Yale University Press, 1991), pp. 6–8; and Hubbs, *Mother Russia*, pp. 143–66 (for a feminine-centered reading).

14 English translations of both essays are available in Ju. M. Lotman / B. A. Uspenskij, *The Semiotics of Russian Culture*, trans. N. F. C. Owen, ed. Ann Shukman (Ann Arbor: University of Michigan Slavic Department, 1984): Lotman/Uspenskij, "The Role of Dual Models in the Dynamics of Russian Culture (Up to the End of the Eighteenth Century)" [1977], pp. 3–35; and Lotman, "'Agreement' and 'Self-Giving' as Archetypal Models of Culture" [1980], pp. 125–40. Translation of the title of the second essay adjusted in the text.

15 See Svetlana Boym, *The Future of Nostalgia* (New York: Basic Books, 2001), pp. 100–08, the subchapter "The Largest Orthodox Church in the World," in ch. 8, "Moscow, the Russian Rome."

16 For more on this fascinating story, see John Garrard and Carol Garrard, "Rebuilding Holy Moscow," ch. 3, *Faith and Patriotism in the New Russia: From Party to Patriarch* (Princeton: Princeton University Press, forthcoming).

17 W. F. Ryan, "Magic and Divination. Old Russian Sources," in *The Occult in Russian and Soviet Culture*, ed. Bernice Glatzer Rosenthal (Ithaca: Cornell University Press, 1997), pp. 35–58, esp. 36.

4 The eighteenth century

1 Alexander M. Schenker, *The Dawn of Slavic: An Introduction to Slavic Philology* (New Haven: Yale University Press, 1995), p. 167.

2 William Edward Brown, *A History of 18th Century Russian Literature* (Ann Arbor, MI: Ardis, 1980), pp. 123–27.

3 David J. Welsh, *Russian Comedy 1765–1823* (The Hague: Mouton, 1966), p. 15.

4 Simon Karlinsky, "Beginnings of Secular Drama: Court Theater and Chivalric Romance Plays," ch. 2, *Russian Drama from its Beginnings to the Age of Pushkin* (Berkeley: University of California Press, 1985), especially, pp. 34–35.

5 *Ibid.*, pp. 123–24. As Karlinsky notes, plays mocking the abuses of serfdom were regularly performed by serf actors in private theatres to domestic audiences. There is no indication that Catherine or her court felt indicted by a depiction of these whims or cruelties in comic operas – any more than consumer-side beneficiaries of capitalism today feel indicted (or implicated) when corporate crooks are caught and punished, or when contemporary films document their misdeeds.

6 For a balanced view of Fonvizin's biography, see the Introduction by Marvin Kantor to *Dramatic Works of D. I. Fonvizin*, trans. Marvin Kantor (Frankfurt: Peter Lang, 1974).

7 In Mira Mendelson's libretto for Prokofiev's *War and Peace*, this rebuke from Mme Akhrosimova to Natasha (Book Two, Part IV, ch. 18) is amplified by Gallophobic references not in the original.

8 Iakov B. Kniazhnin, *Misfortune from a Coach*, in *The Literature of Eighteenth-Century Russia*, ed. and trans. Harold B. Segal (New York: Dutton, 1967), pp. 374–93, quote on p. 384. Translation adjusted.

9 Mikhail D. Chulkov, *The Comely Cook, or The Adventures of a Debauched Woman*, in Segal, *The Literature of Eighteenth-Century Russia*, pp. 26–68; quote on p. 29.

10 Almost alone in the scholarly literature on Chulkov (which tends to condemn both Martona and her milieu), Alexander Levitsky develops this thesis of *The Comely Cook* as a mock novel targeting literary pretensions rather than social injustice. See Alexander Levitsky, "Mikhail Chulkov's *The Comely Cook*: The Symmetry of a Hoax," *Russian Literature Triquarterly* 2.21 (1988): 97–115.

11 Olia Prokopenko, "The Real-Life Protagonist of Mikhail Chulkov's Comely Cook: A Hypothesis," *Slavic and East European Journal* 48.2 (Summer 2004): 225–46.

12 Gitta Hammarberg, "The Literary and Intellectual Context," ch. 1, *From the Idyll to the Novel: Karamzin's Sentimentalist Prose* (Cambridge: Cambridge University Press, 1991), especially pp. 10–12.

13 See Brown, "Russian Prose of the Last Quarter of the Eighteenth Century," *A History of 18th Century Russian Literature*, pp. 544–47.

5 Romanticisms

1 For the convincing case that Pushkin partook only sparingly of European Romanticism and not at all of "Realism" (a term that appeared on the continent and in Russia in its present literary meaning only in the late 1840s), see Boris Gasparov, "Pushkin and Romanticism," in *The Pushkin Handbook*, ed. David M. Bethea (Madison: University of Wisconsin Press, 2005), pp. 537–67.

2 For this transition from court patronage to professionalism via familiar associations, salons, and booksellers, see William Mills Todd III, "Institutions of Literature," ch. 2, *Fiction and Society in the Age of Pushkin: Ideology, Institutions, and Narrative* (Cambridge, MA: Harvard University Press, 1986), pp. 45–105.

3 Yu. M. Lotman, "Liudi i chiny" [People and ranks], *Besedy o russkoi kul'ture* (St. Petersburg: Iskusstvo-SPB, 1994), pp. 18–45, esp. 20.

4 For a fascinating prehistory of Pushkin's duel and the intricacies of his outraged honor, see Serena Vitale, *Pushkin's Button*, trans. Ann Goldstein and John Rothschild (New York: Farrar, Straus and Giroux, 1995), especially ch. 6.

5 This reading of the Onegin–Lensky duel was first laid out by Yury Lotman in his Commentary to *Eugene Onegin*, 1980. See Yu. M. Lotman, "*Evgenii Onegin*. Kommentarii," *Pushkin* (St. Petersburg: Iskusstvo-SPB, 1995), p. 679.

6 Arthur Krystal, "En garde! The history of dueling," *New Yorker* (March 12, 2007), 80–84, esp. 81.

7 For more on "insult" and "honor" as they evolved in Russia from the eighteenth century on to the twentieth, see chs. 1 and 2, in Irina Reyfman, *Ritualized Violence Russian Style: The Duel in Russian Culture and Literature* (Palo Alto: Stanford University Press, 1999).

8 See Ian M. Helfant, "Pushkin as a Gambler," *The High Stakes of Identity: Gambling in the Life and Literature of Nineteenth-Century Russia* (Evanston, IL: Northwestern University Press, 2002), p. 51.

9 James E. Falen, Introduction to his translation of Alexander Pushkin, *Eugene Onegin. A Novel in Verse* (Oxford: Oxford University Press, 1995), p. xii.

10 Capital letters indicate feminine rhymes (double or two-syllable rhymes with stress on penultimate syllable); small letters are masculine rhymes (single-syllable and stressed). See Vladimir Nabokov, "The 'Eugene Onegin' Stanza," in Aleksandr Pushkin, *Eugene Onegin. A Novel in Verse*, trans. Vladimir Nabokov, 2 vols. (Princeton: Princeton University Press, 1975), vol. I, pp. 9–14; and Michael Wachtel, "The Onegin Stanza," ch. 3, *The Development of Russian Verse: Meter and its Meaning* (Cambridge: Cambridge University Press, 1998), pp. 119–22.

11 For an intriguing scene-by-scene exegesis of this pyramidal symmetry, see Irena Ronen, *Smyslovoi stroi tragedii Pushkina "Boris Godunov"* (Moscow: Its-Garant, 1997), esp. the chart on p. 128.

12 Alexander Pushkin, "On Prose," in *Pushkin on Literature*, ed. Tatiana Wolff (Evanston, IL: Northwestern University Press, 1998), pp. 43–44. Translation adjusted. This useful anthology is marred by translation errors and must be used with caution.

13 See Irina Reyfman, "Prose Fiction," in *The Cambridge Companion to Pushkin*, ed. Andrew Kahn (Cambridge: Cambridge University Press, 2006), pp. 90–104, especially 96–99.

14 David Powelstock, *Becoming Mikhail Lermontov: The Ironies of Romantic Individualism in Nicholas I's Russia* (Evanston, IL: Northwestern University Press, 2005), p. 330.

15 Leo Tolstoy, *War and Peace*, trans. Anthony Briggs (New York: Penguin Classics, 2005), vol. II, Part 1, chs. 4–6, p. 340.

16 See Gary Saul Morson, *Hidden in Plain View: Narrative and Creative Potentials in "War and Peace"* (Palo Alto: Stanford University Press, 1987), Part III, esp. p. 210.

17 Anton Chekhov, "The Duel," ch. 19, in *The Duel and Other Stories*, trans. Ronald Wilks (London: Penguin, 1984), p. 111, trans. adjusted.

18 See Reyfman, "How Not to Fight: Dueling in Dostoevsky's Works," ch. 6, *Ritualized Violence Russian Style*, pp. 192–261.

19 Nikolai Gogol, "The Carriage," in *Plays and Petersburg Tales*, trans. Christopher English (Oxford: Oxford University Press, 1995), p. 153.

20 Nikolai Gogol, "The Nose," in *Plays and Petersburg Tales*, pp. 43–44, trans. adjusted.

21 The Russian Formalists loved Gogol. This example is discussed in Boris Eikhenbaum's classic essay "How Gogol's 'Overcoat' is Made" (1918), in *Gogol from the*

Twentieth Century, ed. Robert A. Maguire (Princeton: Princeton University Press, 1974), p. 277.

22 Vladimir Nabokov, *Nikolai Gogol* (New York: New Directions Publishing, 1944), p. 140.

23 For these arguments, see chs. 1 and 2 of Chester Dunning, with Caryl Emerson, Sergei Fomíchev, Lidiia Lotman, and Antony Wood, *The Uncensored Boris Godunov: The Case of Pushkin's Original Comedy* (Madison: University of Wisconsin Press, 2006). The volume contains Antony Wood's translation of all twenty-five original scenes.

24 V. N. Turbin, "Kharaktery samozvantsev v tvorchestve Pushkina," *Nezadolgo do Vodoleya* (Moscow: Radiks, 1994), p. 75.

25 The best translation is in Nikolai Gogol, "The Government Inspector," in *Plays and Petersburg Tales*, trans. Christopher English (Oxford: Oxford University Press, 1995), pp. 245–336.

26 Alexander Pushkin, "The Captain's Daughter," in *Alexander Pushkin: Complete Prose Fiction*, trans. Paul Debreczeny (Palo Alto: Stanford University Press, 1983), p. 337, trans. adjusted.

27 Nikolai Gogol, *Dead Souls*, trans. Bernard Guilbert Guerney, rev. and ed. Susanne Fusso (New Haven: Yale University Press, 1996), p. 247.

28 Stephen Moeller-Sally, "Spreading the Word," ch. 4, *Gogol's Afterlife: The Evolution of a Classic in Imperial and Soviet Russia* (Evanston, IL: Northwestern University Press, 2002), esp. p. 85.

29 October 31, 1853. *Tolstoy's Diaries*, ed. and trans. R. F. Christian, vol. I: *1847–1894* (New York: Scribner's Sons, 1985), p. 75.

6 Realisms

1 D. S. Mirsky, from his discussion of "The Moscow Circles," in *A History of Russian Literature*, ed. Francis J. Whitfield (Evanston, IL: Northwestern University Press, 1999), p. 166.

2 Two excellent books discuss this theme: Adam Weiner, *By Authors Possessed: The Demonic Novel in Russia* (Evanston, IL: Northwestern University Press, 1998), especially ch. 2 on *Dead Souls* and ch. 3 on *Demons*; and W. J. Leatherbarrow, *A Devil's Vaudeville: The Demonic in Dostoevsky's Major Fiction* (Evanston, IL: Northwestern University Press, 2005), especially its opening chapter on Dostoevsky's sources for the demonic in Russian folklore and in Gogol.

3 Fyodor Dostoevsky, *The Brothers Karamazov*, trans. Richard Pevear and Larissa Volokhonsky (New York: Vintage, 1991), p. 648. All references to the novel in the text will be to this translation.

4 *Hadji Murad*, trans. Louise and Aylmer Maude, in *Great Short Works of Leo Tolstoy* (New York: Perennial Classics, 2004), p. 667.

5 For a lyrical evocation of this routine, see "The writer at work," ch. 7 in Jacques Catteau, *Dostoevsky and the Process of Literary Creation*, trans. Audrey Littlewood

(Cambridge: Cambridge University Press, 1989), pp. 173–79. For a glimpse in Joseph Frank's monumental five-volume biography of Dostoevsky (1976–2002), see ch. 8, "A Literary Proletarian," in vol. V: *Dostoevsky: The Mantle of the Prophet* (Princeton: Princeton University Press, 2002), pp. 130–48.

6 On Tolstoy and the graphic revolution, see Michael Denner, "'Be not afraid of greatness...': Lev Tolstoy and Celebrity" (forthcoming in *Journal of Popular Culture* 42.4 [2009]).

7 Maxim Gorky, "Memoirs" [Tolstoy], "A Letter" [1910], in Gorky's *Tolstoy and Other Reminiscences: Key Writings by and about Maxim Gorky,* trans, ed., and intro. Donald Fanger (New Haven: Yale University Press, 2008), p. 51. He has long wanted to suffer, Gorky continues, but "with the plain and, I repeat, despotic intention of intensifying the weight of his teaching, . . . for he knows that this doctrine is not convincing enough." Translation slightly adjusted.

8 Gorky, "Memoirs" [Tolstoy], p. 35 and (from the 1910 letter) p. 63. Gorky's memoirs are vibrant but stylized, and reveal as much about Gorky as about Tolstoy.

9 From Tolstoy to N. N. Strakhov, 5 December 1883 (in *Tolstoy's Letters*, ed. and trans. R. F. Christian, vol. II: *1880–1910* (New York: Scribner, 1973), p. 363). The best brief gloss on this relationship is Robert Louis Jackson, "A View from the Underground: On Nikolai Nikolaevich Strakhov's Letter About His Good Friend Fyodor Mikhailovich Dostoevsky and on Leo Nikolaevich Tolstoy's Cautious Response to It," *Dialogues with Dostoevsky: The Overwhelming Questions* (Palo Alto: Stanford University Press, 1993), pp. 105–20.

10 Chekhov to Aleksei Suvorin, March 27, 1894, in *Anton Chekhov: A Life in Letters*, trans. Rosamund Bartlett and Anthony Phillips (London: Penguin, 2004), p. 324.

11 Mikhail Bakhtin, *Problems of Dostoevsky's Poetics* [1929/1964], trans. Caryl Emerson (Minneapolis: University of Minnesota Press, 1984), chs. 1 and 2; on Tolstoy, pp. 68–73.

12 Fyodor Dostoevsky, *The Double*, trans. by George Bird, in *Great Short Works of Fyodor Dostoevsky* (New York: Perennial Classics, 2004), p. 143.

13 See Deborah A. Martinsen, *Surprised by Shame: Dostoevsky's Liars and Narrative Exposure* (Columbus: Ohio State University Press, 2003), especially her distinction between guilt and shame.

14 On narrative duplicity and the distinction between withholding a story and not knowing it, see Robin Feuer Miller's classic study, *Dostoevsky and The Idiot: Author, Narrator, and Reader* (Cambridge, MA: Harvard University Press, 1981).

15 See the discussion from the chapter "Anti-Dostoevsky," in Nina Gourfinkel, *Gorky*, trans. Ann Feshback (New York: Grove Press, 1960), p. 73.

16 "Drafts for an Introduction to War and Peace" [late December 1865], Draft 3, in Leo Tolstoy, *War and Peace*, ed. George Gibian, Norton Critical Edition (New York: Norton, 1996), p. 1089.

17 For more on Tolstoyan psychology as reflected in narrative strategy, see Gary Saul Morson's classic *Hidden in Plain View: Narrative and Creative Potentials in "War and Peace"* (Palo Alto: Stanford University Press, 1987), the most ambitious attempt to integrate all aspects of this novel into a living worldview.

18 "*Anna Karenina* as a Fact of Special Importance," July–August 1877, in Fyodor Dostoevsky, *A Writer's Diary*, trans. Kenneth Lantz, 2 vols. (Evanston, IL: Northwestern University Press, 1994), vol. II, pp. 1067–77, esp. 1071–72.

19 L. N. Tolstoy, *Resurrection*, trans. Rosemary Edmonds (London: Penguin, 1966), p. 19.

20 L. N. Tolstoy, "Master and Man," in *Great Short Works of Leo Tolstoy*, trans. Louise Maude and Aylmer Maude (New York: Perennial Classics/HarperCollins, 2004), p. 500.

21 Mikhail Bulgakov, *The Master and Margarita*, trans. Diana Burgin and Katherine Tiernan O'Connor (New York: Vintage, 1996), ch. 23, p. 233, trans. adjusted.

22 See Bakhtin's lecture "Lev Tolstoi" as noted down by R. M. Mirkina, in "Zapisi domashnego kursa lektsii po russkoi literature," in *M. M. Bakhtin: Sobranie sochinenii*, ed. S. G. Bocharov and L. S. Melikhova (Moscow: Russkie slovari, 2000), vol. II, p. 239.

23 Leo Tolstoy, *Anna Karenina*, trans. Richard Pevear and Larissa Volokhonsky (London: Penguin, 2000), p. 186. All further references in the text are to this translation.

24 Aleksandr I. Solzhenitsyn, *The Cancer Ward*, trans. Rebecca Frank (New York: Dell Publishers, 1968), p. 310.

25 Bruce Weston, "Leo Tolstoy and the Ascetic Tradition," *Russian Literature Triquarterly* 3 (1972), 297–308.

26 Makar Devushkin to Varvara Alekseyevna, 8 July, in Fyodor Dostoevsky, *Poor Folk*, trans. Robert Dessaix (Ann Arbor, MI: Ardis, 1982), p. 80.

27 Conversation recorded by I. Teneromo and first published in English in the *New York Times*, January 31, 1937, in Jay Leyda, *KINO: A History of the Russian and Soviet Film* [1960] (Princeton: Princeton University Press, 1983), pp. 410–11, esp. 410.

28 "The Raid," from Leo Tolstoy, *The Raid and Other Stories*, trans. Louise Maude and Aylmer Maude (Oxford: Oxford University Press, 1982), p. 25.

29 This seminal reading is by Gary Saul Morson, "The Reader as Voyeur: Tolstoi and the Poetics of Didactic Fiction" [1978], repr. in *Tolstoy's Short Fiction*, ed. Michael R. Katz, Norton Critical Edition (New York: Norton, 1991), pp. 379–94.

30 Margo Rosen, "Natasha Rostova at Meyerbeer's Robert le Diable," *Tolstoy Studies Journal* 17 (2005): 71–90.

31 Mikhail Bakhtin, "Discourse in the Novel," in *The Dialogic Imagination: Four Essays by M. M. Bakhtin*, trans. Michael Holquist and Caryl Emerson (Austin: University of Texas Press, 1981), pp. 286–88.

32 Nikolai Nekrasov, "O pogode" (1859), Part I, "Ulichnye vpechatleniia," "Do sumerek," 2, *Sobranie sochinenii* (Moscow: Khudozhestvennaya literatura, 1971), vol. I, pp. 292–93. The poem "Yesterday . . ." is on p. 94.

33 Chekhov to Aleksei Suvorin, March 27, 1894, in *Anton Chekhov, A Life in Letters*, p. 324.

34 For a discussion of early parodies, see Karl D. Kramer, "Literary Parodies," ch. 2, *The Chameleon and the Dream: The Image of Reality in Čexov's Stories* (The Hague: Mouton, 1970), especially pp. 31–33.

35 See the ruminations by Leonid Heifetz, "Notes from a Director: *Uncle Vanya*," in *The Cambridge Companion to Chekhov*, ed. Vera Gottlieb and Paul Allain (Cambridge: Cambridge University Press, 2000), pp. 91–101, esp. 98. This *Companion*, edited by two drama professionals, is devoted entirely to the plays. My discussion of Chekhov in chapter 6 reverses that priority and attends almost exclusively to Chekhov as short-story writer.

36 Anton Chekhov, "The Lady with the Little Dog," in *About Love and Other Stories*, trans. Rosamund Bartlett (Oxford: Oxford University Press, 2004), p. 173.

37 Anton Chekhov, "Enemies," *The Tales of Chekhov*, vol. XI *The Schoolmaster and Other Stories*, trans. Constance Garnett (New York: Ecco Press, 1986), p. 32.

38 Chekhov, "About Love," in *About Love and Other Stories*, p. 166.

39 Chekhov, "The Lady with the Little Dog," p. 183.

7 Symbolist and Modernist world-building

1 Dmitri Merezhkovskii, "O prichinakh upadka, i o novykh techeniyakh sovremennoi russkoi literatury" [1893], *Polnoe sobranie sochinenii* (Moscow, 1913), vol. XV, p. 259.

2 Ilya Vinitsky, "Where Bobok Is Buried: The Theosophical Roots of Dostoevskii's 'Fantastic Realism'," *Slavic Review* 65.3 (Fall 2006): 523–43, especially 536–37.

3 For a survey of the institutions, philosophers, and literary critics who challenged positivism during these years, see Randall A. Poole, "Editor's Introduction: Philosophy and Politics in the Russian Liberation Movement," in *Problems of Idealism: Essays in Russian Social Philosophy*, trans. and ed. Randall A. Poole (New Haven: Yale University Press, 2003), pp. 1–83.

4 See Vladimir Solovyov, *Lectures on Divine Humanity*, trans. Peter Zouboff, rev. and ed. Boris Jakim (Hudson, NY: Lindisfarne Press, 1995).

5 See Edith W. Clowes, *The Revolution of Moral Consciousness: Nietzsche in Russian Literature, 1890–1914* (De Kalb, IL: Northern Illinois University Press, 1988), esp. chs. 2 and 3 (on Nietzsche's philosophy and its eccentric reception in Russia) and ch. 5 (on Russia's "mystical symbolists"). Quoted phrases on p. 15.

6 Irina Paperno, "Nietzscheanism and the return of Pushkin in twentieth-century Russian culture (1899–1937)," in *Nietzsche and Soviet Culture: Ally and Adversary*, ed. Bernice Glatzer Rosenthal (Cambridge: Cambridge University Press, 1994), pp. 211–32, esp. 213.

7 January 16, 1900, in *Tolstoy's Diaries* ed. and trans. R. F. Christian, vol. II: *1895–1910* (New York: Scribner's Sons, 1985), p. 475. See also the discussion of this letter and its context in Clowes, *The Revolution of Moral Consciousness*, pp. 67–70.

8 See Anna Geifman, *Thou Shalt Kill: Revolutionary Terrorism in Russia, 1894–1917* (Princeton: Princeton University Press, 1993), esp. chs. 1 and 5 (on the criminal, psychopath, and juvenile components of the "new terrorism").

9 Evgeny Zamyatin, "On Literature, Revolution, Entropy, and Other Matters," in *A Soviet Heretic: Essays by Yevgeny Zamyatin*, ed. and trans. by Mirra Ginsburg (Chicago: University of Chicago Press, 1970), pp. 107–12, esp. 107–08.

10 See the discussion of Bely's 1909 essay "The Magic of Words" and its reflection in Bely's novel in Vladimir E. Alexandrov, *"Petersburg," Andrei Bely: The Major Symbolist Fiction* (Cambridge, MA: Harvard University Press, 1985), pp. 101–52.

11 A lucid discussion can be found in J. D. Elsworth, "Bely's Theory of Symbolism," ch. 1, *Andrey Bely: A Critical Study of the Novels* (Cambridge: Cambridge University Press, 1983), pp. 7–36.

12 See Richard A. Gregg, "Two Adams and Eve in the Crystal Palace: Dostoevsky, the Bible, and *We*," in *Major Soviet Writers: Essays in Criticism*, ed. Edward J. Brown (Oxford: Oxford University Press, 1973), pp. 202–08. Gregg makes the point about Cyrillic and Latin alphabets in n. 21, p. 421.

13 Yevgeny Zamyatin, *We*, trans. Clarence Brown (New York: Penguin Books, 1993), Record 9, p. 45. All further references in the text are to this translation.

14 For a good discussion of parallels, see Robert Louis Jackson, "E. Zamyatin's *We*," *Dostoevsky's Underground Man in Russian Literature* (The Hague: Mouton, 1958), pp. 150–57.

15 Translation by Mirra Ginsburg in *A Soviet Heretic*, pp. 21–33, quote on pp. 21–22. See also Stefa Hoffman, "Scythian Theory and Literature, 1917–1924," in *Art, Society, Revolution. Russia, 1917–1921*, ed. Nils Ake Nilsson (Stockholm: Almqvist and Wiksell, 1979), pp. 138–64.

16 Mikhail Bulgakov, *The Master and Margarita*, trans. Diana Burgin and Katherine Tiernan O'Connor (New York: Vintage, 1996), p. 12. All further references in the text are to this translation.

17 Ellendea Proffer, *Bulgakov* (Ann Arbor, MI: Ardis, 1984), p. 526.

18 Dostoevsky, "The Devil. Ivan Fyodorovich's Nightmare," *The Brothers Karamazov*, Book Eleven, ch. 9, p. 642.

19 The two most important essays drawn upon here were published in 1984 in the Tartu school publication *Trudy po znakovym sistemam* 18: Vladimir Toporov, "Peterburg i peterburgskii tekst russkoi kul'tury," repr. in Toporov, *Mif. Ritual. Simvol: Issledovaniia v oblasti mifopoeticheskogo: Izbrannoe* (Moscow: Izdatel'skaia gruppa Progress, Kul'tura, 1995), pp. 259–367 and Yurii Lotman, "Simvolika Peterburga i problemy semiotiki goroda," repr. in Lotman, *Izbrannye stat'i v trekh tomax*, vol. II (Talinn: Alexandra, 1992), pp. 9–21. An English variant of the Lotman essay can be found in Yuri M. Lotman, "The Symbolism of St. Petersburg," *Universe of the*

Mind: A Semiotic Theory of Culture, trans. Ann Shukman (Bloomington: Indiana University Press, 1990), pp. 191–202.

20 See Sidney Monas, "St. Petersburg and Moscow as Cultural Symbols," in *Art and Culture in Nineteenth-Century Russia*, ed. Theofanis George Stavrou (Bloomington: Indiana University Press, 1983), pp. 26–39. I am indebted to this article also for details of the Moscow Myth.

21 Andrei Bely, *Petersburg*, trans. Robert A. Maguire and John E. Malmsted (Bloomington: Indiana University Press, 1978), p. 10. All further references in the text are to this translation.

22 M. M. Bakhtin, "Zapisi kursa lektsii po istorii russkoi literatury" R. M. Mirkinoi, "Blok," *Sobranie sochinenii*, vol. II (Moscow: Russkie slovari, 2000), pp. 343–55, esp. 351–52.

23 Alexander Blok, "Intelligentsia and Revolution" [January 1918], *The Spirit of Music* (Westport, CN: Hyperion Press, 1946: repr. 1973), pp. 7–19, especially 11–13. Translation adjusted.

24 Julie A. Buckler, *Mapping St. Petersburg: Imperial Text and Cityscape* (Princeton: Princeton University Press, 2005), p. 1. See also ch. 4, "Stories in Common: Urban Legends in St. Petersburg," pp. 116–57, and "The Illegible Industrial Text," pp. 179–94.

25 Simon Karlinsky, *Marina Tsvetaeva: The Woman, the World and her Poetry* (Cambridge: Cambridge University Press, 1986), pp. 58–60.

26 Keith A. Livers, "Conquering the Underworld: The Spectacle of the Stalinist Metro," ch. 4, *Constructing the Stalinist Body: Fictional Representations of Corporeality in the Stalinist 1930s* (New York: Lexington Books, 2004), pp. 189–236.

27 Svetlana Boym, "Moscow, the Russian Rome," ch. 8, *The Future of Nostalgia* (New York: Basic Books, 2001), pp. 83–119.

28 Both stories are available in English in Mikhail Bulgakov, *Diaboliad and Other Stories*, trans. Carl R. Proffer (Bloomington: Indiana University Press, 1972): pp. 3–47 and 159–74.

29 See Sabine I. Gölz, "Moscow for Flaneurs: Pedestrian Bridges, Europe Square, and Moskva-City," *Popular Culture* 18.3 (2006): 573–605.

30 Nicolai Ouroussoff, "The Malling of Moscow: Imperial in Size and a View of the Kremlin," *New York Times* (March 15, 2007). The architect-urban designer is British Modernist Norman Foster.

31 See Irina Gutman, "The Legacy of the Symbolist Aesthetic Utopia: From Futurism to Socialist Realism," in *Creating Life: The Aesthetic Utopia of Russian Modernism*, ed. Irina Paperno and Joan Delaney Grossman (Palo Alto: Stanford University Press, 1994), pp. 167–96.

32 For debate over "Taylorism" and industrial futures, see Patricia Carden, "Utopia and Anti-Utopia: Aleksei Gastev and Evgeny Zamyatin," *Russian Review* 46.1 (January 1987): 1–18.

33 Leon Trotsky, *Literature and Revolution*, trans. Rose Strunsky (Ann Arbor: University of Michigan Press, 1971), p. 132.

8 The Stalin years

1 Jochen Hellbeck, *Revolution on My Mind: Writing a Diary under Stalin* (Cambridge, MA: Harvard University Press, 2006), pp. 282–83.

2 See Eric Naiman, *Sex in Public: The Incarnation of Early Soviet Ideology* (Princeton: Princeton University Press, 1997), pp. 135–36. For the debates over Meyerhold's production of Tretyakov's *I Want a Child*, see pp. 109–14.

3 See David L. Hoffmann, *Stalinist Values: The Cultural Norms of Soviet Modernity [1917–1941]* (Ithaca: Cornell University Press, 2003), p. 31.

4 Rufus W. Mathewson, Jr. was the pioneering Western scholar to take these doctrines and their effect on literature seriously; see his *The Positive Hero in Russian Literature* [1958], 2nd edn. (Palo Alto: Stanford University Press, 1975), especially ch. 8, "Marxism, Realism, and the Hero."

5 Abram Tertz [Andrei Sinyavsky], "On Socialist Realism," trans. George Dennis [1960], in Abram Tertz, *The Trial Begins and On Socialist Realism* (Berkeley: University of California Press, 1982), pp. 147–93, esp. 150. Further quoted phrases on pp. 181 and 182. The Russian word translated as Purpose, *tsel'*, also means aim or goal, and resonates with words for wholeness and integrity [*tsel'nost'*].

6 "Soviet Literature. Address Delivered to the First All-Union Congress of Soviet Writers, August 17, 1934," in Maxim Gorky, *On Literature* (Seattle: University of Washington Press, 1973), pp. 228–68.

7 Mathewson, *The Positive Hero in Russian Literature*, p. 122.

8 Petre Petrov, entry on "Socialist realism," in *Encyclopedia of Contemporary Russian Culture*, ed. Tatiana Smorodinskaya, Karen Evans-Romaine and Helena Goscilo (London: Routledge, 2006), pp. 575–77.

9 See the comprehensive discussion in Keith Livers, "Mikhail Zoshchenko: Engineering the Stalinist Body and Soul," ch. 2, *Constructing the Stalinist Body* (Lanham, MD: Lexington Books, 2004), pp. 91–152.

10 For an excellent overview of the functions filled by this hero, see Sheila Fitzpatrick, "The World of Ostap Bender," ch. 13, *Tear off the Masks! Identity and Imposture in Twentieth-Century Russia* (Princeton: Princeton University Press, 2005), pp. 575–77.

11 Fyodor Vasilievich Gladkov, *Cement*, trans. A. S. Arthur and C. Ashleigh (Evanston, IL: Northwestern University Press, 1994), "Autobiographical Note" [undated]. All references are to this edition.

12 Katerina Clark analyzes Gleb Chumalov as a mythical *bogatyr* (although not as a *pravednik*) in *The Soviet Novel: History as Ritual* (Bloomington: Indiana University Press, [1981] 2000), pp. 69–82.

13 See Boris Gasparov, "A Testimony: Shostakovich's Fourth Symphony and the End of Romantic Narrative," ch. 6, *Five Operas and a Symphony* (New Haven: Yale University Press, 2005), pp. 161–79, where the implications of this thesis are discussed for sonata form. In oral presentations, Gasparov has adduced further literary examples, including *Cement*.

14 Régine Robin, *Socialist Realism, An Impossible Aesthetic*, trans. Catherine Porter (Palo Alto: Stanford University Press, 1992), pp. 60–62.

15 For this early career, see Amanda J. Metcalf, *Evgenii Shvarts and his Fairy-Tales for Adults* (Birmingham Slavonic Monographs No. 8, 1979).

16 Yevgeny Schwartz, *The Dragon*, in *Three Soviet Plays*, ed. Michael Glenny (New York: Penguin Books, 1966), Act I, pp. 147–49. The translation, by Max Hayward and Harold Shukman, is free but excellent.

17 Liudmila Filatova, "Konchen bal," *Peterburgskii teatral'nyi zhurnal* No. 39 (2005). http://ptzh.theatre.ru/2005/39/23/.

18 Andrei Platonov, *Dzhan*, trans. Joseph Barnes, from *The Fierce and Beautiful World: Stories by Andrei Platonov* (New York: Dutton, 1971), p. 82.

19 Andrey Platonov, *The Foundation Pit*, trans. Mirra Ginsburg (Evanston, IL: Northwestern University Press, 1994), p. 3. All further references in the text are to this translation.

20 See Thomas Seifrid, "Platonov and the Culture of the Five-Year Plan (1929–1931)," ch. 4, *Andrei Platonov: Uncertainties of Spirit* (Cambridge: Cambridge University Press, 1992), esp. pp. 132–49 for a list of parallels with *Cement*. My examples and conclusions depart somewhat from his.

21 Nikolai Vasilevich Gogol, "Sorochinsky Fair," in *Village Evenings near Dikanka and Mirgorod*, trans. Christopher English (Oxford: Oxford University Press, 1994), pp. 33–34.

22 Katerina Clark, "The Cult of Byron in the Stalinist Late 1930s" [excerpts of two chapters, on the Cult of Byron and the Stalinist Sublime, from her book in progress, *Moscow, the Third Rome*], delivered at "Slavic Historical Mythologies" (University of Pennsylvania, April 27, 2007). Cited by permission.

23 Lazar Fleishman, "The Trials of Hamlet," ch. 10, *Boris Pasternak: The Poet and his Politics* (Cambridge, MA: Harvard University Press, 1990), especially pp. 218–23.

24 Osip Mandelstam, "The End of the Novel" [1922], in *Mandelstam: Critical Prose and Letters*, ed. Jane Gray Harris (Ann Arbor: Ardis, 1979), pp. 198–201.

9 From the first Thaw to the end

1 Two efficient guides to this period, which I draw on here, are Marc Slonim, "The Thaw," ch. 27, *Soviet Russian Literature, Writers and Problems 1917–1967* (Oxford: Oxford University Press, 1969), pp. 293–310, and Josephine Woll, "The Politics of Culture, 1945–2000," in *The Cambridge History of Russia*, ed. Ronald Grigor Suny (Cambridge: Cambridge University Press, 2006), vol. III, pp. 605–35.

2 David Burg and George Feifer, *Solzhenitsyn* (New York: Stein and Day, 1972), p. 96.

3 From "Lendlease," in Varlam Shalamov, *Kolyma Tales*, trans. John Glad (New York: Penguin Books, 1994), pp. 280–81. For a good contrast with Ivan Denisovich, see also "The Lepers" and "Condensed Milk."

4 Aleksandr I. Solzhenitsyn, *The Gulag Archipelago, 1918–1956*, trans. Thomas P. Whitney, I–III (New York: Harper and Row, 1973), p. xii.

5 "Nobel Lecture" [1970], in *The Solzhenitsyn Reader: New and Essential Writings, 1947–2005*, ed. Edward E. Ericson, Jr. and Daniel J. Mahoney (Wilmington, DE: ISI Books, 2006), pp. 512–26, esp. 526.

6 "The Future According to Alexander Solzhenitsyn" [1992], repr. in Tatyana Tolstaya, *Pushkin's Children: Writings on Russia and Russians*, trans. Jamey Gambrell (New York: Houghton Mifflin, 2003), pp. 61–79, esp. 62–63. Translation adjusted.

7 Aleksandr I. Solzhenitsyn, "The Relentless Cult of Novelty and How It Wrecked the Century," *New York Times Book Review* (February 7, 1993), pp. 3, 17.

8 Vladimir Voinovich, *Moscow 2042*, trans. Richard Lourie (New York: Harcourt Brace Jovanovich, 1990), 2nd edn. with a new Afterword by the author, p. 279. In 2002, Voinovich published a brief book entirely on Solzhenitsyn, *Portret na fone mifa* [Portrait against the background of a myth] (Moscow: Eksmo, 2002) with no irony at all.

9 "Repentance and Self-limitation" [1973] is one of Solzhenitsyn's most overtly biblical essays, in theme and tone. *The Solzhenitsyn Reader*, pp. 527–55.

10 "Vladimir Putin pobyval v gostyakh u Solzhenitsyna," *Vesti* (June 14, 2007).

11 *The Solzhenitsyn Reader* was reviewed by Zinovy Zinik in *TLS* March 9, 2007, where the writer's shabby record, in his exile and returnee phase, of denunciations against liberal opponents is taken as proof of Russia's failure to "de-Sovietize." Daniel Mahoney responded in an indignant counter-essay, "Zinovy Zinik and 'The Solzhenitsyn Reader,'" *First Things: The Journal of Religion, Culture, and Public Life* (March 12, 2007).

12 Aleksandr I. Solzhenitsyn, *The Cancer Ward* (New York: Dell, 1968), p. 433.

13 This episode from Yevtushenko's 1998 memoirs is cited and contextualized in Serguei Alex. Oushakine, "Crimes of Substitution: Detection in Late Soviet Society," *Public Culture* 15.3 (2003): 426–51, esp. 427–28. Oushakine's term for Shostakovich's ploy is "transgressive imitation," a "crime of substitution" distinct from deception or imposture that is designed to modify the symbolic structure of one's society, not to elicit martyrdom.

14 Barbara Heldt, *Terrible Perfection: Women in Russian Literature* (Bloomington: Indiana University Press, 1987).

15 Z. Boguslavskaya, cited in Robert Porter, "Female Alternatives – Narbikova, Petrushevskaya, Tolstaya," *Russia's Alternative Prose* (Oxford: Berg, 1994), p. 44.

16 For a biography, see Helena Goscilo, "Ludmila Petrushevskaya," in *Russian Writers since 1980*, ed. Marina Balina and Mark Lipovetsky, Dictionary of Literary Biography 285 (Detroit: Gale, 2004), pp. 220–29.

17 Lyudmila Petrushevskaya, "Our Crowd," trans. Helena Goscilo, in *Glasnost: An Anthology of Russian Literature under Gorbachev*, ed. Helena Goscilo and Byron Lindsey (Ann Arbor, MI: Ardis, 1990), pp. 379–82.

18 Helena Goscilo, "Paradigm Lost? Contemporary Women's Fiction," in *Women Writers in Russian Literature*, ed. Toby W. Clyman and Diana Greene (Westport, CT: Praeger, 1994), pp. 205–28, esp. 219–20.

19 Ludmilla Petrushevskaya, *The Time: Night*, trans. Sally Laird (Evanston, IL: Northwestern University Press, 1994), p. 13.

20 Natalya Shrom, *Literatura sovremennoi Rossii 1987–2003: Uchebnoe posobie* (Moscow: Abraziv, 2005), pp. 126–32.

21 Viktor Erofeyev, "Anna's Body," trans. Leonard J. Stanton from author's manuscript, in *Glasnost: An Anthology of Russian Literature under Gorbachev*, ed. Helena Goscilo and Byron Lindsey (Ann Arbor, MI: Ardis, 1990), pp. 379–82.

22 Mikhail N. Epstein, "Postmodernism, Communism, and Sots-Art," in *Endquote: Sots-Art Literature and Soviet Grand Style*, trans. John Meredig, ed. Marina Balina, Nancy Condee, and Evgeny Dobrenko (Evanston, IL: Northwestern University Press, 2000), pp. 3–31.

23 A good reading from each tradition exists in English: for the liberal-humanist critique, see Ellen B. Chances, "Pushkin House: The Riddles of Life and Literature," ch. 11, *Andrei Bitov: The Ecology of Inspiration* (Cambridge: Cambridge University Press, 1993), pp. 202–24; for the postmodernist interpretation, Mark Lipovetsky, "Sacking the Museum: Andrei Bitov's *Pushkin House*, ch. 2 in *Russian Postmodernist Fiction: Dialogue with Chaos*, ed. Lipovetsky with Eliot Borenstein (Armonk and London: M. E. Sharpe, 1999), pp. 39–65.

24 Andrei Bitov, *Pushkin House*, trans. Susan Brownsberger (Normal, IL: Dalkey Archive Press, 1987), p. 71.

25 See Henrietta Mondry, "The Russian Literary Press, 1993–98: Critics Reach Reconciliation with Their Audience," in *Russian Literature in Transition*, ed. Ian K. Lilly and Henrietta Mondry (Nottingham: Astra Press, 1999), pp. 105–26, especially 112–14.

26 See Lipovetsky, *Russian Postmodernist Fiction*, pp. 197–219; also the discussion by Slobodanka Vladiv-Glover, "Heterogeneity and the Russian Post-Avant-Garde: The Excremental Poetics of Vladimir Sorokin," in *Russian Postmodernism: New Perspectives on Post-Soviet Culture*, ed. Mikhail N. Epstein, Alexander A. Genis, and Slobodanka M. Vladiv-Glover (New York: Berghahn, 1999), pp. 269–98.

27 Sally Laird, "Introduction" to Vladimir Sorokin, *The Queue* (New York and London: Readers International, 1988), p. i.

28 Konstantin V. Kustanovich, "Vladimir Georgievich Sorokin," in *Russian Writers since 1980*, ed. Marina Balina and Mark Lipovetsky (Detroit: Gale, 2004), p. 305.

29 A portion of the first part of *The Norm* (plus summary of remaining episodes) was translated by Keith Gessen in the journal *n + 1*, no. 1 (Fall 2004): 75–95; the "Nose" / norm episode is on pp. 83–86.

30 Interview with Vladimir Sorokin by Anna Narinskaya, "Ya vypolnil rol' kul'turologicheskogo bul'dozera," *Kommersant – Weekend*, June 1, 2007.

31 Alexander Genis, "Borders and Metamorphoses: Viktor Pelevin in the Context of Post-Soviet Literature," in *Russian Postmodernism*, ed. Epstein, Genis, and Vladiv-Glover, pp. 212–24, esp. 207.

32 For this discussion of Pelevin as a second-generation postmodernist (or perhaps not one at all but some transitional, more "sincere" third category), see Ellen Rutten, *Unattainable Bride Russia: Engendering Nation, State and Intelligentsia in Twentieth-Century Russian Literature* (Groningen, 2005), pp. 202–09, esp. 202.

33 For good English-language discussions of Pelevin, see two by Gerald McCausland: his entry "Viktor Olegovich Pelevin" in *Russian Writers since 1980*, ed. Balina and Lipovetsky, pp. 208–19, and "Viktor Pelevin and the End of Sots-Art," in *Endquote*, ed. Balina, Condee, and Dobrenko, pp. 225–37.

34 Vitaly Chernetsky, *Mapping Postcommunist Cultures: Russia and Ukraine in the Context of Globalization* (Montreal: McGill-Queen's University Press, 2007), p. 107.

35 Victor Pelevin, *Oman Ra*, trans. Andrew Bromfield (London: Harboard Publishing, 1994), pp. 26–27.

36 Victor Pelevin, *Buddha's Little Finger*, trans. Andrew Bromfield (New York: Penguin, 2001), p. 23.

37 Lipovetsky, *Russian Postmodernist Fiction*, p. 196.

38 Boris Akunin, *The Winter Queen*, trans. Andrew Bromfield (New York: Random House, 2003), pp. 9–10. All further references in the text are to this translation.

39 For the parameters of sex crimes and for Russian bias against materialist acquisition, see Anthony Olcott, "Crime, Sex and Sex Crimes," ch. 2, *Russian Pulp: The* Detektiv *and the Russian Way of Crime* (Lanham, MD: Rowman and Littlefield Publishers, 2001), pp. 50–63.

40 A. Chekhov / B. Akunin, *Chaika. Komediia i ee prodolzhenie* (Moscow: Mosty Kul'tury, 2000). For a discussion in English, see Volha Isakava, "Postmodernism Revisited: *The Seagull* by Boris Akunin," in *Anton Pavlovich Chekhov: Poetics – Hermeneutics – Thematics*, ed. J. Douglas Clayton (Ottawa: Slavic Research Group at the University of Ottawa, 2006), pp. 267–85.

41 See Leon Aron, "A Champion for the Bourgeoisie: Reinventing Virtue and Citizenship in Boris Akunin's Novels," *The National Interest* (Spring 2004): 149–57. Aron, Director of Russian Studies at the American Enterprise Institute, considers the Akunin boom a moral and sociopolitical triumph, a continuation of the anti-intelligentsia campaign launched by the Idealist authors of the *Landmarks* essays of 1909.

42 "Jasper Rees meets Boris Akunin," *Electronic Telegraph* (UK), April 17, 2004.

43 This point is made by Aron, "A Champion for the Bourgeoisie," p. 149. Akunin's English-language translator (or perhaps publisher) does not include this dedication in its Fandorin Series paperback.

44 Dmitry Prigov, "Dialogue No. 5," from the bilingual anthology *In the Grip of Strange Thoughts: Russian Poetry in a New Era*, selected and edited by J. Kates (Brookline, MA: Zephyr Press, 1999), pp. 260–63.

45 V. B. Kataev, *Igra v oskolki: sud'by russkoi klassiki v epokhu postmodernizma* (Moscow: Izdatel'stvo moskovskogo universiteta, 2002), p. 230.

46 M. M. Bakhtin, "The Art of the Word and the Culture of Folk Humor (Rabelais and Gogol')," in *Semiotics and Structuralism*, ed. Henryk Baran (White Plains, NY: IASP, 1976), p. 293.

Glossary

Pronunciations and definitions of Russian words, names, places, and texts

Page reference is made to the first appearance of the word. Monarchs appear in the list alphabetized according to their first names, and the dates listed indicate the time span of their reign. Most Russian words have a strong primary stress. This is marked by an acute accent over the stressed syllable.

Words

bashmák   shoe; boot, p. 116.

Bédnye lyúdi   *Poor Folk*, title of Dostoevsky's 1846 epistolary novel, p. 237.

Bédnyi vsádnik   "The Poor Horseman," title of a chapter from Andrei Bitov's *Pushkin House* that parodies the title of Pushkin's narrative poem, *The Bronze Horseman* [*Médnyi vsádnik*], p. 237.

blazhénny   blessed one; alternate name for a holy fool, p. 39.

bogatýr   a hero from Russian folk myth, similar to a warrior saint, p. 60.

bolshevík   lit. "majority person," as opposed to "menshevik" ("minority person"); the Leninist wing of the Marxist Socialist-Democratic Party, victorious in 1917, p. 31.

bylína   Russian folk epic, the hero of which is usually a *bogatýr*, p. 60.

chort   devil, imp, p. 35.

chronotope   Bakhtin's neologism for the time-space relationship in narrative, p. 17.

chudák   oddball, misfit, p. 42.

dácha   a cabin or small house, usually rural, used for retreats, p. 32.

detektív   detective novel, p. 243.

diamát   Soviet compound word for "dialectical materialism," p. 197.

Dobroliúbov   "Mr. Lover-of-Good," speaking name from Denis Fonvizin's comedy *The Brigadier* (1769), p. 88.

dogovór   pact; contractual agreement, p. 77.

Dúma   Russian representative governing body, p. 166.

durák   fool, p. 39.

dúrochka   little fool (female diminutive of *durák*), p. 42.

269

dvoevérie   dual-faith; the blend of pagan and Christian *ethoi* in Russian culture, p. 29.

dyávol   devil (more imposing and terrifying than a *chort*), p. 35.

feuilleton   lit. leaf, piece of paper (from Fr.); short, journalistic prose sketch, p. 156.

Gallomania   a frenzy or mania for all things French, ridiculed in eighteenth-century comedies (especially Denis Fonvizin's), p. 82.

Gallophilia   the love of all things French (in contrast to Gallománia), p. 87.

glásnost'   lit. "public voicedness"; first used in reference to lessened censorship during the Great Reforms (1861–64); entered English usage beginning in the mid-1980s, in reference to Gorbachev's liberalization policies in the Soviet Union, p. 77.

grekh   sin, p. 41.

gróznyi   terrible, awesome (in the sense of frightening to one's enemies); refers to "Ivan the Terrible," p. 52.

idéinost'   idea-mindedness (lit. "idea-ness"); one of the tenets of socialist realism, that the "idea" of a work of art should embody the current high-priority party slogan, p. 200.

intelligéntsia   a mixed class based on education and ideological commitment rather than birth or government rank, p. 7.

Kalmýk   Asiatic, Siberian ethnic group, p. 121.

Khanzhákina   "Mrs. Hypocrite," speaking name from Catherine the Great's comedy *O! The Times!* (1769), p. 85.

kitezhánka   a woman from the legendary city of Kitezh, p. 30.

klássovost'   class-mindedness; a tenet of socialist realism, acknowledging the social-class origin of art and obliging it to further the struggle of the proletariat, p. 200.

knízhnik   scribe; bibliophile; bookseller (pl. *knízhniki*), p. 23.

kolkhóz   collective farm, p. 216.

Kóshchnoe tsárstvo   Kingdom of the dead, p. 68.

kost'   bone, p. 68.

Kotlován   *Foundation Pit*. Title of Platonov's 1930 novel, p. 212.

kulák   lit. "fist"; well-to-do peasants who resisted collectivization after 1932, or anyone who profited under the quasi-capitalistic New Economic Plan, p. 51.

kul'túrnost'   culturedness, p. 193.

lésenka   lit. "short flight of stairs"; refers here to a verse form invented by Vladímir Mayakóvsky, p. 8.

l'gat'   to tell a lie, p. 49.

lichína   mask; outward appearance that conceals one's true person, p. 30.

líchnoe (nominative neuter declension of the adjective *líchnyi*)   personal; unique to an individual, p. 30.

líchnost′   personality; implies the moral character of a person, p. 30.

lik [pronounced "leek"]   face, visage, countenance, p. 30.

líshnii chelovék   superfluous man, p. 54.

Litfónd   acronym for "Literary Fund," the financial division of the Union of Soviet writers, p. 198.

litsó   generic Russian word for "face," p. 30.

loshad′-kaléka   crippled mare, p. 155.

lubók   woodcut print, one of the earliest forms of printing the written word in Russia; now often used in the sense of "pulp fiction," p. 73.

lúzha   mud puddle, p. 49.

Lyód   *Ice*, title of a novel by Vladímir Sorókin, p. 240.

magícheskii kristáll   lit. "magic crystal"; crystal ball used for telling fortunes, a famous image from Chapter 8 of *Eugene Onegin*, p. 105.

magnitizdát   recordings of illegal music smuggled into the Soviet Union and distributed illicitly, p. 238.

Mát′-syrá-zemlyá   Moist-Mother-Earth [Russian order is "Mother – Moist – Earth"], p. 61.

Médnye lyúdi   "Bronze Folk," title of a chapter from Andréi Bítov's *Pushkin House* that parodies Dostoevsky's epistolary novel, *Poor Folk* [*Bédnye lyúdi*], p. 237.

Médnyi vsádnik   *The Bronze Horseman*, a narrative poem by Aleksandr Pushkin, p. 237.

Milón   "Dear One," speaking name from Denis Fonvizin's comedy *The Minor* (1781), p. 86.

mit′kí   eccentric followers of artist Dmitry Shagin in the 1970s; painters, poets, filmmakers, and performance artists with an anti-work ethic, p. 42.

Mitrofán   "Mama's Boy" (Greek), speaking name from Denis Fonvizin's comedy *The Minor* (1781), p. 86.

Moskvá   Moscow, p. 183.

nachináetsia   begins, is beginning, p. 164.

naródnost′   people- or folk-mindedness; a value precious to Slavophile thinkers in the nineteenth century and revived as a socialist realist concept in the 1930s, suggesting that art should be accessible and appealing to the masses by drawing on their traditions, language, melodies, rhythms, and values, p. 200.

nechístaya síla   unclean force. One of many euphemisms for the devil, p. 61.

nédorosl′   "minor," a young man in tsarist times who had not yet passed the literacy exam qualifying him for obligatory civil service – and for marriage, p. 86.

Nepústov   "Not-Shallow," speaking name from Catherine the Great's comedy *O! The Times!* (1769), p. 85.

nogá   foot, leg, p. 242.
nóvyi slog   "The new style," p. 94.

Óchered'   *The Queue*, a novel by Vladímir Sorókin, p. 239.
ócherk   sketch (as a literary genre popular during the second half of the nineteenth century, a brief descriptive narrative in the Realist style), p. 156.
ogón'   fire, p. 62.
oknó   window, p. 61.
óko   eye, p. 61.
Old Believer   one who refused to accept the official reforms of the Russian Orthodox Church under Patriarch Nikon in the seventeenth century, p. 30.
Orgbyuró   acronym for the Organizational Bureau of the Union of Soviet Writers, p. 198.
óttepel'   Thaw; period of diminished arbitrary government persecution, such as the post-Stalin years under Khrushchev, p. 220.
Ottsý i déti   *Fathers and Children* (novel by Ivan Turgenev), p. 55.

partíinost'   party-mindedness; a socialist realist concept whereby every act is a political act and the source for all correct knowledge is the Communist Party, p. 200.
Peresméshnik íli slavénskie skázki   *The Mocker, or Slavic folk tale*, p. 91.
perestróika   lit. "Restructuring"; liberalizing reforms in the Soviet Union under Mikhail Gorbachev in the 1980s, p. 18.
Petrúshka   tragicomic hero of Russian puppet theatre, related to the tradition of Pierrot, Punch and Judy, etc., p. 40.
pleténie slovés   lit. word-weaving – an aesthetic technique associated with pre-modern Russian prose texts that involves assonance, alliteration, and repetition to produce a rhythmic, lyrical effect, p. 81.
plut   (pronounced *ploot*) rogue, rascal, Russian *picaro*, p. 47.
Polóvtsians   pagan tribes to the southeast of Kiev in medieval times, p. 44.
popútchiki (pl.)   lit. "fellow travelers," a term coined by Leon Trotsky in the early 1920s to refer to non-Bolshevik or apolitical writers who were nevertheless not hostile to the new regime, p. 196.
póshlyi   vulgar, trivial, banal, p. 49.
póshlost'   vulgarity, banality, p. 50.
poshlyák   a vulgar, banal or trivial person, usually with commercial or consumer values, p. 49.
Právdin   "Mr. Truthful," speaking name from Denis Fonvizin's comedy *The Minor* (1781), p. 86.
právednik (f. *právednitsa*; pl. *právedniki*)   righteous person, p. 29.
proizvól   arbitrary political will or license; the exercise of power for its own irrational sake, or to intimidate, p. 194.
Proletkúlt   acronym for "proletarian culture," a radical organization of writers from the urban working class that flourished for several years after the Revolution, p. 195.

prorók prophet, p. 109.
Prostakóva "Mrs. Simpleton," speaking name from Denis Fonvizin's comedy *The Minor* (1781), p. 86.

Raskól 17ᵗʰ C. schism in the Russian Orthodox Church, p. 59.

samizdát lit. "self-publishing," the underground circulation of texts in Soviet-era Eastern and Central Europe, p. 238.
samovár lit. "self-cooker," a metal urn with spigot and internal tube for boiling water for tea, p. 32.
samozvántsvo lit. self-naming, pretendership, as in "pretender to the throne," usurper, p. 118.
Shinél' "Overcoat." Title of a short story by Nikolai Gogol, 1842, p. 117.
shut (pronounced *shoot*) jester, p. 39.
shútka joke, p. 41.
skaz the literary device of a folksy, oral, usually digressive narrator, p. 201.
skázka folk tale; fairy tale, p. 60.
skomorókh (pl. *skomorókhi*) traveling minstrel, p. 39.
Skotínin "Mr. Pig," or "Brute," speaking name from Denis Fonvizin's comedy *The Minor* (1781), p. 86.
Slavophile nineteenth-century writers and lay philosophers opposed to borrowing from other national traditions and favoring a uniquely "Russian" culture untainted by the West, p. 12.
slúchai chance, p. 105.
smekh laughter, p. 41.
sobór synod, assembly; cathedral, p. 61.
sobórnost' togetherness; a sense of spiritual, ideological, or cultural togetherness, p. 31.
Sófya "Wisdom," speaking name from Denis Fonvizin's comedy *The Minor* (1781) and also *The Brigadier* (1769), p. 86.
sotsiál'nyi zakáz social command, p. 193.
soyúz union, p. 198.
Starodúm "Old Thought," speaking name from Denis Fonvizin's comedy *The Minor* (1781), p. 86.
stólnik a high-ranking official responsible for serving the tsar at table, p. 48.
stránnik (f. *stránnitsa*) wanderer, p. 36.
strastotérpets passion-sufferer, p. 62.
Svoi krug "Our Crowd" (title of Lyudmíla Petrushévskaya's short story), p. 232.

tamizdát lit. "published elsewhere," works smuggled out of the Soviet Union and published in the West, p. 238.
toská melancholy, grief, anguish, p. 50.
tsarévich son of the tsar (prince, in the Western sense), p. 41.
tsélostnost' wholeness, p. 31.

váshe prevoskhodítel'stvo   Your Excellency; the appropriate mode of address for third and fourth ranks in the Table of Ranks, p. 101.

váshe vysokoblagoródie   Your High Honor; appropriate for sixth, seventh, or eighth rank, p. 101.

váshe vysokoprevoskhodítel'stvo   Your High Excellency; appropriate for the first or second rank in the Table of Ranks, p. 101.

váshe vysokoródie   Your Highly Born; appropriate for the fifth rank in the Table of Ranks, p. 101.

vertét'sya   to revolve, spin, p. 62.

Véstnikova   "Tattler," speaking name from Catherine the Great's comedy *O! The Times!* (1769), p. 85.

vlast'   power (political), p. 23.

vodá   water, p. 62.

vózdukh   air, p. 62.

"Vprok"   the title of Platonov's short story, "For Future Use," p. 203.

vrémya   time, p. 62.

vruchénie sebyá   self-giving, the giving or "handing over" of oneself without the motive of personal gain, p. 77.

yuródivy (f. yuródivaya)   holy fool, p. 39.

yuródstvo Khristá rádi   holy foolishness for the sake of Christ, p. 41.

zapíski   notes or diary entries, p. 11.

zastói   Stagnation; usually refers to the years of cultural and economic stagnation under Brezhnev (1970s–84), p. 220.

zemlyá   earth (as in soil), p. 62.

zhitié [pronounced "zhitiyéh"]   saint's life (hagiographic text), p. 62.

People

Afanásiev, Aleksándr Nikoláevich (1826–71)   Russian collector of fairy tales, p. 68.

Akhmátova, Ánna Andréyevna (1889–1966)   p. 30. Works by: "Requiem."

Akímov, Nikolái Pávlovich (1901–68)   p. 210.

Aksákov, Sergéi Timoféyevich (1791–1859)   p. 45. Works by: *Family Chronicle.*

Akúnin, Borís (pseudonym of Grigóry Chkhartishvíli, b. 1958)   p. 97. Works by: *Azazel'* [Eng. *The Winter Queen*]; *Seagull, The: A Comedy and its Continuation.*

Alexánder Névsky (r. 1236–63)   p. 59.

Alexánder Románov I (r. 1801–25)   p. 24.

Alexánder Románov II (r. 1855–81)   p. 12.

Alexander Románov III (r. 1881–94)   p. 132.

Avvakúm, Protopop (1620–82)   p. 45. Works by: "The Life of Archpriest Avvakum, Written by Himself."

Bábel, Isaák Emmanuílovich (1894–1941) p. 47. Works by: *Red Cavalry*.
Bakhtín, Mikháil Mikháilovich (1895–1975) p. 15.
Behrs, Sófya Andréyevna (later S. A. Tolstáya) p. 151.
Belínsky, Vissarión Grigórievich (1811–48) p. 14.
Bély, Andréi (pseudonym of Bugáev, Borís Nikoláevich, 1880–1934) p. 17. Works by: "Magic of Words, The"; *Petersburg*.
Berdyáev, [Nicolas] Nikolái Aleksándrovich (1874–1948) p. 22. Works by: *Russian Idea, The*.
Bítov, Andréi Geórgievich (b. 1937) p. 17. Works by: *Pushkin House*.
Blok, Aleksándr Aleksándrovich (1880–1921) p. 182. Works by: "Intelligentsia and Revolution, The"; *Twelve, The*.
Borís Godunóv (r. 1598–1605) p. 59.
Borodín, Aleksándr Porfírievich (1833–77) p. 44. Works by: *Prince Igor*.
Bródsky, Jóseph Aleksándrovich (1940–96) p. 220.
Bryúsov, Valéry Yákovlevich (1873–1924) p. 243.
Bulgákov, Mikháil Afanásievich (1891–1940) p. 16. Works by: "Adventures of Chichikov, The"; "Diaboliad"; *Fatal Eggs, The*; *Heart of a Dog*; *Master and Margarita, The*.
Búnin, Iván Alekséyevich (1870–1953) p. 221.

Catherine Románova [Ekaterina Romanova] I (r. 1725–27) p. 93.
Catherine Románova [Ekaterina Romanova] II (the Great) (r. 1762–96) p. 80. Works by: *O! The Times!*
Chaadáev, Pyotr Yákovlevich (1794–1856) p. 4.
Chapáyev, Vasily (1887–1919) p. 243.
Chékhov, Antón Pávlovich (1860–1904) p. 12. Works by: "Black Monk, The"; "Culprit, The"; "Death of a Clerk, The"; *Duel, The*; "Enemies"; "In the Ravine"; "Lady with a Pet Dog"; *Little Trilogy* ("About Love"); "Anna On the Neck"; "Calamity, A"; "Tedious Story, A"; "Name-Day Party, The"; "Peasants"; *Seagull*; "Steppe"; *Three Sisters*; *Uncle Vanya*; "Ward Number Six".
Chernétsky, Vitály p. 15.
Chernyshévsky, Nikolái Gavrílovich (1828–89) p. 36. Works by: *What Is to Be Done?*
Chukóvsky, Kornéy Ivánovich (1882–1969) p. 207.
Chulkóv, Mikháil Dmítrievich (1743–92) p. 27. Works by: "Bitter Fate, A"; *Comely Cook, The*; *Mocker, The*.

Daniél, Yúly Márkovich (1925–88) p. 220.
Deníkin, Antón Ivánovich, General (1872–1947) p. 29.
Derzhávin, Gavríla Románovich (1743–1816) p. 13.
Dolgorúkaya, Natálya (1714–71) p. 45.
Dostoévsky, Fyódor Mikháilovich (1821–81) p. 4. Works by: *Brothers Karamazov, The*; *Crime and Punishment*; *Demons*; *Diary of a Writer*; "Dream of a Ridiculous Man"; *Double, The*; *Idiot, The*; *Notes from Underground*; *Poor Folk*; *White Nights*.

Ehrenbúrg, Ilyá Grigórievich (1891–1967)   p. 220. Works by: *Thaw, The.*
Éikhenbaum, Borís Mikháilovich (1886–1959)   p. 16. Works by: "How Gogol's 'Overcoat' is Made"; *Young Tolstoi, The.*
Éisenstein, Sergéi Mikháilovich (1898–1948)   p. 66. Works by: *Alexander Nevsky.*
Épstein, Mikháil Naúmovich (b. 1950)   p. 15.
Eroféyev, Venedíkt (1938–90)   p. 35. Works by: *Moscow to the End of the Line.*
Eroféyev, Víktor (b. 1947)   p. 236. Works by: "Anna's Body"; *Russian Beauty*; "Russia's *Fleurs du mal*"; "Wake for Russian Literature, A."

Fadéyev, Aleksándr Aleksándrovich (1901–56)   p. 221.
Fáinzelberg, Ilyá Arnóldovich (1897–1937)   p. 202. Works by: *Golden Calf, The*; *Twelve Chairs, The.*
Fonvízin, Denís Ivánovich (1745–92)   p. 86. Works by: *Brigadier, The*; *Minor, The.*
Fyódorov, Iván (d. 1583)   p. 59.

Gíppius, Zináida Nikoláevna (1869–1945)   p. 74.
Gladkóv, Fyódor Vasílievich (1883–1958)   p. 65. Works by: *Cement.*
Gógol, Níkolai Vasílievich (1809–52)   p. 13. Works by: "Carriage, The"; *Dead Souls*; *Diary of a Madman*; *Government Inspector, The*; "Nose, The"; "Overcoat, The"; *Selected Passages from a Correspondence with Friends*; "Sorochinsky Fair."
Goncharóv, Iván Aleksándrovich (1812–91)   p. 72. Works by: *Oblomov.*
Górky, Maksím (pseudonym of Peshkóv, Alekséi Maksímovich, 1868–1936)   p. 13. Works by: *Mother*; *On Literature.*
Griboyédov, Aleksándr Sergéyevich (1795–1829)   p. 100. Works by: *Woe from Wit.*
Grigóry Otrépiev (Dmítry the Pretender) (1605–06)   p. 106.

Iskandér, Fazíl Abdúlevich (b. 1929)   p. 53. Works by: *Sandro from Chegem.*
Iván IV (the Terrible) (r. 1533–84)   p. 52.
Ivánov, Vsévolod Vyacheslávovich (1895–1963)   p. 47. Works by: *Armored Train 14–69.*

Jakobsón, Román Ósipovich (1896–1982)   p. 15.

Karamzín, Nikolái Mikháilovich (1766–1826)   p. 27. Works by: *History of the Russian State*; *Letters of a Russian Traveler*; "Poor Liza."
Katáev, Evgény Petróvich (1903–42)   p. 202. Works by: *Golden Calf, The*; *Twelve Chairs, The.*
Katáev, Valentín Petróvich (1897–1986)   p. 25. Works by: *Time, Forward!*
Kharms, Daníil (1905–42)   p. 53. Works by: *Elizabeth Bam.*
Khlébnikov, Velemír (1885–1922)   p. 81.
Knyazhnín, Yákov Borísovich (1742–91)   p. 89. Works by: *Misfortune from a Coach.*
Korolénko, Vladímir Glaktiónovich (1853–1921)   p. 29.
Kúrbsky, Andréi Mikháilovich, Prince (1528–83)   p. 52.

Lérmontov, Mikháil Yúrievich (1814–41)   p. 12. Works by: *Hero of Our Time*; "Prophet."
Leskóv, Nikolái Semyónovich (1831–95)   p. 46. Works by: *Enchanted Wanderer, The*; *Left-Handed Craftsman, The* [*Levshá*].
Lótman, Yúry Mikháilovich (1922–93)   p. 15.
Lukín, Vladímir Ignátievich (1737–94)   p. 83.

Mandelstám, Nadézhda Yákovlevna (1899–1980)   p. 9.
Mandelstám, Ósip Emílievich (1891–1938)   p. 52. Works by: "Stalin Epigram."
Marshák, Samuíl Yákovlevich (1887–1964)   p. 207.
Mayakóvsky, Vladímir Vladímirovich (1893–1930)   p. 7. Works by: *Bedbug, The*.
Merezhkóvsky, Dmítry Sergéyevich (1865–1941)   p. 29. Works by: *Anti-Christ. Peter and Alexis*; "L. Tolstoy and Dostoevsky"; "On Reasons for the Decline of Contemporary Russian Literature, and on its New Tendencies."
Meyerhóld, Vsévolod Emílievich (1874–1940)   p. 189.
Mikháil Románov (1613–45)   p. 59.
Mírsky, D. S. [Dmítry Svyatopólk] Prince (1890–1939)   p. 23. Works by: *History of Russian Literature, A*; *Pushkin*.

Nabókov, Vladímir Vladímirovich (1899–1977)   p. 4.
Nekrásov, Nikolái Alekséyevich (1821–78)   p. 153. Works by: *On the Weather*.
Néstor (Chronicler) (*c.* 1056–after 1113)   p. 65. Works by: "Life of St. Theodosius."
Nicholas Románov I (r. 1825–55)   p. 53.
Nicholas Románov II (r. 1894–1917)   p. 63.
Novikóv, Nikolái Ivánovich (1744–1818)   p. 84.

Olésha, Yúry Kárlovich (1899–1960)   p. 57. Works by: *Envy*.

Pánin, Nikíta Ivánovich, Count (1718–83)   p. 86.
Pashkévich, Vasíly Alekseyevich (1742–97)   p. 89.
Pasternák, Borís Leonídovich (1890–1960)   p. 195. Works by: *Doctor Zhivago* (Appended "Poems of Yury Zhivago" "Hamlet"); *Hamlet*.
Paul Románov I (r. 1796–1801)   p. 63.
Pelévin, Víktor Olégovich (b. 1962)   p. 28. Works by: *Chapayev and Emptiness* [Eng. *Buddha's Little Finger*]; "Life and Adventures of Shed Number XII, The"; *Life of Insects, The*; *Oman Ra*; *Yellow Arrow, The*.
Peter Románov I (the Great) (r. 1682–1725)   p. 11.
Peter Románov III (r. 1762)   p. 100.
Petrushévskaya, Lyudmíla Stepánova (b. 1938)   p. 224. Works by: "Our Circle"; *Three Girls in Blue*; *Time Night, The*.
Pilnyák, Borís (pseudonym of Borís Andréyevich Vogáu, [1894–1937])   p. 22.
Platónov, Andréi Platónovich (1899–1951)   p. 20. Works by: *Dzhan*; "For Future Use"; *Foundation Pit, The*; *Happy Moscow*; "Homecoming, The."

Pleshchéyev, Alekseí Nikoláevich (1825–93)　p. 157.

Polevóy, Borís Nikoláevich (1908–81)　p. 242. Works by: *Story of a Real Man*.

Pólotsky, Simeón (1629–80)　p. 51. Works by: "Merchant Class, The."

Praúdin, Anatóly Arkádievich (b. 1961)　p. 211.

Prígov, Dmítry (b. 1940–2007)　p. 17.

Prokófiev, Sergéi Sergéyevich (1891–1953)　p. 3. Works by: *Story of a Real Man*; *War and Peace*.

Pugachóv, Emelyán Ivánovich ([1740]–75)　p. 80.

Púshkin, Aleksándr Sergéyevich (1799–1837)　p. 1. Works by: *Boris Godunov*; *Bronze Horseman, The*; *Captain's Daughter, The*; *Eugene Onegin*; *Journey to Arzrum, A*; "Little Tragedies" (*Miserly Knight, The*; *Mozart and Salieri*; *Stone Guest, The*); "Prophet"; "Queen of Spades, The"; *Ruslan and Lyudmila*; *Tales of the Late Ivan Petrovich Belkin* ("Shot, The"; "Stationmaster, The").

Radíshchev, Aleksándr Nikoláevich (1749–1802)　p. 27.

Raspútin, Valentín Grigórievich (b. 1937)　p. 13. Works by: *Farewell to Matyora*.

Rímsky-Kórsakov, Nikolái Andréyevich (1844–1908)　p. 29. Works by: *Invisible City of Kitezh and the Maiden Fevronia, The*; *Koshchey the Deathless*.

Ryúrik (r. c. 862–79)　p. 59.

Saltykóv-Shchedrín, Mikháil Evgráfovich (1826–89)　p. 51. Works by: *Golovlyovs, The*.

Scriábin, Aleksándr Nikoláevich (1872–1915)　p. 60. Works by: *Mysterium*.

Shágin, Dmítry Vladímirovich (1957–)　p. 42.

Shalámov, Varlám Tíkhonovich (1907–82)　p. 225. Works by: *Kolyma Tales*.

Shelgunóv, Nikolái Vasílievich (1824–91)　p. 14.

Shklóvsky, Víktor Borísovich (1893–1984)　p. 6. Works by: "Art as Device."

Shólokhov, Mikháil Aleksándrovich (1905–84)　p. 9. Works by: *Quiet Don, The*.

Shostakóvich, Dmítry Dmítrievich (1906–75)　p. 116.

Shukshín, Vasíly Makárovich (1929–74)　p. 42.

Shvarts, Evgény Lvóvich (1896–1958)　p. 203. Works by: *Dragon, The*; *One Night*.

Sinyávsky, Andréi Donátovich (1925–97)　p. 39. Works by: *Ivan Durak*.

Sologúb, Fyódor Kuzmích (1863–1927)　p. 17. Works by: *Petty Demon*.

Solovyóv, Vladímir Sergéyevich (1853–1900)　p. 168. Works by: *Lectures on Divine Humanity*.

Solzhenítsyn, Aleksándr Isáevich (b. 1918)　p. 23. Works by: *Cancer Ward, The*; *First Circle, The*; *Gulag Archipelago*; *One Day in the Life of Ivan Denisovich*; *Rebuilding Russia*; "Relentless Cult of Novelty and How It Wrecked the Century, The"; *Two Hundred Years Together*.

Sorókin, Vladímir Geórgievich (b. 1955)　p. 237. Works by: *Blue Lard*; *Ice*; *Norm, The*; *Queue, The*; "Sergei Andreyevich."

Stravínsky, Ígor Fyódorovich (1882–1971)　p. 222.

Sumarókov, Aleksándr Petróvich (1717–77)　p. 83. Works by: *Hamlet*; "Second Epistle."

Suvórin, Alekséi Sergéyevich (1834–1912)　p. 133.

Svyatopólk (the Accursed) (r. 1015–19)   p. 63.

Tchaikóvsky, Pyotr Ilyích (1840–93)   p. 7. Works by: *Eugene Onegin; Queen of Spades, The.*
Tertz, Abram (pseudonym of Sinyávsky, Andréi Donátovich) (1925–97)   p. 199. Works by: "What Is Socialist Realism?"
Tolstáya, Tatyána Nikítichna (b. 1951)   p. 227.
Tolstóy, Lev Nikoláevich (1828–1910)   p. 1. Works by: "About Life"; "About Relations between the Sexes"; "About Religion"; "About War"; "Alyosha the Pot"; *Ánna Karénina; Childhood; Confession; Cossacks, The;* "Death of Iván Ilyích, The"; "Devil, The"; "Father Sergius"; "God Sees the Truth, But Waits"; *Hadji Murad;* "Kreutzer Sonata, The"; "Master and Man"; *Power of Darkness, The;* "Prisoner of the Caucasus"; "Raid, The"; *Resurrection;* "Sevastopol in December"; *War and Peace;* "What do People Live By?"; *What is Art?;* "Why do People Stupefy Themselves?"
Tretyakóv, Sergéi Mikháilovich (1892–1939)   p. 194. Works by: *I Want a Child.*
Trótsky, Lev Davídovich (1879–1940)   p. 190. Works by: *Literature and Revolution.*
Tsvetáeva, Marína Ivánovna (1892–1941)   p. 6. Works by: "Verses about Moscow"; "Verses to Pushkin."
Turgénev, Iván Sergéyevich (1818–83)   p. 4. Works by: *Diary of a Superfluous Man; Fathers and Children; Nest of Gentlefolk, A; On the Eve; Rudin; Sportsman's Sketches, A;*
Tynyánov, Yúry Nikoláevich (1894–1943)   p. 15. Works by: "Toward a Theory of Parody."

Uspénsky, Borís Andréyevich (b. 1937)   p. 76.

Vasilénko, Svetlána Vladímirovna (b. 1956)   p. 42. Works by: *Little Fool.*
Vladimir, Prince Svyatoslávovich (the Great) (r. 980–1015)   p. 59.
Voinóvich, Vladímir Nikoláevich (b. 1932)   p. 228. Works by: *Moscow 2042.*
Volóshin, Maksimilián Aleksándrovich (1877–1932)   p. 29.

Yevtushénko, Yevgény Aleksándrovich (b. 1933)   p. 230.

Zamyátin, Evgény Ivánovich (1884–1937)   p. 49. Works by: *Islanders, The;* "On Literature, Revolution, Entropy, and Other Matters"; "Scythians?"; *We.*
Zhukóvsky, Vasíly Andréyevich (1783–1852)   p. 100.
Zóshchenko, Mikháil Mikháilovich (1895–1958)   p. 192. Works by: *Before Sunrise; Youth Restored.*

Places

Angara, River   p. 13.
Arzrúm   p. 28.

Bashkír, Steppe   p. 45.
Belomór ["White Sea"] Canal   p. 225.
Bóldino   Pushkin's estate, where he had two legendarily productive autumns, p. 106.
Borodinó   site of an extremely bloody battle between the Russians and Napoleon's army near Moscow in 1812, p. 150.

Caucasus, Mountains   p. 28.
Chechnya   p. 13.
Chernígov   p. 72.
Chud (pronounced *chood*), Lake   p. 59.

Dnieper, River   p. 175.
Don, River   p. 175.
Dushanbé   formerly Stálinabad, in Soviet Tajíkistan, p. 210.

Ekibastúz   Soviet prison camp, p. 224.

Kazán   p. 72.
Kiev   former capital of *Rus'*, now capital of Ukraine, p. 44.
Kítezh   (pronounced Keetezh), p. 29.
Klopskó   A monastery located near the northern city of Novgorod, p. 63.
Kolymá   p. 225.

Leningrad   Soviet name for St. Petersburg from 1924–91 (see also Petrograd, St. Petersburg), p. 42.

Magnitogórsk   p. 25.
Moscow   p. 1.
Múrom   p. 72.

Nóvgorod   p. 40.

Ob', River   p. 45.
Oká, River   p. 72.
Oryól   p. 74.

Petersburg   St. Petersburg (see also Petrograd and Leningrad), p. 28.
Petrográd   Slavic equivalent of the Germanic-sounding Petersburg ("Peter's city"), so renamed in 1914 by Nicholas II as a patriotic move during World War I, p. 15.

Riga   p. 72.

Sakhalín Island   a penal colony north of Japan,   p. 133.
Sevastópol   battle site in the Crimean War,   p. 125.

Smolénsk   p. 74.
St. Petersburg   original name for the former capital of Russia, p. 1.
Stalinabád   now Dushanbe, in Tajikistan, p. 210.
Svetloyár, Lake   p. 29.

Tobólsk   p. 45.
Túla   city South of Moscow, p. 131.

Ufá, region   p. 45.
Urál (Mountains)   p. 45.

Vladivostók   p. 53.

Yálta   coastal city on the Black Sea in Crimea, p. 159.
Yároslavl-Vólga, region   p. 29.
Yásnaya Polyána   estate where Count Leo Tolstoy was born and buried, p. 131.
Yenesei River   p. iv.
Yershaláim   "Jerusalem," in Bulgakov's *Master and Margarita*, p. 176.

Guide to further reading

General background and useful reference

Brown, Edward J., *Russian Literature since the Revolution* (Cambridge, MA: Harvard University Press, 2002).
Brown, William Edward, *A History of Eighteenth-Century Russian Literature* (Ann Arbor, MI: Ardis, 1980).
  A History of Seventeenth Century Russian Literature (Ann Arbor, MI: Ardis, 1980).
Cornwell, Neil, ed., *The Routledge Companion to Russian Literature* (New York: Routledge, 2001).
Fedotov, George P., *The Russian Religious Mind*, 2 vols. (Blemont, MA: Norland, 1975), vol. I: *Kievan Christianity, the 10th to the 13th Centuries*, and vol. II: *The Middle Ages, the 13th to the 15th Centuries*.
Haney, Jack J., *An Introduction to the Russian Folktale* (Armonk, NY: M. E. Sharpe, 1999).
Hubbs, Joanna, *Mother Russia: The Feminine Myth in Russian Culture* (Bloomington: Indiana University Press, 1988).
Karlinsky, Simon, *Russian Drama from its Beginnings to the Age of Pushkin* (Berkeley: University of California Press, 1986).
Kelly, Catriona, *A History of Russian Women's Writing 1820–1992* (Oxford: Clarendon Press, 1994).
Mirsky, Prince D. S., *A History of Russian Literature from its Beginnings to 1900* (Evanston, IL: Northwestern University Press, 1999).
Moser, Charles, ed., *The Cambridge History of Russian Literature* (Cambridge: Cambridge University Press, 1992).
Rzhevsky, Nicholas, ed., *The Cambridge Companion to Modern Russian Culture* (Cambridge: Cambridge University Press, 1998).
Smorodinskaya, Tatiana, Helena Goscilo, and Karen Evans-Romaine, eds., *Encyclopedia of Contemporary Russian Culture* (London: Routledge, 2006).
Terras, Victor, ed., *Handbook of Russian Literature* (New Haven: Yale University Press, 1990).
  A History of Russian Literature (New Haven: Yale University Press, 1991).

Wachtel, Michael, *The Cambridge Introduction to Russian Poetry* (Cambridge: Cambridge University Press, 2005).

Zenkovsky, Serge A., ed., *Medieval Russia's Epics, Chronicles, and Tales* (New York: Dutton, 1974).

Biographies of Russian writers featured in this book

Bartlett, Rosamund, ed., *Anton Chekhov: A Life in Letters*, trans. Anthony Phillips (New York: Penguin Books, 2004).

Binyon, T. J., *Pushkin: A Biography* (New York: Alfred A. Knopf, 2003).

Curtis, J. A. E., *Manuscripts Don't Burn: Mikhail Bulgakov. A Life in Letters and Diaries* (London: Bloomsbury, 1991).

Fanger, Donald, *Gorky's Tolstoy and Other Reminiscences: Key Writings by and about Maxim Gorky* (New Haven: Yale University Press, 2008).

Fleishman, Lazar, *Boris Pasternak: The Poet and his Politics* (Cambridge, MA: Harvard University Press, 1990).

Frank, Joseph, *Dostoevsky*, 5 vols. (Princeton: Princeton University Press, 1976–2002).

Freeborn, Richard, *Dostoevsky (Life and Times)* (London: Haus Publishing, 2003).

Karlinsky, Simon, *Marina Tsvetaeva: The Woman, the World and her Poetry* (Cambridge: Cambridge University Press, 1986).

ed., *Anton Chekhov's Life and Thought: Selected Letters and Commentaries* (Evanston, IL: Northwestern University Press, 1997).

Kelly, Laurence, *Lermontov: Tragedy in the Caucasus* (New York: Tauris Parke, 2003).

Kochetkova, N. D., *Nikolai Karamzin* (Boston: Twayne Publishers, 1975).

Lyngstad, Sverre, and Alexandra Lyngstad, *Ivan Goncharov* (New York: Macmillan, 1984).

Maude, Aylmer, *The Life of Tolstoy*, 2 vols. (Oxford: Oxford University Press, 1987).

Mochulsky, Konstantin, *Dostoevsky*, trans. Michael A. Minihan (Princeton: Princeton University Press, 1971).

Moser, Charles A., *Denis Fonvizin* (Boston: Twayne Publishers, 1979).

Nabokov, Vladimir, *Nikolai Gogol* (New York: New Directions, 1961).

Proffer, Ellendea, *Bulgakov* (Ann Arbor, MI: Ardis, 1984).

Rayfield, Donald, *Anton Chekhov: A Life* (New York: Henry Holt and Co., 1997).

Reeder, Roberta, *Anna Akhmatova, Poet and Prophet* (New York: Picador, 1995).

Roskin, A., *The Life of Maxim Gorky* (New York: Fredonia, 2002).

Rowe, William Woodin, *Leo Tolstoy* (Boston: Twayne Publishers, 1986).

Russian Literature in the Age of Pushkin and Gogol, ed. Christine A. Rydel [Dictionary of Literary Biography, vol. 205] (Detroit: Gale, 1999).

Russian Novelists in the Age of Tolstoy and Dostoevsky, ed. J. Alexander Ogden and Judith E. Kalb [Dictionary of Literary Biography, vol. 239] (Detroit: Gale, 2001).

Russian Writers since 1980, ed. Marina Balina and Mark Lipovetsky [Dictionary of Literary Biography, vol. 285] (Detroit: Gale, 2003).

Scammell, Michael, *Solzhenitsyn: A Biography* (New York: Norton, 1986).

Thomas, D. M., *Alexander Solzhenitsyn: A Century in his Life* (New York: St. Martin's Press, 1998).

Wilson, A. N., *Tolstoy: A Biography* (New York: Norton, 2001).

Russian literary criticism for the non-specialist relevant to the framework of this book

Bakhtin, Mikhail, *The Dialogic Imagination: Four Essays by M. M. Bakhtin*, trans. Michael Holquist and Caryl Emerson (Austin: University of Texas Press, 1981).

   Problems of Dostoevsky's Poetics, trans. Caryl Emerson (Minneapolis: University of Minnesota Press, 1984).

Balina, Marina, Nancy Condee, and Evgeny Dobrenko, eds., *Endquote: Sots-Art Literature and Soviet Grand Style* (Evanston, IL: Northwestern University Press, 2000).

Brandist, Craig, *The Bakhtin Circle: Philosophy, Culture and Politics* (London: Pluto Press, 2002).

Epstein, Mikhail N., *After the Future: The Paradoxes of Postmodernism and Contemporary Russian Culture* (Amherst: University of Massachusetts Press, 1995).

Erlich, Victor, *Russian Formalism: History, Doctrine* [1955], 3rd edn. (New Haven: Yale University Press, 1980).

Jakobson, Roman, *Language in Literature*, ed. Krystyna Pomorska and Stephen Rudy (New York: Belknap, 1990).

Lipovetsky, Mark, with Eliot Borenstein, eds., *Russian Postmodernist Fiction: Dialogue with Chaos* (Armonk and London: M. E. Sharpe, 1999).

Lotman, Yu. M., and Boris Uspensky, *The Semiotics of Russian Culture*, trans. N. F. C. Owen, ed. Ann Shukman (Ann Arbor: University of Michigan Slavic Department, 1984).

Shklovsky, Viktor, *Theory of Prose*, trans. Benjamin Sher (Normal, IL: Dalkey Archive, 2000).

Index